W9-BGX-714

modern
elementary
science

TEACHER'S EDITION

modern elementary science

Abraham S. Fischler

Samuel S. Blanc

Mary Nicholas Farley

Lawrence F. Lowery

Vincent E. Smith

HOLT, RINEHART AND WINSTON, INC.
New York   Toronto   London   Sydney

Authors

Dr. Abraham S. Fischler is James Donn Professor of Education, Dean of Graduate Studies and Director of the Social and Behavioral Sciences Center at Nova University in Fort Lauderdale, Florida. Dr. Fischler has co-authored numerous elementary and Junior High School science textbooks and has also written extensively in a great many science journals and bulletins over the past fifteen years.

Dr. Sam Blanc is Associate Professor of Education at the San Diego State College and was a classroom teacher for nineteen years. He was the science Coordinator of Junior High Schools for eight years in the Denver School System and Director of Science and Math at Cajon Valley School District in California. Dr. Blanc has written numerous books and articles in science education.

Mary Nicholas Farley is Associate Professor of Physics and Lecturer in Education at Georgian Court College in Lakewood, New Jersey. Sister Mary Nicholas is former Dean of Women at Georgian Court College, has taught elementary school science, and was an Elementary School Principal for twelve years. She has also written a number of elementary science programs and has been a consultant in education in a wide variety of innovative educational programs.

Dr. Lawrence F. Lowery is the Testing Teacher and Evaluator for Elementary School Science Projects at the University of California. He has authored numerous elementary school science books for children and has written a great many science articles for elementary school teachers. Dr. Lowery was formerly a Teacher—Principal in the Oakland Unified School District in Oakland, California.

Dr. Vincent Edward Smith is teaching full time at Sarah Lawrence College, preparing a book-length manuscript on the history of the laws of nature and is a Seminar Associate at Columbia University. Dr. Smith has co-authored an entire elementary school science series and has authored numerous publications and articles in journals and encyclopedias.

Copyright © 1971 by Holt, Rinehart and Winston, Inc.
All rights reserved.
Printed in the United States of America
ISBN: 0-03-072120-2   1234567890   071   98765432
Parts of book formerly copyrighted 1963-1966
under the title *Science and Life*
and 1966 under the title *Science, a Modern Approach*

Consultants

Dr. Lyman C. Hunt, Jr. is Professor of Education and Director of the Reading Center at the University of Vermont. Dr. Hunt has taught elementary school and has published several journal articles on reading. He has addressed numerous educational organizations and interested civic groups across the nation on the subject of reading.

Dr. John N. Shive is Manager of Science Lectures and Demonstrations of Bell Telephone Laboratories, Inc. Dr. Shive is the author of three textbooks in Physics, specializing in wave behavior and electronics. He has written high school science articles, and has given lectures for various educational and civic groups.

Mr. Leonard Simon is the Acting Assistant Director of the Bureau of Curriculum Development in New York City. He has taught mathematics on both the Junior High and Senior High School level. Mr. Simon has instructed at such schools as New York University, Bronx Community College, and City College of New York. Mr. Simon has also written a number of elementary mathematics books for young children and is the co-author of a highly successful elementary school mathematics program.

Dr. Walter Steidle is the Chief of the Program Development Section for elementary and secondary education, for the United States Office of Education. He was the State Supervisor for the State of Delaware and became top specialist of Science for the United States Office of Education. Dr. Steidle has written numerous magazine articles on elementary school science, and was given the honor of being awarded the title of Congressional Fellow from 1968-69.

Dr. Joel Warren is Professor of Life Sciences at Nova University in Fort Lauderdale, Florida. He has occupied various University teaching positions over the past thirty years. Professor Warren has written numerous articles in the general fields of microbiology and infectious diseases.

Illustrated by

Tim and Greg Hildebrandt
Dave Hodges
Richard Loehle
Raul Mina Mora

Contents

Introduction

What is science?

Generally when people use the word science, they refer to theories and laws about our world; for example, the "atomic theory" or "the Law of Gravity." People who know such theories and laws are said to know science. When used in this sense, the word science is a "noun."

The word science has also become associated with a particular way of approaching reality. People talk about using a scientific approach to find the cause of cancer or of using scientific methods to analyze a social problem such as the causes of school dropouts. Used in this way, the word science has a "verb" connotation; it is used to characterize processes that people employ to solve problems. Science as a "noun" denotes an achievement; science as a "verb" denotes logical operations leading to the achievement. Gilbert Ryle[1] has pointed out the difference between *knowing that* something is so (for instance knowing that the earth is round), and *knowing how* to prove the point. Science as a "verb" denotes science as a knowing how.

The conclusions of science must always be tested in experience. Yet experience alone—what Feigl[2] calls "raw feels", are not science. If experience were science, all men would be scientists because no man can escape having experiences. Primitive man, for example, had experience of the night-time sky, yet we do not call him a scientist. The ancient Babylonians, however, used mathematical tables to predict where the planets would be from one night to the next. These people were scientists; they were astronomers. How did they differ from primitive man who just had experience of the sky? One difference is that the Babylonians questioned their experience. They asked *why* or *how* the planets move. The first stage of scientific inquiry is one of asking questions based on experiences one has. There is no science so long as man passively submits to experience. For science to take place, man the knower must first initiate something, even if it is only the question, "What is it all about?"

After the initial questions are asked, a scientist thinks of different ways of answering the questions. He deduces what would be observed if this or that answer were true. For example, if a difference between living and non-living things is that living things grow, then living things will increase in size from time to time. Through observa-

viii

tion or experimentation, our answers to scientific questions are checked. When possible, measurements are made. For example, an exact way of knowing whether or not a living thing has grown is to measure its size periodically. The answer which agrees with experience is accepted, and the answers which do not agree with experience are rejected.

Thus, among the stages of a scientific approach to a problem are the formulation of a question, giving various answers to the question, deducing from each answer consequences that can be checked with experience or observation, using experience or observation to test what we have deduced, and then accepting the answer which experience confirms, rejecting the others.

Other subject matter areas, such as sociology, historical research, or philosophy, do not always lend themselves to the kind of controlled experiential testing possible in the natural sciences. However, in any investigation carried on by the human mind there are questions, deductions, and some kind of test. It is subject matter, not method, which makes science different from other kinds of knowledge and one kind of science different from another. Nevertheless, subject-matter should not be allowed to set science apart from the humanities. George Sarton[3], the foremost historian of science in our century, has written, "It is irritating to meet classical scholars and men of letters who seem to think that they are the guardians of culture, ancient and modern, and yet who do not see, nor try to see, the whole world of beauty which science is steadily unfolding under their very eyes. . . . A true humanist must know the life of science . . ."

We cannot neglect what is described by science as a "noun." Yet the authors of *Modern Elementary Science* believe that the "verb" implication of science is far more important than the "noun" connotation. From this point of view, *Modern Elementary Science* embodies a science program which has as a primary goal the developing of the intellectual processes by which man gains knowledge. Knowing *how* is emphasized as the only means, in science, to knowing *that*. For students who use this series, science becomes an approach to subjects rather than a heap of facts. By focusing on the processes of gaining knowledge, we give the students an opportunity to "learn how to learn." The program stresses the questionings involved in science. It emphasizes the testings of answers. Jerome Bruner[4] has cautioned against "the myth that advanced knowledge is the result of wizardry. The way to battle this myth is in the direct experience of the learner—to give him the experience of going from a primitive and weak grasp of some subject to a stage in which he has a more refined and powerful grasp of it. I do not mean that each man should be carried to the frontiers of knowledge, but I do mean that it is possible to take him far enough so that he himself can see how far he has come and by what means."

What are process skills?

What are the processes and process skills involved in using a scientific approach to subject matter? A process is a procedure, and a process skill is a *knowing how* to use that procedure in Ryle's sense. In science, *knowing that* something is so is the result of a process. To *investigate* might be characterized as a process. It is a highly complex one, however, that involves several more basic processes, for example, *observing*. By observing, we are not referring to a simple sensation. You ask your students to observe a bird's nest; you would hardly ask them to sense a bird's nest. When you ask your students to observe, you want them to rely heavily on their senses, but you also want them to pay special attention to certain features of the object under study. Observing is (a) an attentive activity that we (b) originate to try to (c) discover something. Observing is thus more complicated than it might appear to be at first glance. Observing is the centering of attention on what we already know or suspect. *Identifying* is paying attention to an unfamiliar object to isolate it from other objects. *Describing* is a more sophisticated skill. It requires that the parts of the experienced object be articulated. One can observe a bird's nest as a whole; to describe it requires attention to its parts. Equipped with the skills for describing objects, the student is ready to look at these objects in relation to each other. The process involved here is *comparing*. The objects compared will be seen to have likenesses and differences, and there can now begin a process of *classifying*. When objects are arranged in groups on the basis of similarities and dissimilarities, the student can better find out what the object under study is. Thus, he is *defining*. When we find out what an object is, we next want to know why it is, and from here on science learning involves more sophisticated processes, such as *inferring, predicting* and *explaining*, which combine many of the previously-mentioned processes. *Measuring, recording* and *testing* of hypotheses are used as much as possible at all levels and in all phases of science learning. It would be a mistake to think that these processes are employed in any fixed or absolute kind of order. Moreover, in any sophisticated process, the more elementary processes are presupposed.

Is there an order in science learning?

It is a first principle of all learning that knowledge proceeds from the known to the unknown. We would certainly not expect an elementary school student to write a book until he has mastered the alphabet, learned how to read and write, learned to arrange thoughts into paragraphs and paragraphs into chapters. Each of these skills requires a certain physical, emotional, intellectual, and social readiness before it can be developed, and the teaching of any skills must be arranged in such a way as to take the student's readiness into account. There is science learning proper to more mature stages of education such as high school or college, but when it is arranged in accordance with the background and age of the students, science learning can also be appropriate to the elementary school. As Bruner[5] says, any subject may be taught "in some intellectually honest form to any child at any stage of development."

As a learner advances from the known to the unknown, he moves from what is closer to direct experience to what is more remote, from the concrete to the more abstract, or from what is easy to what is difficult. There are ways of describing our progress in learning subject matter. But science learning can also be described in terms of a sequence from simpler processes to more sophisticated ones. For example, we cannot expect a student to be able to infer and explain the subtle meanings in Shakespeare's writings, until he has had the direct life experiences necessary to recognize and understand these meanings. For such a reason, the authors have arranged the process skills, as well as the content, in sequence. As can be seen from the Scope and Sequence charts on pages xx-xxxi, the processes taught at earlier levels are closest to the student's own experiences. Simpler processes such as observing, describing, identifying, and grouping predominate in the earlier books, while more sophisticated processes such as inferring, predicting, and explaining are most evident in later books. This sequence of skills can be thought of as a "vertical development" of skills —that is, the students proceed from a lower order of sophistication to a higher order. In addition, we have sequenced a "horizontal development" of skills, by which we mean that skills taught at early levels are employed and reinforced at the higher levels even as new skills are being introduced.

How is Modern Elementary Science organized?

Each text in the series contains three or four units of study, which are further sub-divided into a number of lessons. Each lesson is a natural teaching unit, representing about one week's work. The principle that learning proceeds from the known to the unknown is applied within each lesson, within the units of a given book, and within all the books in the series. Thus, you will find that content in the lower grades deals with concepts and ideas which are most familiar to students and that the level of abstractness increases in the higher grades. In every unit, and book, we proceed from the macro-physical world to the micro-physical. We proceed from what is spatially near us to what is spatially remote. We study the present before we study the remote past. This type of organization parallels the vertical development of process skills discussed earlier.

In addition, horizontal development of concepts has been carefully considered. Science content is traditionally divided into three main categories: the *life sciences* (including zoology, botany, and anatomy and physiology); the *physical sciences* (physics and chemistry); and the *earth sciences* (geology, meteorology, and astronomy). In *Modern Elementary Science*, content is sequenced so that the students study from each of these main categories each year. The depth and breadth of the specific subject matter changes each year; yet each unit in a given text relates to units studied in previous grades and to those which follow. In this way, the concepts taught are broadened, reinforced, and extended. The Scope and Sequence chart will help you see how this organization is carried through and how the content in your grade level fits into the total scheme of the series.

How are the units organized?

Each unit begins with a photograph reflecting the theme of the unit. In grades 4, 5, and 6, a historical introduction to the content of the unit is also included. Both of these elements are primarily motivational, intended to arouse curiosity and bring previous but related experiences to mind.

The lessons within the units follow the pattern and plan we labeled "scientific approach" earlier. That is, each begins either by providing experiences from which questions can be raised or by directly raising questions which recall experiences relevant to the unit.

After a question is posed, various answers to the question are considered and then experiments and tests are carried out in an attempt to find a solution. These activities are arranged so that, in accordance with Piaget's[6] findings in psychology, the student proceeds from concrete observations to more abstract generalizations. Finally, answers are accepted or rejected on the basis of the results of the activities. To help the students synthesize their observations and experiences, reading plateaus appear periodically within each lesson. Because both content and process development are based almost exclusively on activities that the students perform, those students whose reading abilities may not be up to grade level are not penalized in this program. Technical terms are not introduced until the appropriate concepts have been developed.

One word of caution is essential at this point. If students are to carry out the activities, equipment is necessary. We have tried to keep the equipment to a minimum and to suggest inexpensive material wherever possible. The Teacher's Edition lists, at the start of each lesson, the equipment necessary to perform all the activities in the lesson. It is essential that this material be available in order for the students to carry out the activities in the text.

How can you evaluate your science program?

Evaluation in science should be a continuous, on-going process. To keep it continuous, a teacher must have records of each child's behavior while he is engaged in science experiences. Such records are best taken from direct observations of the child. Other evaluative information may be obtained through tests which are designed to measure particular objectives. These informal and formal evaluations are built into our program. Each time a child or a group of children engages in an activity, you have an ideal opportunity to observe what is occurring. This means that every minute of the day you will be evaluating in an informal way. Whenever you discuss the results of an activity with a particular group of students, you are actually conducting an informal interview.

More formal evaluation includes a series of questions at the end of each lesson and unit. These questions require the children to engage in some process, which, in turn, helps them to use what they have learned in different, but related, situations.

Both written tests and check lists can be a part of your science program. We have not included any objective, "one-word-answer-type" written tests in either the texts or the Teacher's Editions because we believe that you are in a better position to design such tests—tests which are geared to your own individual class needs. However, we are including a check list which you can use to develop individual progress profiles for each of your students. We hope this evaluation check list will help you look for and evaluate signs of growth in the children's process skills. This list is general and is intended to help you evaluate the effect of the total program rather than any specific lesson. It can be used frequently, as dictated by the nature of your class.

Evaluation Check List

> forms intelligent guesses and/or hypotheses
>
> shows open-mindedness in pursuit of solutions to problems
>
> desires to search for and find solutions to problems
>
> extends and expands his interests independently
>
> detects similarities and differences, discrepancies and inconsistencies
>
> uses a variety of resources in searching for information
>
> organizes information after sifting, classifying, selecting, and bringing together his data
>
> draws meaningful conclusions from his observations

generalizes about ideas he has learned through experiences

offers original ideas to supplement those supplied by the text, the teacher, and other students

asks thoughtful, perceptive questions pertinent to the material being studied

expresses ideas freely using vocabulary and concepts presented in the text

is able to complete an activity or experiment once he has begun

works efficiently on his own and with others

exercises care in taking notes and recording data

What is your role?

The teacher, by virtue of his background and educational experience with the subject matter, can plan a logical route that a pupil must take to apply the proper processes and thus get to his destination within the subject matter itself. The pupil would not get there on his own, except rarely and by accident. Without your help, the pupil would not know what experiences to seek out nor in what order. He needs help even in raising the right questions. Thus, even at the level of experiences, the pupil needs direction and encouragement if he is to attain scientific understanding of the material world and if he is to learn the ways of attaining useful information. You can help him choose and execute the appropriate processes.

As a teacher, you are the one who stimulates, encourages, guides, listens, questions, and inspires. At times, you may find it difficult to withhold answers to the questions raised by the students or in the text. You may be tempted to tell a child just how to proceed in order to solve a problem. It is important that you encourage students to find their own methods and derive their own solutions, using their own data. By your teaching this way, no student is made to feel that science is too hard for him. No student feels his suggestions or ideas are irrelevant. Each student gains a sense of self-esteem as his ideas are considered and discussed with the rest of the class. By teaching, rather than telling, you will be helping your students learn how to go on learning for the rest of their lives.

How is the teacher's edition organized?

The Teacher's Edition of *Modern Elementary Science* has been designed, both visually and in terms of content, to be as useful a tool as possible. There are many more suggestions for each unit than could possibly be used by any one teacher. This abundance of material has been provided to allow you as much flexibility and creativity as possible. It is strongly recommended that you read all the material for each unit well in advance of teaching it. This will allow you to alter the basic and optional material to the needs of your class so that, before you begin teaching the unit itself, you may gather equipment, reference books, and films for yourself and the students.

The reference materials which precede the Teacher's Edition to the student pages include: Science Information for the Teacher, Unit Generalizations, New Words for the Student, Scientists, Books for the Student, Books for the Teacher, Films, Bulletin Board suggestions, and Optional Equipment.

Following this introductory material are student pages, reduced in size, surrounded by pertinent teacher notes and suggestions. At the top of the pages are the basic lesson plans, including:

> *History of the Idea:* This appears only on the first page of each new unit. It provides additional historical background for you and suggests ways of introducing the unit.

> *Overview:* This appears at the beginning of each lesson and it briefly outlines the purpose and content of the lesson.

> *How to Begin:* Ways of starting the lesson are suggested. They are suggestions only, of course, and are not intended to limit you in any way.

> *Procedure:* The procedure for conducting the lesson includes specific directions for activities, responses to text questions and responses to Testing Your Ideas questions. Procedural material pertinent to a given student page appears on the top of that page.

The side margins in the Teacher's Edition, with the exception of the listing of process skills and materials for each lesson, are of a different nature than the material at the top of the pages. This marginal material includes optional rather than basic suggestions and notes. The content and process skills for each grade level have been selected on the basis of what is considered average for that grade level. However, we are well aware of the fact that an "average" class contains students who are far above grade level in reading ability and conceptual development, as well as students who are below grade level in these areas. The marginal material provides for these students as well as providing supplementary materials for your average students. Suggestions for using specific items in these marginal materials are included to help you judge how best to use them.

The unit at a glance Appearing only once in the unit, this is a brief statement about the content and purpose of the unit. It also points out

a. The human mind goes from hazy, vague notions about objects to notions that are more clear and distinct.

b. The macrophysical is always treated before the microphysical.

c. What is spatially near us is treated before what is spatially remote.

d. The present is studied before the study of the remote past.

Terms are not employed until the corresponding concepts have been developed. Science learning is not memorizing terms but building ideas. We try to avoid technical terms when possible, but there is a vocabulary which a student must learn to understand science and speak to scientists. However, this vocabulary is subordinated to conceptual development. The conceptual scheme (Conant) is more important than the word that labels it.

The processes involved in science learning are taught throughout. These processes have been named in the text in connection with each activity. The student thus learns methods as well as subject matter.

Questioning techniques are stressed. Telling is reporting. It is indoctrination. It deadens the mind rather than quickens it. Questions create a hunger in the learner for what is to be presented. Thus they make the materials relevant to him. They encourage him to search. They prod him to be active. They ensure that learning will be internalized and, therefore, genuine.

There is a horizontal order among our books. Each unit in a later book has a relation to what was studied in a unit or units of earlier books. By organizing the series in this way, the learner's grasp of what was studied earlier is progressively deepened.

There is a vertical order within each book. As explained in the Teacher's Edition, the units of a particular book have been arranged according to a definable pedagogical order. Both content and process skills are taught sequentially, from the less complex to the more complex.

Hypotheses are distinguished from verified propositions. Where questions are unsettled, it would be a mistake to propose a final solution. For example, no attempt is made to teach the atomic theory but only to suggest it.

Simplifying can never be falsifying. Even though the content is simplified, the science taught throughout the series is accurate. Thus, the student who studies from our series will not have his learning contradicted in high school or college.

Our tests are learning devices. There are reviews and other features of unit endings, but each unit has a test designed to extend the students' comprehension of the principles involved.

Our titles are in the form of questions. Here again we are attempting to arouse interest. No title contains a term that has not already been defined.

Our series promotes team learning. We suggest that the activities in many cases be conducted in groups and be followed by group discussion. In addition to its values at the elementary level, such a format shows the student how science today usually works. Rarely today do individual scientists perform single experiments. Rather, scientists work in teams and consolidate their efforts.

There is a quantitative thread running through the series. This is so not only because problems are being worked out mathematically in every lesson, but also because the basic quantitative concepts of science are developed; e.g., elliptical motion, frequency, volume, pressure, etc.

Attention is paid to the history of science. This is not merely a rhetorical ornament designed to arouse the interest of students. When we learn the history of an idea, we are learning what the state of a question is. This is an important part of science learning. We learn how difficult it is to achieve truth. We learn that science is an emotional human activity, not a machine-like movement.

Attention is paid to the philosophy of science. This emphasis does not appear explicitly, but care has been taken in the use of concepts, the choice of terms, and the methods of proof to keep the series in accord with a sound philosophy of science.

Science as a humanity is explored. Science comes from man. The scientist is often as creative as the artist. Though science does not tell the whole story of man, it tells us a great deal about ourselves, about our place in nature, about our own bodies, and about the strengths and weaknesses of the human intellect.

Reading plateaus are included. These summarize, deepen and extend the science learning which the student has previously achieved.

A complete range of annotations is included in the Teacher's Edition. This phase of the Teacher Edition is designed to enrich the effectiveness and versatility of the program by providing supplemental teaching aids.

The artwork combines human as well as scientific values. Persons, young and old, are portrayed as human beings in human situations, while scientific accuracy is also stressed. Since science learning involved bringing human beings into contact with science, the art work maximizes pedagogical effectiveness.

Aesthetically the artwork stands on its own. All art pieces, photographs, and design elements were chosen from the standpoint of artistic excellence, as well as scientific accuracy.

How to use the
Scope and Sequence Charts

The charts on the following pages describe the scope and sequence development of the *Modern Elementary Science* program. There is a separate chart for each grade level. The charts are designed to illustrate both the horizontal and vertical development of the program. The horizontal component is divided into the three major disciplines: life, earth and physical, depicted by three color bands. Reading horizontally across each chart, you are presented with the contents for each unit, the process skills to be derived for each lesson, and the generalizations to be developed. Reading vertically, for each grade level, you will see how the process skills and unit generalizations proceed from the familiar to the less familiar and from the simpler to the more complex.

At every grade level, material previously developed is maintained and extended. Thus, by comparing the charts you will know what was presented to your pupils in the previous year, as well as what they are expected to learn in the following year.

The list of process skills and contributing principles has been abbreviated on each chart to allow room for a representative sampling of the scope and sequence for each grade level. A complete listing of process skills for each grade level will be found in the Teacher's Edition for the appropriate grade.

1

Contents	Process Skills

PHYSICAL

A WORLD FULL OF THINGS

Shapes — Recognizing shapes as like or unlike.
Sizes — Observing differences and likenesses in object sizes.
Colors — Recognizing the three primary colors.
Sounds — Making loud and soft sounds.
Hard and soft — Observing and comparing different textures.
Rough and smooth — Observing different textures.
Hot and cold — Describing objects in terms of temperature.
Wet and dry — Feeling objects having sticky, wet, and dry textures.
Tasting — Tasting several solutions and describing them.
Smelling — Describing the smell of various substances.
Grouping shapes, sizes, and colors — Describing objects according to size, shape, and color.
Grouping what we hear — Listening to different sounds and identifying them.
Grouping what we feel — Comparing and grouping objects according to texture.
Grouping what we taste — Comparing and classifying foods by taste.
Grouping what we smell — Locating and grouping smells.
Observing — Observing and describing likenesses and differences.

EARTH

CHANGES YOU CAN SEE

Weather changes — Observing shapes of clouds.
Wind moves things and changes things — Defining wind as moving air.
Temperature changes — Observing movement of objects due to wind.
Water changes — Observing that weather changes produce temperature changes.
Wind and water change things — Measuring temperatures with thermometers.
Children grow and change — Observing the forms which water takes.
Moving and measuring — Observing effects of wind and water on soil and rocks.
Shadows change — Describing changes which take place as children grow.
Wheels help to move things — Learning how to stay healthy.
Magnets move some things — Observing one's own ways of moving.
Measuring the distance an object has moved.
Observing that shadows move and change in size and shape.
Observing that wheels or round objects move easily.
Observing that magnets will move some objects.

LIFE

LOOKING AT ANIMALS AND PLANTS

Looking at animals — Describing the physical characteristics of animals.
Animals move — Identfying animals by their physical characteristics.
Animals grow and change — Describing and grouping animals according to movement.
Animals at the farm — Observing how animals change in growth.
Animals at the zoo — Caring for young animals and watching them change.
Where animals live — Describing how farm animals are cared for.
Looking at plants — Recognizing the needs of animals.
Caring for plants — Observing the physical surroundings of animals.
Warm air and plants — Observing shapes, sizes, and colors of plants.
Water and plants — Describing differences among plants.
Light and plants — Observing how plants grow.
Where plants grow — Caring for plants.
Comparing plants given a sufficient amount of water with plants given ample water.
Comparing plants that grow in a cold place with plants that grow in a warm place.

We can find out information through our senses.

We have five senses—seeing, hearing, feeling, smelling, and tasting.

   A. Seeing is a way to find out information.
   B. We see with our eyes.
   C. Hearing is a way to find out information.
   D. We hear with our ears.
   E. We can hear different types of sounds such as high and low, loud and soft, pleasant and unpleasant.
   F. Feeling is a way to find out information.
   G. We can feel with any part of our bodies.
   H. We can feel different sensations such as smoothness and roughness, wetness and dryness.
   I. Smelling is a way to find out information.
   J. We smell with our noses.
   K. Tasting is a way to find out information.
   L. We taste only four flavors with our tongues.
   M. Different substances have different tastes.
   N. Smells make foods taste differently.

Objects can be classified on the basis of their physical characteristics.

   A. Objects have different characteristics.
   B. Objects can be compared by their different characteristics.
   C. Objects with similar characteristics can be grouped.
   D. The grouping of objects helps us understand them better.
   E. We can organize what we see by shape, size, and color.
   F. We can organize the sounds we hear by the way they sound.
   G. We can organize the objects that we touch by feel.
   H. Smells are difficult to organize.
   I. We can organize foods and drinks by taste.

Objects physically interact and change.

   A. Weather changes.
   B. Water changes.
   C. Wind and water change and move things.

Changes in objects can be measured.

   A. The distance an object moves can be measured.
   B. Children grow and change, and this change can be measured.

The positions of objects change.

   A. Shadows change in size and position throughout the day.
   B. Some objects can be moved by wheels.
   C. Some objects can be moved by magnets.

Animals can be identified by their characteristics.

   A. Animals are recognized by their appearance.
   B. Animals move in different ways.
   C. Animals grow and change.

Animals may be cared for.

   A. Animals need food, water, and shelter in order to live.
   B. Some animals are kept on farms, some in zoos, and some in homes as pets.

Different animals live in different environments.

   A. Animals make and live in different homes.
   B. Some animals live in water, some on land.

Plants can be identified by their characteristics.

   A. Plants vary in size, shape, and color.
   B. Plants grow and change.

Plants may be cared for.

   A. Plants need water in order to live.
   B. Heat and cold affect the growth of plants.
   C. Light and darkness affect the growth of plants.

2

Contents   Process Skills

LIFE

MORE ABOUT ANIMALS

Furry animals
Caring for a hamster
Birds
Caring for wild birds
Turtles and other animals
Caring for a lizard
Frogs and other animals
Caring for a frog
Fish
Keeping fish
Insects
Keeping insects
Grouping animals

Defining the term "mammal."
Observing basic characteristics of mammals.
Caring for and handling mammals in the classoom.
Defining the term "bird."
Distinguishing birds from other animals.
Observing the characteristics of a bird.
Caring for a bird.
Defining the term "reptile."
Distinguishing reptiles from other animals.
Observing the growth of live reptiles.
Caring for lizards in a terrarium.
Defining the term "amphibian."
Identifying the characteristics which form the group called amphibians.
Observing the growth of live amphibians.
Caring for tadpoles and/or other amphibians.

EARTH

EXPLORING WATER AND AIR

Looking at water
How much water
Things that float
Working with water
Making water work
How water is stored
Where water comes from
How water gets dirty
Water in the air
Finding out about air
Air takes up room
Feeling air move
Weighing air
How air gets dirty

Describing some physical characteristics of water.
Observing that water takes up space and has weight.
Measuring water by volume and weight.
Weighing liquids and solids.
Determining which objects float and which sink.
Constructing a water wheel which will do work.
Describing the relationship of water pressure to depth.
Describing how water flows from a higher to a lower place.
Observing and describing the three states of matter.
Recognizing an important water source.
Observing that in water some substances dissolve, some mix, and some settle out.
Explaining verbally the water cycle.
Demonstrating evaporation and condensation.
Demonstrating the presence of air.
Demonstrating that air takes up space.

PHYSICAL

THINGS TO HEAR, SEE, AND FEEL

Hearing and seeing
Making sounds
Where sounds come from
Sending sounds through wood and metal
Making different sounds
Changing sounds
Things that move back and forth
Sending sounds through water
Inside your ears
Looking at shadows
Using your eyes
Looking at light
Looking at lenses
Watching light bend
Watching light bounce
Inside your eyes

Introducing the unit on sound, light, and heat.
Discovering that echoes are sounds which bounce.
Categorizing sounds in various non-scientific ways.
Discovering that sound travels through solid objects.
Producing various sounds in different ways.
Using various materials to make high, low, or soft sounds.
Defining the term vibration.
Discovering that sounds travel through water.
Observing a model of the eardrum and its function.
Recognizing that light comes from a variety of sources.
Providing experiences with transparent objects.
Providing experiences with translucent objects.
Observing that light can be controlled by lenses.
Defining the term refraction.
Defining the term reflection.
Observing that eyes are of many shapes and colors.

Animals may be kept and cared for as pets or for study.

Mammals have identifiable characteristics.
  A. Mammals have fur or hair on their bodies.
  B. Most mammals live on land.
  C. Most mammals bear their young alive.
  D. Young mammals are cared for by their parents and are fed milk from their mothers.
  E. Young mammals resemble their parents.

Birds have identifiable characteristics.
  A. Birds have feathers covering their bodies.
  B. Most birds can fly.
  C. Birds have wings instead of front legs.
  D. The feet and bills of birds are specially designed to help them get food.
  E. Young birds hatch from eggs usually laid in nests.
  F. Young birds are cared for by their parents.
  G. Young birds resemble their parents.

Reptiles have identifiable characteristics.
  A. Reptiles have dry scales covering their bodies.
  B. Most reptiles live on land.
  C. Young reptiles hatch from eggs which are laid on land.
  D. Reptiles do not care for their young.
  E. Young reptiles resemble their parents.

Amphibians have identifiable characteristics.
  A. Amphibians have moist skin.
  B. Amphibians live on land and in water.

Fish have identifiable characteristics.
  A. Fish have slippery scales covering their bodies.
  B. Fish live in water.
  C. Most young fish hatch from eggs laid in water.

Insects have identifiable characteristics.
  A. Insects have three body parts.
  B. Insects have six legs.

Water has identifiable properties.
  A. Our senses can be used to identify the properties of water.
  B. Water (in its pure state) is a colorless, tasteless, odorless liquid.
  C. Water does not have a shape of its own; it takes the shape of its container.
  D. Water takes up space and has weight.
  E. Water has a surface which acts like a skin and supports weight; the skin surface tension can be reduced.
  F. Water exerts pressure.
  G. Some things dissolve in water, others do not.
  H. Moving water has force and can do work.
  I. Water changes into a solid when it is frozen; ice changes into a liquid when it is heated.

Air has identifiable properties.
  A. Our senses can be used to identify the properties of air.
  B. Air (in its pure state) is a colorless, tasteless, odorless gas.
  C. Air does not have a shape of its own; it takes the shape of its container.
  D. Air takes up space and has weight.
  E. Air is all around us; it is found inside solids and liquids.
  F. Air exerts pressure.
  G. Air contains water vapor, smoke particles, and dust.
  H. Moving air has force and can do work.

Sounds have identifiable characteristics.
  A. Sounds are caused by vibrating objects.
  B. Some sounds are made by blowing, plucking, or tapping.
  C. Some sounds are loud and some are soft.

Sounds travel in air, water, and solids at different speeds.
  A. Sounds travel in waves that spread out in all directions.
  B. Sounds travel through air, water, and solids.

Sounds can be reflected and absorbed.
  A. Sounds can be directed to a particular place.
  B. Sounds bouncing back cause echoes.
  C. Sounds can be absorbed.

The ear is an organ of the body that receives sound.
  A. The outer ear picks up sound.
  B. Two ears are better than one for locating sounds.
  C. The eardrum vibrates when sound strikes it.

Light has certain characteristics.

Light travels through air, water, and clear solids at different speeds.

Light can be reflected and absorbed.

The eye is an organ of the body that receives light.

Heat energy may come from many sources.

Some burning substances that produce heat can be used as fuels.

Heat changes the temperature of a substance.

There are different kinds of thermometers.

Most materials expand when heated and contract when the heat is removed.

Heat travels through solids by conduction.

Some solids conduct heat better than others.

3

Contents	Process Skills

Generalizations

Roots have identifiable characteristics.
  A. In most plants, the root grows at base of stem.
  B. Plants can be grouped by their roots.

Some new plants can be propagated from roots.

The parts of a root function to keep a plant growing.
  A. Roots anchor plants and hold the soil in place.
  B. Roots absorb water and minerals from the soil.

Stems have identifiable characteristics.
  A. The stems have definite characteristics.
  B. Plants can be grouped by their stems.

The stem parts function to keep a plant growing.
  A. The stem is the part which supports other organs.

  B. Stems conduct liquids from the roots to other organs.

Leaves have identifiable characteristics.
  A. Leaves have characteristic shapes.
  B. There is a correlation among leaf shapes and vein patterns.
  C. Leaves have characteristic margin patterns.
  D. Plants can be grouped by their leaves.

Some leaves are designed to aid plants in special ways.

Flowers and cones have identifiable characteristics.

Parts of a flower function to produce more offspring.

Seeds have identifiable characteristics.

In germination an embryo breaks from a seed and grows into a new plant.

Rocks have identifiable characteristics; rocks may be grouped on the basis of similar characteristics.
  A. Some rocks are heavy and some are light.
  B. Different rocks have different colors.
  C. Some rocks are smooth and some are rough.
  D. Some rocks are hard and some are soft.
  E. Some rocks are layered, some are made up of smaller pieces stuck together, and some are made of a solid material.

Rocks are formed through the forces that wear down and build up the earth's surface.
  A. Melted rock deep in the earth, called magma, squeezes up between layers of solid rock.

  B. Igneous rocks are formed from hardened magma.
  C. Sedimentary rocks form through the deposition of sediments which are pressed and cemented together.
  D. Metamorphic rocks are formed when heat and pressure change igneous and sedimentary rocks.

Soil is composed of a thin layer of mineral, animal, and vegetable matter.
  A. Heat and cold cause rocks to break into pieces.
  B. Running water and wind cause rocks to wear away.
  C. Soil is made from small pieces of rock mixed with plant and animal materials.

A machine is a man-made device which changes one kind of motion into another kind of motion.
  A. Force is any push or pull on an object that causes that object to move.
  B. Effort is the force used to move something.

Levers are simple machines used to make work easier by helping to lift loads with less effort.
  A. A lever is a rigid bar that is free to pivot or turn around a fixed point.
  B. The balance point (fulcrum) is the fixed point around which a lever pivots or turns (usually the resting place for a bar lever).

Pulleys are simple machines which may be used to increase force and/or change the direction of force.

Inclined planes are simple machines which may be used to raise an object from one level to another with less force.

Gears are simple machines which may be used to transfer forces from one part of a machine to another part.

Wheels and axles are simple machines which may be used to move a load farther than a lever can.

Simple machines are often used together to make more complex machines.

Solid is one of three states of matter.
  A. Solids have definite shapes.
  B. Solids melt into liquids when heated.

Liquid is one of three states of matter.
  A. Liquids generally take the shape of their container.
  B. Liquids evaporate into gases when heated.

Gas is one of three states of matter.
  A. Gases generally fill any container in which they are placed.

  B. Most gases cannot be seen.

Each solid substance has identifiable characteristics.
  A. Many solid substances are too similar to tell apart with only our senses.
  B. Indicators are substances which can be used to identify the characteristics of similar solid substances.

Each liquid substance has identifiable characteristics.

Each gaseous substance has identifiable characteristics.

4

Contents	Process Skills

LIFE

ANIMALS, PLANTS, AND PLACES

What are some habitats of living things?
What is the kind of habitat in which you live?
What lives in the habitat of a pond?
What animals and plants live in the sea?
What plants and animals live on mountains?
How do animals and plants live in other regions?
How do some animals survive seasonal change?
How do other living things change habitat?
How are living things protected from their enemies?
How are animals and plants prepared for the future?
Are some kinds of animals and plants no longer on earth?

Duplicating natural habitats of plants and animals.
Examining plants and animals in a small area.
Observing the habits of animals in an outdoor habitat.
Collecting living organisms found in ponds and streams.
Observing animal and plant life at seashore.
Identifying plants and animals of a mountainous habitat.
Identifying living things of a desert habitat.
Comparing how plants and animals change seasonally.
Explaining bird and animal migration.
Investigating how plants and animals spread seeds.
Describing protective devices of plants and animals.
Investigating the reproductive powers of living things.

YOUR GROWING BODY

What foods do you need?
What happens to the food we eat?
What happens to digested foods?
What happens when food and oxygen combine?
How does your body move?
What is healthy growing?

Choosing foods from each of the four basic food groups.
Identifying foods having essential nutrients.
Describing how the body is organized in systems, organs, tissues and cells.
Explaining how the digestive system functions in the ingestion, digestion, and absorption of nutrients.
Describing how the heart pumps blood.
Identifying what is brought to and from body cells.
Describing the respiratory system.
Describing the urinary excretory system.
Describing the bones as a support for the body.
Explaining how the muscular system produces movements.

PHYSICAL

HEAT AS ENERGY

Can heat cause changes?
What other changes can heat cause?
How does heat travel through solids?
How does heat travel through liquids and gases?
How does heat travel through space?
How do we measure temperature?
Are there different thermometers?
What is heat?
Is heat a form of energy?
How is heat energy connected to motion?

Observing changes of state caused by heat.
Observing expansion and contraction of solids, liquids, and gases when heated and cooled.
Identifying the conditions needed for burning.
How does heat travel through solids?
Observing convection currents.
Defining reflection and absorption.
Comparing sensations of heat and cold.
Marking (calibrating) a liquid thermometer.
Comparing the Fahrenheit and Celsius thermometer scales.
Calibrating a homemade gas thermometer.
Measuring a change in temperature caused by friction.

EARTH

THE CHANGING EARTH

What changes can we see on the earth?
How does wind cause changes on the earth?
How does water change the surface of the earth?
How does temperature cause change?
How could mountains be made?
How does the earth change suddenly?
How does man change the surface of the earth?

Showing that the earth's surface is changing.
Observing the effects of running water, wind, and ice.
Investigating how wind changes the earth's surface.
Describing prevention of topsoil and seashore erosion.
Describing how running water can wear away land.
Explaining how land areas and shorelines are eroded.
Describing how freezing and melting cause erosion.
Describing how pressure causes ice to melt.
Inferring how glacier movements change the surface.
Describing the process of mountain formation.
Explaining how mountains occur through faulting.
Explaining the cause of earthquakes.

Plants and animals can be found in a great variety of environments. Each living kind exists only in certain environments.

  A. Plants and animals live in habitats in which they can obtain food and water.

  B. Plants and animals live in habitats in which they are protected from their enemies.

  C. Plants and animals live in habitats in which they can reproduce more of their kind.

Some plants and animals respond to seasonal changes.

  A. Some birds and mammals change color seasonally.

  B. Some animals hibernate during cold weather.

  C. Some animals estivate during hot, dry weather.

Plants and animals are adapted to their environments for survival.

  A. Many seeds are adapted to be dispersed by means of wind or animals.

  B. Many animals are adapted for protection by being able to move quickly.

Man has learned ways to use plants and animals.

  A. Man uses plants for food, shelter, and clothing materials.

  B. Man uses animals for food, work, and clothing materials.

Man has only recently begun to understand how the human body takes in and utilizes food substances.

The human body must have proper foods to carry on its functions. Several types of substances are found in foods.

The human body is made up of many systems, or groups, or organs. The digestive system contains the body parts which work together to break food down into smaller particles for use in the body.

The respiratory system contains the body parts which work together to take air into the lungs and expel it from them.

The circulatory system contains the body parts which work together to move the blood through the body.

The excretory system contains the body parts which work together to eliminate the waste products of digestion.

The nervous system contains the body parts which work together to sense stimuli and cause muscles to act.

The skeletal system contains the body parts which give support to the body and protect its vital organs.

The muscular system contains the body parts which work together to produce motion.

The gain or loss of heat can cause physical changes.

  A. Most materials expand when they gain heat and contract when they lose heat.

  B. Many materials change state when they gain or lose heat.

Heat can cause chemical changes.

  A. Heating can separate a complex substance.

  B. Heating can combine simple substances to form a new, complex substance.

Heat travels from a hotter to a cooler place.

  A. Heat travels in solids by conduction.

  B. Heat travels in fluids by convection.

  C. No medium is required for heat travel by radiation.

Temperature is the measure of the degree of hotness or coldness of a substance.

  A. The sense of touch does not enable us to determine temperature accurately.

  B. The thermometer is an instrument that is used to measure temperature accurately.

Heat is a form of energy.

  A. Heat is associated with motion.

  B. Heat is capable of doing work.

  C. Heat energy can be transformed into other forms of energy; other forms of energy can be transformed into heat energy.

The surface of the earth is constantly changing.

  A. Some changes in the earth's surface take place rapidly.

  B. Some changes in the earth's surface take place very slowly.

Changes in the earth's surface may be physical or chemical.

  A. Wind is air moving over the earth's surface.

  B. Wind changes the earth's surface by carrying away dry soil and sand and depositing them elsewhere.

  C. Wind-driven sand changes the earth's surface by carving and eroding land surfaces.

  D. Water flows from high places to lower places over the earth's surface.

  E. Flowing water changes the earth's surface by wearing away land surfaces and depositing sediment.

  F. Ocean waves change the earth's surface by wearing away shorelines.

Unbalanced forces under the earth's surface cause mountain formations and earthquakes.

  A. Pressures in the earth raise blocks of crust and fold the surface into mountains.

  B. Pressures in the earth cause blocks of crust to shift along deep faults, causing earthquakes.

5

Generalizations

Through adaptation, various structures of animals keep the animal alive and growing.

A. An animal's type of motion depends upon the arrangement of the muscles.

B. Animals are adapted to find and capture food in their environments.

C. Animals are adapted to obtain oxygen from their environments.

D. Animals are adapted to protect them against predators in their environments.

E. Animals reproduce by sexual or asexual means to provide new generations.

Through adaptation, various structures of plants operate in special ways to keep the plant alive and growing.

A. Plants are adapted to respond to certain environmental conditions.

B. Stems conduct liquids and dissolved minerals between the parts of the plant.

C. Leaves have tiny openings through which respiration takes place.

D. Leaves manufacture food by using the energy of sunlight (photosynthesis).

E. Many plants are adapted to protect themselves.

The atmosphere regulates the amount of solar energy reaching earth and is affected by solar energy.

A. Temperatures on earth vary daily and seasonally.

B. The thermometer measures changes in temperature.

Air occupies space and has weight; it exerts pressure.

A. The pressure of air on an object is equal to the total weight of the column of air above the object.

B. Air exerts pressure in all directions.

The movement of air from one place on earth to another, due to unequal air pressures, causes winds.

The heat of the sun causes water on the earth to change into water vapor in the air.

A. Heat causes water to evaporate.

B. Moisture in the air condenses into clouds.

Weather predictions are based on information collected at weather stations all over the world. Information from weather stations describes major air masses and their direction and speed.

Water as matter occupies space and has weight; it exerts pressure. The pressure of water on an object is equal to the total weight of the column of water above the object.

Water in different areas of the oceans differs in temperature and in salt content.

A transfer of electrons from one object to another builds up a potential difference and a charge.

A. Electric charges are built up by friction by adding or removing electrons in the objects being rubbed.

B. Electrically charged objects attract uncharged (electrically neutral) objects.

A charged object exerts a force in the space around it; this space is called its electric field.

A. The repellent force between two objects having like charges is evident before the objects touch.

B. The attractive force between two objects having unlike charges is evident before the objects touch.

Electrons tend to flow from an object with an excess of electrons to one that has a deficiency of electrons.

A. The potential difference between electrodes in an electric cell produces a flow of electrons.

B. The potential difference in an electric cell is produced by chemical action between the electrodes and the electrolyte.

A circuit is a pathway for an electric current.

Magnetism is a property of certain natural and man-made materials.

The space around a magnet in which the magnetic force exists is its magnetic field.

The material substances of the earth can be changed.

A. In a physical change, the substance itself remains the same after as before the change.

B. In a chemical change, different substances result.

Air is an important example of matter in a gaseous state.

Heating is important in the study of chemistry.

A. Burning is a chemical change.

B. The boiling points of substances help identify them.

Water is an example of matter in the liquid state.

A. Much of the water found in nature is hard water.

B. Water is a universal solvent.

Solids can be formed from solutions.

A. A solution is a homogeneous mixture of substances.

B. Crystals can be made from solutions.

All earth substances are made up of particles.

A. The smallest particle of a compound, and of most elements as found in nature, is the molecule.

B. Molecules are made up of atoms.

6

Contents   **Process Skills**

Observing plant dependence on bacteria and molds.
Observing and identifying carbon in plants.
Inferring animal-plant interdependence in respiration.
Explaining the significance of green plants in the food web.
Investigating animal dependence on green plants.
Identifying predators within a food web.
Explaining how predators help maintain a balance of nature.
Identifying parasitic relationships in the balance of nature.
Describing how organisms of the same species cooperate.
Identifying territorial behavior in birds.
Explaining the importance of plants as primary producers.
Identifying the ways in which plants are useful to man.
Identifying the ways in which animals are useful to man.
Identifying the ways in which man upsets the balance of nature.
Explaining prevention of air and water pollution.

Observing sound-producing objects for sound production.
Observing compressional motion of various materials.
Observing physical properties of waves.
Defining crest, trough, frequency, and amplitude.
Inferring that the loudness of sound is related to the amplitude of
    swing of a vibrating source.
Observing vibrating objects for the relationship of frequency and
    pitch.
Inferring that light travels in straight lines.
Observing how light reflects.
Observing how light reflects from mirrors.
Inferring that light bends from one medium to another.
Comparing convex and concave lenses.
Observing passage of light through a prism.
Comparing light absorption and reflection materials.
Comparing the particle and wave theory of light.

Locating reference points for sky and horizon observation.
Recording apparent motion of the sun during the year.
Locating the "North Star" as a reference in the night sky.
Comparing star positions at different times.
Observing that only spherical objects cast round shadows.
Defining constellations.
Observing certain constellations to determine star movement.
Identifying one or more planets in the night sky.
Explaining how the rotation and the revolution of the tilted earth
    result in day and night and the seasons of the year.
Applying a technique for solar observation.
Comparing the sun and the moon in size, distance, motions.
Inferring apparent monthly change of shape of moon.

Describing motion in distance and time.
Observing the path of moving objects.
Defining straight-line motion.
Observing how objects begin to move.
Inferring that force is needed to start motion.
Observing how forces affect speed.
Observing how forces affect direction of motion.
Observing the motion of falling bodies.
Identifying gravity as a force.
Observing the effects of friction on motion.

Generalizations

Animals and plants are interdependent.
  A. Green plants depend on non-green plants.
  B. Plants depend on animals for existence and growth.
  C. Animals depend on plants.

Cooperative and competitive behavior promote a population balance.
  A. Predator-prey and parasite-host relationships help to keep animal populations constant.
  B. Some animal species compete for territory.
  C. Some animals compete for position of rank. This behavior insures that the best-adapted members of the species will survive to reproduce.

Some animals live cooperatively in permanent groups.

Some animals live cooperatively in temporary groups.

Man is a part of the community of animals and plants.
  A. Man uses plants for food, medicine, clothing, materials, and work.
  B. Man can upset the balance of nature through overpopulation, overconsumption, and pollution.
  C. Man has a responsibility to see that natural resources are conserved.

Sounds are produced by vibrating objects.
  A. "Frequency" is the number of vibrations per second.
  B. Sound vibrations travel in waves and in all directions.
  C. Sound waves travel in air, solids, and water.

Sound waves have identifiable characteristics.
  A. The top of a sound wave is called the crest; the height from the surface level is called the amplitude.
  B. The loudness of a sound increases with amplitude: the greater the amplitude, the louder the sound; the smaller the amplitude, the smaller the sound.
  C. The pitch of a sound increases with the speed of vibrations: the greater the frequency, the higher the sound; the less the frequency, the lower the sound.

Light is produced by many sources.
  A. The sun is our primary source of light.
  B. Light may be produced by fire or other luminous sources.
  C. Light travels from a source in all directions.

Light has identifiable characteristics.
  A. Light ordinarily travels in straight lines.
  B. Light can be reflected: the angle of reflection equals the incoming angle.
  C. Light can be refracted: it bends when passing from one medium to another with a different density.
  D. A convex lens converges light rays.
  E. A concave lens causes light rays to diverge.
  F. A prism separates white light by refracting the colors of which it is made.
  G. The color of an object depends upon which colors are transmitted, reflected and absorbed.

Early scientists thought that the sun, moon, planets, and stars moved around the earth; modern scientists have shown that the earth and other planets revolve around the sun.
  A. The planets appear to move in a path against the background of stars; at times the planets appear to move backwards in the sky.
  B. Models may be used to demonstrate that the earth and other planets revolve around the sun.

The relative motions of the sun, earth, moon, and planets bring about phases.
  A. The earth, moon, and other planets are seen by reflected sunlight.
  B. Differences in the moon's appearance are caused by changes in the relative positions of the sun, earth, and moon.

The relative motions of the sun, earth, and moon bring about eclipses.
  A. An eclipse of the sun occurs when the moon's shadow falls upon the earth.
  B. An eclipse of the moon occurs when the earth's shadow falls on the moon.

The solar system is but a tiny part of the total universe.
  A. Meteors are streaks of light in the sky caused by pieces of mineral matter that enter the earth's atmosphere and burn up.
  B. Comets are masses of frozen particles which move in elliptical orbits around the sun.

Motion is a property of all objects and occurs when unbalanced forces act on them.
  A. The speed of a moving object is determined from the time elapsed and the distance covered.
  B. Time and distance can be measured in many different units.

There are different kinds of motion.
  A. Straight-line motion is motion of an object traveling in a straight line.
  B. Uniform motion is motion of an object traveling in a straight line and at a steady speed.

The motion of an object is dependent upon force.

All objects within the gravitational field of the earth are affected by the force of gravity.

Frictional forces absorb energy and prevent motion.

All objects possess the property of inertia which affects their movement.

unit one
Animals, Plants,
and Places

unit one

Animals, Plants, and Places

SCIENCE INFORMATION FOR THE TEACHER

In a broad sense this unit is a study of the relationships of plants and animals to their environments. The planned experiences of the unit allow for a great diversity of activity. In the unit children observe various animals living in their natural habitats, as well as in simulated habitats. They recreate in the classroom common types of natural environments. By observing plants and animals in their environments, children become aware of the characteristics of living things. By creating simulated habitats, they develop an understanding of the basic needs of living things and the nature of compatible relationships between living things and their habitats.

As the children carry out the activities of the unit, they discover that although the types of habitats in which living things live differ greatly, all living things have certain basic needs which must be satisfied in their particular habitats. Animals live in habitats that provide them with food, oxygen, water, favorable conditions of temperature, and a reasonable amount of protection for themselves and their young. Plants too, live in habitats in which they can obtain nutrients, water, light, and some protection.

The children develop their understanding of continuity and change in this unit. They learn that populations of plants and animals continue, but they also learn the reason for this continuance: that the given animal or plant population has adapted to its environment and the changes in it. They learn that protective coloring and markings, for example, are evolutionary changes that have taken place over a long period of time.

All the activities of the unit are designed to encourage independent discovery by the children. As they observe plants and animals in their natural habitats, and in aquariums and terrariums in the classroom, they observe both similarities and differences in plant-animal-environment relationships. As they observe the living things in a woodland environment, for example, they compare frogs and toads. Through such observations they learn to compare, group, and categorize a great variety of living things.

Through such independent discoveries, they also observe the interdependence and interaction of living things. As they observe the eating habits of animals, children see that animals are dependent upon other animals and on plants for food. They observe other evidences of interaction and interdependence, for example, the hermit crab making use of vacant shells of snails, and seeds being spread by animals.

The children also make firsthand observations of the adaptations of organisms to their environments. For example, they observe the protective coloration of a frog. They see what happens to living things when conditions in their environments change or when they are placed in unnatural surroundings. They observe how living things respond to certain stimuli.

To make a full study of living things, one must see them in their natural surroundings. Not only are animals and plants affected in countless ways by the environment, but also they greatly modify the environment of which they are so important a part. This interaction of animals and plants with their surroundings is a subject of increasing interest to biologists.

Only a few of the limitless ways in which animals and plants are adapted to their surroundings are discussed in this unit. As soon as the student is aware of the principle involved, he should be encouraged to look for examples both by reading and in actual observation of animals and plants in their natural surroundings. Observations of this kind take much time and patience before they begin to become meaningful. It is not immediately evident that the environment might offer some explanation as to why some plants are wind-pollinated while others are pollinated by insects. Nor may one understand immediately why some animals living in fresh flowing water lay eggs that sink to the bottom, while some saltwater animals lay eggs that float on the surface.

We call the surroundings in which an organism normally lives its habitat. The habitat of a plant or animal will be an environment where the organism can find the means to satisfy its life needs—enough water, food, and air, proper conditions of light and temperature, and protection from its enemies. If a change should occur in the environment, making it difficult for members of a species to meet one or more of these needs, the species must adapt or die. Adaptation among the higher plants and animals is not a matter of individuals but generations. Organisms whose genetic make-up helps them to survive to reproductive age in an environment will pass on their genetic advantage to their offspring. In the course of many generations, a well-adapted population builds up. As the environment continues to change, those plants and animals within the population which can keep up with the changes are, again, the ones which will survive to reproduce a new generation.

Plants must be able to nourish themselves and reproduce in order for a plant species to survive in its environment. Water and light are two primary needs for the nutrition of green plants. The root of a germinating plant must reach down through the soil to seek the water and dissolved minerals which the plant will need later to produce food. The primitive leaves of the germinating plant must reach up through the soil to find the light so that photosynthesis can take place. Both movements are the young plant's responses to stimuli. Growth reactions determined by the direction from which a stimulus is applied are called tropisms. The root's response is a positive one—growing toward the stimulus and influenced by gravity. The leaves' response is a negative one—growing away from the stimulus of gravity. The response toward gravity is affected by a substance in the plant's cells that increases the rate of cell growth on one side of the root or stem.

Once the plant has broken through to the surface, additional stimuli come into play. Light, for example, is very important. Response to light (phototropism) is a phenomenon familiar to the classroom teacher, who knows that windowsill plants must be turned periodically if they are not to grow "all to one side." Differing light requirements of plants should be well known, too. Some plants thrive in a great deal of direct sunlight and will flourish in open fields; others will be found in nature growing in the shade of trees or tall shrubs. These plants live in different environments.

The kinds of species that will survive in an environment is limited by temperature. Tropical plants differ from arctic species, and both differ from temperate species. Within the temperate zone, plant species must be adapted to seasonal changes in temperature. Winter is a critical time for green plants since photosynthesis stops as the temperature nears the freezing point. Most woody plants such as trees and shrubs flourish during the spring, summer, and fall, and enter a period of inactivity or dormancy during the cold winter months. These plants lose their leaves, and their sap recedes to parts of the plant where it will not become frozen. This represents an adaptation to temperature.

The color change that precedes leaf loss in many trees is indirectly influenced by temperature change. In the warm months of the growing season, chlorophyll is continually being used up and replaced in the leaves. Autumn temperatures alter the rate of chlorophyll production and pigment formation. The predominant green substance yields to "autumn colors." Yellow and orange pigments, present in the leaf but previously masked by the chlorophyll, become evident. Red pigment is produced in cell sap as a result of cool weather and increased atmospheric water.

Evergreen trees retain their leaves throughout the winter. The leaves are usually waxy and needle-shaped for maximum protection against the cold. Even in the evergreens, metabolic activity almost stops during the winter.

Most non-woody plants are unable to survive the winter, and must possess other means of continuing the species. Some die, having produced seeds that are able to weather the winter cold. The seeds will germinate only when the temperature is again favorable to growth. Other plants die above ground, but have underground roots or stems from which new growth will develop in the spring.

For animals, too, the environment must provide adequate food and water, favorable temperature conditions, and some measure of concealment from enemies.

Plant-eating (herbivorous) mammals have flat grinding teeth which break down the tough plant fibers of their food. Seed-eating (herbivorous) birds have a muscular gizzard containing gravel and sand which serves a similar purpose. Meat-eating (carnivorous) animals are equipped for capturing prey. Birds with sharp beaks and talons, and mammals with claws and tearing teeth are common among carnivores. Some animals change their eating habits as they mature. The tadpole is a herbivore; the adult frog a carnivore. The change in diet requires a change in the digestive apparatus. Animals that eat both plants and animals are called omnivores.

Animals, like plants, must be adapted to seasonal changes in temperature if they are to survive. Some escape the temperature extremes of summer heat and winter cold by entering a state of inactivity in which their bodies' demands are greatly reduced. In winter, a few mammals and many reptiles and amphibians undergo hibernation, a state in which body metabolism is reduced to a minimum. A hibernating animal becomes active again only when increased environmental temperature speeds up the many processes once again. Summer dormancy, called estivation, is not so deep a state and lasts for a shorter period.

For those animals that must actively endure heat and cold, other adaptations are necessary. Many mammals grow coats of thick, short hair in autumn, shedding the extra hair in spring. The winter coats of these animals may differ in color from their summer coats. Seasonal change in a coat color serves the animal as camouflage in the seasonally changing environment. Many animals are colored to blend with their surroundings, an adaptation that increases the animals' chances of survival.

Migration of birds is an adaptation to seasonally changing environment that may be related to seasonal changes in the length of the day. Many birds of temperate regions fly south to tropical or semitropical environments when the days begin to shorten in autumn. In the lengthening days of spring, they return north to their breeding grounds. The timing of migration appears to be controlled by changes in the birds' internal chemistry, in response to changes in length of the day.

When we examine a habitat, we will find it populated by organisms that are well adapted to take advantage of it. The community of life on a mountain contains sure-footed goats that live on the sparse vegetation of mountain pastures, and hardy trees whose trunks resist the high winds and whose roots take firm hold in the cracks of rocky slopes. The plants that succeed in the desert are thick-skinned and spiny-leaved to hold in the precious moisture their roots must find deep in the ground. Desert animals conserve water by avoiding the dehydrating heat of noon; they seek their food in the cool of night. Non-air-breathing water animals, needing oxygen as air breathers do, have organs (gills) to extract dissolved oxygen from water as our lungs extract it from the air. Air breathers that live in water have a much greater ability to store oxygen in their bodies than do the land air breathers.

Not only are plants and animals adapted to the places in which they live; they can and do modify their surroundings. The layer of soil that covers dry land is, in fact, produced in large part by the action of plants and animals on weathered rock. Plants draw minerals from the soil to use in their own life processes. The living plant holds the soil in place with its roots; when dead, the plant returns its minerals to the soil and enriches the soil with the products of its decay. The earthworm and other burrowing animals tunnel through the soil, aerating it and loosening it for the passage of plant roots. Living animals add to the fertility of the soil by manuring it; the decomposed bodies of dead animals further enrich it. The relation here of plants, animals, and environment is very complex.

We owe our means of survival on the earth's surface to the interaction of plants, animals, and environment. The soil, in part built by plants and animals from the rocky crust, supports the plants that feed us and the animals on which we depend for food, clothing, service, and much more. We speak in the unit of food chains, but this is a simplification. It would be more accurate to speak of food webs, for we eat many kinds of plants and animals, and each thing that is food for us is nourished in turn by other living things.

Unless man has a proper regard for all forms of life and for the earth which sustains life, he will exploit the earth rather than use its resources in an appreciative and conservative way. The student should be led to understand how the good things of the earth are produced and how to use them without destroying them. Ultimately, their removal would be to man's own undoing. Studying the interaction of living things and the environment will help to develop a sense of the community of living things.

This unit, "Animals, Plants, and Places," allows the teacher considerable latitude to develop or restrict the various themes discussed. Discussion of the examples given should be encouraged. Collections of materials suggested by the examples should be accompanied by physical assignments. Mathematical surveys can be performed. For example, various tree leaves may be measured for length and width. Tables of data may be prepared, averages found, and so on. Encourage systematic data recording and discussion of the data. Science is continually asking the questions, why, how, when, what. Students should be brought to realize that science is not a collection of facts to be memorized, but rather a method for developing new knowledge.

Generalization I

Plants and animals can be found in a great variety of environments. Each living kind exists only in certain environments.

Contributing Principles

A. Plants and animals live in habitats in which they can obtain food and water.
B. Plants and animals live in habitats in which they are protected from their enemies.
C. Plants and animals live in habitats in which they can reproduce more of their kind.
D. Different plants and animals are found at different elevations in mountain environments.
E. Many plants and animals live in desert environments.
F. Many plants and animals live in and around pond environments.
G. Many plants and animals live along shallow seashore environments.
H. Many plants and animals live in deep ocean environments.

Generalization II

Some plants and animals respond to seasonal changes.

Contributing Principles

A. Some birds and mammals change color with changes in the seasons.
B. Some animals hibernate during cold weather.
C. Some animals estivate during hot, dry weather.
D. Many plants become dormant during the winter.
E. Many birds migrate great distances each spring and fall.

Generalization III

Plants and animals are adapted to their environments for survival.

Contributing Principles

A. Many seeds are adapted to be dispersed by means of wind or animals.
B. Many animals are adapted for protection by being able to move quickly.

C. Many animals are adapted for protection by outer body coverings.
D. Many animals are adapted for protection by their coloring and markings.

Generalization IV

Man has learned ways to use plants and animals.

Contributing Principles

A. Man uses plants for food, shelter, and clothing materials.
B. Man uses animals for food, work, and clothing materials.

before you begin

NEW WORDS FOR THE STUDENT

This list contains science words that will arise in the course of the unit. Mastery of the vocabulary is not essential. Use this list to help your students understand what they read. Do not require memorization of its contents.

carnivores meat-eating animals, such as dogs, cats, and lions

climate an average of weather conditions over a long period of time

community a group of plants and/or animals that live together and depend on each other in a given area

environment all the forces of nature acting on a living thing

food chain the order in which living things supply food for one another

food producers the green plants which produce food by the process of photosynthesis

habitat the natural environment in which plants and animals usually live

herbivores plant-eating animals such as horses, cows, and sheep *interdependence* the way in which living things affect and depend on each other

life processes the main body activities necessary for life in all living things

photosynthesis the process by which green plants produce food materials

population the number of all species of a plant or animal found in a specific area

protective coloration the variations in color which help protect animals from their enemies

scavenger an animal which feeds on dead or decaying materials

tundra a vast, treeless plain encircling the arctic region where the subsoil is frozen all year round

BOOKS FOR THE STUDENT

Amos, William H., *The Life of the Pond.* New York. McGraw-Hill, 1967.

Austin, Elizabeth S., *Penguins: The Birds with Flippers.* New York. Random House, 1968.

Bentley, Linna, *Plants That Eat Animals.* New York. McGraw-Hill, 1968.

Billington, Elizabeth T., *Understanding Ecology.* New York. Warne, 1968.

Brandhorst, Carl T., and Robert Sylvester, *The Tale of Whitefoot.* New York. Simon and Schuster, 1968.

Busch, Phyllis S., *Lions in the Grass: The Story of the Dandelion, A Green Plant.* Cleveland. World, 1968.

Busch, Phyllis S., *Once There Was a Tree: The Story of the Tree, A Changing Home for Plants and Animals.* Cleveland. World, 1968.

Cook, Joseph J., and William L. Wisner, *The Nightmare World of the Shark.* New York. Dodd, Mead, 1968.

Earle, Olive L., *Strange Fishes of the Sea.* New York. Morrow, 1968.

George, Jean Craighead, *The Moon of the Monarch Butterflies.* New York. Crowell-Collier, 1968.

Hawes, Judy, *Why Frogs Are Wet.* New York. Crowell-Collier, 1968.

Hess, Lilo, *The Curious Raccoons.* New York. Scribner's, 1968.

Hoff, Alice L., *Earth's Bug-Eyed Monsters.* New York. Norton, 1968.

Kellin, Sally Moffit, *A Book of Snails.* New York. Scott, 1968.

Knight, Maxwell, *The Small Water Mammals.* New York. McGraw-Hill, 1968.

Lauber, Patricia, *Bats: Wings in the Night.* New York. Random House, 1968.

Leskowitz, Irving, and A. Harris Stone, *Animals Are Like This.* Englewood Cliffs, N. J. Prentice-Hall, 1968.

Lindemann, Edward, *Some Animals Are Very Small.* New York. Crowell-Collier, 1968.

McCoy, J. J., *House Sparrows: Ragamuffins of the City.* New York. Seabury, 1968.

Pfadt, Robert E., *Animals Without Backbones.* Chicago. Follett, 1967.

Pringle, Laurence, *Dinosaurs and Their World.* New York. Harcourt, Brace & World, 1968.

Raskin, Edith, *The Fantastic Cactus: Indoors and In Nature.* New York. Lothrop, Lee and Shepard, 1968.

Rosen, Ellsworth, *Spiders Are Spinners.* Boston. Houghton Mifflin, 1968.

Shapp, Martha, and Charles Shapp, *Let's Find Out About Snakes.* New York. Watts, 1968.

Silverstein, Alvin, and Virginia B. Silverstein, *Unusual Partners: Symbiosis in the Living World.* New York. McGraw-Hill, 1968.

Wood, F. Dorothy, *The Cat Family.* New York. Harvey House, 1968.

BOOKS FOR THE TEACHER

Blanc, Sam S., Abraham S. Fischler, and Olcott Gardner, "The Relationships of Life," pp. 305–340, *Modern Science: Earth, Space, and Environment.* New York. Holt, Rinehart and Winston, 1967.

Blough, Glenn, and Julius Schwartz, "Living Things," pp. 209–394, *Elementary School Science and How to Teach It.* New York. Holt, Rinehart and Winston, 1964.

Gaga, Peter C., *Science in Elementary Education.* New York. John Wiley, 1966.

Hone, Elizabeth, *Teaching Elementary Science,* ed. Paul F. Brandwein, New York. Harcourt, Brace & World, 1962.

FILMS

Adapting to Changes in Nature　　　　　10 minutes　B&W/color　JF
Shows how living things are able to survive in various types of environments by adapting to different changes as they occur.

Animals' Homes　　　　　11 minutes　B&W/color　EEF
Shows where various animals live and explains why animals build their homes where they do. Includes scenes showing where trap-door spiders, squirrels, raccoons, skunks, woodchucks, and wood mice live.

Animals at Night　　　　　11 minutes　B&W/color　EBF
Presents a study of various nocturnal animals, pointing out their physical characteristics, habits, and adaptations to their nighttime environment. Shows the habits of insects, worms, toads, salamanders, snakes, bats, beavers, porcupines, and raccoons.

Animals—Ways They Eat　　　　　11 minutes　B&W/color　EBF
Pictures the adaptations of various animals that enable them to catch and eat the food necessary for their survival. Shows amebas, snails, crabs, fish, birds, giraffes, cows, and other animals.

Animals—Ways They Move   11 minutes   B&W/color   EBF
Shows different ways animals move, such as running, hopping,
crawling, swimming, climbing, gliding, and flying. Shows bison,
ostrich, kangaroos, rabbits, grasshoppers, inchworms, snails, eels,
sea lions, flying squirrels, and herons.

Adaptations of Plants and Animals   13 minutes   B&W/color   COR
Illustrates adaptations that enable living things to protect themselves
and to obtain food. Emphasizes the point that the principle of adaptation is essential to survival of plants and animals.

Animal Communities and Groups   11 minutes   B&W/color   COR
Gives examples of two ways animals live. Shows animals that live
in groups: cliff swallows, elk, bison, beavers, and quail—and animals
that live in communities: ants and termites.

Animals Protect Themselves   11 minutes   B&W/color   COR
Shows that some animals have adaptations for self-protection such
as their ability to run, their color, or their structure. Others have
defensive adaptations, such as the odor glands in a skunk. A number
of adaptations are seen.

Life Between Tides   11 minutes   B&W/color   EBF
Explains that living things along seashores and in tidepools must be
able to adjust to both a water and air environment in order to survive. Shows adaptations in clams, seaweeds, barnacles, limpets,
mussels, starfish, anemones, and others.

How Animals Live in Winter   11 minutes   B&W/color   COR
Shows how animals are adapted to live through the winter by means
of hibernation, protective coloration, or migration. Compares winter
and summer habitats of snowshoe rabbits, raccoon, skunk, badger,
and deer.

How Nature Protects Animals   11 minutes   B&W/color   EBF
Illustrates typical defensive adaptations of animals. Shows many
adaptations, such as running, swimming, climbing, and flying; shows
how protective coloration serves to protect some animals from their
enemies.

Wonders in the Desert   11 minutes   B&W/color   CF
Describes habits and adaptations that enable the jackrabbit, burro,
tortoise, and mouse to survive in a desert environment.

Wonders in a Country Stream   11 minutes   B&W/color   CF
Shows fish, a garter snake, insects that walk on water, and a damsel

fly. Illustrates their adaptations for life in a water environment; also shows views of frogs, newts, and a baby turtle.

Wonders in Your Own Backyard   11 minutes   B&W/color   CF
Shows habits of earthworms, house spiders, millipedes, sowbugs, and snails. Close-up photography shows many interesting adaptations of these animals.

A Plant Through the Seasons   11 minutes   B&W/color   EBF
Shows the changes that take place in a plant as the seasons change. Traces through the life cycle of the plant.

Plants That Live in Water   11 minutes   B&W/color   COR
Surveys plants that live in streams and ponds. Shows close-ups of the smaller plants. Explains how the water habitat meets the needs for survival.

Seasonal Growth in Plants   11 minutes   B&W   YAF
Explains the difference between annual, biennial, and perennial plants. Discusses why plants shed leaves, how the formation of buds takes place, and why leaves change color in the fall.

We Explore the Desert   11 minutes   B&W/color   COR
Surveys animals that live in the desert with good close-ups. Explains how desert plants are adapted to conserve water. Shows that the desert comes to life at night when the temperature drops.

CF	Churchill Films
COR	Coronet Films
EBF	Encyclopaedia Britannica Films
JF	Journal Films
YAF	Young America Films

BULLETIN BOARDS

Where Do Animals Live?

Put up in a random order pictures or drawings of various animals and of different kinds of habitats. Let the children link the animal to its home by means of a colored cord. For example, show squirrels living in fields, deer in forests, and so forth.

What Do I Eat?

Put up pictures of a number of animals and of a number of the foods they eat. Have the class illustrate the food chain by linking the primary food to the intermediate animal and the intermediate animal to the ultimate consumer. For example, one food chain might consist of plants, rabbits, and coyotes; another of seeds, mice, and owls.

What Kind of Climate Can I Live In?

Show pictures of typical climatic regions, such as deserts, swamps, grasslands, temperate forests, and polar regions. Have the students bring in cutouts of plants and animals that would be found in these regions. Let each child explain why his plant or animal belongs in a certain region. If he is right, let him put up the picture in the proper place.

What Kinds of Plants and Animals Live on Mountains?

Put up a diagram or chart of a steep mountain slope, showing the life zones. Put up pictures of plants in the appropriate life zones. Have the children bring in pictures of typical mammals and birds that live in each zone and pin them in place.

DISPLAYS AND EXHIBITS

Make dioramas of different kinds of habitats. For a background use plaster covered with soil, twigs, and plants. Animal and bird pictures can be pasted on cardboard and then cut out for the diorama. Small models of animals can be purchased at the dime store and painted appropriate colors. Let the class discuss ways in which the animals are adapted for survival in that habitat.

Display a collection of birds' nests. Let the students tell what kinds of birds must have nested in each one. (Nests may be collected after the breeding season, because most birds do not use a nest more than one season.)

Terrariums showing various types of life conditions (desert, woodland, swamp) should be set up around the room. See pages 20–21 of this teacher's edition for further suggestions.

A balanced aquarium should be in the room at all times. Encourage the children to observe the living things in it and to tell how they get food and oxygen. See pages 28–29 of this teacher's edition for suggestions.

A saltwater aquarium is an interesting exhibit for showing various kinds of tidepool life. Directions for making one can be found in most high school laboratory manuals or in books dealing with aquaria. See also suggestions on pages 36–38 of this teacher's edition.

THE HISTORY OF THE IDEA

The opening statements of this unit show a vital connection exists between our world and the living things in it. A cactus plant can grow in the deserts of Arizona but not in the rain forests of Brazil. The oyster and clam communities can flourish in the sea but only if the population of the starfish is controlled.

This connection is not commonly appreciated. Indeed, the science of ecology or the study of living things and their environment did not have serious beginnings until the late nineteenth and the early twentieth centuries, although its origins can be traced back to the natural history of Aristotle. Today, however, ecology touches many fields, such as taxonomy, physiology, biochemistry, geography, and psychology.

The story of the peppered moth prepares the child to see that the survival, change, and development of a living thing are related to its habitat. The point of the story may be elaborated if the children

studying the picture

The children may be encouraged to recognize that the picture of the rabbit and the lizard, as well as the picture of the coral and the fish, not only show particular animals but particular places as well. *To have the children discover the importance of place, ask them why they would not find a rabbit or a lizard in the picture of the coral and the fish, or vice versa.* Rabbits and lizards are land animals, and fish are water animals. You can at this point also discover in general terms how well or how poorly individual children are prepared to study animals, plants, and places, or how well the children are inclined to observe, question, discover, or infer. Studying these pictures through questions should at the outset establish inquiry as a tool to pursue learning.

are asked to consider why some animals and plants are at home in the sea, while others are at home on land. Why does the polar bear have white fur? Why can some animals and plants live in very cold places while others cannot?

The children need not be expected to answer these questions immediately. The questions are designed to open lines of inquiry to be developed as study of the unit progresses. A discussion, however, is hoped to suggest that in the lives of animals and plants surroundings play a necessary and influential role.

You are familiar with plants and animals. But have you ever noticed the place in which they live? Have you ever thought that there might be a link between living things and their surroundings? Let's look at a certain place and a particular animal, the peppered moth, living in it.

The peppered moth lives near the industrial city of Manchester, England. Before 1845, the moth was light colored with some dark spots. Birds, the moth's enemy, had difficulty seeing it as the moth rested on light tree bark. The color of the moth helped it blend in with its surroundings. In 1845, however, a black peppered moth was captured. It was a new variety. Could the black moth live in light-colored surroundings?

Manchester was rapidly becoming an industrial center, and factory chimney soot had darkened the grey tree bark. Black moths resting on this bark were hard to find, and birds found the light moths were easier to see and eat. Within fifty years almost all kinds of peppered moths in the area of Manchester were of the black variety.

Animals and plants are suited to the places in which they live. These places are called habitats (HAB-i-tats). Many animals and plants must live in special places where they can obtain food and water, where they can protect themselves, and where they can reproduce.

Some animals are more at home in forests, while others are most at home in open fields. Think of some plants and animals you find on a desert. Can you name some plants and animals that live only in water? Would a cow eat the same food as a tiger? Why can some animals live in cold places while others cannot?

You will be studying animals and plants in their surroundings. There are many ways that animals and plants are suited to live in fields or in woods, on mountains, or on deserts, and in fresh water. Each plant or animal lives in the habitat that is best for it.

3

the unit at a glance

The conceptual scheme of this unit is defined by the questions ecology answers. Ecology can be thought of as the study of the distribution of animals and plants, for distribution itself expresses the relationship of living things to their surroundings. To study distribution is an observational process. One must observe the many kinds of habitats and the kinds of animals and plants living in their particular surroundings. Therefore, this unit first answers the question *what*. To this information, the process of inference may be applied, and we may say that living things are adapted to their surroundings. The question of *how* can then be answered. The answers to *what* and *how* become the basis for the study of functional biology in Book Five.

OVERVIEW

This section emphasizes that in order to keep living animals and plants in a classroom properly, the conditions of the natural habitat must be duplicated as closely as possible. The main activity is the building of a woodland terrarium and caring for it in a classroom. Animals can also be added to the terrarium. Plants and animals can also be observed at home, and their individual differences and requirements can be determined from careful observation.

process skills

Duplicating natural habitats of plants and animals in the classroom

Selecting plants and animals which are appropriate to the various habitats

materials

various leaves, fish tank, small pebbles, sand, garden-rich soil, small woodland plants, small woodland animals, glass cover for terrarium

how to begin

You can initiate the discussion of natural habitats by asking the children to tell how they care for their pets at home. Have them discuss what their pets eat and how they provide for their pets' needs. Ask the students if any of them have unusual pets at home that need special food and special care. Discuss why there are many kinds of living things that the youngsters could not care for at home because of the special requirements of those things.

WHAT ARE SOME HABITATS OF
LIVING THINGS?

Some of your observations of plants and animals can be done at home or in the classroom. Dogs and cats are common pets. You probably would not bring a pet to school, but you can study it at home. What other animals besides dogs and cats do people keep as pets?

What differences do you notice between cats and dogs? Are all dogs alike? How do they differ? Are all cats alike? How are they different? Find out what cats eat. Find out what dogs eat.

procedure

Ask the children, one by one, to name as many different animals as they can. After they have exhausted their inventory of animals, tell them to think of where each of these animals lives. With the students' help, list on the chalkboard some of these typical places (habitats). Introduce the term, *habitat,* and divide the class into as many groups as the main habitats listed on the board (forest habitat, desert habitat, field habitat, mountain habitat, pond and stream habitat, ocean habitat). Let the groups of children make drawings of typical plants and animals found in each of the habitats.

The children can be helped to think about important similarities and differences of living things if asked to reflect on animals or plants with which they are familiar. Dogs usually eat a variety of meat or meat-like foods, dry cereals, and water. Cats can thrive on a diet of fish, meat, and milk. Dogs more heavily depend on an acute sense of smell than do cats.

The children may not be aware of the fact that the great variety of plants implies a variety of needs. In contrast to green plants, non-green plants, such as some kinds of mushrooms, grow best with no sunlight. Among green plants, proper amounts of sunlight and water required depend upon the particular kind of plant at hand.

(continued on page 20)

1/Observe

Make a list in your notebook of different kinds of pets as shown in the following table.

Kind of Pet	Body Covering	Kind of Food
1. Dog	Fur	Meat
2. Cat	Fur	Meat, Fish
3.		
4.		
5.		

Do plants also differ in how they look? Do they all need the same care? Do most plants you know grow better in bright sun? Do some plants grow better in shade?

studying the picture

Ask the children to compare the flowers on the plant in this picture. *Does each flower have the same number of petals? Are the color patterns alike or different? Have the children infer how the color and general appearance of the flowers might help the plant survive in a natural habitat.* The colors may be attractive to insects in the habitat; the insects may pollinate the plant as they move about on the flower.

5

In 3/Investigate, the youngsters learn how to build a simple terrarium. The building of a woodland terrarium can be done as a single class project or several can be made by each group of children. If more than one terrarium is to be made, the class can be divided into groups of six to eight. Have the students bring in small woodland plants and be sure they bring in some of the soil surrounding the plants. The type of plants will vary with each geographical area.

Have the children provide the pebbles, sand, and garden soil for the terrarium. They can use moss to cover one area of it. Provide a small, shallow area of water if frogs or toads are put into the terrarium.

After the terrarium is built, have the youngsters share in caring for the plants and animals in it. Have them use a pane of glass to cover the terrarium and help keep the moisture from completely evaporating. The children can provide for any animals they keep

responses to 2/compare

1. All have stems and veins. Edges may be smooth, toothed, or indented. Some may have fuzzy or velvety surfaces. Some are long and bladelike, some oval or rounded.

studying the picture

Ask the children how many animals they can find in the aquarium. Ask how many different kinds they can identify. Have them count the number of different plants they see. *Ask how the plants and rocks might be beneficial to the animals in this habitat.*

2/Compare

Collect some leaves from different plants. Draw their outlines. Observe how they differ in size and shape. Are there any similarities? ■

Observing plants and animals can be an exciting experience in your classroom. Let us make a typical plant and animal habitat in the following activity.

3/Investigate

A field terrarium in your classroom is a good place for observing the habits of some small animals. An empty fish tank will make a good container. First, put a layer of small pebbles about an inch deep in the bottom. Now place a half-inch layer of sand over the pebbles. Finish with an inch of garden-rich soil.

in their woodland terrarium. Have them find out if there is any special care needed for the particular animals they have.

The students can report periodically to the entire class on how the terrarium and the plants and animals it contains are doing. What is most important is that the children learn that what they are doing is duplicating as closely as possible a particular habitat for the plants and animals they are keeping in their woodland environments in their classrooms.

(continued on page 22)

Collect your plants from a wooded area. You can get low-growing plants like ferns, mosses, and other small plants. Leave some of the soil around the roots when you dig up ferns or mosses. Keep the soil moist around the plant roots until you have planted them in the terrarium.

Water your terrarium well. The water should be about halfway up the layer of pebbles. Keep your terrarium almost completely covered with a glass plate. This covering will help to conserve the moisture needed by the plants, and they will not have to be watered as often.

Now your terrarium is ready for some animals. A toad, if you can get one, is an interesting animal to observe. You can feed it earthworms. How does the toad eat? A toad's tongue is sticky. Watch the action of the tongue as you feed an earthworm to the toad. You may want to get other animals for your terrarium. A frog, small garter snake, salamander, or a turtle also makes a good terrarium pet. Find out what kind of food your terrarium animal will need. Why should you not put too many animals in your terrarium? ■

7

responses to 3/investigate

1. The toad's tongue is attached at the front of the mouth. The toad flips its tongue out and captures an insect, then flips its tongue back and swallows the insect.

2. Too many animals in the terrarium will upset the natural balance between the animals and their environment.

note

A few pieces of rock or wood for the toad to hide under should be placed along the sides of the terrarium. The toad will feed on live flies, beetles, and other insects, but will rarely take food that is not moving. To feed a toad you may dangle a live insect in front of the toad's mouth. Children will be interested to see how rapidly the toad's tongue flips out to capture the food.

21

The last statement of Testing Your Ideas best explains why the cactus plant died.

Testing Your Ideas should not merely be used to examine the student's understanding of the lesson or to summarize for him the lesson's major points. These questions should also be used to develop the student's powers of thought. To this end you might have the students state why the false explanations of the cactus' death are false. You should also have the students state why the last statement is true. For example, they may refer to instances in which a living thing other than a cactus dies without proper surroundings. A cactus houseplant does not need to be watered frequently because water is stored in the plant.

optional activity

To observe the habitat of earthworms and the function of these animals, make a box two sides of which should be made of glass about one foot long and one foot high. The ends of the box should be made of wood about three inches wide and one-half inch thick. Fill the box with soil to a height of nine inches and put in a few earthworms. Cover the glass sides with black paper and let the "wormarium" stand for a few days. When the paper is removed, the children should be able to see how earthworms burrow underground. The children can observe that the worms loosen the soil. You may ask the children if they can imagine how the burrowing earthworms help root-plants grow and branch.

In order to keep plants and animals alive in your classroom, you must try to provide the things they would have in their natural habitat. A frog in your terrarium would need a small pan of water so that it could keep its skin moist. If you were growing plants that should have a lot of sun, you would place them on a window sill instead of in a shady place. Since cactus plants grow naturally in the desert, would they need much water? In each case you try to make the new habitat as much like the natural one as possible.

TESTING YOUR IDEAS

A cactus was planted in rich, brown soil, shaded from the sun, and watered twice a day. The cactus died. Which of the following reasons best explains why the plant died?

A cactus may die of a disease.
A cactus usually has a short life.
A cactus never survives outside of a desert.
A cactus usually can only live and grow in a habitat which meets its needs.

8

OVERVIEW

The children learn to use their powers of observation when examining plants and animals in an open area outdoors. Here they get an opportunity to see how well they can examine a specific section to look for plant and animal varieties. As the students look for animals, ask them to notice what food the animals eat and what are some of their habits. It is important for the youngsters to realize that only by careful and studious observation can they see all the animals and plants in a specific outdoor area.

how to begin

Instruct the children on the proper way to begin observing living things outdoors. First, they should realize that plant and animal species should not be destroyed by carelessness. If they are going to take samples of plants, they should remove the samples carefully, leaving some of the soil around the roots. Animals should be taken only if they can be cared for properly in the classroom or at home. Ask several students to look up local wildlife regulations.

(continued on page 24)

WHAT IS THE KIND OF HABITAT IN WHICH YOU LIVE?

You can continue your study of living things and their surroundings near your home or school. If there are fields or open lots nearby, you might find some wild flowers and grasses. Do you know what we usually call these wild flowers and grasses? If you say they are weeds, you are correct! Since weeds are growing in their natural habitat, they grow very fast. If you have a garden, you pull out the weeds to protect the plants you are trying to grow. Name some other places where you have observed weeds growing.

process skills

Carefully examining the plants and animals in a small geographic area

Observing the habits of animals in an outdoor habitat

materials

notebooks, pencils, magnifying glass*, binoculars*

---

* one per team

Regulations that provide for the protection of animals and plants will differ from state to state, and the children should become familiar with those that pertain to their own area.

procedure

At this point the students should be ready to discover that their immediate environments offer examples of specialized habitats. In many of our larger cities, the school may lack immediate surroundings in which livings things may be found. If this is the case, encourage the children to go to vacant lots, parks, and other areas where plants and animals may be found. There is a great variety of life to be discovered even in some very unlikely places. Let the youngsters help you identify some of these specialized habitats by discussing with them where they have noticed plants and animals near their homes, on the way to school, or in other areas.

For 4/Observe, have the children divided into teams of about six to eight students. Let each team choose a captain who will be responsible for recording the name and number of the animals and/or plants the teams observe. The children can decide what they will look for—either plant or animal

studying the picture

Have the children describe the coloration of the insect shown. *Ask them how the coloration might be helpful to the insect.* It serves as camouflage against backgrounds of similar coloring. Ask the children to describe other animals which are protected by their coloration.

for your information

Rabbits eat rough plant foods, which they chew with a grinding, sideways motion of the lower jaw.

Walking through a field, you may see a rabbit hop quickly through the grass and then stop to eat. What does a rabbit eat? There will be food and shelter for each kind of animal you find in the field.

Under an upturned stone you may see fat, white worms, called grubs. These are young beetles. In a moist area, you might find salamanders or earthworms. Take a look under a large rock. You can study the plants and animals living in your schoolyard, an empty lot, in a park, or small open area. Let us see how many plants and animals we find in one area.

4/Observe

Before you go out into the area, you should be organized into teams. Decide what each team will look for. Several animals can be assigned to each team. There may be insects, spiders, sparrows, toads, squirrels, cats, chipmunks, rabbits, and many other animals in the open area you select for study. Other teams will look for plants such as trees, shrubs, grasses, ferns and mosses. The captain of each team will record the name and number of the animals and plants that his team finds. ■

species. They can divide the animals into birds, insects, and small mammals. Plant groups can be divided into trees, shrubs, flowering plants, and weed varieties. It would be better for the children to record the plants and animals they find with descriptions, naming the familiar ones and then using a field guide when they return to the classroom to identify those they did not know. Leaf samples can be gathered for identification. The class should notice the type of soil the plants grow in—sandy, rich loam, or clay soil.

Before each group starts out, re-emphasize that careful observation is of the utmost importance. Also stress the idea that conservation of plants and animals is a constant necessity and that the examination of living things in the field should observe conservation rules and ideals. When the children return to class with their notes and any specimens they may have gathered, they can discuss and compare what they have found. They can see how many varieties of plant and animal life were observed. Using field guides, they can try to identify as many species as possible. See how the teams compare as to how well they have recorded their observations and as to how descriptive they have been. They can add some of their specimens to any existing woodland terrarium in the classroom or at home.

(continued on page 26)

Looking for plants and animals needs careful observation. When first going out to look, you may think there is little to find. Upturned rocks might reveal tiny insects. Ant hills may be found when you brush aside grass. Careful looking is the key to a successful hunt.

On your next field trip you could select one animal for study. The squirrel is one of the most common animals around many homes or in parks in certain parts of the United States. So many of these furry animals live in city parks that many of them are almost as tame as dogs or cats. Even if these park squirrels were not fed peanuts and popcorn, they would not grow hungry. They are well suited for finding the food they need. Look at the picture of the squirrel. What do you think it can eat? Note the shape of its teeth.

When you spot a squirrel, watch to see what food it is collecting or eating. Notice how it climbs a tree. Could you climb a tree that fast? How do its sharp claws help the squirrel? What use to the squirrel is its bushy tail as it jumps from one branch to another?

optional activity

Insects which have been collected on the field trip may be kept in an insect terrarium. Roll a square of wire screen into a tube eight inches in diameter and stand it in a cake pan filled with plaster of Paris. When the plaster is dry, the screen will be held in place. Another cake pan can be used for the top of the cage. Put a few inches of sand, some twigs, and a shallow jar lid of water in the bottom of the cage. Ask the children to observe the activities of the insects.

for your information

A squirrel eats nuts, twigs, and rough plant foods. Its sharp claws enable it to hang onto trees, and its tail keeps balance.

11

25

Before having the children do 5/Observe, ask them about animals with which they are familiar. While some of the most common house pets may initially spring to mind, hopefully the students may become aware that they are familiar with a wider range of animals than their first thoughts imply. Moreover, the variety of experience of the children should be shared. Perhaps one child may be familiar with a particular animal not an intimate part of his classmates' experience and might be encouraged to speak about it. If this is so, the characteristics of the animal might be compared with those of an animal the children all know well. In light of this comparison, features that are common to most animals, and that therefore are important to notice, may be decided upon. This discussion may suggest how animals differ from each other. Then, a child observing a familiar animal may become more acutely aware of its particular identity.

The first statement of Testing Your Ideas is true and should suggest that a living thing is always linked with a particular place to live. The second statement has been made sufficiently general so that, hopefully, it will be true for everyone in your class. The third statement is true. The answers to the fourth and fifth statements will vary depending upon your geographical area. In most areas, they both would be false.

responses to 5/observe

1. Some animals use their legs for capturing food or holding food.

optional activity

Have a pair of children work together. Each pair can find an area of soil approximately two feet square. Let them turn over the soil and smooth it down. Have them observe it each day. Let them observe the plants which appear first. They can map their area by placing a piece of plastic over it on four stakes, and then marking on the plastic sheet each plant's position and the date it appeared. In this way, the class can keep track of the number and variety of plants. The students can use different colored pencils for each type of plant. They can also observe the types of animals which enter and leave (or make a home in) the environment.

5/Observe

You may want to observe a bird, a kitten or some other familiar animal. Write down the observations you make of the animal you select for study. Describe the size, shape and color of the animal. How many legs does it have? Do any animals use their legs for something besides moving? Notice the food an animal eats. Find out where the animal spends most of its time. ■

TESTING YOUR IDEAS

Which of the following statements are true about the area in which you live?

The area in which you live is a particular habitat.
Your area has special habitats in it, such as an empty lot, a woods; a park, pond or garden; an apartment house, a home; a flower pot, fish tank, or bird cage.
Your area is part of a larger habitat.
The weather in your area is practically the same all year round.
There are many kinds of animals and plants in the area in which you live.
The kinds of animals in your area are the same whatever the time of year.

OVERVIEW

The children continue to use their powers of observation in gathering living organisms. Here they observe the variety of life found in a pond or small stream. They will use more specialized techniques for gathering specimens and identifying and observing them. Again, it is important that the students' observations be accurate and detailed. Conservation measures should again be stressed and the class reminded of them and their importance to our natural wildlife.

how to begin

Use a filmstrip in color to show the varieties of life found in freshwater areas at various seasons of the year. The filmstrip will show the children the proper way to begin their observation and collection of freshwater plants and animals. The youngsters can also be introduced through the filmstrip to the variety of living things to be found in a pond or freshwater stream.

WHAT LIVES IN THE HABITAT OF A POND?

You will be able to observe and study hundreds of living things if you live near a freshwater pond, a small stream, or near a park which has a body of water where living things might grow. Ask an adult to go with you. Each time you go exploring you will discover something interesting and new. Pond exploring can be an adventure. The kinds of plants and animals you discover will depend on the size of the pond, its location, how deep it is, and many other conditions. The plants and animals you find may be different from those your classmates find in other ponds.

process skills

Observing and collecting living organisms found in ponds and streams

Using power of observation to describe accurately plants and animals found in freshwater areas

materials

collecting containers (jars, bottles, all with lids)°, microprojector or microscope, field guides

Frogs' eggs may be purchased inexpensively at a biological supply house.

° one per team

13

procedure

The activities up to this point have led the class to discover something about plants and animals living in dry-land habitats. But there are many interesting varieties of life to be found in ponds and streams. Since water habitats may not exist near the school or community, the children should be encouraged to study pond life individually or in small groups. The animals collected can be brought to school in small jars with screw lids. Discuss with the students the necessity for keeping the animals in water taken from the pond. Treated water used in the school or at home usually has too much chlorine in it for pond life to thrive. Lead the class to understand that substances in the water, its oxygen content, microscopic plants, etc., are all factors necessary for forms of pond life to live.

studying the picture

Ask the children to look carefully at the pond area and locate places that seem to be good for the protection of various animals. Have the children give rationales for the places they suggest.

Ask them from which direction the sun comes. Have them discuss the advantages and disadvantages of the shadow areas cast by the sun.

An ordinary pond is a small body of water fed by a small stream or spring. Its edges are overgrown by plants whose roots grow in the moist soil or mud. Most ponds are not very deep. Some plants grow in the water at the pond's edge. Still other plants are able to grow on and beneath the surface of the pond.

Since pond life is always changing with the seasons, the time of year you decide to visit a pond is important. What is a good time to explore a pond in the region where you live? What is the poorest time of the year? In many parts of our country, the first sign of spring is the appearance of skunk cabbage

Tadpoles, salamanders, and insects searching for food may hide under rocks or plants or in the mud. Scientists study plants and animals in their natural habitats to discover the relationship of a living thing to its total environment. Some important environmental factors include the food supply, light, heat, cold, and altitude. Relationships of the living thing to other plants and animals are also studied.

It is necessary to collect samples of plants and animals for indoor study in order to examine internal structures and to test reactions to controlled environments.

The best times to see a pond's animal and plant life is during the spring and summer months. Nevertheless, life in and near a pond during the fall is still active.

(continued on page 30)

along the banks of ponds and streams. Cattails and other plants rise out of the shallow water where their roots are anchored in the muddy bottom. Farther out from the shore, duckweed and pond lillies float on the surface of the water.

There are many places for animals to hide and many sources of food in ponds. Can you think where tadpoles, salamanders and insects searching for food might be hiding? In trying to obtain food, many animals are in danger of being eaten themselves. All these pond dwellers are carrying on a battle to stay alive.

Think of some ways in which changes of season might cause pond life to become different.

Cold, rain, periods of dry weather, chemicals in the water, and changes of season can affect pond life.

Why do some scientists study plants and animals in their natural habitats? Why is it sometimes necessary to collect samples of plants and animals for further study indoors? You may want to study some pond animals in your classroom by doing the next activity.

15

optional activity

Re-create a bog or swamp environment. To produce a swamp environment, use bog soil or make a base of sand, peat, and gravel in equal parts about two inches deep. Place a pan of water on a gentle slope of earth to make it easy for animals to climb in and out. Mosses, ferns, Venus's flytraps, and pitcher plants would be appropriate for this environment. To make an attractive display, place the taller plants in the back and on the sides. Try to avoid overcrowding, but arrange everything so that no bare earth shows. After planting, sprinkle the terrarium with water and cover it with a glass top to maintain the water cycle. Frogs, newts, tadpoles, salamanders, and turtles will live in this moist, marshy habitat. Most of these animals will prefer live food such as insects, mealworms, and moths.

6/Investigate should give an impressive sample of microscopic animals, especially if the area chosen for study is rich in duckweed or small flowering plants. Abundant plant and animal life indicates a healthy pond. Desmids, diatoms, blue-green algae, insect larvae, and peritrichs are usually present. Also rotifers and hydra are likely to be found. The chance of finding each kind of animal is great if individual teams of six to eight children collect a sample. All these animals might easily be identified to the student through the use of a filmstrip or a well-illustrated book. Some of these sources are listed in the bibliography. The student's familiarity with these animals, however, is not as important as is knowing that duckweed is a significant influence in the surroundings of the animal life thriving under it. Almost all animals in the duckweed habitat are attaching forms that move along the roots to feed on bacteria and algae. Found commonly in areas usually free of predators that might feed on microscopic life, duckweed also supplies oxygen to the attached animals.

responses to 6/investigate

1. Insect larvae, protozoa, and hydras may be seen. The children should not be held responsible for the names of these animals.
2. Animals may be seen attached to roots to feed on bacteria and algae.
3. Plants supply oxygen.
4. Duckweed usually grows in areas free of predators, but fish, frogs, and water insects may be found.
5. The plant provides a source of food and protection.

studying the picture

Have the children describe the animals that they see. *Ask if the picture represents the correct size of the animals or if the size has been reduced or magnified.* Have them provide rationales for their answers. The bottom picture in the margin is a magnification of the top picture.

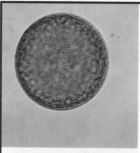

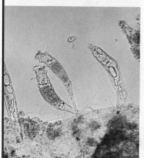

6/Investigate

Walk along the edge of a pond or any other shallow body of fresh water. Look for some duckweed, as is shown in the picture, or a small, flowering plant. They are usually found in quiet, sheltered, shoreline areas. Collect some of the plant and some of the water below it. Use a jar which you can cover with a lid. With your teacher's help, examine the water with a microscope or microprojector. Do you find any tiny animals among the plant? Do you see any of them clinging to the roots? How does the plant help these animals breathe? When you collected the plant, did you see any animals that might eat the creatures that you found? Why is the plant a good habitat for these living things? ■

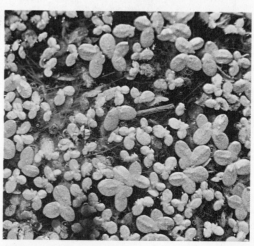

On this field trip, frogs, water insects, water fleas, worms dug from the muddy bottom, and plants of various kinds may be collected for a pond aquarium. Stress that only a few specimens should be taken from their natural habitat. Help the students through the use of field guides to identify any plants and animals they collect which they cannot readily name.

Ask the students to compare a frog's coloring with the colors in its natural environment. Such protective coloration helps the frog hide from its enemies.

(continued on page 32)

The variety of animals found in a pond may be great. It may range from those that can be seen only with a magnifier to those as large as fish. Your collection will be just a small sampling of pond animals.

Walking along the shore of most ponds in spring or summer, you can hear and see frogs splashing in the water. Some pond frogs have bright green heads and darker green backs. Their bellies are white, and the throats of the male frogs are often bright yellow. Can you explain why the coloring of a frog helps it hide from its enemies?

Frogs play an important part in pond life. Like many other pond animals, frogs go through many body changes during their lives. Frogs start as tiny eggs covered with a jelly-like covering. These eggs can be

17

optional activity

Aquatic insects make an interesting group of animals for classroom study. Prepare a gallon jar by putting several inches of sand in the bottom, and by planting a few water plants in the sand. Add pond water, and collect water insects, such as dragonfly nymphs and damsel flies, and water striders. Keep them in the aquarium for the children to observe. Push some sticks into the sand so that they slant up to the sides of the jar above the water level. This is needed for insects which emerge from the water as they complete their metamorphosis from nymph to adult.

It may be interesting for the students to realize how curiously different the frog is from other animals, since it is adapted to two far different environments at different times in its life. Living in the water during the early stages of its life, the frog is well adapted to a water environment, since it has, for example, gills for breathing and a tail for swimming. The development of lungs makes it adapted for land, but its skin, diet, and webbed feet show the frog to be still a citizen of a pond-like habitat. The frog is a water-land animal, an amphibian. Ask the children how the frog is uniquely different from most animals in terms of its life cycle.

Dams built by beavers may slow the flow of streams and bring that freshwater habitat closer to the conditions of a pond-like environment. Life in streams and ponds becomes less active in the winter than in the summer, reacting to a change in temperature.

optional activity

The children can use a freshwater aquarium to grow tadpoles into frogs. Since the time it takes for tadpoles to change into frogs is often longer than the class cares to wait, this process can be hastened by feeding the tadpoles pieces of minced thyroid glands obtained from a slaughter house. This makes the frogs smaller than they normally would be, but it speeds up the process and fascinates the children.

found among the water plants of the pond in the spring or early summer. The dark spots in the jelly mass are frog eggs from which tadpoles will grow.

Tadpoles live like fish during their early lives. They have gills and can get oxygen they need from the pond water. In the next few weeks the tadpoles will grow legs, develop lungs, and gradually lose their tails. They develop from the tadpole stage into frogs.

Tadpoles feed on small plants in water. They can be called vegetarians (veh-juh-TAIR-ee-unz) because they eat only plants. If you can catch some tadpoles and observe them in your classroom, you can see what they eat. Put some water plants into your aquarium. Tadpoles will also eat small pieces of lettuce.

Suppose you put tadpoles in the aquarium with bigger fish. What do you think would happen to some of the tadpoles? The diet of tadpoles changes as they

18

Be sure the children understand what is being asked in Testing Your Ideas. We are not concerned with which of the statements is true, but rather, with which of the statements best explains why a pond is considered a special habitat. In fact, all the statements are true about a pond. Only the last statement, however, relates to the idea that a pond is a special habitat.

grow larger. When they change into frogs, they eat earthworms, caterpillars, and insects.

Is the animal and plant life in streams like that in ponds? It may change more in streams since pond water moves less. There are many kinds of freshwater fish found in streams. Trout fishing in a stream is a great sport for fishermen. Sometimes streams are blocked by beavers building dams. How do you think such dams might affect plant and animal life in streams? Would the seasons change life in streams? How does plant and animal life differ as the temperature of their habitat becomes higher or lower?

TESTING YOUR IDEAS

Which of the following statements best explains why a pond is a special habitat?

A pond is a place where animals and plants live and grow.
Animal life in a pond battles to stay alive.
In a pond, there are many different kinds of plants.
Some animals and plants are not likely to be found anywhere else except in a pond or pond-like habitat.

note

If tadpoles were put into an aquarium that contained fairly large fish, the fish would probably eat some of the tadpoles.

OVERVIEW

The ocean environment of plants and animals will be one not readily available and accessible to most children. The youngsters will not be able to get their experiences first-hand unless they live along a seacoast. Saltwater aquariums can be set up in the classroom to provide firsthand observations. The special requirements of life in the ocean are pointed out in this section. The way that plants and animals adapt themselves to living in a saltwater environment is discussed.

how to begin

The use of a good color film or filmstrip will serve to introduce the children to this section. Firsthand observations will be difficult to provide, so audio-visual aids are helpful here for classroom use. Have youngsters in the class discuss any plants and animals they may have seen on trips to seashore areas.

process skills

Observing and identifying the variety of both animal and plant life contained along the seashore and in the ocean
Describing the adaptations which living organisms in saltwater have made in order to survive in their environment

materials

oysters, clams, saltwater aquarium

WHAT ANIMALS AND PLANTS LIVE IN THE SEA?

Salt water is the home of many animals that could not live in a freshwater pond habitat. There are shellfish that are interesting to study along the ocean shoreline. These are animals with soft bodies that are protected by hard coverings or shells. Such animals make their shells as they grow.

procedure

Since many children will not be close to ocean areas where live shellfish can be seen, they might have to rely on a local fish market for their specimens. A good seafood store can supply you with fresh clams, oysters, scallops, lobsters, and crabs. Oysters are not available all year long, but clams usually are. Even if you just obtain a few fresh, unopened clams, it will provide an exciting firsthand opportunity for children who may have only seen clams in chowder or fried and already prepared.

7/Describe provides the class with some idea of the nature of saltwater animals through examination of clams or oysters. You will also want to rely on aids to do this. A saltwater aquarium can be set up in the classroom for daily observations. Discussion can center around the great variety of plant and animal life found in the oceans of the earth. Point out the differences in structure of animals found in saltwater environments and the large number of such animals that are used as food sources. Try to emphasize that the structures found on many of these animals protect them against their enemies.

(continued on page 36)

Have you ever eaten oysters or clams? Do you know what a living oyster or clam looks like? If you live near a seashore, finding shellfish on the beach is an interesting experience. Be sure to visit the seashore when the tide is low and the plants and animals living in that kind of habitat are not covered with water. Check in the rocky or muddy areas.

7/Describe

Oysters and clams remain in one spot instead of moving around. The shells of oysters are rough and bumpy. Do these shells look like anything you have ever seen before? How do you think an oyster or clam gets its food since it doesn't move from place to place?

Try to open a clam or oyster. Why are the shells so difficult to open? When you eat scallops, clams, or oysters, you are eating some of the strong muscles that hold together the two halves of the animal's shells. How do such muscles protect these shellfish? ■

The soft-bodied hermit crab may also be found near the seashore. It doesn't make its own shell. The crab finds an empty snail shell and crawls into it. If

21

studying the picture

Ask the children to compare and contrast the animals they see in the picture. The clam's hard shell, for example, protects its soft body. *Ask them to observe at least one feature of each animal which makes it particularly adapted to a sea habitat.*

responses to 7/describe

1. Oysters and clams feed on microscopic organisms that are carried by the tide.
2. The shells are held tightly closed by strong muscles inside the shell.
3. Muscles open and close the shell and, thereby, protect the soft body-parts.

The students can use the library to obtain information about life in saltwater since in most cases first-hand experiences will be limited to those children either living along coastal areas or to those who may have visited a seashore area. Encourage the writing of special reports on the ocean as a source of food today and on the possibility of someday using forms of seaweed as a food source.

Many different articles about the sea and the life in it may be collected by the children. It may be interesting for them to gather reports about how the rapidly growing starfish population is reducing the clam population. Articles may also be gathered about animals which destroy the microscopic life which builds coral reefs. If the living coral is destroyed eventually the coral reef protecting an island may be worn away. How strange it would be if an island were worn down because life in the sea was unbalanced.

The sea turtle and the land turtle differ in the structure of the legs. Also, some sea turtles grow to larger size than any land turtles.

The coloring of the flounder makes it hard for enemies to see it. The method of swimming of the flounder increases its visibility.

(continued on page 38)

for your information

The spiny skin of the starfish is its major protection, although this animal is eaten by gulls and various fish. Some varieties of starfish protect themselves by living beneath the surface of the sandy sea bottom.

In addition to whales, mackerel and herring for their entire lives feed on plankton which makes its own food from water, carbon dioxide, and the aid of sunlight. Plankton is also the chief supply of food for young fish which, when they grow older, feed on larger animals and fish.

you know what a hermit is, decide whether these crabs are well named. Starfish and brightly colored sea urchins covered with prickly spines are seashore dwellers. Of what use are its spines to the sea urchin?

Sea animals are well adapted to their natural habitat. Often their structure is such that enemies are discouraged from eating or attacking them. How would a starfish repel its enemies?

The plants that are most common in the ocean are so small that they can be seen only with a microscope. These tiny plants are algae (AL-jee). Free-floating algae and microscopic animals form plankton (PLANK-tun). Which animals do you think live on plankton? Would you believe that a whale uses plankton as food?

22

Some algae are anchored to rocks and sand. They grow into large plants, called kelps (KELPS). The kelps have stems as long as 100 feet. Air bladders on the stalks of these plants keep the kelps afloat in the water. Most algae plants are green, but some varieties of kelps are red or brown.

23

optional activity

Set up a saltwater aquarium. The aquarium parts should be protected with asphalt paint at all points where water contacts metal. A special twenty-gallon tank built for this purpose is recommended. The tank should be placed so that it is not exposed to direct sunlight. Spread several layers of wax paper under the tank to protect the surface on which it rests from the salt water, and prop up the tank if it doesn't stand steady.

Spread several inches of washed gravel or sand on the bottom of the tank and put a saucer or a piece of glass on the sand so that the force of the incoming water used to fill the aquarium does not disturb the sand. Fill the tank with tap water.

For saltwater aquariums, fresh sea water is best. Artificial sea water, however, can be made by dissolving 10 ½ ozs. of pure table salt, 1 ½ ozs. of magnesium chlor-
(continued)

Plants and animals fitted for life in the ocean are algae, some varieties of which lack chlorophyll and do not need sunlight, and deep sea fish, whose bodies have high inside pressure; some have structures that glow and give off light.

Remember that the adaptations of an animal or plant to a particular environment are expressions of a living thing's dependence on its environment. To be adapted to a particular environment means to be unable to live without the essentials of that environment. This fact forces one to ask if animals and plants can change, and, if so, how much, and finally by what means. These questions are suggested in later lessons.

The first statement of Testing Your Ideas is false and should suggest that the sea is a particular habitat for particular kinds of animals. The second statement,

optional activity

(continued)

ide 1 oz. Epsom salts, and ½ oz. of plaster of Paris in every three gallons of water. Water that evaporates should be replaced. Otherwise the water which does not evaporate will become excessively salty and will lessen the oxygen content. A mark made at the original water line will help you keep track of the evaporation. The temperature of saltwater aquariums should be kept at about 65°F.

Start the aerator pump and make sure air is coming out through the filter and carbon particles. Adjust the bleed valve so that the stream of air bubbles from both outlets is steady.

Add salt mix to the water in the proportions given. Start with about five gallons of water so that salinity can be brought to the desired level by adding more salt. Allow the salt to dissolve and mix with the water for several hours. Float a hydrometer in the water

(continued)

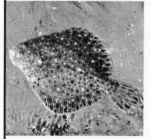

The turtle in the photograph lives in the sea. A sea turtle has legs that are flattened like paddles. What is the difference between the sea turtle and the land turtle? When sea turtles are ready to lay eggs they come out of the water and onto the land. Then they return to the sea. Later on, the newly hatched turtles find their way to the ocean.

On the ocean floor are flat fish that are very specially suited to living in this habitat. The flounder in the picture is such a flat fish. The upper side of its body is dark like the floor of the ocean. How is this coloring helpful to the flounder? Do you know where the eyes are in a flounder? If you say on both sides of the head, you are wrong! Both eyes are on one side, the upper side of the fish. The flounder swims in a strange way with its body tilted to one side. How do you think this way of swimming is helpful to the flounder?

When the young flounder is hatched from the egg, it swims like any normal young fish. Its eyes are

24

which is false, should point out that the similarity between the sea turtle, kelp, and flounder is a common habitat. The third statement which is true should suggest that the sea is a habitat as is a pond. That the sea has special habitats within it should be brought to mind by the fourth statement which is true. The fifth statement is false and discussion should focus on the fact that different seas can be substantially different environments.

on opposite sides of its head. When the young fish is about one inch long, one of its eyes begins to change its position. For example, the eye on the right side of the fish's head will move across to the left side, until both eyes are on the same side. This strange movement takes only about three or four days.

How many other plants and animals do you know that are especially fitted for life in the ocean?

TESTING YOUR IDEAS

With which of the following statements do you agree?

The sea is a good home for any kind of water animal or plant.

The sea turtle, kelp, and flounder are all entirely different living things and have nothing in common at all.

The sea is like a pond, because both are particular habitats.

The sea is like the area in which you live, because both have special habitats within them.

Some seas are warmer than others. But the animals and plants in these different seas are the same in kind.

to check salinity of the solution. The desired reading is 1025, but any reading between 1020–1030 is satisfactory. Add more salt if the reading is too low. The hydrometer should be left in the tank so that a reading can be taken each day. If the reading gets above the desired point because of evaporation of water, add more tap water to lower the reading.

A clear glass cover should be kept on the aquarium to avoid spray and splashing water which might corrode any metal it touches. Do not use a wooden cover. Consult sea life books for care and feeding instructions. Sea water animal life should exist for a long time in this type of aquarium. Change the glass wool in the filter when it gets grimy. Do not put in too much wool, but be sure it covers the entire surface of the carbon granules.

OVERVIEW

Most of this section will not be suitable for providing firsthand experiences. Mountainous areas will be available only to those children living close to such geographical regions. The main emphasis is on how animals and plants adapt themselves to living on mountain slopes. The various regions (life zones) from the bottom to the top of a mountain are discussed, showing the types of plants and animals at the different levels of altitude.

process skills

Identifying the different types of plants and animals that live in a mountainous habitat

Describing the adaptations which living organisms have made to live and survive in mountainous areas

materials

how to begin

The students who have visited mountain areas can describe to the class the plant and animal life they have observed there. Some of the parents of those children might have collections of color slides that could be made available for classroom showing. Discussions based on these firsthand experiences can be extended by providing photographs of plants and animals which live on mountains. A filmstrip and film can also be shown to extend these second-hand learning experiences.

WHAT PLANTS AND ANIMALS LIVE ON MOUNTAINS?

Have you ever climbed or driven up a high mountain? It might have been one of the great mountains in the western part of the United States. Did you feel any change in the temperature as you traveled higher? Did you see regions in which the plants were different colors along the way up?

When you stand at the foot of a high mountain and look up, you will see regions of different colors. There may be several shades of green, brown, and gray.

procedure

Lead the children to describe the differences in plant life they observed from the lower to higher elevations (grasses, forests, brush, small scrubby plants) if they have visited mountains. Let the class speculate on how these changes in climactic conditions and plant growth affect animal life found in mountainous regions (heavier fur coats, adaptations to food).

Have the children make natural habitat reproductions. They might look at pictures of animals in such surroundings before constructing their own habitat representations. Encourage the class to use source books for information. Some children might also remember habitat scenes they saw in a natural history museum. Try to have each child make his own natural habitat reproduction or have the students work in groups of four or less. When all the habitats are finished, the children can make oral reports to the class describing the plants they have included, some of the habits of the animals shown, and how these animals' color blends into the natural habitat background.

(continued on page 42)

Some of the highest mountains in North America are white on the top because they are capped with snow. This snow does not melt even in the summertime. When traveling up such a mountain, you can see that the changing colors mark off different parts of the mountain, which we call life zones. How do you think the different climates might affect the plants and animals living on the mountain?

At the foot of the mountain there may be fields with much green grass. Forests of oak, pine, and evergreen surround these fields. Animals, such as chipmunks and rabbits, may be running about looking for food. Different kinds of birds can also be seen.

Higher up on the mountain, the deeper green color that you noticed from the bottom of the mountain is made by forests of tall evergreen trees. Large pine cones may be scattered over the ground. Gophers run out of their burrows. Fish may be found in a pool of water fed by a mountain stream. The black and brown bears on this part of the mountain may catch fish for their next meal, or they may look for berries and nuts.

27

optional activity

To help the children understand that the different zones in a mountain region have different climates and that, therefore, the distribution of life on a mountain may be as varied as is the distribution of life from temperate to arctic regions of the earth, have the children make a list of what features plants and animals might require to live in each zone.

Discuss with the class some of the adaptations other than color blending of animals living on mountains. Some examples would be thickened fur coats of animals adapted to the cold near mountain tops, the hoof of the mountain goat enabling this animal to climb rocky, mountainous areas, and the large wings of eagles helping them fly to heights where they can safely build their nests.

Animals and plants found at different levels of a mountain include rabbits and chipmunks living in grassy meadows or deciduous forests; higher up, bear might be found living in evergreen forests; still higher, mountain goats would live in a zone of small, low-growing plants. At the top of the mountain birds such as the finch, and in the Rockies, the mountain chickadee and junco are found in various seasons.

studying the picture

Ask the children if the slope of the hill seems to have any affect on the growth of the plants and trees. In spite of the slope, most plants and trees grow vertically.

optional questions

Ask the children what a timberline is. It is the line above which no plant life will grow. *Ask them to imagine why plant life does not grow above the timberline.* The wind and cold are too harsh an environment for most trees and plants.

Farther up, there are rugged cliffs. Small plants, with long, thin roots can grow in the cracks of these rocks. Mountain goats live on this rocky land. How do their small feet help them? Would the trees on this part of the mountain be tall or short? Why?

No trees will grow above a certain height on a mountain. There is a definite line where the trees end. This height is called the timberline. From the timberline to the top of the mountain, the rocky slopes are often covered with snow much of the year. Even so, there are animals that live on this part of the mountain. Small birds called finches eat insects and seeds that the wind blows onto the snow. Other birds, such as the mountain chickadee and the junco in the Rockies, nest at the top of the mountains. They move down in the wintertime to the foothills.

28

Where plants and animals live depends on temperature and on the availability of food, water, and enough oxygen for breathing.

The top of a very high mountain resembles a polar region in the presence of ice, snow, and cold.

Polar animals include seal, walrus, polar bear, and whale.

Only the last statement of Testing Your Ideas is true.

Gather pictures of the animals and plants you might see if you traveled up a peak of a high mountain. Make a notebook of them and divide them into those you would expect to see at the various life zones on the mountain. Describe some of the animals and plants. Which are the different animals and plants found at different levels?

What do you think determines where particular plants and animals live? The living things found at various mountain levels must be able to survive the conditions present at the level at which they live.

Why is the climate at the top of a very high mountain like that at the North Polar region? Can you name animals at this polar region that you would not find on a mountain?

The class should be encouraged to bring in magazine cutouts of plants and animals from each life zone and to tack the cutouts to a large mountain silhouette. A summary activity of this lesson as well as preparation for coming lessons might be managed. Each child could explain why he or she chose a particular animal or plant for a particular life zone. Moreover, the children might also be asked to point out what habitats, such as the desert or sea, do not appear on a mountain. To expose the children to seasonal change and migration, ideas that will shortly appear in following lessons, ask them what might happen to the plants and animals in a particular life zone if winter or summer changes the zone's climate.

TESTING YOUR IDEAS

With which of the following statements do you agree?

A mountain is one kind of habitat with only one kind of climate.

Animals and plants which live near or on a mountain usually can live on any part of it.

A mountain is a good habitat for any kind of animal or plant.

Since a mountain is a habitat, it is like the area in which you live, or a pond, or the sea.

OVERVIEW

Animals and plants which live in extremely cold, hot, or dry areas must make special adaptations to compensate for these conditions. The construction of a diorama showing a polar environment and a desert terrarium helps the children to relate to these special adaptations and, in the case of the desert plants and animals, provides them with a first-hand observational experience.

process skills

Identifying the variety of living things present in a desert habitat
Describing the adaptations which plants and animals make for living in a desert environment

materials

fishbowl, sand, cactus plants, garden soil, horned toad, lizard, pan of water, shovel*, gallon jar*, ants and soil from an ant hill, rubber band*, heavy black cloth or paper*, food crumbs, candy, cardboard box*, paints, scissors*

---
* one per team

how to begin

Ask the children if they have ever been out for a walk, heard the chirping of a nearby bird, and then attempted to locate the bird. Have them discuss their experiences. Some children will no doubt have attempted this and found it difficult. Ask why they had trouble finding the bird. Since most birds' colors blend with the background foliage, you can bring out the idea of color adaptations as a prelude to the text discussion of the color adaptations of polar animals.

HOW DO ANIMALS AND PLANTS LIVE IN OTHER REGIONS?

Polar bears are the largest land animals of the North Polar region. They live in icy regions the year round, but they are well suited for living in such cold lands. These animals have very thick coats of fur. Polar bears have a layer of fat under their skin which also helps to keep in the heat of their bodies. These bears are good swimmers and can swim in the cold arctic waters. They can withstand the freezing temperatures because of their heavy coat of oily fur and the fat layer underneath. The polar bear has heavy pads of fur on the soles of its feet. How would this fur help the polar bear walk over ice without slipping? Would you like to see what a polar habitat looks like? Let's do the next activity to find out.

procedure

Ask the children how well the polar bear is suited to his surroundings. Make a list of particular features of this animal such as its color, its thick fur, its heavily padded feet. The fur pads on the polar bear's feet enable it to walk on ice because they provide friction. Then, have the children indicate how these features enable the polar bear to live in his arctic surroundings. Some emphasis upon this animal's color will prepare the children for the lesson about how animals are protected from their enemies.

(continued on page 46)

8/Compare

Bring in a cardboard box. Paint the inside of the box white, the color of a polar habitat. Now cut out paper animals living in this habitat. Color them so they will blend in with the background. How does the color of an animal help it in its natural habitat? ■

If it were not for the blending in of many animals with the colors of their habitat, they would have a very difficult time escaping enemies or approaching their prey. Animals which have colors adapted to their habitat have been able to survive better than those that did not. Do you now understand why most polar bears have white fur? How does this color help the polar bear? This animal lives mostly on seals and fish, but polar bears also eat birds and foxes. Some of these animals are as white as the polar bear. Arctic foxes are white. An arctic bird, called the ptarmigan (TAR-mi-gan), has white feathers in the winter but gets brown feathers in the spring. Do you think food is hard to find in winter at the polar regions? Why must meat-eating polar animals be skillful hunters?

31

studying the picture

Have the children describe the coloration of each animal in terms of the environment in which it was photographed. *Ask how easy or difficult it would be for a predator to see the animals.* Have the children look for other photographs depicting camouflaged animals.

responses to 8/compare

1. When an animal is colored or marked like its surroundings, it is camouflaged from its enemies.

The students will probably be more familiar with plants and animals discussed in this section than in some of the other habitat relationships. Have the class name typical plants and animals which are found in the dry plains or the desert regions of our country. List these on the board and let the children speculate as to the adaptations each form of living organism shows (cactus plants have long, thin roots to absorb water, and spines instead of leaves to reduce water loss; desert kangaroo rats spend the hot days in deep tunnels and obtain all their water by eating seeds and plant matter). The adaptations of the camel to dry, desert conditions are explained in detail in the textbook. The important idea which the class should discover here is that the more extreme the conditions are in the environment, the greater the variations found in the plants and animals adapted to live in these habitats.

(continued on page 48)

studying the picture

Have the children note that the camel's features are adapted to enable it to live in a desert environment. For example, its eyes have overhanging lids and long lashes which shield them from the bright sunlight. Tell them that its nostrils can be opened and closed to protect it from the blowing sand in storms. Have the children find other photographs of camels and discuss other adaptive features (e.g., broad feet to keep it from sinking into the sand; padded knees which protect it when kneeling).

Although there are no trees at the North Pole, there are some familiar plants growing there. Mosses and other small plants are able to grow in these cold arctic regions.

Why do you think animals and plants living in very dry land areas are usually very different from those that live on mountains, at the North Pole, or in fields? To survive all living things must have water. Since deserts have very little rainfall, do you think that desert animals and plants must have special ways of finding and saving water?

Camels can live without water for several days and sometimes as long as a month. They are well adapted to life in the desert. A thirsty camel may drink 20 gallons of water at one time. The camel can store this water in its muscles. Do you think the camel stores water in its hump? This thought is a common error. The hump on a camel's back is fat which is used as stored food.

Camels sometimes get water, as well as food, from plants such as cactus, which grow well in a desert habitat. What type of roots would these plants have? Why are the stems of the cactus so large?

A camel can walk over the soft hills of sand easily with its large, spongy and flat feet. This animal has long, thick eyelashes, and slit-shaped nostrils that can be closed tightly. How would these be useful to a camel in a sandstorm? A camel is able to get along in its desert habitat because its body is adapted to desert conditions.

One of the best known North American plains animals is the coyote (KY-oht). The coyote is a member of the wolf family. It is a good hunter and will eat rabbits, mice, ground squirrels, lizards, snakes, birds, and insects. It may also live on cactus and the beans of the mesquite (mes-KEET) plant when other food is scarce.

optional activity

To observe lizards, place them in a wire cage made of mesh big enough to let flies in. A little sugar syrup in the cage will attract flies so that the lizards can feed on them. There should be a pan of water and a few sticks or stones in the cage for the lizards to hide under. Keep the cage in a warm place, but not in direct sunlight. The lizards and the inside of the cage should be sprayed once a week with lukewarm water.

In 9/Describe the students will need to consult source books to complete the activity. 10/Observe will give the children an opportunity to study the conditions found in a desert terrarium. After the youngsters have constructed their desert terrariums, they can observe the living things in them. Have the children record carefully how much water they give the plants weekly and be sure they are cautioned not to overwater them. Members of the class can take turns feeding the desert animals and providing them with live food in the form of insects if there are any available at that time of year.

You may at this point in the lesson have the children describe the climatic conditions about which they have thus far read. List the conditions on the blackboard as the children suggest them. The class should understand that almost all desert regions are dry, windy, usually hot during the day, and extremely cold at night.

Ask the children to suggest reasons why animals build underground homes. (Underground homes are built to provide protection from heat and cold as well as protection from natural enemies.)

(continued on page 50)

studying the picture

Long roots of the mesquite allow this plant to reach water far below the desert's surface. With sufficient water, the tender green leaves of the mesquite become a source of water during the dry season for animals such as the jack rabbit.

The mesquite, like the cactus, is specially suited to desert life. In Death Valley, California, mesquite plants have roots 30 to 100 feet long. Why are such long roots needed? How do the long roots of some desert plants help desert animals?

9/Describe

Use pictures to make a notebook of animals that live on the deserts of North America. What plants live there? How is each plant and animal fitted to live in this dry climate? ■

The important adaptations that desert plants and animals have enable them to make use of the little water present. Each variety of desert life has its special structure to make this water adaptation. You can see such structures in the animals and plants if you make a desert terrarium.

10/Observe

First, get a few small cactus plants, some sand, and a large fishbowl. Put a layer of garden soil into the fishbowl before adding the sand. Add a sand layer of about two inches and place your cactus plants in it. A horned toad or a lizard will be a suitable animal for your terrarium. The cactus will not need to be watered more than once a week. Provide a small pan of water and some live ants or other small insects to take care of the food needs of your terrarium animal. ■

responses to 9/describe

1. Some plants that live on the desert of North America are the cactus, sagebrush, tumbleweed, yucca, and the creosote bush.
2. Some plants have small leaves with thick outer layers to conserve water. The needles of the cactus bush are its leaves; they preserve the plant's water by presenting little surface area to the desert's heat. Some animals are fitted to this environment by burrowing during the day.

The construction of an ant colony in 11/Observe takes more care and skill and is better done as a class project. The children should be encouraged to observe the ant colony carefully, to draw pictures of tunnels made by the ants, and to take notes on the behavior of the ants. Have the students make a list of the many kinds of desert plants and animals that are familiar to them. Encourage the class to look up information about each plant and animal, stressing the more unfamiliar species. Have the youngsters find out the structural adaptations of these plants and animals, both familiar and unfamiliar, which help them to survive in the hot and dry desert environment.

(continued on page 52)

note

Keep in mind that desert plants such as cacti decay and become moldy from too much water. In caring for your terrarium, try to imitate nature as much as possible.

If you build the ant colony in 11/Observe, this colony can be used as a source of food for the toads, lizards, and salamanders in the desert habitat.

Your terrarium is intended to provide desert conditions for the plants and animals within it. Therefore, you should provide the animals with live food such as flies. Toads and snakes prefer such food. If you cannot find live food for the toad, use small bits of meat. Man-made habitats should follow closely the ones nature provides.

Some animals live in underground burrows and dens. Foxes, wolves, skunks, coyotes, and prairie dogs are among such animals. Even an owl might nest in the empty burrow of a skunk or fox. Burrowing animals in the desert may live underground during the hot day and come out to hunt for food at night. What might be some other reasons why animals build underground homes?

36

Fox dens may be as deep as 10 feet underground. The cubs are born there. The den has a storage room and a lookout place. Why must the fox be on the lookout for other animals?

Ants have more unusual underground nests than most animals. There are so many skilled workers among ants that they can have nests with many rooms that are connected by tunnels. Some ants build roads and tunnels. Other ants are like woodworkers and carve passages through pieces of wood.

Other ants may be like farmers. Some of them grow plants to feed the colony. One kind of ant milks plant sap from insects called aphids (AY-fids). Aphids suck the sap from plants. When stroked by an ant, the aphid gives a drop of plant sap in a form called honeydew.

11/Observe

You can watch ants in a colony. Get a shovel and a gallon jar and begin to dig around an ant hill. Fill half the jar with loose soil. Dig at least a foot deep

Small rodents called gerbils can be found in almost any pet store and can be put in a small aquarium. Cover the bottom of the aquarium with wood shavings and provide a raised wooden platform for a food dish. Cover the aquarium with a wire mesh cover and suspend a water bottle from it. Gerbils eat seeds and are especially fond of sunflower seeds. These animals need little water and minimal care. Change the shavings about every three weeks and provide food and water as needed. If you put a cardboard tube in the aquarium, the gerbils will shred it and use it for a nest. Very active animals, they are amusing to watch. They are about four inches long with a tail of almost equal length.

The second statement of Testing Your Ideas is true. A habitat may be a flowerpot or bird cage or a cage in the zoo or any place where a living thing may thrive and carry on its life. The children might have fun simply listing habitats unlike the popular ones they have read about. You may possibly attempt to have the children realize that the concept of habitat is not unlike that on smaller boxes within larger boxes. For example, a neighborhood may be part of a city which is part of a country which is part of a continent and so on. Have them speculate on how a change in a "larger box" or habitat may affect a change in a habitat contained in it.

responses to 11/observe

1. With a heavy metal lid on the jar, the ants would not be able to breathe.
2. The first ant will find the candy by chance and will communicate his discovery to another ant, who will then find it much more quickly.
3. Yes, there is evidence that communication is taking place among the ants.

note

In regard to 11/Observe, note that the time interval between the second and third ants reaching the candy is likely to be shorter than that between the arrival of the first and second. Encourage the children to try to explain this observation.

into the side of the ant hill. Scoop up the dirt and pick out the ants and their eggs. If you see a very large ant, be sure to capture it for your colony. This is the queen ant. Put the ants and the eggs into the jar. Cover the jar with a cloth held by a rubber band. Why would it be wrong to cap the jar with a metal lid?

Wrap heavy black cloth or paper around the bottom half of the jar to keep out sunlight. The ants will then build their tunnels against the side of the jar. Unwrap the jar each day and observe the ants.

Food crumbs and a few drops of water should be added every few days. Put a small piece of candy in the jar. Note how long it is before the first ant finds the candy. How much time did it take for the second ant to find it? Do you think ants let each other know about food in the jar? ∎

Ants work so closely together that we call them social animals. They divide the colony into kinds of ants who have specific jobs. For such simple animals they build very fine colonies. Ants are strong and can move objects many times their weight.

TESTING YOUR IDEAS

Which of the following statements is true?

Forests, ponds, seas, mountains, the polar regions, deserts, and plains are all the habitats there are.
There are as many habitats as there are places where living things may live and grow.

OVERVIEW

This section is one in which the children can use their daily observations of how plants and animals change with the seasons to understand how these changes affect living things. It is important that the children concern themselves with the visual changes that are evident among plants and animals with each of the four seasons.

how to begin

Ask the children to make a chart comparing the ways various plants and animals look during the different seasons. The chart can be a class project with each child contributing information, drawings, and pictures cut from magazines.

HOW DO SOME ANIMALS SURVIVE SEASONAL CHANGE?

Nature comes back to life in the springtime in most areas. There is a great change in the appearance of things after the cold winter is over. What are some of the changes you can see in trees and bushes from day to day as the weather gets warmer? You could make a bulletin board display of some of the signs of spring. What is happening as these changes are taking place?

process skills

Comparing how plants and animals change their appearance and living processes with the change in seasons

materials

large fishbowl°, 10–15 adult crickets°, apple, lettuce, sponge°, cloth°, string, pan°, ice cubes, heater or radiator, thermometer°, dark cloth°, frog°, jar°, lid°, rich soil from under dead leaves, flowerpot°, twigs from flowering shrubs

----
° per team

procedure

Discuss with the youngsters the way the environment differs from summer to winter (temperature, rain and snow, wind, etc.). Ask them if animals are able to adapt in some ways to the changes in seasons (some animals do and some do not). The textbook explains how some animals change the color and thickness of their fur or feathers with a change in seasons. Let the children name other animals which show a seasonal change in coloration (weasel, ptarmigan, snowshoe rabbit, ermine). Ask the class if changes in temperature affect animals in other ways.

Discuss the "cricket-thermometer" with the children before they start doing 12/Compare. The students should keep accurate notes as they do this experiment.

(continued on page 56)

for your information

Some kinds of male birds use their plumage to "advertise" themselves during the mating season. The less colorful patterns of the female help the female to blend with its surroundings, making the nest upon which she perches more difficult to find by natural enemies.

During the spring season dogs and cats gradually lose their thick winter coats of fur. In the far north ptarmigans and snowshoe rabbits change their white winter coats to brown spring ones. Birds leave their winter homes and fly north. Some song birds also change their colors. Male birds usually grow brighter-colored feathers. What do you think may be the reason for this color change? After the male bird finds a mate, he often helps the female build a nest and care for the young birds.

Frogs and fish become more active in the spring. Turtles and snakes begin looking for good places to lay their eggs. Why do they lay their eggs at this time of the year?

Moths, butterflies, and other insects appear again in the spring. How many different kinds of insects can you find? What appears to be the most important factor in bringing about the changes of spring? Explain how warm weather affects you. Did you know that crickets are fairly good thermometers? They chirp more rapidly as the weather gets warmer. When the weather gets very hot or fairly cold, they do not chirp at all. You can observe crickets in the next activity.

12/Compare

Get a large fishbowl or other container. Put about two inches of loose dirt in the bottom of the bowl. Put 10 or 15 adult crickets in the bowl. If you cannot find crickets, you can buy them at a store that sells fishing bait.

Put some water in the lid of a small jar for the crickets. Place a piece of sponge in the lid so they

40

1. The crickets should slow their chirping as the temperature gets colder.
2. As the temperature becomes warmer, the crickets should speed up their chirping.
3. Crickets do chirp in the dark.

will not drown in the water. Put pieces of apple and lettuce in the bowl for the crickets to eat. Cover the top of the bowl with a cloth. Tie a string around the mouth of the bowl to keep the cloth in place. Now place your cricket bowl in a pan of ice cubes. Wait several minutes until the cricket bowl cools. What do you notice happening as the bowl gets colder and colder?

Put the bowl near a radiator or heater. Do the crickets chirp when they get very warm? Get a thermometer and measure the temperature at which the crickets stop chirping. Cover the cricket bowl with a dark cloth. Do the crickets chirp in the dark?

It was once thought that the chirping of crickets was due to their rubbing their legs together. After careful observation it was found that the chirping was due to the rapid beating of their wings. They do rub their legs together, but this rubbing does not cause the chirping.

41

An experience to determine the effect of temperature on the activity of a frog is carried out by the children in the next activity 13/Observe. This activity might be done at home if a refrigerator is not readily available at school. Possibly a container cooled with ice could be used by the class instead of a refrigerator.

The woodchuck is a true hibernator. It falls into a torpor, a state of "suspended animation." The heartbeat and respiration of the hibernating woodchuck are greatly reduced. Its body temperature is little above that of its surroundings. For this reason, it hibernates below the frost line. Some animals freeze during hibernation. The true hibernating animal does not eat during this time. Moreover, a hibernating frog is insensitive to pain, while a sleeping frog will react to a pin prick.

There are many degrees of inactivity. A bear's heartbeat and breathing are not slowed down appreciably during its winter sleep. When food becomes scarce, the bear goes to sleep. But it may wake up on

optional questions

Have the children compare the reactions to cold temperatures of an animal such as a dog or a cat to the reactions of an animal such as a cricket or frog. *Ask the children which animal tends to remain active in cold weather and which becomes sluggish. Ask them to compare the body temperature of a dog or cat during cold weather to atmospheric temperature.* Most probably the children have petted or frolicked with a dog or cat during cold weather and can recall the animal's warmth. *Keeping activities 12 and 13 in mind, ask them if the body temperature of the crickets and frogs might have dropped as the "outside" temperature dropped.* Inquire if the children can conclude that some animals' body temperature is the same as their surrounding's, while other animals' body temperature remains the same regardless of the temperature outside.

Cold weather causes some animals to become inactive. Others are affected by the hot weather. The ground hog and the woodchuck are among the animals that sleep through the long, cold winter. This resting in winter is called hibernation (hy-ber-NAY-shun).

A hibernating animal is like an animal in deep sleep. But there are some differences. Its heart beats very slowly. Its body temperature is lowered and it breathes very little. Many frogs, too, sleep through the cold winter. If you can get a frog, you can cause it to become sluggish by lowering its body temperature. To see what happens, let's do the next activity.

warmer days during the winter and go out in search of food. Mother bears give birth to their babies in midwinter.

The bear, who may sleep for weeks at a time, sleeps continuously, different from man. While man's bodily activities, such as respiration and heartbeat, do slow down, his temperature remains about the same and digestion does not stop.

Not adapted to face the hot months of summer in the desert, the ground squirrel must estivate (spend the summer in a dormant condition).

(continued on page 58)

13/Observe

Put a frog in a jar. Punch air holes in the lid. Add a small amount of water to the jar to keep the frog's skin moist. Place the jar in the refrigerator over night, but not in the freezer. Notice the frog's movements when you remove the jar from the refrigerator. 1How long is it before the frog begins to move at all? Put the frog on its back and touch it gently. 2Is the frog able to get up? Record how long it takes the frog to become active. ■

Doctors have been able to perform some new operations on human beings because they can lower the temperature of the body. The lowered body temperature helps the doctors perform delicate operations they could not otherwise do. The lowered temperature causes the body functions to slow down much the same way as the frog's.

The winter sleep of a bear is somewhat different from hibernation. The bear's breathing and heartbeat slow down, but its body temperature remains high. If the weather is mild, the bear may wake up in midwinter and then go back to sleep until spring.

Man, too, must sleep. He usually sleeps part of every day. Is his sleep like that of the bear? Do you think man's temperature drops when he sleeps? Do you think his heartbeat slows down? Would man's digestion almost stop, the way a bear's does?

Man does not hibernate, but scientists are hoping that he may in the future. Doctors, as we mentioned before, can slow down a man's heartbeat and his breathing by cooling his body. This slowing down is done in order to make brain and heart operations less dangerous to the patient. Perhaps, if man can be made to

43

optional activity

Another activity to suggest how animals react to temperature may be done with guppies. Fill two glass jars with water and put in some water plants. After a few days, place a pair of guppies in each jar. The females are usually gray and bigger than the smaller, more colorful males. Put a lamp provided with a 200-watt bulb over one jar. Have the children keep a record of the number of guppies born to each pair. Let the children speculate as to why there are fewer guppies born in warm water than there are born in water at room temperature.

responses to 13/observe

1. Answers will vary.
2. No.

The activity 14/Compare can be done in groups of about five or six children. Each group should keep separate notes on its container of soil and any changes observed in the soil. Forcing a twig to blossom from a flowering shrub can be done in the classroom or at home. Just be sure to caution the children not to cut twigs before there are tight buds on them. This precaution will insure blossoming when the twig is placed in water and put in a sunny place. Careful observation will aid the students in this activity. They can draw before and after pictures of the twig which show the different stages in the forcing of the blossoms.

In Testing Your Ideas, the students will have to infer the possible reasons for the slow-up of bodily functions during hibernation. Hopefully, some students will realize that these bodily processes require energy, and food is an animal's source of energy. While hibernating, an animal cannot secure food. If its bodily processes continued at their normal rate, the animal's stored fat would not be able to supply enough energy and the animal would die.

responses to 14/compare

1. The plants sprouted from the seeds that lay dormant in the soil.
2. The twig should bloom.
3. Attempts to force a twig cut during the fall to bloom will fail.

hibernate, he could travel into outer space with less food, water, and air than he would need if he were awake and moving around. It will take many years of traveling for man to reach some of the other planets. It would not be such a tiring journey if he could hibernate along the way.

Some animals will pass the summer in a sleepy state. This resting in summer is called estivation (ess-tuh-VAY-shun). Snails and frogs may become inactive or estivate when the weather is very hot.

Some reptiles also may behave in the same way. The ground squirrel of Southern California both estivates and hibernates. This little animal may begin resting in July and sometimes remains this way until the following spring. How might this long rest help the squirrel?

Plants, too, go through periods of inactivity. Some appear to be dead during the winter. We call the plant's seasonal inactivity dormancy (DAWR-mun-see).

Many plants shoot up in the springtime. Where are they during the winter? Do all of them come from seeds? What parts of the plant remain in the soil during the winter months? You will find out about plant dormancy in the following activity.

14/Compare

You can show that there are seeds, roots, and stems in the soil ready to come to life when the weather gets warmer and the soil gets enough moisture. Dig up some rich soil from under dead leaves and put it in a flowerpot. Take out any green plants that are already growing in the soil. Water the dirt in the flowerpot. After about a week look to see if there are any plants growing in the container. Where did they come from?

Cut a twig from a flowering tree or bush which hasn't yet bloomed. Keep it in water. What happens? 3 Would the same twig have bloomed if it had been cut last fall and put in water? ■

Taking twigs from flowering shrubs and putting them in water is called forcing. This can be done with plants such as forsythia (for-SITH-ee-uh) and most of the flowering fruit trees. It must be done in springtime and may take a few weeks for the blossoms to come out.

TESTING YOUR IDEAS

What reasons can you suggest to explain why the heartbeat, temperature, and breathing rate of hibernating animals are lowered?

for your information

Biennials and perennials are adapted to the changing seasons and live through the winter in an inactive state, resuming growth and foodmaking in the spring. In order to survive during the winter, the plants must store food during the summer. This food is used to nourish the plant in the spring until the leaves begin their work.

OVERVIEW

The movement of animals from one place to another includes the migration of birds. This is a change that occurs in the fall and spring. By observation the children can notice the birds which migrate and those which remain throughout the year.

how to begin

Rely on personal experiences that the children might have had in seeing great numbers of birds flying in formation either in late fall or early spring. Question the youngsters as to the season of the year in which they saw such flocks and have them describe the pattern that the birds made as they flew overhead. Begin to discuss the reasons why birds would leave their regular habitat when the seasons change.

process skills

Explaining why birds and other animals migrate from one place to another

materials

field guides for birds

HOW DO OTHER ANIMALS SURVIVE SEASONAL CHANGE?

Many birds move from one part of the country to another and even from one country to another in the fall and spring. Name the birds that you see around your home all winter. These are called winter residents. What birds return for the spring and summer? These are called summer residents.

Redstarts, cliff swallows, and grosbeaks fly north from Mexico and Central and South America to nest in Canada and the United States. The ruby-throated hummingbird flies across the Gulf of Mexico from Central America back to the eastern part of the United States to nest. Whippoorwills that spend their winter in the southern tip of Florida return to raise their young in New England. Can you figure out how many miles some of these birds fly? Would you like to take such a long trip each year?

procedure

Discuss with the class possible reasons why birds migrate. Migrations may be due to food needs, changes in climate, or breeding habits. A great many birds fly long distances in the spring, then nest and raise their young in a new home. They return to warmer climates in the fall. It is difficult to determine why some birds leave a good food supply and warmth in the tropics to migrate to breeding grounds in the far north. It is easier to point out to the children the logic of the southward migration of insect-eaters when cold weather kills their food supply. The reason why water birds fly south before the ponds and lakes freeze over can be clearly understood when explained to the children.

The whippoorwill during its migration flies about 1500 miles. But the arctic tern may migrate 8,000 miles, spending seven months each year on the wing.

(continued on page 62)

Why do you think some people spend their winters in Florida? What makes birds take such long trips? Animals are said to migrate (MY-grayt) when they move in large numbers from one place to a distant place.

Man does not fully understand the reason why birds leave their summer homes and fly hundreds of thousands of miles to another place. When the birds leave the North, there is still plenty of food for them, and the weather has not yet turned cold. We say the birds migrate at a certain time because of an inner urge called instinct (IN-stingkt).

To find out about their patterns of migration scientists trap birds and put bands on their legs. Each band has a number to identify the bird. There are instructions on this band for anyone who captures the bird or finds it dead. If you find such a bird, you are asked to write the Bureau of Biological Survey, U.S. Dept. of Agriculture, telling where you found the bird

47

for your information

There are certain general routes followed by birds in migrating. Birds of the Mississippi Valley usually follow a path which leads them to western Louisiana and northwestern Florida and across the Gulf of Mexico. Birds that nest in the Central United States migrate over a land route, usually wintering in Mexico or Central America. The Atlantic Flyway is traveled by such birds as the golden plover, which spends its summer in Labrador and its winter in South America.

In 15/Record the students are asked to name the birds that they usually see all winter. Responses will differ in each geographical area, and it will be important to use field guides to help the class identify birds by their correct names. The list of summer residents will be much longer than the list of birds seen during the winter months when food is scarce. If any of the children have bird feeding stations set up near their homes, they might be able to draw pictures of the birds they see during the season this section is studied. Possibly they might be able to take photographs as well.

The example of salmon migration is a familiar one, and here the reason is clearly that of reproduction of the species. It is thought that salmon eggs develop better in freshwater than in saltwater. Some mammals also migrate. The trips are shorter for animals such as bighorn sheep and elk, but the purpose, a better food supply, is the same as for many birds.

(continued on page 64)

responses to 15/record

1. During winter when insects die, or remain underground or in nests, birds retire to warmer climates in which insects thrive.

2. Birds in a yard differ from birds in a wooded area because of the different needs these two areas meet.

3. The female has dull-colored feathers so that the bird may blend with her surroundings when eggs are being hatched or when the female is feeding the young.

and the number on its band. By such methods, scientists have found out much information about the migration routes of birds. Can you recognize some of the birds presently in your area?

15/Record

Make a list of birds in your area that are winter residents and a list of those that are summer residents. Do you think that insect-eating birds will be around during the winter? Why not? What do the birds eat during the winter? Why are the birds in your yard different from those in a wooded area? If you wish to observe birds at short range, use the method of "squeaking." To squeak, loudly kiss the back of your hand. Try to remain still. On occasion and particularly during the breeding season, you may find a dozen or more birds will come to inspect the noise you are making. Draw pictures of the birds around your home. Use these for a bulletin board display. To identify birds you cannot easily name, you may with the help of your teacher find them in a book about birds.

You will have to notice the different markings of these birds and their colors to help identify them. Usually the male bird has the brighter colors. Think of why the female would not have brightly-colored feathers. ■

We cannot fully explain migration. One theory says that birds know it is time to migrate when the days begin to shorten in the northern regions. But birds are not the only animals which migrate. It is even harder to explain the migration of some fish, such as the salmon.

Salmon spend years feeding and growing in the ocean. When fully grown, they return to the fresh water where they were hatched. Large numbers of salmon swim up rivers against rapid currents at certain seasons of the year. In their upstream journey they may leap up waterfalls as high as 12 feet. Did you know fish could jump? Measure 12 feet. Can you jump as high as a salmon?

for your information

The poorwill of southern California, a member of the whippoorwill family, is known to exhibit an inactive state close to hibernation. Its body temperature drops about 36°, respiration becomes nil, and no heartbeat can be detected. But spring temperatures stir the bird to flight.

The answer to Testing Your Ideas is that migration is a means of adapting to surroundings. The children might be led to understand that migration is an adaptation to surroundings if you suggest that only those animals survived which were able to move from inhabitable places to areas in which they could survive.

for your information

Some species of salmon travel to the headwater of a stream, while other species spawn just a mile or two above a stream's saltwater line. The king salmon has been found in fresh water more than 2,500 miles from the sea. After spawning, the salmon drift downstream and die, but no one knows if any one of these fish has ever lived to spawn more than once.

If the salmon successfully make this dangerous trip, the female lays eggs and the male covers them with a whitish fluid from his body called milt (MILT). This act of covering the eggs is called spawning. If we can find out why it is better for salmon eggs to be laid in fresh water, we may discover the reason why these fish make such a difficult journey.

TESTING YOUR IDEAS

Animals migrate from one place to another because a) some animals are travelers b) migration is a means of adapting to surroundings c) all animals at one time or another migrate.

50

OVERVIEW

Dispersal is a means by which living things change their habitat accidentally. The occurrence of living things on the island of Surtsey which arose from the sea in 1963 is offered as an illustration of dispersal. The chance migration of seeds by wind, water, and by animals as well as the dispersal of animal life are all offered as important ways in which habitat is changed.

how to begin

Ask the children if they have ever noticed soil which, for the first time, has been planted with grass seed. Then, ask if they have noticed dandelions or crabgrass growing on the same plot of land months later. Point out that no crabgrass or dandelion seeds were originally planted. How did these weeds get there? In urban areas, questions relating to dispersal may be asked about weeds and animals, such as insects, found in dirt lots or parks.

HOW DO OTHER LIVING THINGS CHANGE HABITAT?

Before November 1963, off the southwestern islands of Iceland, there was nothing but the seas of the North Atlantic. But on November 14, 1963, the waters boiled with smoky activity. For almost a year and a half, a fiery birth pushed land above the ocean's surface. An island had risen from the sea about half the size of Central Park in New York City. The island was named Surtsey (SURT-see).

process skills

Investigating how plants and animals spread their seeds by wind, water, or animals
Observing animals and plants that inhabit a new environment because of dispersal

materials

garden soil, pan*, oven, water

_____
* one per team

51

procedure

Though dispersal is a common event, the fact that it occurs by chance is unusual in an environment governed by order. Without man, all life has spread by dispersal. Dispersal is limited only by the needs of living things and how an environment satisfies them.

The island of Surtsey offers a dramatic example of dispersal, for virgin soil becomes the home of its first land plant which came to the island by accident. The text of the discussion of Surtsey makes this fact clear, though the children should be asked what carried the seed of the sea rocket to the island. To re-inforce the inference being made here, sea having carried the seed, ask the class to speculate upon the seed's requirements to withstand salt water and the North Atlantic's cold temperature. It should be made clear that a living thing to survive and to be dispersed must withstand the differences of new surroundings.

In 16/Observe the children are dealing with dispersal by means of wind. Possibly the only growth they might get is that of weeds and only if the pan of soil is left out for an extended time would they find insects in the soil.

Depending on the season of the year when this section is studied, the children could make a seed

responses to 16/observe

1. Children might find insects or animals in the soil. If they do not, the possibility of the soil showing animal life is a matter of time and should not be eliminated from the minds of the children.
2. Again, children should find plants growing in the soil after a few weeks.
3. The seeds may have gotten to the soil by wind dispersal or by animals carrying them.
4. It is possible that the seeds may have been carried by the wind.

Surtsey had no plant or animal life. Some birds and seals came to use it as a resting place. During the early days of June, however, a scientist found a wonderful thing in the moist soil near the edge of the island's lagoon. A small, green coastal plant called a sea rocket had taken root. Its picture appears on this page. Surtsey was nourishing a living thing, but from where had the sea rocket come? How did it get to the island? An activity will begin to help you answer these questions.

16/Observe

Put some garden soil in a pan. Heat the pan in an oven for one hour at 400°F to kill any plant or animal life present. Then, place the pan outdoors. Continually moisten the soil. Do any insects or animals find their way to the soil? Do you find after several weeks plants growing in the soil? How did the plants get there? Were the plant's seeds carried to the soil by the wind? ■

collection showing the structures various kinds of seeds have for dispersal. During late spring the dandelion is a common example of how a mere light breeze can blow the seeds about after the yellow flower has changed to a white puffball. Use the examples mentioned in the text to show other structures seeds have for easy dispersal. The main methods of seed dispersal are: (1) being carried by the wind—milkweed, dandelion; (2) shooting out from a pod—beans, peas; (3) being eaten by birds or animals—cherries, grapes; (4) being carried on the outside of animals—burrs, sticktights; (5) being carried by water—sea rockets, coconuts, water lilies.

Some seeds can be carried by wind. The milkweed seed has little silky hairs growing out of its covering. These tiny hairs are like parachutes that help the seed travel. Cattails, which grow along ponds and streams, also have "flyaway" seeds.

The seed of the sea rocket has no parachute, however. The sea rocket grows along Icelandic shores and can also be found on North American coasts. But its seeds cannot be carried by wind. To reach the shores of Surtsey, the seed had to be carried by water. Accidentally, a seed from a sea rocket, possibly from a nearby island, drifted to Surtsey and took root.

Your activity showed you that wind can carry seeds. The example of Surtsey showed you that water can carry seeds. Animals can carry seeds, too. A bird

53

studying the picture

Have the children identify the type of seed dispersal represented by each of the line drawings in the margin.

The top drawing (dandelion), the middle drawing (maple), and the photograph (milkweed) show seeds that are wind dispersed. The poppy pod (second from the top) has openings in the top of the pod. As the plant sways back and forth in the breeze, seeds sift out and fall to the ground. The burr (second from the bottom) clings to clothing or an animal's fur. The pods in the bottom drawing (touch-me-not) burst open when touched and fling their seeds out.

The answer to Testing Your Ideas is that this type of dispersal occurs by chance.

will pick up a cherry, carry it for some distance, eat the soft part, and then drop the seed. Sometimes animals may migrate from one country to another on ships or airplanes. All of these kinds of migration we call dispersal (dis-PER-sal).

In time, Surtsey will be covered with green plants. Seals, insects, and other animals will come there, too. By dispersal, living things will have changed their old habitat for a new one.

TESTING YOUR IDEAS

Plants change their habitat by means of wind or by being carried by animals. Some animals change their habitat by being carried by ship or airplane. Such a change occurs a) by instinct b) by chance.

54

OVERVIEW

Living organisms, both plants and animals, have structures which protect them against natural enemies and predators. Two of these protective devices are blending colorations and mimicry of undesirable species. Many animals protect themselves by natural habits which prolong their lives. Animals usually protect their young by caring for them until they can fend for themselves.

The students will probably be able to answer most of the motivational questions on this page. The frog, fish, horse, and tiger are all capable of very swift movement as protection from their enemies. The tiger's teeth and claws, the clam's shell, and the swordfish's "sword" are all used for the animals' protection and defense.

how to begin

Ask the children to recall any animals they have seen use their color to blend into their surroundings. If the youngsters cannot recall any, suggest some examples that might remind them of ones they have seen. The class might also be able to bring in pictures which would illustrate color blending of animals with their surroundings for protection.

process skills

Describing the various protective devices of plants and animals

Describing some of the habits animals utilize to protect themselves and their young

materials

walking stick*, jar with cover*, leaves, twigs, green, red, and white toothpicks

---

* one per team

HOW ARE LIVING THINGS PROTECTED FROM THEIR ENEMIES?

So far you have studied animals and plants in their physical surroundings. Their physical surroundings also include other living things. Animals and plants must be protected from other living things.

The best means of protection for many animals is their ability to run, fly, or swim quickly. Most birds have no other way to defend themselves. The cottontail rabbit in the eastern part of the United States and the jack rabbit of the western prairies hop so fast that they often get away from dogs or foxes. Swimming is the means used by some animals to escape their enemies. What happens when you try to catch a frog on the side of a pond? How do fish escape dangerous enemies?

Think how horses, tigers, and clams protect themselves. How does a swordfish use its "sword"?

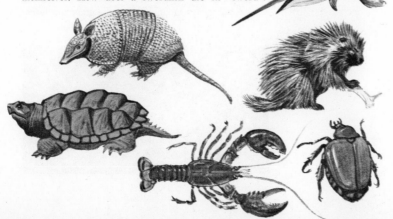

procedure

Ask the children if they ever dropped a small object on a woolly rug. Let them describe whether they had trouble finding it or not. They might have had the same sort of experience finding spilled green peas on a spatter-type pattern kitchen linoleum. The idea here is to have the class discover the principle that an object colored like the rug or the linoleum would be harder to find than one of a contrasting color. Ask the students to name animals that are protectively colored. Let them speculate on other ways that animals are adapted for protection. By reading the text, the children will find that there are three main ways: (1) by rapid movement; (2) by claws, teeth, stinging parts, etc.; and (3) by color and shape.

17/Observe, which examines the walking stick against a background of leaves and twigs, will test the youngsters' powers of observation and show them an excellent example of mimicry and the blending into the background of an insect. Have them look at the walking stick by itself and then against the

studying the picture

Have the children use a hand lens to examine the thorns along the stem of the rose. *Ask them if the thorns are alike in size and shape.* No, they are not. *Ask the class if the thorns are arranged in a pattern to benefit the plant.* Yes, they are arranged to afford maximum protection for the plant.

Many animals have their outer coverings for protection. The shells of armadillos, turtles, clams, and oysters, the quills of porcupines and hedgehogs, and the hard coverings of beetles help these animals protect themselves against enemies.

Plants also have protective coverings. Bark is the tough covering of trees. The pineapple protects the juicy fruit underneath with an outside covering that looks much like armor. Thirsty animals in the desert stay away from cactus plants because of their spines. The thorns of rose, raspberry, and blackberry bushes keep animals away. In what other ways do plants protect themselves?

Many animals are hidden from enemies by their coloring. Such coloring is called protective coloration. A polar bear, for example, is difficult to see against the white snow because of its white fur. Fish living near the surface of the water, and especially those swimming in the open sea, are steel-blue on the back. How does this coloring protect the fish? Is it easy to see a frog near a pond? Why?

Color hides many insects from their enemies. Grasshoppers may be as green as the grass and leaves

56

twig and leaf background so that they can see the shape of this insect. If walking sticks are not common, have the children look for praying mantises or other insects which have protective shape and color.

A fish that is steel blue on the back and a frog sitting near a pond both blend with their environments, and are thus protected.

Plants with protective devices include those which cause skin irritations if touched, those which are poisonous and cause serious illness or death if eaten, and those which have an unpleasant odor.

(continued on page 72)

they feed upon. A twig-shaped insect, the walking stick, is green during the springtime when feeding upon young green plants. When the leaves fall in autumn, the color of the walking stick changes to a rusty brown. This color change hides the walking stick from its enemies. In the next activity, observe how hard it is to see a walking stick.

17/Observe

Put a walking stick in a jar with leaves and twigs. Let in air by punching several holes in the cover of the jar. Bring the jar to school. At first, your classmates may think you have only leaves and twigs in the jar. They will have to look carefully to see the walking stick. ▪

57

note

To have the children associate protective coloration with the role played by environment in an animal's life, ask them how the peppered moth and the changes the moth underwent might be examples of protective coloration.

Once students are made aware of protective coloration, they may find many examples of it in their neighborhoods. Tree hoppers may be mistaken for thorns on a twig. The wing pattern of the pine tree moth makes it inconspicuous on the dark colored bark.

18/Compare gives the students a fine chance to see how blending coloration makes objects difficult to find. They can then apply this concept to the way that animals blend in with their background habitats for protection from their enemies.

The examples of warning coloration given in the text are most likely to be familiar to the children, even city children. All will probably know the wasp and the skunk. How do we use color as a warning? (Red stop signs, edges of stair treads painted yellow, fire call boxes painted red.)

(continued on page 74)

optional activity

If chameleons are available, students may check divergent theories about the cause of this animal's change in color. While it has been popularized that the color of a chameleon's habitat determines the lizard's color, biologists feel color changes are determined by temperature.

Divide the class into four or five groups, and have each group place its chameleon on brown, green, and gray objects. Then, have them place the animal on warm objects of the same color. Observe in which case the animal changes color.

Man has learned from nature to use color to hide objects he doesn't want seen. This is the art of camouflage (KAM-uh-flahzh). Buildings cannot be easily seen from an airplane when they are colored or covered to blend in with the surrounding scenery.

Some animals change color with the seasons, but others can change color in a few minutes. A flounder resting on a sandy ocean bottom will be evenly colored. If it swims to a place where there are stones and pebbles, the flounder will take on a spotted appearance that blends with the surroundings.

The ability to change color has made the American chameleon (kuh-MEE-lee-uhn) very well known. This little lizard will turn brown or green. The chameleon will change color according to temperature. These color changes are not sudden but take several minutes each

58

time to occur. Find out about blending coloring in the following activity.

18/Compare

Scatter three dozen toothpicks on a grassy area. Use 12 green, 12 red, and 12 white toothpicks. Each student can time himself as to how long it takes to find all the green toothpicks. Keep a chart of the numbers of each kind of colored toothpick found. Which were the easiest to find? Why? In what way does your finding more of one colored toothpick than another show how protective coloring works? ■

The toothpicks that were easiest to find did not blend with their background. It follows that those animals that blend in with their backgrounds are more difficult to see and can more easily escape their natural enemies.

Hornets, and other insects that sting, are usually yellow and black. Would you catch yellow and black insects in your bare hands? Why not?

The European fire-bellied toad produces certain substances from its skin which give it a bad taste. The toad has black markings on its legs and a bright red belly. When a stork or other bird flies down to catch the toad, it flops over on its back. The bright color warns the stork that this is a bad-tasting toad and it flies away.

Stripes on the back of a skunk are thought to be a fair warning of this animal's presence. The skunk's stripes are therefore called warning coloration. The skunk sprays its enemies with a bad-smelling liquid. How can you recognize a skunk?

responses to 18/compare

1. The red and white toothpicks are easiest to find.
2. The red and white toothpicks contrast with the green of the grass.
3. Objects colored or marked like their surroundings are more difficult to see than objects the color of which contrasts with that of their surroundings.

for your information

While yellow and black markings are popular among wasps, bees, and yellow jackets, their predators, such as birds, do not instinctively recognize the colors' significance. Each new generation of predators must learn through painful experience which colors are menacing and which are not.

Beavers build dams to slow a stream's flow, enabling these animals to build a lodge in quiet waters safe from predators. Having the appearance of a mound of sticks, the lodge is hollow, and it is entered through an underwater tunnel. Draw on the blackboard a cross-section of a hollow lodge with its underwater entrance. Ask the children how the lodge is built in mid-water and how its entrance protects the beaver from enemies.

Some animals, when confronted by an enemy, pretend to be dead. The enemy is repulsed by the "dead" animal and leaves it alone.

In Testing Your Ideas the answer to the first question is that protection is necessary. The answer to the second question is that a living thing's protection may be influenced by its surroundings.

for your information

Scientists have yet to discover why beavers slap the water with their large, flat tails. This behavior is popularly recognized to be the beaver's signal for danger. Sometimes the sound does cause all beavers in the colony to scurry to their lodge. However, it is equally true that at times the noise causes no alarm among these animals.

Habits help animals protect themselves. American beavers cut down trees with their sharp teeth. The trees are used to build dams in ponds or streams. Mud, sticks, and stones are used to dam up part of a stream or river to form a pond. The beavers build their homes within the pond. These dams sometimes change the direction of water flow and cause flooding of surrounding land. Dams built by beavers may last for several years.

When faced with danger, some animals pretend to be dead. How would this pretense help an animal to escape its enemies? One animal in our country which is noted to pretend to be dead or hurt when an enemy approaches is the hog-nosed snake. The snake may hiss and attack. But it also may turn over on its back and pretend to be lifeless.

Some young birds, like the bobwhite, stay very still when their mother gives the signal that danger is near. This action is called "freezing". Until the mother bobwhite gives the baby birds the signal that all is clear, they remain "frozen". When she goes out into a field, the mother bird runs some distance from the nest before flying. You will not find the nest at the spot from which the mother bird flew. Why do you think she runs this distance before flying up?

TESTING YOUR IDEAS

Living things may have a tough covering, live in shells, be fast runners, have sharp teeth, or may be colored to blend with their surroundings. These features a) do not help living things in any way b) are helpful but not needed c) are necessary protection.

Different animals are protected from other living things in different ways. The kind of protection a living thing may have a) may be influenced by its surroundings b) may not be influenced by its surroundings.

61

for your information

The mother bobwhite runs from her nest before flying to mislead an approaching predator about the location of her young.

OVERVIEW

As animals and plants are adapted to winter, so too are they adapted through reproductive powers to the problem of preserving their kind. The discussion makes clear that reproduction is the means by which living things are adapted to an environment in which all living things die. The importance of the young is, therefore, established, and a discussion of how animals care for their young is next presented.

how to begin

Ask the children what would happen to living things if no young could be produced. Allow them to speculate on what would occur if no cats could have kittens, if no dogs could have puppies, or if no flowers could produce seeds from which other flowers grow. Allow them to discuss what the importance of the young is. You may aid the discussion if you ask what finally happens to all animals and plants.

process skills

Explaining how animals and plants are prepared for winter
Investigating the reproductive powers of living things
Comparing how different animals care for their young

materials

6 lima beans*, jar*, water, knife*, flowerpot*, dark soil

_____
* per team

HOW ARE ANIMALS AND PLANTS PREPARED FOR THE FUTURE?

Living things, prepared for winter, usually survive. The oak, elm, birch, and maple trees lose their leaves in the fall. The green of spring becomes the brown of winter, and the growth of plants stops. Beets and carrots have, however, stored food in their roots, and the white potato has an underground stem of stored food it can use to begin growth next spring.

The squirrel busily tucks nuts away in a hollow oak tree for his meals in the coming months. Gnawing mammals and man store up food for the winter. Beavers store pieces of bark and wood in the bottom of a pond so that they will have food even when the pond's

procedure

Suggest that our environment is one in which new things eventually die but whose kind is renewed.

Squirrels store nuts in the ground. Some of the nuts are overlooked and may eventually grow into trees, thus preserving the species.

19/Investigate should be done by each child. After soaking overnight, two or three lima beans may be distributed to each student and carefully dissected under adult supervision. The remaining beans may then be planted in large metal containers which are about three inches deep. The plants should begin to poke through the soil in three or four days and should be watered lightly daily. The plants should be allowed to mature to show that these new lima bean plants produce new seeds. This observation is extremely important to have the children understand how the plant is preserved.

(continued on page 78)

surface and everything above ground are frozen. Squirrels, chipmunks, and beavers are busy in autumn storing food and preparing their homes for winter.

One half pint of wheat, a quart of hazel nuts, two quarts of buckwheat, and a few dozen acorns were the storehouse contents of one chipmunk. Holes are dug in the ground by squirrels for the nuts they eat during the winter. Some forget where they stored their nuts. How does this help the trees from which the nuts came?

Animals and plants, however, have a different kind of winter in their lives. This different winter is that all living things will someday die. What must happen to have animals and plants remain on earth? How have animals and plants adapted to a habitat in which living things die? The following investigation will help you answer this question.

19/Investigate

Obtain six lima beans. Notice the shape of the bean, that it is divided into halves, and that there is a small nub or bump on one side. Soak the beans in a glass of water overnight to loosen the halves and the bean's outer skin. On the following morning, remove the beans from the water. Hold one of the beans between your fingers with the nub of the bean face down on the table. Carefully separate the halves of the bean with a knife. Be sure that your teacher or an adult is present when you do this activity. 1 What do you find between the halves of the lima bean seed? 2 Do you find a new lima bean plant?

Now plant the remaining lima bean seeds in a container five inches deep filled with dark brown soil.

63

responses to 19/investigate

1. Between the halves (called cotyledons) is an embryo plant. 2. The embryo plant will grow into a new lima bean plant, although at this stage it is probably not recognizable as such.

(continued)

Discuss parental care with the children and again point out some of the textbook examples of such care among different animal species. The youngsters might be able to recall from their own experience with pets how the young were cared for until they were able to go off by themselves.

(continued on page 80)

responses to 19/investigate

(continued)

3. Seedling plants should have appeared.
4. Yes.

Plant the beans about an inch beneath the soil, and water the beans lightly every day. Wait a few days. **3** What do you see growing in the container? **4** Do you see new lima bean plants? ■

From the lima bean seeds grow new lima bean plants. In turn, these new plants will produce new seeds with new plants in them. By making new plants like the old which will in time die, plants are adapted to death.

Animals are adapted to death, for they can produce young, too. One day when the young are adults, they also will produce new animals of the same kind. What is the importance of seeds, new plants, and new animals? What would happen if animals and plants could produce young no longer? The making of new living things is the way animals and plants have adapted to surroundings in which all living things die.

The young must be cared for in some way. While most fish and water animals spend little time caring for their young, they lay many eggs in one season. One oyster may lay millions of eggs. Most of the eggs and many of the young oysters will be eaten by fish. But enough will grow into adults.

There are a few exceptions to the general rule that water animals do not care for their eggs and young. Male stickleback (STICK-ul-back) fish seem to plan carefully for their young. The male alone first builds an underwater nest. He brings in a female stickleback only when he has completed the nest. The female swims away after laying the eggs and doesn't return. The male moves his tail to keep a stream of fresh water flowing over the eggs. This water provides oxygen for the eggs. After six days, the eggs will hatch. The little fish are kept together by the male and protected until they are large enough to go off by themselves.

optional activity

To compare the germination rates of various seeds, line the bottom of a large cookie tin with several layers of toweling paper and moisten thoroughly. Spread rows of different seeds, such as beans, peas, radish, corn, etc., on the toweling and press the seeds down firmly. Cover the cookie tin with another cookie tin. Keep this in a dark place at room temperature. After three days, the children should make daily observations to record which seeds are germinating, and the differences in growth of the seedling plants.

for your information

The male stickleback has the entire responsibility for the care of the young. After preparing the nest, he invites in several females until he has a sufficient number of eggs. After the young are hatched, he cares for them, bringing them back to the nest in his mouth if they should stray away.

The children might be tempted to view parental care as a product of affection. While this idea is not undesirable, parental care seen as an adaptation to environment is an important lesson. Ask the children to name some animals which require parental care. Animals with which the children are familiar, such as a dog or cat, or those animals the children have read about in the text, such as a lion or porpoise, may spring to mind. Ask them what would happen if no parents were available to care for the young. Ask the children if the environment of the young can care for them as their parents do. Finally, ask if the young survive because the parents fulfill their offsprings' needs until a certain age.

The answer to Testing Your Ideas is that living things, for their kind to be preserved, must be able to have young. The other answers apply to individual animals, but not to species.

for your information

The time of parental care within the class of mammals varies greatly from species to species. The tiny deer mouse usually spends about one month with its young, while the elephant spends two years. Generally, the larger the mammal the longer the time of parental care required. Man, of course, is an exception to this rule.

Whales and porpoises also take good care of their young. They give birth to live young. They do not lay eggs like most other swimming forms of life. Baby blue whales are 25 feet long at birth. The young whales gain about 200 pounds each day. Until the young whale is six or seven months old, its food is the milk of its mother. She protects her young from other animals during this period.

The mothers of lion and bear cubs protect and train them for almost two years. Five years is the length of time elephant babies stay close to their mothers. What is the name of the most helpless baby that comes into the world? If you say man, you are right! How many years does it take before a child can get along without parents? Think what would happen to you if you had to care for yourself without help from your mother and father.

TESTING YOUR IDEAS

All kinds of animals and plants must someday die. To preserve their kind on earth, living things must a) store food for the winter months b) protect themselves from all other living things at all times c) be able to have young.

for your information

Some male animals aid in the care of the young, while others, such as the rabbit and some fish, may kill their offspring. The male gorilla will guard the home at night to protect the female gorilla and her young.

OVERVIEW

Various changes in environment due to climate, weather, or other reasons can drastically affect plants and animals. Those species that adapt to or survive these changes continue to remain on earth. The others suddenly or gradually die out. Man himself may be one cause of vanishing animal and plant species. The importance of conservation of plant and animal species is stressed and man's important role in conservation is discussed in this section. Food chains are an integral part of the natural environment, and disruption of these chains can have adverse effects on any particular species of plant or animal.

how to begin

Give the students a list of plant and animal species that are now extinct and have them look in the library to learn how and why these species disappeared from the earth. Within the last forty years some plant and animal species have dwindled in number. Discuss the cause of the near extinction of these species. Try to get pictures to show the class of plant and animal varieties once abundant and now no longer present.

process skills

Describing the effect of changing environmental conditions on the survival of a plant or animal species

Discussing the importance of conservation of natural life in any particular geographical area

materials

terrarium with plants and animals, weed seeds, crop seeds, soil, flowerpot or wooden box° (If it is difficult for the children to obtain weed seeds, you can purchase such seeds from any biological supply house.)

° one per team

ARE SOME KINDS OF ANIMALS AND PLANTS NO LONGER ON EARTH?

We know from a study of bones found in the earth that many millions of years ago there were huge reptiles called dinosaurs (DIE-no-sawrz) living on the earth. None is alive today.

We do not know all the reasons why the dinosaurs died out. Changing weather may have been one of them. The weather may have become too hot for the dinosaurs to live. As the great ice sheets covered areas of the earth, perhaps it became too cold for them

procedure

Let the youngsters speculate as to what might happen to life in this country if a great ice sheet or glacier once again covered the North American continent. (Cold would kill many forms of temperate plants and animals; man's food sources would disappear; man would probably migrate to a warmer climate, etc.) Ask the children if we have any way of knowing what animals once lived on earth which are no longer present (fossil remains, fossil prints, etc.). Let the class conclude that changed environmental conditions have a gradual effect on living things in any particular part of the world.

In taking care of a classroom terrarium and observing the living things in it, the youngsters will become acquainted with the basic needs of living things and the conditions necessary for their survival. Lack of satisfaction of any of these needs can cause damage to the living organisms. Some plants are able to survive better than others, and when the children cultivate weed seeds and crop seeds in 20/Observe, they will learn this fact. Ask the students to discuss weed growth in gardens at home and the differences they see between weeds and the plants they are cultivating. Perhaps a field trip can be arranged during which the class will visit a vacant lot to examine weed growth.

(continued on page 84)

---

to get enough food. We know from our observations today, that weather has a very important effect on the lives of animals.

Many animals that cannot adapt to weather changes die every year. The hibernating turtle will freeze during the winter if it does not dig below the frost-line when making its winter home. Toads in hibernation will die if the land dries out. Floods and high water force rabbits and rattlesnakes from their burrows. What do you think happens to those that do not get out of their burrows? What happens to seeds that do not get enough moisture and soil? Find out in the next activity with weed and crop seeds.

20/Observe

Some plant varieties may prevent the growth of others. Your teacher will give you the same number of weed seeds and crop seeds to plant in a pot or box.

69

Have the children take leaf samples of the more prevalent weed species. Then have the youngsters use guidebooks in the classroom to try and identify the weeds they have collected. Discuss selective weed-killers and how they are of help to the gardener and the farmer.

In 21/Interpret the children examine their terrarium to find out if any plants or animals have died. If possible, they must determine the cause of death.

Have them check whether enough water and sunlight was provided for the plants. Did they over- or under-feed the animal or give it the wrong food? Was water lacking or too abundant? The failure to meet plant or animal needs generally is the cause of the death of living things.

The discussion of food chains in the textbook should help the students understand that every living thing on earth is affected in some way or another by

responses to 20/observe

1. The weed seeds grow faster than the crop seeds.
2. Weeds grow faster and impede the growth of crops.

optional activity

Cover part of a geranium (or other houseplant) leaf with a small square of black paper. Tape one corner of the paper with a little Scotch tape so the paper is held securely in place.

Expose the plant to bright sunlight. Water the plant sufficiently.

Lift the paper and describe what happened to the covered part of the leaf after four days, after one week, and after two weeks.

①Which seeds grow faster?②Why do farmers have to get rid of weeds? ■

Weeds usually are strong plants. They take from the soil the nourishment needed by other plants. Weeds will take over an area if allowed to spread. Other plants and all animals will die if not given proper care and needed requirements. Relate this fact to the care of living things in a terrarium in the next activity.

21/Interpret

You have made a terrarium in your classroom or at home. If you have one, make a report on the plants and animals in it. If any of the animals or plants died, try to find out why. Did you have food and oxygen for the animals? Was there enough water for the plants? ■

Sometimes plants will appear to have all the things they need for good growth and still not do well. It has been found that some varieties of plants need specific minerals in the soil for them to do well. Without these minerals they do not reach their best growth. The use of proper fertilizers can often provide these missing minerals.

Plants and animals will die if they do not have the surroundings to which they are suited. If they are to survive, all the important needs must be fulfilled in their living and non-living environment.

Charles Darwin (1809-1882), a famous English scientist, once said that the amount of clover seed produced in one season depends on the number of cats living near the clover fields. This statement sounds strange until you listen to Darwin's reasoning.

Darwin

other living things. After they have read the account of Darwin's observation of the relationship of cats to clover seed, ask the class to describe other similar relationships of organisms (bees and fruit trees, birds and insects, ladybird beetles and aphids, etc.).

In the food chain illustrated at the top of the page, if there were an increase in clover hay the cost of clover hay should decrease, thus lowering the farmer's expenses. The cost of meat should then also decrease.

(continued on page 86)

Cats eat the field mice which feed on bumble-bees. The bumblebees help the clover so that it will produce seeds. When there are many bumble bees to help the clover plants, there is enough clover seed, and a large clover crop the next season. Clover hay is used by farmers to fatten their cattle.

These plant and animal relationships are called food chains or food webs. Think of another food chain and try to follow it as far back as you can.

Man stands at the top of many food chains. In the above example, how would the cost of meat be affected by an increase in clover hay?

Fish we eat are another good example of food chains. Man eats the big fish which eat the smaller ones. Little fish eat tiny water animals which feed on tiny water plants. Do you know where the tiny water plants get their food?

71

for your information

Algae are the great manufacturers of food for animals and man. These and other green plants harness the energy of the sun in carbohydrates and other food-stuffs and thus provide the energy and matter needed by animals. As raw materials, plants use waste products of animals (carbon dioxide and water) and thus the same elements are recycled through the plant and the animal.

The domestication of animals and plants introduces man as a factor in the environment of living things. To begin a discussion of this subject, ask the children to give examples of both animals and plants which have been domesticated. List these examples on the blackboard. Then, ask the children what needs of mankind the domesticated animals and plants satisfy. Animals are mainly raised for food and raw materials, but do not ignore the other roles animals play such as protection, scientific research, hobbies, and companionship. Plants too are raised for food and raw materials but are also cultivated for research and for their own beauty.

Having established that animals and plants are domesticated by man to meet his needs, ask the children how far man can domesticate animals. Ask the class if they know of any animal which cannot be domesticated. Tell the children that a popular observation among wolf breeders is that this animal cannot be house-broken. Ask the children if they can name an unusual housepet. Suggest to the class that while many animals can be raised and domesticated, many, many others can only be raised and not tamed. You

All animals were wild hundreds of thousands of years ago. They traveled over the earth searching for food and water. Later on, man began to tame some of these wild animals. The dog was probably the first animal to be tamed. Dogs may have been only companions at first. Man then found that these animals could help protect him.

Can you name some other kinds of domestic animals? What benefits does man receive from them?

may finally ask the class if they have ever heard of any animal which cannot even be raised in captivity. Ask them if there is any animal which will only breed when living in its natural environment. There are animals, such as the three-toed sloth, which have been raised with difficulty and only for a short period of time in an environment which exactly duplicated their natural habitat. It is believed, however, that it is only a matter of time and knowledge about an animal and its habitat which limits the kinds of animals that can be domesticated.

(continued on page 88)

Animals tamed by man supply him with many of the important things he needs. Animals helped man to do much of his work before the invention of modern machines. However, some of these animals are valued by man for their beauty or their amusing habits. The ancient Egyptians originally tamed the cat as a house pet. Anyone who has a pet monkey or has seen one enjoys their playful ways.

Man provides domestic animals with food and shelter in exchange for the benefits they give him. He cares for them if they become sick and protects them from their enemies. Most domestic animals have lived with man for such a long time that if allowed to run wild, they could not take care of themselves.

Domestic animals are only a small number of the different kinds of animals on the earth. Think of some of the wild animals that are highly valued by man.

studying the picture

Ask the children to what use man has put each of the domesticated animals shown. Also ask the class what animals have been replaced by man's inventiveness. The engine has replaced the horse and donkey, and man-made fibers now compete with the wool from sheep.

73

The use to which man has put animals and plants can be a good introduction to man's misuse of his environment and the living things in it. Ask the class to consider how wisely man has tended to animals, plants, and their places. Point to whatever local misuse of surroundings there might exist in your area. Ask the children if they know or have read of other misuses. Mention those animals such as the passenger pigeon, the heath hen, the sand-shoal duck, and the masked bobwhite which man has made extinct. Almost extinct is our national symbol, the bald-headed eagle, as well as swallow tail kites, whooping cranes, prairie chickens, and the California condor. Fighting for existence are the bobcat, lynx, red wolf, and moose and over a hundred other kinds of animals which man has threatened. Bring to class pictures of some of these animals. Then help the children locate the habitats of these animals on a map of the United States. Ask the children what might happen to the animals whose food chains incorporate those animals which are few in number.

In addition to threatening wildlife, man has laid waste great forests without replacing them. Ask the children how the destruction of a forest can harm the animals living in it. Ask them if an animal can thrive if its habitat is ruined.

(continued on page 90)

for your information

You can obtain pamphlets, films, and other materials useful in teaching conservation from sources such as National Parks Service, National Audubon Society, U.S. Forest Service, 4-H Club, state conservation departments, and county agricultural agencies.

Minks or foxes raised on ranches for their fur are not really tame. A ranch fox or mink would be able to survive in the wilderness.

The land was rich with forests, wild animals, fertile soil, and other natural resources when settlers first arrived in North America. These resources seemed so great that the American settlers believed that they would last forever. Forests were cut down to clear farmland and the wild animals were shot for food. The soil was often used unwisely and in time it became much less fertile. Great amounts of forest and grassland were destroyed by carelessly started fires.

74

Many wild animals were displaced from their natural habitats each time that man moved into a new area. Others were killed carelessly. For example, the American buffalo once roamed the plains in herds of many thousands. By the 1880's their total number became much smaller. Buffalo were often killed by the thousands, merely for the sport of the hunters.

The passenger pigeon was another North American animal that once was present in great numbers.

75

Water and air pollution is a misuse of environment and can upset the complex balance of nature just as a link made extinct in a food chain can affect the wildlife associated with it. Perhaps, this particular misuse of natural resources will quickly be understood by the class to be a direct threat to man's own existence.

At this point, ask the class to make up their own minds about how wisely man has tended his surroundings and the living things in it.

Ask them what they would do to change man's misuse of his environment, if they agree that man is not using it wisely. Could laws be passed? How would they be enforced? What laws should be passed?

Man is the most adaptable of animals because he can establish surroundings to suit his needs.

All the statements of Testing Your Ideas are true. You should ask the children for examples of each of the statements.

John James Audubon (1785-1851), the famous naturalist, reported in 1813 having seen a flock of passenger pigeons so huge it took three days for them to pass by. Not one passenger pigeon is alive today. They were all killed by hunters and changed conditions in their habitats.

Many people realized by the 1880's that the nation's resources were being used up rapidly by man's greed and carelessness. Such people wanted to stop the wasteful use of our resources. In order to protect our forest lands, wildlife, and other resources the conservation movement was started.

A powerful supporter of this movement was President Theodore Roosevelt. Help came from him to make conservation popular during his years as President (1901-1909). Many forest lands were put under government control, land for national parks was set aside, and hunting and fishing laws were passed. Are there any wild animals living near your area? Can they be hunted? Find out the legal seasons for fishing and hunting.

Animals and plants live in every kind of habitat, from the wettest to the driest, from the hottest to the coldest. It is not the same plants and animals that live and do well in these different climates. Each animal and plant lives in the place to which it is best suited.

Roosevelt

76

Man is very different from all the other animals. He alone can live almost anywhere on earth. Man can change his surroundings to suit him. Even though man cannot live without air to breathe, he doesn't have to stay where air is naturally present. Taking his atmosphere with him, man can travel under the ocean or far out into space. Clothing is made by man and he builds houses to protect him from the weather. He provides a comfortable climate in his house by heating or air-conditioning.

When man changes his surroundings to suit him, he must be careful not to ruin the land or harm the animals living on it. His responsibility is to use the natural world carefully so that it can be used and enjoyed by future generations. The more each individual learns about plants and animals, and about the ways they depend upon each other, the better he will be able to meet this responsibility.

TESTING YOUR IDEAS

With which of the following statements do you agree?

Changing weather conditions over a long, long period of time on earth have killed certain kinds of animals.

Changing weather conditions over a short period of time may kill some animals.

Man is the one animal who can directly change his environment.

Man can be a threat to animals and plants.

SUMMING UP THE UNIT

review

The answers to review questions are listed below:
   A: 4, 5, 7, 8, B: 7, C: 1, 3, D: 2, E: 4, 5, 6, 7, 8, F: 3, 6, 7.

self-test

Two of the major points in this unit are that particular living things need a particular environment and that a radical change in the environment can mean the extinction of a species. The point of this question is to suggest a lesson beyond these two ideas, i.e., that living things can adapt to some kinds of substantial environmental change.

SUMMING UP THE UNIT

REVIEW

Below are listed particular statements about living things and general statements about living things. Which of the general statements about living things helps to explain each of the particular statements? A general statement may explain more than one particular statement.

Particular Statement	General Statement
1. The fur of the polar bear is white.	A. A habitat is a place where living things live and grow.
2. Milkweed seeds have "parachutes."	B. Some animals change their habitat by migration.
3. In spring, the ptarmigian looses its white feathers and grows brown ones.	C. The color of animals is influenced by their surroundings.
4. Both a mountain and a flower pot are habitats.	D. Dispersal occurs by chance.
5. Cactus grows in desert surroundings.	E. Proper surroundings meet the needs of living things.
6. In winter, frogs hibernate.	F. Some animals and plants have adapted to seasonal change.
7. Salmon swim to fresh water at certain seasons.	
8. Some fish need warm water.	

78

The children might be encouraged to begin a discussion of their own on the subject of the self-test. Ask those children who have been to a zoo to describe the animals they saw and if they think anything was done to make the animals feel at home.

A woodland terrarium was to be built by a science class. Dick and Barbara were chosen to build it. They knew living things need certain surroundings. But Dick grew tired of the idea of a terrarium.

"You know," he said to Barbara, "My uncle took me to a zoo yesterday. I saw zebras and elephants—all kinds of animals. They were all in the middle of the city, and all were brought from Africa. How come they can live here?" Barbara suggested animals perhaps could make a change.

"Do you mean adapt?" Dick asked.

How do you think animals from Africa can live in the city?

Find out how various seeds have been adapted so that they can travel from place to place. Collect play some of these seeds.

You are a State Forest Ranger. What plants and animals do you find in your region? What is the habitat of each? How can you protect these plants and animals?

You are a teacher planning to take your class on a field trip to study plants and animals. Where can you go? What will you see there? What plans should you make?

79

unit two
Your Growing Body

unit two

Your Growing Body

SCIENCE INFORMATION FOR THE TEACHER

The growth and development of our bodies is something people seem to take for granted. Our growth is so gradual that we usually are not aware of the changes taking place. Children probably do not give much thought to the marvelous workings which go on inside their bodies to maintain health and produce proper growth. Youngsters are often told, "Eat this or do that, so you will grow big and strong." But most children do not know why adults tell them to cultivate this health habit or avoid that one. In this unit the students receive a general introduction to some of the fascinating aspects of how the body is constructed and how man, as an organism, is able to carry on many of the complex tasks necessary for life.

To study as basic a function as body growth, as well as to understand its relationship to nutrition and health, we must consider the functioning of the human organism as a whole. In such an approach to the study of health, human beings must be treated as units. We are more than mechanical bodies. We are living organisms which have an intellect.

To understand how the body grows and develops, it is necessary to understand the relationship between the food we eat and the way the body digests the food and uses it in the cells. Sound nutrition contributes to the proper growth and health of the organism. It permits the best possible development and functioning of human beings. The establishment of intelligent eating habits has a lifelong effect on health. Thus, the focus of this unit is on a sense of health, or total well being of the body, with additional reference to the phenomenon of growth.

To understand as fully as possible the relationship between what we eat and how the body functions, various classes of foods and good eating habits are stressed. The children discover how food is digested, how it is carried to the cells in the various tissues of the body, how it is assimilated into the cells, and how it is used to carry on the life processes necessary for good health and proper growth. Thus, learning what food does in the body should help the youngsters understand the need for eating well-balanced meals and making intelligent food selections.

Digestion occurs in stages and takes place at various sites in the digestive tube. Digestion is primarily a function of the mouth, stomach, and intestines. These organs make up a long tube through which food passes, nutrients are selected, and wastes are discarded. In the digestive tract a number of physical and chemical changes take place in the food we eat. Carbohydrates are changed into simple sugars; proteins are digested into peptides and amino acids; and fats are changed into fatty acids. Thus, the process of digestion breaks down the complex foods we eat into their component parts, which are absorbed into the blood stream.

Digestion of starches begins in the mouth as the food is chewed and mixed with certain chemical substances present in the saliva. When food is swallowed, it is moved to the back of the mouth and forced into the gullet where wavelike contractions convey the food to the stomach. The stomach is a muscular sac in which gastric juices inhibit the action of the saliva on the swallowed starches and begin the breakdown of proteins. Digestion is completed in the small intestine where food is acted upon by secretions of the intestinal glands and of the pancreas and liver. The final stages in the breakdown of proteins into amino acids, of carbohydrates into glucose, and of fats into fatty acids and glycerol occur here.

The walls of the intestine are lined with numerous finger-like projections called villi. These are microscopic in size and increase the absorptive surface exposed to the digested food to about ten times the skin surface of the body. When glucose, amino acids, and fatty acids have been absorbed through the villi into the blood capillaries which line them, indigestible food residues pass into the large intestine. During digestion, the food must be in a liquid form so that the different digestive fluids may act on the various food substances ingested. In the large intestine water is reabsorbed and the thick fluid which enters the large intestine gradually becomes solidified material, the feces. In addition to food residues, the feces contain waste materials filtered out of the blood in the liver, a considerable number of intestinal bacteria, and discarded cells from the intestinal lining.

Oxygen and digested food materials pass through the thin walls of the air sacs in the lungs and the villi in the intestine respectively, and enter the minute capillaries that line these organs. The blood in the circulatory system then acts as a means of transportation and distribution of the materials needed by the cells. Among the cells of the body tissues the capillaries form a network. Essential nutrients and oxygen pass through the capillary walls into the fluid which bathes the cells of the body. From the surrounding fluids, the cells absorb the materials they need to carry on their specific activities. For example, the cells oxidize glucose for energy or store it in various cells for future use. Amino acids are recombined into body protein to repair and increase the number of cells. Fatty acids are used for energy, or are recombined with glycerol to form the characteristic layers of body fat.

Thus, the actual living processes occur in the cells. The cells take in oxygen and nutrients from the blood, use them as needed, and give off to the blood carbon dioxide, water, nitrogen, and broken down cell material in the process. The wastes pass into the fluids surrounding the cells and are then absorbed into the blood plasma. These wastes are carried to excretory organs which remove them from the body. Carbon dioxide and water are exhaled from the lungs. The urinary wastes are filtered out of the blood as it passes through the kidneys and are excreted in the form of urine. The main purposes of this whole process of ingesting and digesting food are to supply the cells with energy foods for movement, and to provide materials for repair and growth of the cells.

To hold all parts of the body together, we have a skeleton of bones which forms a framework. Different tissues and organs are attached to the skeleton. The contractions and relaxations of the voluntary muscles attached to the bones produce the familiar motions in the outer parts of our bodies. Among the many functions necessary to life, the action of the involuntary muscles inside the body produces the digestive movements, breathing action, and the pumping of the heart.

The growth of the bones is one measure of the way the body grows. Bones grow longer, broader, and thicker. The body deposits minerals in the microscopic spaces among the living bone cells. This action replaces cartilage, building up the infant skeleton with minerals for strength and hardness. However, not all cartilage is replaced. In a few places in the adult skeleton, such as in the tip of the nose or the pads between the bones, cartilage is retained. The required minerals must be supplied in the diet as the body is growing. Body growth may continue for about 25 years, and the deposition of minerals in the bones continues throughout life. The skeleton forms a framework for the body, protects delicate organs, and provides places of attachment for the muscles.

The control of all our body activities is dependent on the action of the brain, spinal cord, nerves, and other sense organs making up the nervous system. Through these organs, our life activities are coordinated, and the organism functions as a unit.

Although the children will be studying about the digestive, circulatory, respiratory, excretory, skeletal, muscular, and nervous systems in this unit, they should understand that all these systems are functioning simultaneously in the body. All the cells, tissues, organs, and systems must work in harmony for life to proceed and for the human organism as a whole to be able to maintain a state of good health and to grow and develop properly. The unitary character of man as an organism should be stressed, even though for purposes of study the whole is divided into parts.

Man is an organism and, like all organisms, has basic needs for survival, development, and growth. In this unit the children discover what these needs are and how their bodies are organized to carry out the activities which will meet these needs. The children become aware of the fact that the organism carries out its life processes by means of a complex of interacting systems.

The method used in this unit as elsewhere in the series is that of discovery. The student is introduced to a topic and then is led to form conclusions about it by taking part in activities designed to help the concepts grow.

The emphasis of this unit is on the well-being and growth of the body. The children discover that from the moment of birth, their bodies have been developing and changing. Yet such growth and development have depended upon a complex of interrelated body activities. The youngsters learn, for example, that the first need of the body is for energy—that it gets energy from the oxidation of food materials in the cells. However, the provision of energy depends on the interrelated activities of many systems. The digestive, circulatory, respiratory, excretory, muscular, skeletal, and nervous systems are all involved.

As the children become aware of these interactions, they also become aware of the concept of variety and pattern. They learn that activity and change are characteristics of life processes. Changes occur in the body continuously. Cells are replaced, and materials are changed from one form to another. Yet there is a pattern to these changes. There is a continuous cycle of life-sustaining activities.

The planned experiences of the unit help the students recognize the variety and pattern in human development. Children learn that human beings differ; yet for all human beings, there is a typical pattern of growth from infancy to childhood, from childhood to adolescence, and from adolescence to adulthood.

The activities of the unit are designed to help the children develop good habits of observation and interpretation. The youngsters feel some of the body structures and observe body activities.

Generalization I

Man has only recently begun to understand how the human body takes in and utilizes food substances.

Contributing Principles and Sub-principles

A. The body is made up of many substances.
B. Foods supply the substances used by the body.
C. A balanced diet includes foods from four basic groups: milk, meat, vegetables and fruit, and cereal.

Generalization II

The human body must have proper foods to carry on its functions.

Contributing Principles and Sub-principles

A. The body is made up of many substances.
B. Foods supply the substances used by the body.
C. A balanced diet includes foods from four basic groups: milk, meat, vegetables and fruit, and cereal.

Generalization III

Several types of substances are found in foods.

Contributing Principles and Sub-principles

A. Carbohydrates and fats are the main energy foods.
    1. The presence of starch can be determined by an iodine test.
    2. The presence of fat can be determined by a grease spot test.
B. Proteins are the main foods used in the building and repairing of body tissues.
    1. The presence of protein can be determined by odor and chemical tests.
C. Vitamins and minerals are needed to regulate body processes and aid body growth.
    1. The presence of minerals can be determined by a heat test.
D. Water is needed to carry substances to and from the body tissues.

Generalization IV

The human body is made up of many systems, or groups, or organs.

Contributing Principles and Sub-principles

A. Each organ, or part of a system, has certain functions.
B. Each organ is made up of tissues which contain cells.

Generalization V

The digestive system contains the body parts which work together to break food down into smaller particles for use in the body.

Contributing Principles and Sub-principles

A. Digestive glands produce juices (enzymes) that help change food.
B. In the mouth, food is crushed and mixed with saliva.
C. In the stomach, food is churned and mixed with digestive juices.
D. In the small intestine, the digestion of food is completed and the absorption of its active components into the blood stream takes place.

Generalization VI

The respiratory system contains the body parts which work together to take air into the lungs and expel it from them.

Contributing Principles and Sub-principles

A. Air is moistened, cleaned, and warmed as it is drawn into the body through the nose on its way to the lungs.
B. Oxygen from the air passes into the blood through tiny air sacs in the lungs.
C. Carbon dioxide from the blood passes into the air through tiny air sacs in the lungs.
D. The movement of the diaphragm and the rib muscles helps the body inhale and exhale.

Generalization VII

The circulatory system contains the body parts which work together to move the blood through the body.

Contributing Principles and Sub-principles

A. The heart pumps the blood to all parts of the body.
B. The blood flows in a continuous stream through the body.
C. The blood absorbs digested food products from the intestine.
D. The blood absorbs oxygen and gives off carbon dioxide in the lungs.
E. The blood carries waste products from the tissues to the excretory system.
F. The lungs get rid of carbon dioxide and water.

Generalization VIII

The excretory system contains the body parts which work together to eliminate the waste products of digestion.

Contributing Principles and Sub-principles

A. The large intestine and rectum remove undigested food.
B. The kidney and bladder get rid of water and liquid waste.
C. The skin gets rid of water and mineral waste.

Generalization IX

The nervous system contains the body parts which work together to sense stimuli and cause muscles to act.

Generalization X

The skeletal system contains the body parts which give support to the body and protects its vital organs.

Generalization XI

The muscular system contains the body parts which work together to produce motion.

Contributing Principles and Sub-principles

A. Voluntary muscles attached to the bones produce motion in the body.
B. Involuntary muscles function automatically and no conscious effort can affect them.
C. Good posture helps the skeleton and muscles develop properly.

**before
you
begin**

NEW WORDS FOR THE STUDENT

This list contains science words that will be introduced in the course of the unit. Mastery of the vocabulary is not essential. Use this list to help your students understand what they read. Do not require memorization of its contents.

air sacs microscopic sacs in the lungs in which the exchange of oxygen and carbon dioxide in the blood takes place

arteries blood vessels which carry the blood away from the heart to all parts of the body

auricles (also called atria) the two chambers making up the upper part of the heart into which the blood returns from the body and from the lungs

capillaries microscopic blood vessels forming a network in all the tissues of the body at which the exchange of nutrients and wastes with the cells of the body takes place

carbohydrates a class of food containing carbon, oxygen, and hydrogen, which are the main sources of energy for body activities

carbon dioxide a gas produced in the oxidation of carbohydrates; produces energy which is excreted from the lungs as a waste product

cartilage an elastic tissue forming the first skeleton in the body and making up the soft parts of the skeleton in later life

diaphragm the large sheetlike muscle separating the chest cavity from the abdominal cavity; functions in breathing movements

digestive juices fluids containing chemical substances which act on foods to break them down during the digestive process

hemoglobin a red-colored protein substance within the red blood cells which transports oxygen in the blood

involuntary muscles the muscles making up the internal organs of the body and which function without conscious control

joints the places in the skeleton where bones are fastened together so that movement can take place

ligaments the strong bands of connective tissue which hold the bones together at the joints *motor nerves* nerves which carry signals from the brain and spinal cord to the muscles and glands

mucous membrane a moist tissue which produces mucus and which lines the optic socket and the respiratory and digestive systems in the body

nutrients essential food elements needed to supply the body with materials for energy and growth

oxidation the chemical process in which food combines with the oxygen in the cells to release energy

plasma the liquid part of the blood, composed largely of water, in which nutrients and waste materials are dissolved and transported

proteins a class of food containing nutrients which supply materials for the growth and repair of cells in the body

reflex action an involuntary movement of voluntary muscles which protects the body from harm

sensory nerves nerves which carry signals from the sense organs to the spinal cord and brain

system a term applied to a group of organs in the body which perform a related function

tendons the tough bands of tissue which connect the muscles to the bones

urinary wastes waste products produced by the cells and excreted in the urine

veins blood vessels which return the blood from the body to the heart

ventricles the two chambers making up the lower part of the heart which pump the blood to the body and the lungs

villi microscopic projections of the inner wall of the small intestine through which digested materials are absorbed into the blood

vitamins a class of food containing chemical substances needed by the body for proper growth and health

voluntary muscles the muscles making up the outer parts of the body; usually under conscious control of the brain

BOOKS FOR THE STUDENT

Adler, Irving and Ruth, *Taste, Touch, and Smell.* New York. John Day Company, 1966.

Brandenberg, Aliki, *My Five Senses.* New York. Thomas Y. Crowell, 1962.

Dietz, David, *All About Great Medical Discoveries.* New York. Random House, 1960.

Follett, Robert, *Your Wonderful Body.* Chicago. Follett Publishing, 1961.

Gramet, Charles, *The Wonder That Is You.* New York. Abelard-Schuman, 1962.

Gruenberg, Benjamin and Sidonie, *The Wonderful Story of You.* Garden City, New York. Doubleday, 1960.

Keen, Martin, *The Wonders of the Human Body.* New York. Grosset and Dunlap, 1966.

Lauber, Patricia, *Your Body and How It Works.* New York. Random House, 1962.

Riedman, Sarah, *Food for People.* New York. Abelard-Schuman, 1961.

Showers, Paul, *How Many Teeth?* New York. Thomas Y. Crowell, 1962.

Showers, Paul, *Your Skin and Mine.* New York. Thomas Y. Crowell, 1965.

Weart, Edith, *The Story of Your Blood.* New York. Coward-McCann, 1960.

White, Anne T., *Secrets of the Heart and Blood.* Champaign, Illinois. Garrard Publishing, 1965.

BOOKS FOR THE TEACHER

Blanc, S., A. Fischler, and O. Gardner, *Modern Science: Man, Matter, and Energy.* New York. Holt, Rinehart and Winston, 1967. "Energy for the Body," pp. 305–328; "Functions of the Body," pp. 333–362; "Growth of the Body," pp. 367–387.

Blough, Glenn O., and Julius Schwartz, *Elementary School Science and How to Teach It,* New York. Holt, Rinehart and Winston, 1969. "The Human Body and How It Works," pp. 209–329.

Gega, Peter C., *Science in Elementary Education.* New York. John Wiley and Sons, 1970. "Human Growth and Nutrition," pp. 413–425.

Hone, Elizabeth B., Alexander Joseph, and Edward Victor, *A Sourcebook for Elementary Science.* New York. Harcourt, Brace & World, 1962.

FILMS

About the Human Body   11 minutes   B&W/color   CF
Discusses the more important systems in the body and shows how they function. Explores the skeletal, muscular, nervous, circulatory, digestive, and respiratory systems.

Digestion in Our Bodies   11 minutes   B&W/color   COR
Shows the main organs of digestion and traces the process. Explains why food must be digested before the body can use it and why correct eating attitudes and habits are important.

Exploring Your Growth   11 minutes   B&W/color   CF
Explores the process of growth. Explains how food is digested and transported to the body cells, and how the cells grow and divide to produce body growth.

Food That Builds Good Health   11 minutes   B&W/color   COR
Shows how eating proper foods contributes to the building of a healthy body. Compares the effects on the body of a good diet and a poor diet. Shows the main types of foods that should be in a good diet.

Growing Up—Preadolescence   11 minutes   B&W/color   COR
Illustrates variations in rates of normal growth among boys and girls. Explains the effects of the endocrine glands in controlling growth and shows proper health measures which aid growth.

Growing Up Day By Day   11 minutes   B&W/color   EBF
Points out that some children grow faster than others and that factors such as rest, diet, and exercise can affect growth. Stresses that in growing up children must learn to take responsibility for their own health.

Heart, Lungs and Circulation   11 minutes   B&W/color   COR
Explains how the heart, lungs, and blood vessels work together. Uses fluoroscopic films to show some of these actions actually taking place. Emphasizes the need for maintaining a healthy heart and lungs.

Learning About Our Bodies   11 minutes   B&W/color   COR
Shows the major organs of the body. Uses fluoroscopic films to show how the various parts of the body function. Explains that the body must be kept in good condition to work properly.

Muscles and Bones of the Body   11 minutes   B&W/color   COR
Describes the functions of the bones and muscles. Shows how tendons and muscles are attached to bones and how the joints function to allow movement. Explains the difference between voluntary and involuntary muscles.

Nutritional Needs of Our Bodies   11 minutes   B&W/color   COR
Shows how food meets the body's basic needs. The four basic food groups are illustrated, and the nutrients which they contain are shown. The uses of the nutrients in the body are discussed.

Understanding Vitamins   14 minutes   B&W/color   EBF
Explains what vitamins are and why they are necessary for good health. Tells about the natural sources of important vitamins in the diet and reveals some of the effects of a vitamin-poor diet. Tells about the discovery of vitamins.

Your Nervous System   11 minutes   B&W/color   COR
The general parts of the nervous system are shown and the way the muscles and the glands are controlled by this system is explained. The sense organs and their relation to the body activities are discussed.

CF   Churchill Films
COR   Coronet Films
EBF   Encyclopaedia Britannica Films

BULLETIN BOARDS

Co-ordination

Display pictures of children carying on various activities such as walking, running, swimming, and climbing. Ask the youngsters to imagine that they had to use machines to do these things. Let them speculate as to how the body is able to carry on all these activities.

What Foods Keep Us Healthy?

After the students have completed the first lesson of this unit, they can review and summarize their learnings with this bulletin board. First, review the four basic food groups necessary for good nutrition and then have the students make a placard naming each group (Meat Group, Milk Group, Bread Group, Vegetable Group). These placards can divide the bulletin board into sections and the children can then bring in pictures cut from magazines or hand-drawn which illustrate foods from each of the groups.

What Is Inside Our Bodies?

Display in random order pictures or drawings of various body organs. Do not label them. Have the students identify any organs they may recognize and explain their functions. Plan to follow up this discussion with others as the unit study continues.

Where Does the Blood Go in the Body?

Make an outline drawing of the body and let the children cut out various organs from colored paper (heart, lungs, stomach). Let them pin the cutouts in place on the outline drawing as they learn about organs in this unit. Let the youngsters use colored yarn to trace the circulation of the blood from the heart and back again.

Where Do Messages Go in the Body?

Display pictures or drawings of the brain, spinal cord, sense organs, and muscles. When they have finished this section of the unit, let the students use colored yarn to show the pathway of a nerve impulse—how the impulse is received by a sense organ, is transmitted to the spinal cord and/or brain, and returned to a muscle. Through discussion and demonstration help the class understand that the nervous system controls all activities in the body and that the brain is a master control.

Where Does Our Food Come From?

There are two basic sources for all our food (other than water): animals and plants. Have the students make placards with each of these titles. Then have them collect pictures of animals and plants that supply us with food and group them under the appropriate heading on the bulletin board.

THE HISTORY OF THE IDEA

The opening discussion of this unit presents the concept that, historically, man has needed an adequate and continuing supply of nourishing food. This has always been a basic confrontation of the human species, and, in fact, of all living things. To stay alive, one must eat; to stay well, one must eat well. Food had to be grown, raised, and hunted; ways of preserving food for consumption during periods of scarcity had to be devised. Methods of manufacturing food products from plant and animal sources had to be invented, and proper distribution of foods to people in remote or isolated areas had to be worked out. Concepts of nutrition in the modern sense evolved from observation and experimentation, and gradually diseases related to deficiencies in the diet began to be understood. The need for sanitary, pathogen-free, and dirt-free food supplies became apparent with the growth in medical knowledge and became feasible with advances in food technology. Credit must be given to modern methods in the various food industries as well as improvements in transportation for the availability of sufficient, health-developing foods for large rural and urban populations in the United States. Not so fortunate, however, is the food situation in the rest of the world; rescue from starvation of many of the world's populations

studying the picture

Inform the children that the two photographs on this page are related in a particular way and that you wish to have the class tell you how they are related. *Have the class describe what the children are doing in the first picture. Then, ask the class what eating has to do with the children playing.* The class should conclude that one must eat in order to live and grow. Try to relate the text on page 83 of the student edition with the picture which shows the children having lunch. *For example, ask the class what kinds of food the children are eating and in what amounts.*

attends upon still greater progress in agriculture and food technology abroad.

The study of anatomy and physiology has progressed from unsophisticated beginnings in earlier cultures to the profundities of biology at levels where the study of the cell involves chemistry and physics of the most abstract order. Among the ancient Greeks, medicine was a flourishing art, practiced by scientist-physicians such as Hippocrates. Experience, observation, and conjecture, often of a searching, well-aimed nature, served to form a growing body of teachings concerning human life in health and sickness.

The medical practice of the ancients also involved an interest in anatomy and physiology. Studies of animals through dissection fed the ancients' concepts of human structure and function. Human dissection was not always legal, and since only animals were available for study, some distorted notions resulted. Physicians such as Galen promoted ideas about anatomy and physiology which persisted for centuries, but which were eventually refined by later observers such as Vesalius, who made anatomical drawings of great exactness. Early biological scientists had to contend with the ignorance and superstition of many of the authorities who often enough persecuted and harassed them.

Have you ever wondered how the food you eat helps you to stay healthy and grow strong? Do you think that all kinds of foods in any amount are good for you? Do some foods make you healthier than others? Are some foods unhealthy to eat?

In the history of man, food has been a most important problem in different ways. You might imagine the first way food could be a great hardship — having enough to eat. During one period of the Roman Empire long ago, people chose to drown themselves rather than to starve. But even today some countries have very little food. Yet, is the amount of food you eat all that is important about food? Is it possible that to live and grow you need many different kinds of food in the right amounts?

For many years people knew very little about the way food helped them grow. They did not understand why some foods were better for them than others. They did not realize that a correct diet is needed to stay healthy and grow strong. Before people learned how to keep food from spoiling, they ate the food they could easily get. Meats and foods from grain could be had most of the year. But only in summertime were there plenty of fresh fruits and vegetables. At the times of year when people could not get much fresh food, they became easily tired or even sick. Children did not grow well. Some people died. In some countries at the present time, people may not be always hungry, but they are not healthy. They may have only a few kinds of food to eat, but to be well they need other kinds.

Today, many people may in some parts of the world overeat. If you eat too much, might you grow strong and healthy? Eating too much can be as great a problem as having too little food or not eating the right kinds.

Do you think a proper diet is necessary to live and grow strong?

the unit at a glance

The growing body is presented as a unit of interdependent systems, themselves made up of smaller units, which work together to form a living whole. The theme which unites the various parts of this idea is food—its kinds, its digestion and oxidation, and its uses, such as movement and growth. Since this subject cannot be directly observed, the process of inference comes into full play.

OVERVIEW

The background discussion for the section serves as an introduction to the unit and leads into a consideration of the four basic food groups. Whenever possible throughout this unit, refer to "the human organism" rather than to the human body in order to develop the concept, without using the term, that man is a single, open, dynamic reality. This first lesson should call the pupils' attention to the basic problem of securing enough of the right kinds of food in order to support life and health. After this initial discussion, the students are introduced to the five main classes of foods.

how to begin

Have the class read as homework the text through the discussion of the basic food groups. Start a discussion of man's need for food by asking the students how long they think they would stay alive and comfortable without a) clothing, b) shelter, c) food, d) water. Guide the discussion to the need for food and water, bringing out the relationship between having an adequate supply of the right kinds of food and the feeling of well-being and contentment that we all desire.

process skills

Identifying foods from each of the four basic food groups each day
Identifying foods in which essential nutrients are found
Performing tests for some of the common nutrients found in foods

materials

photograph of student as baby, recent photograph of student, tin can*, cardboard, tincture of iodine (drugstore variety), eye droppers*, small dish*, thick pieces of string, brown wrapping paper, kitchen tongs, candle or alcohol burner, hot plate, metal dishes (tops from jars), platform scales, feathers

In addition, the following foods will be needed for various activities in this section: sugar, potato, bread, apple, cooking oil, butter or margarine, lean meat, cheese.

* one per team

WHAT FOODS DO YOU NEED?

Do you think there is something in fresh foods that helps you grow well and stay healthy? In this unit you will study about food and your growing body. In the first activity it might be fun for you to see how much you have grown.

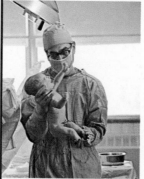

1/Compare

Bring to class a picture of yourself as a baby or as a small child. Also bring a recent picture of yourself. Put the pictures side by side to find out how you have changed. How much have you grown since the first picture was taken? How could you find out how much weight you have gained? What do you think helps you grow and keep healthy?

Imagine what would happen if there were no more food in the world. How would you feel if you did not have food every day? All the food you eat daily makes up your diet (DIE-uht). A diet that gives you the proper amounts of each food you need is called a balanced (BAL-unst) diet. One of the best ways to make sure you have a balanced diet is to plan your meals so that you eat the right kinds of food every day. What kinds of food do you think are needed in a balanced diet?

procedure

In activity 1/Compare on page 84, have the children bring in pictures of themselves as babies and pictures of themselves now. Let the students discuss the changes which have taken place, such as increased size and weight. Ask the children to place their pictures on a bulletin board and see how many of their peers can identify the picture correctly. Point out that all living things grow and develop. Ask the children what is needed in order to grow well. They should be able to conclude that good, fresh food is needed. Bring out the point that proper growth and health depend on good nutrition.

Discuss with the youngsters the picture on page 85 of the family at dinner. Ask the class to name some of the foods on the table. Point out that the proper selection of meat, vegetables, bread, milk, and fruit can provide this family with a good, balanced diet.

The next topic concerns the types of foods which should be eaten to produce a balanced diet. The text presents the concept of the four basic food groups. Bring out the point that good nutrition results if several servings of each of the four basic types of foods are eaten each day.

(continued on page 114)

Look at the picture of a family eating a meal. What different foods are they eating? Do you see the meat, bread, butter, and vegetables? These are foods from four important food groups. The Milk Group includes milk, butter, cream, cheese, and ice cream. The Meat Group contains meat, fish, and poultry. The Bread Group includes bread, cereals, cakes, and pastries. The Vegetable Group is made up of vegetables and fruits.

The foods in these four groups contain the things which people need to be healthy and strong. Which two food groups come from animals? Which two come from plants? Do you know what most of the animals we use for food eat? Why can you call green plants the source of all food in the world?

85

responses to 1/compare

1. Answers will vary.
2. This question is motivational. Ask the children to name things they need to live and grow properly (food, sleep, exercise).

studying the picture

Have the children name the foods and food groups shown in each picture.

The next topic introduces the students to the idea that substances in foods fall into specific categories, such as carbohydrates, proteins, fats, minerals, and vitamins. The class may not be familiar with the terms "carbohydrates" and "proteins." Therefore, point to common foods containing these substances. Be sure the children understand that no single food contains all the necessary nutrients. But milk, even though lacking in Vitamin C and iron, is the closest to a complete food. The text helps the youngsters find out what these nutrients are, how they can be identified, and what they are used for in the body.

In activity 3/Describe, the children find out that heat, a form of energy, is released when sugar burns. Be sure to use only a small amount of sugar on the cardboard so that the sugar will ignite. The can will get hot, but it can be touched on the outside without burning the fingers. The discussion following the activity lets the class infer that more carbohydrates are used by the body during the cold weather and during hard work. In both cases, the body needs excess amounts of energy foods.

(continued on page 116)

studying the picture

In each picture have the class discover an example of each of the four basic food groups.

2/Classify

Make up a page in your notebook for each of the four food groups. Look in magazines around your house to find pictures of different kinds of food. Cut out these pictures and paste them on different pages so that you have one page for each of the four food groups. Label each page according to its food group. ■

As you look at the pictures that you put in your notebook, you can see that many foods we eat belong to more than one food group. For example, a stew may be made from meat, fats, and vegetables. Or a cake may contain flour from wheat, butter, sugar, and milk. As you choose what to eat every day, you should have foods from each of the four main food groups.

The four main food groups are made up of many different foods. Each food may be made up of different materials. Because the different materials found in foods help us in different ways, we give them special names. You will learn more about these materials and their names as you do the activities in this part of your book.

For our bodies to have "go-power," we need a special kind of food. The "go-power" is called energy, and we need it for work and play. Its source is a special kind of food called a carbohydrate (cahr-bo-HIE-drayt). Sugars and starches are carbohydrates that we use every day. They are found in bread, cereals, potatoes, fruits, and, of course, sugar itself. Let us see if we can get some heat energy from sugar.

3/Describe

Put a piece of thin cardboard on top of any empty, clean tin can. Put a little pile of sugar in the middle of the cardboard. Have your teacher light the cardboard with a match so that it begins to burn and causes the sugar to burn also. After the burning sugar drops into the can, *carefully* touch the outside of the can. ■

Ask the children which of the carbohydrate foods shown are normally part of their diet. Ask them if all the foods shown taste the same. Try to lead them to the conclusion, that although these foods taste differently, they all contain carbohydrates.

responses to 3/describe

1. The children should note that the can is hot and that heat has been produced by the burning of the sugar.

In activity 4/Compare, some foods are tested for starch by dropping an iodine solution on them. The ordinary tincture of iodine found in drug stores will work well here. If the food contains starch, the iodine will turn blue to purple. Ask the children to test other food items for starch. Be sure the youngsters include non-starch foods, such as dissolved candy or pieces of meat, so that they can compare what happens to the color of the iodine. The students should record their results in a notebook and indicate the presence or absence of starch by writing *yes* or *no* in the proper column.

The next type of nutrient considered is fat or oil. Fats and oils are a more concentrated form of energy food. They are digested more slowly than carbohydrates. Not over twenty percent of the diet should be made up of fats. They are an important source of energy, and some fats, such as butter, also provide certain vitamins in the diet.

In activity 5/Observe, the children again note that an energy food will burn and give off heat. It may be necessary to ignite the wick with a candle flame to start it burning. But once started, it will continue to burn until the oil is used up. To put out the flame, cover the dish with a can or jar to cut off the oxygen supply. *Do not pour water on burning oil.*

(continued on page 118)

responses to 4/compare

1. The color of the iodine turns blue-black. Even the smallest trace of starch will show up as a blue color. Help the class understand that some foods have a much higher starch content than others.

Carbohydrates give us some of the energy that we need to live, grow, and work. When the weather is cold, do you think you need more or less carbohydrates? Do you use more energy when you work hard or when you are resting?

You can sometimes tell if sugar is found in a food by tasting it. It is not as easy to tell if starch is present. The following activity will help you discover which common foods contain starch.

4/Compare

Take a slice of raw potato, a piece of white bread, and a piece of cut apple. Put a drop of iodine on each of these foods. What happens to the color of the iodine on each piece? This change in the color of iodine on a particular food is a test for starch. Starch is one kind of carbohydrate. ■

Bring other foods to class and test them for starch, as before. In your notebook make a list like the one below of the foods that you tested and record your results.

Name of Food Tested	What Color Changes Take Place?	Does the Food Have Starch?
Potato	blue-black	Yes

Another kind of food we use is fat. As you learned earlier, a food substance that "burns" gives off energy. Let us find out if a fat or an oil is an energy food.

5/Observe

Your teacher will put a small amount of cooking oil or melted butter in a small dish. A thick string will

note

5/Observe should be done as a teacher demonstration to insure student safety.

In the next activity, 6/Compare, a spot left by fat is compared with one left by water on a piece of brown paper. When butter or margarine is tested, the spot should be translucent when held up to the light. This effect is not seen with a water spot after it dries out. This difference is important because the water spot serves as a control in the test.

The children should make a list in their notebooks of the foods tested for fats. The presence or absence of fats or oils should be shown by writing *yes* or *no* in the proper column.

In the discussion of proteins in the textbook, the point is made that in order to build and repair tissue in the body, the diet must include proteins daily. Proteins are not stored in the body. Hence, a new supply is needed every few days. Depending on the source, proteins differ from each other. No one food contains all the proteins needed by the body. To insure good nutrition, a variety of foods containing proteins must be eaten.

(continued on page 120)

responses to 5/observe

1. The oil-soaked wick will burn.
2. Fat or oil is a good source of energy.

be dipped into the oil so that the string becomes soaked. Your teacher will then lift the end of the string up to form a wick and light it with a match. What do you see? 2 Is fat or oil a good source of energy? ■

Which main food groups do you think are sources of fats or oils in your diet? Let us see how you can tell if a food has fat in it.

6/Compare

Rub a piece of butter or margarine on a piece of brown wrapping paper. Hold the paper up to the light and look at the spot on the paper. Now add a drop of water on the same piece of paper next to the grease spot. Hold the paper up to the light again and compare the two spots. 1 What is the difference between the grease spot and the water spot after they dry? The spot left by the butter or margarine is a test for fats. Why is the water spot important? Test other foods for fats or oils. In your notebook make a list like the one below for the foods you test. ■

Name of Food Tested	Observations	Does it Have Fats?
Butter	grease spot	Yes

Fats are found in plants in the form of oils. Corn, soybeans, nuts, and olives are good sources of plant oils. We use animal fats in the form of lard, butter, and cream. Egg yolk, bacon, and cod-liver oil are also good sources of animal fat.

Your body uses carbohydrates and fats for energy. But while you are growing and working, different parts of your body, such as the muscles, skin, and glands, are slowly being worn out. To repair the worn-out parts, you must also have foods which contain proteins (PRO-teenz).

Meat, poultry, fish, eggs, and milk have all the proteins necessary for proper health and good growth. Vegetable foods, such as peas, beans, nuts, and cereal also contain proteins, but not enough to meet the protein needs of the body. From which group should you daily select food in order to supply the body with all the proteins it needs?

An easy way to test for proteins in food is to burn a small piece of the food and to notice how it smells. Let us try this test in the next activity.

91

responses to 6/compare

1. The difference between the grease spot and the water spot is that the grease spot is lastingly translucent.
2. The water spot is used as a control to show that grease spots produce a spot that will not disappear.

119

An easy way to find out if a food has protein in it is to burn the food, as described in activity 7/ Observe. The presence of a protein is indicated by the characteristic pungent odor which is smelled when hair or feathers burn.

A more sophisticated test for proteins is described below, as an optional activity.

Minerals are the next type of nutrient described in the textbook. In the chart, the children will see listed some of the most important minerals in human nutrition, together with good food sources, and their uses in the body.

Ask the children how they think minerals appear in the body. Lead them to understand that minerals are part of other substances in the body and are not found by themselves in living things. For example, you may tell them that iron is part of the blood, but that iron is not found freely floating in the blood. A

optional activity

Use the "biuret reaction" to test for protein. Add powdered copper sulfate to water until its color becomes light blue. A solution of potassium hydroxide should be prepared in another jar. Using a plastic spoon, add 1 tsp. of potassium hydroxide to 4 oz. water in the jar. Stir until pellets are dissolved. Use caution not to allow this strong alkali to touch skin or eyes. To a small amount of skim milk add one or two tablespoons of the solutions of copper sulfate and the potassium hydroxide. The presence of proteins will be indicated as the milk turns blue violet. Heating is not required.

7/Observe

Your teacher will hold a feather in a candle flame for a few seconds until the feather begins to burn. Note the way the feather smells when the flame is blown out. Watch your teacher hold a piece of lean meat in the flame with a pair of kitchen tongs. Compare its smell with that of the burning feather. Describe the smell. This is a test for proteins in food. ■

The foods you eat have carbohydrates and fats to provide energy, and proteins for repair and growth.

Another group of food substances you need is called minerals (MIN-ur-uhlz). Minerals help make your body healthy by building strong bones, hard teeth and healthy blood. Two common minerals are iron and copper, but, of course, you do not eat iron nails or chew pieces of copper wire! The minerals in the foods you eat are in forms that you can use. They are a part of many foods, but they are not even noticed. The table on page 93 shows you some of the common minerals that you require. Can you tell which food group is a good source of minerals?

suitable way this idea may be directly implied is to point out a food which contains iron, such as spinach, and ask the children if they have ever directly seen free iron in the food. Point out the fact that the mineral is combined with other substances in the food in much the same way as minerals are combined with other substances in the body.

(continued on page 122)

Common Minerals in Foods

Mineral	Uses in Body	Food Sources
Calcium	Helps build strong bones and teeth; helps work of heart and muscles	Milk, cheese, beans, cauliflower
Copper	Helps work of blood; needed by tissues for growth	Liver, shrimp, bran, mushrooms, peas
Iodine	Used in controlling many activities of the body	Iodized table salt, sea foods
Iron	Used in blood to carry oxygen to tissues	Kidney meat, liver, spinach, whole wheat
Phosphorus	Helps form strong bones and teeth; used in tissues	Liver, beans, cheese, whole wheat, peas
Sodium	Helps in controlling body activities	Beef, table salt, bread
Sulfur	Used in making tissues in the body	Meat, fish, eggs, peas

The presence of different minerals in foods is hard to test. But the next activity will show you that foods contain minerals.

optional activity

This activity will help the class understand why milk is considered a nearly perfect food. It contains everything necessary for proper nutrition except iron and vitamin C. Get a pint of milk that is not homogenized and remove all of the cream. Test the cream for fats (grease spot test). Heat the milk until it is lukewarm and curdle the milk with vinegar. Pour the curdled milk through filter paper folded in a funnel. Test the part that remains on the paper for protein (copper sulfate test). Boil the liquid that has passed through the paper and then pass this liquid through a clean filter paper. Again test the part that remains on the paper for protein. Boil the remaining liquid in the top of a double boiler until the liquid evaporates. Allow the material that is left to cool and have the class taste it. The remaining substance should taste sweet, indicating carbohydrates.

In activity 8/Observe, the presence of minerals can be shown when a small piece of bread or cheese is burned up completely. Use a metal lid from a jar as a dish since it will be ruined. The dish must be heated over a very hot flame so that all the material in the food is burned away. The ash that is left is the mineral content of the food. The other nutrients have been burned away. Tests for specific minerals are beyond the scope of elementary science.

The youngsters should understand that minerals are essential nutrients because they are used by the body in many of the life processes. Minerals are necessary ingredients in body fluids; they are needed in the formation of bones and teeth; and they are essential for the growth of cells in the body.

Most of the children will probably have heard of vitamins. Let them name some of the vitamins that they are familiar with. Discover if any of the children

responses to 8/observe

1. The non-mineral substances have been burned away.

8/Observe

Put a small piece of bread or cheese in a plain metal dish, such as the lid from a jar. Your teacher will place the dish on a hot plate set on "high" or over a flame until all the food is burned up and the material in the dish stops smoking. The white or grayish ash in the bottom of the dish is made of minerals. What do you think has happened to all the other substances in the food? ■

You can see by looking at the table on page 93, that minerals are used for many purposes in the body. Although they are used in very small amounts, they help you to stay healthy and grow strong. By eating a balanced diet, you will have all the minerals you need.

Besides carbohydrates, fats, proteins, and minerals, another group of food materials you need is known as vitamins (VY-tuh-minz). These are found in many different foods and are needed, much like minerals, for you to stay healthy and grow strong. If a person does not have proper vitamins in his diet, he may develop certain diseases.

can tell what vitamins do for us. Then, let them read the part of the lesson which deals with vitamins.

After the children have studied the text, let them name some foods which contain vitamins. Help them understand that the lack of one or more vitamins can cause disease. Ask them to discuss some of these diseases, such as rickets, and the foods that should be eaten to avoid them.

(continued on page 124)

Many years ago sailors had little to eat during long trips besides dried meat and hard bread. They did not have fresh fruits or vegetables. The sailors often became ill with a disease called scurvy (SKUR-vee). This disease causes bleeding gums, loss of weight and a general feeling of weakness. Many sailors died because of scurvy. After many years it was discovered that eating oranges, lemons, and limes would prevent this disease. We now know that these and other fruits have a substance in them which we call Vitamin C.

In other parts of the world, some people liked to polish the brown covering off the rice that they ate. The people who ate such polished rice and little else very often became nervous and weak, lost weight, and could not work. When the rice was polished, something important was rubbed off. This something in the brown coat is what we call Vitamin B. Lack of Vitamin B in the diet causes a disease called beriberi (BER-ee-BER-ee).

95

You can test for the presence of Vitamin C in foods. Mix 20 drops of boiled starch and 2 drops of ordinary iodine in one cup of water. This mixture is blue in color. Drop a piece of citrus fruit into the liquid. The color of the liquid fades out and becomes lighter. This change in color shows that citrus fruit contains Vitamin C. Test bread, eggs, tomatoes, meat, fruit juices, and candy in the same way.

The children should be asked to read the discussion. It is important that they understand that vitamins are not actually foods or a replacement for foods. Vitamins, as a group, aid the body in using other nutrients properly. Point out that a lack of vitamins over a long period of time may result in deficiency diseases. Scurvy is mentioned in the textbook. Other diseases caused by a lack of specific vitamins are: beriberi (lack of Vitamin B_1), rickets (lack of Vitamin D), keratitis (lack of Vitamin A).

The importance of water to life is stressed in the next discussion. Water may be ingested directly or as a part of the food materials we eat. As a solvent, water dissolves most materials and passes them into the blood. Water aids in digestion, waste removal, and cooling the body. The students will know that more water is lost from their bodies when they work hard and perspire than when they are at rest. Children probably need about eight glasses of water per day to replace the water which is lost. Most youngsters

optional questions

Ask the children if they know how else they can get vitamins other than by eating foods which contain these substances. To encourage responses, ask the class if they have ever taken vitamins in pill form.

The substances we call vitamins are usually named with letters of the alphabet. If you look at the label on most boxes of dry cereal, you will see the names of the minerals and vitamins found in these foods. As long as you eat a balanced diet, you will get all the minerals and vitamins necessary for good health.

One other material you need every day is water. Water does not directly supply materials to build or repair body parts, or to furnish energy. But you must have water to stay alive. Most of the body fluids, including blood, are made up of water. Water acts to dissolve food and waste materials and carry these materials to and from different parts of the body. Most of the water you need is gotten from drinking liquids, but many foods, such as fruits and vegetables, also supply water. Let us find out how much water some foods have.

lose between three and five pints of water daily through the excretory system.

In activity 9/Observe, it is necessary to have a balance to weigh the food before and after drying it out. If a balance is not available, one may be made with a 12-inch ruler, string, paper cups, and by using B-B shot as weight. Notch the sides of the ruler at the six inch mark and firmly tie a length of string around the ruler at the notches. Tie a paper cup to the notched one and eleven inch marks of the ruler. The length of string used to tie the cups should be equal. This apparatus may then be tacked to the underside of a wooden desk or door jamb. To weigh the apple before and after drying, B-B shot may be used as a counter-balance. After the food is dried out, find out how much less it weighs than before. The difference will give the children the weight of the water in the food tested.

This activity will help the children understand that fruits and vegetables are a source of water. However, the class should understand that we get most of the water we need by drinking it.

(continued on page 126)

9/Observe

Weigh a slice of freshly cut apple or potato carefully. Watch your teacher put the piece of food in a metal dish and warm it over a flame so that it becomes dry. The food should not be burned. Your teacher will heat it until there is no further loss of weight. Other foods can be tested in the same way. Use the headings below to make a table in your notebook. Write down the results of your tests. ■

Food Tested	Weight of Dish and Food Before Heating	Weight of Dish and Food After Heating	Weight of the Water Lost

note

Some of the foods which may be used in 9/Observe are potatoes, melons, pears, and oranges.

for your information

Over 90 per cent of blood plasma is water. Water is an important part of all body fluids. Since water is a liquid, it transports important materials from one place to another in our bodies.

97

In Testing Your Ideas each child should be given a chance to prepare his or her own menu for breakfast, lunch, and dinner. The children should be encouraged to suggest foods of their own choosing instead of using all of the foods listed in the text. Care should be taken to note what foods have been selected and in what food group they have been placed. The children might note, with your assistance, what minerals or vitamins are contained in the selected foods. The mineral chart on page 93 is an easy reference.

The substance we drink daily that cannot be placed in any food group is water.

Because water is so important to you in carrying on your life activities, you should drink plenty of water every day. Do you know how much water you lose from your body each day? Have you ever noticed how thirsty you get when you work hard and perspire a lot? You do not have to worry about drinking too much water. Every living thing uses what it needs and gets rid of the water it does not use.

TESTING YOUR IDEAS

Listed below are the four basic groups and some of the foods you may find in them. Try to plan a balanced menu for breakfast, lunch, and dinner. From the foods listed, it is possible to make other foods, such as a sandwich, stew, or cake. Not all the foods listed need be used, and you should add some of your own. An important substance we daily drink cannot be placed in any of the groups. Can you name it? Compare your menu with those of your classmates.

Meat Group	Milk Group	Bread Group	Vegetable Group
bacon	milk	flour	grapefruit
beef	cream	cereal (hot, cold)	potato
liver	butter (margarine)	rice	peas
fish	cheese	white, rye, or whole wheat bread	tomato
chicken	yogurt		string beans

98

OVERVIEW

This section develops the idea that the food we eat is absorbed into the blood stream. The food is traced in its journey through the digestive system from the time it enters the mouth to the time that waste materials are excreted. The digestive changes that take place in the food to change it from the form in which it is eaten into the form which can be used by the cells are described. From the discussion and activities the children should understand that the human organism is a working whole, composed of systems and organs which interact to carry on life processes.

Note that the order of the treatment in this entire unit goes from the familiar to the unfamiliar, from whole to parts, from organism to systems, to organs, to tissues, and finally to cells.

how to begin

Have the children feel the inside of their mouths by moving their tongues. Let them describe what they note (teeth, moist linings, saliva, walls of cheeks, etc.). Ask the youngsters why they think their mouths are constructed the way they are.

(continued on page 128)

WHAT HAPPENS TO THE FOOD WE EAT?

Your body is growing. Inside your body are many parts which you cannot see. Each carries out a life activity for the body. They all work together to keep you living and growing. Each living thing whose parts act together as a unit is called an organism (OR-gan-izm). Some organisms have a few parts. Other organisms are much more complicated. The human organism, such as you, has many, many parts. For the parts to carry out their activities, they must be in good condition. Although your body has many parts all working at different jobs, you are one single organism. Those parts that work together to carry on one life activity form a body system (SIS-tem). Though you are one single organism, you have many systems. For example, the bones of your body form a strong movable framework. This framework gives your body the shape you see when you look in a mirror. The bones taken together are called the skeletal (SKEL-uh-t'l) system. Can you name some of the other systems in the body? If not, you will find out about them later.

Just as an organism like you is made up of systems, each system is made up of different parts, called organs (OAR-gunz). The stomach, for example, is an organ of the digestive system. Organs work together in helping the system do its job. In turn, each organ is made up of special materials called tissues (TISH-yooz). Your bones, your heart, and skin are each made of different types of tissue.

99

process skills

Describing verbally how the body is organized in terms of systems, organs, tissues, and cells

Explaining how the digestive system functions in the ingestion, digestion, and absorption of nutrients

materials

tweezers*, scissors*, microscope slides*, microprojector if available, or microscope, eye dropper*, tongue depressors**, 3 glass jars with lids*, tincture of iodine (drugstore variety), grater*, rubber tube about ½ inch diameter*, glass marble to fit*, 2 pans, hot plate, 2 test tubes*, Benedict's solution (available in drugstores), plastic straw*, modeling clay, small drinking glass*, charts of human body, if available

Supply when needed: onion, unsalted crackers, white bread, lean meat, raw potato, meat tenderizer, starch, fresh egg

---

* per team
** one per student

Examination of the mouth should lead to the conclusion that the mouth is designed to take in food and start the process of digestion. Let the children help you list on the board ways in which food is acted on in the mouth (chewed, ground up, mixed with saliva, moved by tongue, etc.). Ask them to explain why they think this is necessary (it is the first step in digestion). Let the class speculate on what happens to the food after it is swallowed (it moves through the digestive system and undergoes a number of changes). This should lead into a discussion of the main parts of the digestive system.

procedure

Refer again to the charts or model of the body, or to the drawings in the textbook, and ask the children what they think the body is made up of. The point to bring out is that the human organism is a living thing made up of a number of interacting structures which function together to maintain life. Making this point should lead to a discussion of the main body systems, organs, and tissues making up the body. Refer to the charts and models of the body, if they are available, in describing these structures.

responses to
10/demonstrate

1. The onion skin tissue is a whole made up of similar parts called cells.
2. Important features, which the class can see with a microscope or microprojector and which are shared by each cell, are the cell wall which surrounds the cell, the cell body, and the nucleus, a large, spherical shape near the center of the cell body.
3. Important differences between the cells will depend on the particular specimen seen. Cells in the midst of division possibly might be observed.
4. The children should have no difficulty seeing the gelatinous cell body and the nucleus.

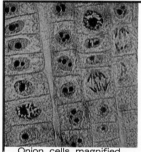
Onion cells magnified 600 times by a microscope magnified 60 times

10/Demonstrate

Peel off a piece of onion skin. Try to get the piece as thin as possible. Put this piece of onion skin on a moistened glass microscope slide. With your teacher's help, look at the piece of onion skin under a microscope or with a microprojector. Is the onion skin tissue one solid sheet, or is it made up of many parts? How are these tiny parts alike? How are they different? What can you see inside?

11/Observe

You can observe the tissue that forms the moist lining of your cheek. Your teacher will provide you with a clean tongue depressor and a glass slide. Using an eye dropper place a single drop of water on the

The idea of cells as the basic units of structure in the body is introduced next. Since cells are microscopic in size, the children will have difficulty in visualizing them. A good approach is to use rectangular blocks of wood or modeling clay and arrange them like bricks in a wall to convey the idea that cells fit together in a pattern and are three dimensional in shape. (However, the analogy must be corrected since bricks do not form a true unit like an organism.)

Activity 10/Demonstrate can be done easily if a microprojector is available. Prepare the slide of onion skin, as described in the textbook. A drop of iodine on the onion skin will help the youngsters see the nuclei of the cells.

Ask the youngsters where cells are found in the body. They should be able to generalize that the entire body is made up of cells. Point out that the cells are continually being replaced as old ones wear out. As the body grows, new cells are added. Explain that a cell takes in food, water, and oxygen and gives off waste products (carbon dioxide, water, and urea in the form of broken-down cellular material). In a cell the raw materials are food, water, and oxygen. The product is new cell growth, energy, and wastes. Activity 11/Observe should clearly suggest that like the onion skin the human body is made up of cells also.

(continued on page 130)

slide. Now, gently scrape the inside of your cheek with one end of the tongue depressor. Rub the wooden stick several times against the lining of your cheek and touch it to the water on the slide. Your slide is now ready, with your teacher's help, for study under a microscope or a microprojector. 1 How does what you see compare with what you saw in the onion? Add a drop of iodine to your slide and observe the tissue again. 2 What do you see this time? ■

All tissue is made up of many tiny units much like the ones you have seen. These units are called cells. They sometimes look as if they were bricks in a brick wall. But because your body is a unit, the cells are not like bricks; they work together in a very special way since you are one single organism. Cells are put together in a regular pattern in each different tissue. Your entire body is made up of millions and millions of cells which grow and multiply as you grow.

Can you guess what a cell needs to keep it alive? If you guess that it must have the food materials we learned about, then you are right. Cells use food. But an apple, a slice of roast beef or a piece of chocolate cake cannot be used by your body as they are. Quite a few changes must take place before it can be used by the cells. The activity in which food is broken down

responses to 11/observe

1. The children can observe that the lining of the cheek is, like the onion skin, tissue made up of cells.
2. The cells of the cheek lining will absorb the iodine and can then be more clearly seen.

Cells of cheek lining

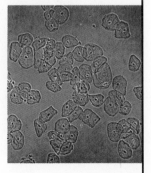

In discussing the mouth as the beginning of the digestive tube, ask the students to take hold of their tongues with clean tissue paper and try to swallow. This is difficult to do. The tongue must move back and upward against the roof of the mouth for swallowing to take place comfortably. Pass out small mirrors and let the children look at their teeth. Discuss the baby teeth and the permanent teeth which they have. The class should understand that the function of the teeth and tongue is to grind up food and mix it with saliva so that the food can be swallowed. Point out that the more thoroughly food is chewed, the more quickly the nutrients can be used by the body. Bring out the value of oral hygiene in preventing tooth decay.

The digestive process begins in the mouth. Activity 12/Explore lets the students experience a change in taste as starch is acted upon by saliva and changed into a form of sugar. When the bread or cracker is chewed and mixed with saliva, the children should detect a sweet taste. This action takes place only on starchy foods in the mouth. Hence, a piece of meat will not be affected in the same way.

(continued on page 132)

responses to 12/explore

1. The answer to the first question is a matter of observation.
2. The cracker, if mixed thoroughly with saliva, should taste sweet.
3. If a piece of hamburger is entirely mixed with saliva and chewed, no change in the meat's taste is noticed.

and dissolved so that it can be used by the cells is called digestion (die-JEST-shun).

Your cells use the materials in foods that are necessary for life. New cells grow. Energy for your growth comes from your food. To provide each cell the food that it needs in a form it can use is the job of the digestive system. The next activities will help you to understand more about digestion.

12/Explore

Put a piece of unsalted cracker or white bread in your mouth and chew it. Hold the chewed food in your mouth without swallowing it for a few minutes. Do you taste something different from the original taste? What does it taste like? Repeat the test with a piece of meat. Do you get the same results? ■

Digestion begins in the mouth. As soon as food is put into the mouth, the food begins to change. When you chew a bite of white bread, what changes do you notice?

102

The moisture in your mouth, called saliva (suh-LIE-vuh), wets the food as you chew it and begins to change it. Starch is found in bread and is changed by the saliva into a kind of sugar.

Your tongue is very important in tasting and chewing food. The tongue moves the food around in the mouth as it is chewed, so that the teeth can crush and grind the food. After the food is chewed well, the tongue pushes the food to the back of the mouth so the food can be swallowed. The next time you eat, pay attention to the movements of your tongue from the time food is put into your mouth until the food is swallowed. Do you think it makes a difference whether food is chewed well or not? Do the next activity to see if you can find out.

13/Compare

Cut a peeled, raw potato into three pieces of the same size. Partly fill three jars with water. Put one piece of potato in the first jar. Cut the second piece of potato into 15 or 20 pieces and put them into the second jar. Rub the third piece of potato on a grater to make the pieces very fine. Put these pieces into the third jar.

note

Activities 12 and 13 provide tangible evidence that the body changes food. The class can infer therefore that the body cannot use food directly, but must change or digest food to use it.

131

Let the class do activity 13/Compare, which tests for the presence of starch after pieces of potato are shaken in water. Iodine is used on the resulting solutions (starch granules are dissolved in the water) to see how much starch is present. The deeper and darker the blue-black color produced, the greater is the relative amount of starch present in the solution. The children should infer that just as the solution from the finest pieces of potato showed the greatest degree of change, the greatest amount of change in the mouth occurs when the food is chewed thoroughly.

Take a chewed cracker and place it in a test tube. Add a small amount of either of the above solutions and heat gently over a flame. If sugar is present, the color will change from blue to green to orange.

(continued on page 134)

responses to 13/compare

1. The jar with the finely grated potato should show the darkest blue-black color.
2. The differences in color show that the more thorough the chewing or mixing of food with saliva, the greater the change in the food.

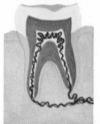

Now, put the lids on the jars and shake each jar for a few minutes. Remove all the pieces of potato from the water, using a strainer if necessary. Now add 10 drops of iodine to each jar and compare the color of the liquid. Describe any differences you see in the depth of color in three jars. Which of the jars showed that more starch was released? What does this activity show you about chewing your food well? ■

You need strong teeth to chew your food properly. Therefore, you can see why you should take care of your teeth and brush them well. Teeth are hard and much like bones, but a tooth that is broken or has a cavity in it will not grow together as a bone will. Teeth are covered with the hardest material found in the body. Even this hard material depends on the food you eat.

Everyone has two sets of teeth during his life. We call the first set the baby teeth, and there are 20 of these. Do you still have some of your baby teeth? We

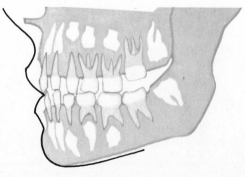

104

132

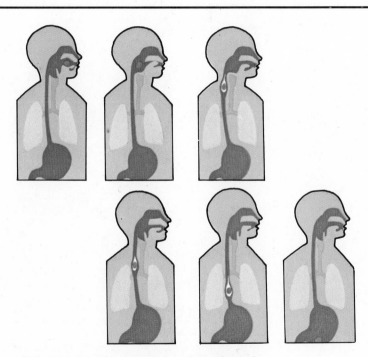

Have the children swallow. *Ask them to note the position of the tongue in the mouth as they swallow.* With the help of the pictures, they can note that the tongue is pressed against the roof of the mouth. Have them swallow once again. *Ask them if they pause in their breathing when they swallow.* With the help of the picture, show them that the passage to the lungs is blocked by a flap of tissue as either food or saliva passes over the tube opening leading to the lungs. *Ask them why this opening is closed.* The closure prevents food and other materials from passing into the respiratory area.

call the second set the permanent teeth. As the teeth of your second set begin to grow, they push against the baby teeth causing them to loosen and come out. Most people will have 32 permanent teeth when they grow up.

Chewed food is swallowed by passing through a long muscular tube leading to the stomach. Liquids pass very quickly through this tube. The chewed foods are moved down to the stomach by a special wave-like action of muscles which make up the tube. You can see how this action takes place by doing the next activity.

105

In teaching about the digestive tube, one should be sure to discuss the rhythmic, wavelike series of contractions which move the food along the tube. Activity 14/Illustrate will help the class understand this wavelike motion by seeing how the marble moves through the tube as the hand presses behind it. The children should understand that as a result of this action, swallowed material passes along the food tube to the stomach regardless of the body position.

In discussing the stomach, one of the main ideas to present is that this organ is a muscular baglike structure in which food is churned and mixed with digestive juices produced in the stomach so that the food becomes a thick, soupy mass. The digestive juices in the stomach are very acidic. This acidity stops the action of the saliva on the food and begins the digestion of proteins.

The churning action of the stomach can be illustrated by putting pieces of bread and a little water into a large rubber balloon and squeezing the balloon vigorously for a few minutes. Pour the contents into a glass of water to show the class how the churning action breaks up the food and mixes it with the digestive juices.

(continued on page 136)

14/Illustrate

Put a marble in a rubber tube. Squeeze the tube to make the marble move through it. The marble moves somewhat like the way food moves through the tube that leads to the stomach. ■

To get the food into other organs where it will be changed even more than in the mouth, the muscles in front of the food relax, while the muscles behind the food contract. Thus, the food is squeezed along. This wavelike action of the muscles allows you to swallow even though your head may be lower than your stomach. In animals with long necks, such as giraffes or swans, food often moves first downward then upward to the stomach.

The food, as it moves along, enters the stomach (STUM-uck). The stomach does not grind up food the way the mouth does. But in the stomach food is mixed with juices from special organs that help in digestion. These digestive juices begin to break down foods. The churning action of the stomach, together with the way the digestive juices act on food, changes

106

134

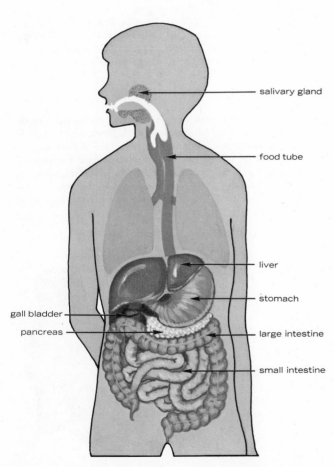

salivary gland

food tube

liver

stomach

gall bladder

pancreas

large intestine

small intestine

107

studying the picture

The children can observe from the picture of the digestive tract that it is a whole made up of parts. *Ask them to name the individual parts of the digestive tract. Then ask them what part the teeth, tongue, and mouth play in digesting food. What role does the food tube play? Ask them about the role of the stomach. Then ask them if each part of the digestive tract works toward a common end; i.e., to digest food. Ask them if this common end links each part of the digestive tract to form a system.*

Activity 15/Observe lets the children see how a digestive substance found in meat tenderizer will break down the fibers in meat. The water in a jar to which the tenderizer has been added will be cloudy from the partly dissolved meat. Another jar will show little change. The second jar is needed as a control in the activity.

The next activity, 16/Observe, also lets the students see how a digestive juice works. This time they use saliva produced in their own mouths and note the action on a starch solution. The action of the saliva will change the starch to a form of sugar in a few minutes if the solution is placed in hot water (37° C). This change is shown by using Benedict's solution, a substance available in any drugstore. When added to a starch solution, the Benedict's solution does not change color. But when added to a solution of sugar formed by the digestion of starch and heated, the color changes to reddish-orange. The Benedict's solution should also be added to the saliva alone as part of the control. Since saliva was added to only one test tube, the children should get a positive test for sugar in that tube only.

(continued on page 138)

responses to 15/observe

1. The water to which tenderizer was added looks cloudy. The water in the other jar shows little change.

note

Some children may be interested in a more clearly defined meaning of the word "changes" as it applies to changes in food. This word may be more clearly defined if you lead the children to suggest that the food must be put into a form in which the organism can use it.

most of the food we eat into a thick, soft material. This thick liquid material leaves the stomach and goes into another organ called the small intestine (in-TESS-tin) where more changes take place. Let us see if we can find out how these changes take place.

15/Observe

Boil some lean meat until it is tender. Cut the meat into small pieces about 1/4 inch square. Fill two small jars half-full of water and put a few pieces of meat in each one. Add a pinch of meat tenderizer to one jar and put the lids on both jars. Place the jars in a warm place overnight. Compare the liquid in the two jars the next day. Describe what you observe. ■

The changes you see are caused by a digestive material which is sold as a meat tenderizer. Your body produces a number of these digestive materials which act very much like meat tenderizer. Juices containing the digestive materials are made in the body by special organs called glands (GLANDZ). There are digestive glands in the mouth, in the stomach, and in the small intestine. There are digestive juices that help break down carbohydrates, fats, and proteins. Do the next activity to find out more about digestion.

16/Observe

Watch your teacher boil about a cup of water and add a level teaspoon of starch. The mixture should be stirred until the starch dissolves and forms a cloudy mixture. To one test tube add a teaspoon of saliva to the mixture. To the other test tube add a teaspoon of water. Shake the test tubes and put them in a pan of warm water for ten minutes. Now add a few drops of Benedict's solution to each test tube. Your teacher

109

Since the production of digestive juices is triggered by the brain, which responds to the stimulus of sight, smell, or even just the thought of food when one is hungry, the thought of flavorful food should make the mouth water. The youngsters should realize that when the mouth waters, other digestive juices in the digestive tube are also being produced.

In teaching about other organs of the digestive system, the most important features are the great length of the small and large intestine. their great absorptive surfaces, and the glands which produce the digestive fluids.

Using the charts or models of the body if available, point out the main glands, such as the liver, which is above the stomach in the upper part of the abdomen, and the pancreas, found attached underneath the stomach. After the youngsters have read the textbook, ask them to explain what happens to the

responses to 16/observe

1. When Benedict's solution is added to the solution without saliva there is no color change. When it is added to the solution *with* saliva the color changes to reddish-orange.
2. No.
3. Saliva turned the starch into sugar, the same process that takes place during digestion.

should heat the water to boiling. ①Note what happens to the color of the liquid in each test tube. Describe what happens. This color change shows that simple sugar is present. ②Did you find sugar in both test tubes? ③Explain your answer. ■

Saliva is a digestive juice produced by glands in the mouth. Does the thought of a nice, juicy hamburger make your mouth water? If this happens, the digestive glands are getting ready to digest food that you might eat. The smell of food cooking, or the sight of food when you are hungry makes the glands begin producing digestive juices.

The liquid food that passes from the stomach into the small intestine mixes with digestive juices produced by glands in and outside the small intestine. The glands outside the intestine are the liver (LIV-uhr) and pancreas (PAN-kree-uhs). Their digestive juices complete the digestion of carbohydrates, fats, and proteins.

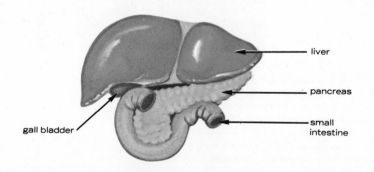

gall bladder

liver

pancreas

small intestine

food in the small intestine. They should understand that digestive glands other than those in the walls of the small intestine produce digestive juices which act on food in the small intestine.

Ask the children what happens to the digested food products in the small intestine (they are absorbed into the blood). Activity 17/Explain illustrates the principle by which food passes from the intestine into the blood. When a liquid passes in one direction through a thin membrane, the process is called osmosis. This is shown by water in the jar passing through the "skin" of an egg and mixing with the material inside the egg. As the pressure builds up here, some of the material from the egg is forced up into the straw. The students should keep a record of how long it takes the liquid to reach a certain height in the straw.

(continued on page 140)

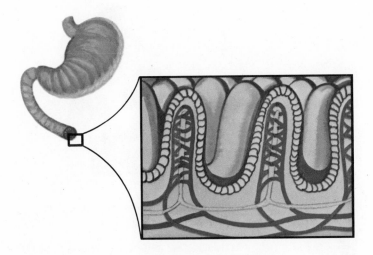

The breakup of food in the small intestine is the last step in digestion. As the wavelike action of the muscles continues to move the food along, tiny blood vessels in the walls of the intestine take in the digested food. The food you eat becomes part of your blood. The digested food is now in a form that the cells can use as it is carried along with the blood. How can the food pass through the walls of the intestine? Let us see if we can find out.

17/Explain

Carefully crack the shell on the large end of a fresh egg and peel away some of the shell. Do not break the thin "skin" just under the shell. Take a small glass

optional activity

You will need powdered pepsin (from a drugstore), vinegar, cooked egg white, cooked lean meat, jars.

Make a solution of artificial digestive fluid by mixing a pinch of pepsin in a cup of warm water. Add a few drops of vinegar and stir. Put some pieces of egg white in two jars, and some pieces of cooked meat in two other jars. To two of the jars add some of the artificial digestive juice. To the other two jars add the same amount of water. Leave the jars in a warm place overnight. Compare the cloudiness of the liquid in the jars the next day. The digestive juice in the first two jars should have broken down the egg white and the meat so that the liquids are cloudy. The jars with the water in them should show very little action. Let the children test other food substances in the same way.

The transfer of nutrient materials in solution from the small intestine into the blood stream occurs by osmosis and diffusion. Thus, when there is a greater concentration of nutrient materials in the intestine than in the blood capillaries, absorption occurs from the intestine into the blood. Tell the class to think of a sponge soaking up water. The sponge is like the wall of the intestine, and the water represents the nutrients being taken up.

That the large intestine is a place where undigested materials are stored temporarily and where water is reabsorbed into the blood should be pointed out. Review the structure and function of the entire digestive system by identifying and discussing the parts shown in the drawing on page 107.

Point out that the large intestine differs from the small intestine in that it is thicker in diameter, is shorter, and does not have villi. Note also that the movement of materials is slower here than in other parts of the digestive tube. The passage of materials through the large intestine may take from 12 to 24 hours. Food is not digested in the large intestine. Its

responses to 17/explain

1. The water passes through the egg membrane ("skin"). As water enters the egg, some of the material in the egg is forced into the straw.

2. In order to pass through cell walls, food must be in liquid form.

jar in which the egg will fit without touching the bottom and fill the jar with water until it comes halfway up the side of the egg.

At the other end of the egg make a small pinhole through the shell and "skin." Fasten a short piece of clear plastic straw over the hole with modeling clay so that the seal is airtight. Put the peeled end of the egg in the water. Observe the straw every 15 minutes. Keep a record of your observations. Can you explain what happens? You have made a model that shows something about the way digested food passes into the cells of your body. In what form would food have to be in order to pass through the "skin" of your cells? ■

You may wonder why we call the small intestine "small" when it seems to occupy so much of the body. It is called small, not because it is short but because it is narrower than the large intestine. The large intestine is wider than the small intestine, but it is also shorter.

most important function is to reabsorb water that is in the waste material before that material leaves the body.

Emphasize the fact that drinking plenty of liquids and eating a balanced diet which includes fruits and vegetables is the normal way to keep material moving through the digestive tube. In spite of the many advertised remedies, the digestive system can function normally if a person is in good health.

(continued on page 142)

The main part of digestion is completed within the small intestine. The soft, wet material that passes into the large intestine is made up mostly of things that the body cannot digest. In the large intestine water is taken back into the blood stream so that only soft, solid wastes are left.

The wavelike action of the muscles moves the solid wastes slowly along the large intestine. The wastes finally reach the end of the digestive system. The large intestine has an opening at its end to the outside of the body, and the undigestable wastes are passed out through this opening.

Think of all that happens in your body after you eat!

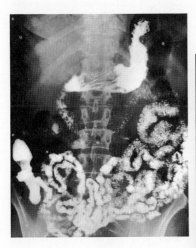
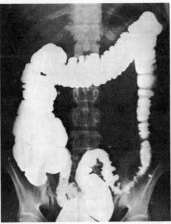

113

optional activity

You will need powdered pancreatin (from a drugstore), baking soda, cooking oil, jars.

Make a solution of artificial digestive fluid similar to that produced in the intestine by mixing a pinch of pancreatin in a cup of warm water. Add a pinch of baking soda and stir. Put a teaspoon of cooking oil in each of two jars. To one jar add the artificial intestinal juice. To the other jar add the same amount of water. Leave the jars in a warm place overnight. Compare the way the oil is distributed in the liquid in the two jars the next day. The jar with the artificial digestive juice should show that the oil is emulsified (mixed with the water in tiny droplets). The jar with the water should have the oil unaffected and floating on top of the water. The latter jar is the control for the activity. Let the students test other foods to see if they are digested in artificial intestinal juice.

In Testing Your Ideas, the first column best shows the order of the parts of the digestive system. The first statement of the second part of Testing Your Ideas is not true because the stomach is not a gland. The second statement is untrue, as is the third statement.

optional activity

You will need red cabbage, a bowl, 1 cup of boiling water, a wooden spoon, a clean, empty bottle, a medicine dropper, white vinegar, and household ammonia.

Shred 2 or 3 cabbage leaves and place the shredded cabbage in the bowl. Pour the boiling water over the shredded cabbage and let it stand for about one hour. Use the spoon to squeeze as much juice as possible from the cabbage.

Pour this purple liquid into the bottle. You can use the cabbage juice to test foods for the presence of acid.

Pour a little cabbage juice into two clean glasses. Cover one glass and leave it undisturbed. This is your control. Add vinegar, drop by drop, to the other glass. Use a medicine dropper. Observe.

Compare the colors of the control and the acid cabbage juice. Vinegar turns the purple juice to red. Any food that turns the purple juice to red contains acid.

Which of the following lists shows the order of the parts of the digestive system?

mouth	mouth	mouth	food tube
food tube	stomach	food tube	mouth
stomach	food tube	stomach	stomach
large in-testine	small in-testine	small in-testine	small in-testine
small in-testine	large in-testine	large in-testine	large in-testine

With which of the following statements do you agree?

Two of the most important glands of the digestive system are the pancreas and the stomach.

All foods may be directly used by the body.

All parts of the foods we eat are completely digestible.

OVERVIEW

The section dealing with the circulatory system discusses the structure of the heart and the composition of the blood. Blood is shown to be the main transporting tissue in the body, carrying food and oxygen to the cells and removing liquid waste products from the cells. The function of the heart in pumping blood through the body is studied. Also the movement of a typical drop of blood as it makes a circuit in the body is traced, first in body (or system) circulation and then in lung (or pulmonary) circulation.

how to begin

Refer to a chart of the body or use a model of the heart and hold it up in front of the class. Ask the children if they recognize the picture or model as a heart; ask them of what kind of tissue it is made (it is a large muscle). Discuss with the class the main purpose the heart has in the body (it acts as a pump to keep the blood moving in the blood vessels). Ask the youngsters if they know what is inside the heart and blood vessels (blood).

(continued on page 144)

WHAT HAPPENS TO DIGESTED FOODS?

The digestive system has the job of breaking apart solid food and changing it into liquid so that it may be used by all of your cells. How do you suppose the digested food gets from the tube where it is digested to the cells of your fingers, toes, arms, and legs? How do you think the liquid food gets to every part of your body? The system that gets food to all parts of your body is made up of tubes, a hollow pump, and blood. Food materials enter the blood by passing through both the cells of the small intestine and the cells that make up the smallest blood tubes.

Blood is pumped to all parts of the body by the action of the heart. The heart pumps blood by contracting its muscles. The heart is a powerful muscle with four parts through which the blood flows. Each time the heart beats, the muscles contract and about one-fifth of a cup of blood is pumped to your body.

To find where the heart is located in your body, let us do the next activity.

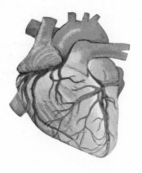

18/Locate

Make a loose fist with your left hand. Place it over the center of your chest and pull your fist slightly to the left. Point your thumb toward your right shoulder to make sure your fist is in the right position. This is about the location of the heart inside your chest. Now

115

process skills

Describing how the heart pumps blood to all parts of the body

Describing how blood flows in a continuous stream throughout the body

Identifying the materials transported to and from the body cells

materials

cardboard tubes (empty paper towel cores or mailing tubes are excellent)°, watch with a second hand°, charts of the body and a model of the heart, if available

---

° one per team

Try to get the class to determine the relationship between the heart and the blood (the heart pumps the blood). Ask the children what they think happens to the blood when it is pumped out of the heart (it goes to all parts of the body). Have the class read the introductory pages of this section in the text and go on with the discussion.

procedure

Hold up a water-soaked sponge and squeeze some of the water out of it. Ask the children if they remember what the blood picks up from the small in-

testine (digested food materials). Explain that the blood, like the sponge, picks things up and lets them go. Squeeze the sponge again and let the class see that the water goes out. Explain that the blood picks up materials from one part of the body and carries them to other parts. The children should understand that the circulatory system is a transporter and distributor of materials to be used by the body. These materials pass from the blood stream through the capillary walls into the fluids which bathe the cells in the tissues. In the cells the nutrient materials are used to build and repair tissues and to release energy.

Activity 18/Locate lets the students visualize where the heart is and how it sounds as it beats. Of

responses to 18/locate

1. Using the cardboard tube, a student should have no trouble hearing his classmate's heartbeat.
2. A person at rest usually has a steady heartbeat.
3. At this point the child is not expected to know exactly what each beat of the heart means, except that each beat indicates the heart is pumping blood.

place a cardboard tube against the chest of another student and put your ear to the tube. What do you hear? Can you hear the other student's heart beating? Is it beating at a steady rate? What is happening to the blood each time you hear a beat? ■

The main job of the heart is to act as a pump which keeps the blood moving through the body. If you listen carefully, you can hear a "lub" sound and a "dup" sound in each beat. These sounds are caused by the opening and closing of folds of tissue that act as one-way doors in the heart. The one-way doors called valves (VALVZ) serve to keep the blood flowing in one direction. The speed of this pumping action depends on your body activity.

The heart pumps blood to the lungs where it takes in oxygen from the air you inhale. The blood then returns to the heart. Next, the blood goes out to all other

course, if a stethoscope is available, it should be used. But a cardboard tube, as indicated in the textbook, will allow the children to hear the heart sounds quite clearly. The "lub" sound is due to the contraction of the ventricles and the closing of the valves between the auricles and ventricles. The "dup" sound is caused by the closing of the valves between the ventricles and the aorta and the pulmonary arteries. The youngsters should be able to hear the heart beating with a steady, rhythmic beat. Of course, each time the heart beats, blood is forced out into the body.

Proceed to the topic of the circulation of the blood in the body. Very briefly, blood flows 1) from the heart to the lungs, 2) from the lungs back to the heart, 3) from the heart to all other parts of the body, 4) from the body back to the heart. The cycle is repeated continuously.

The main knowledge to be gained is that the heart is a hollow muscle with four chambers through which the blood flows in a regular route. The heart is like a pump which continues to beat during the entire life span of an individual. When it stops for any appreciable time, death occurs.

(continued on page 146)

parts of the body. It picks up digested food from the small intestine and takes it to the cells of the body. The blood also picks up liquid waste which it carries to the organs that dispose of it.

How is the heart able to do all these things? Look at the picture of the heart on this page. You can see four "rooms" in which the blood collects. Facing another student, you can think of his heart as having a right side (to your left) and a left side (to your right).

As the heart begins its beat, the blood moves through the valves from the top rooms into the bottom rooms. Then as the beat continues, the blood moves out of the lower rooms into blood tubes that carry it to all other parts of the body. When the heart relaxes at the end of its beat, some blood comes back into the room on the upper right side of the heart. This blood collects from the body parts. At the same time, blood collects in the upper left room as it comes from the lungs. Then, on the next beat, the action is the same

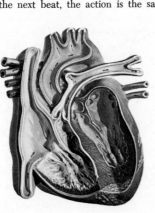

studying the picture

Ask the children where the blood goes when it leaves the bottom right room of the heart. It goes to the lungs. *Then, ask from where the blood has come when it enters the top left room.* It has come from the lungs. *Next, ask the children if they see a difference in the color of the blood in the two different upper rooms of the heart.* Blood in the right upper room is blue, and blood in the left upper room is red. *Ask if it is not possible that the color means a change has taken place in the blood while it was in the lungs.* Yes, a change might have taken place in the lungs. This conclusion will help the children to understand the text on page 119.

117

In activity 19/Count the students place their fingers on the inside of their wrists so as to feel their pulse. The pulse is due to the surge of blood throughout all the arteries as a result of the heartbeat. Use a watch with a second hand and, telling the class when to start and stop, let the children count their pulse for one minute. Youngsters at this age should average 80–85 beats per minute when they are sitting down. After they exercise, the pulse rate jumps up significantly.

In activity 20/Compare the children should note that there is a time lag of a fraction of a second between the pulse felt in the neck and the one in the ankle. This lag is due to the difference in distance these points are from the heart. It takes time for the blood to move from one point to another.

Optional activities should be used to reinforce the child's understanding of the subject matter. Each is designed to illustrate an important concept already established in the foregoing text.

(continued on page 148)

responses to 19/count

1. A pulse count between 80–85 beats per minute is considered to be the average for children.
2. The number of beats per minute should increase substantially after the children exercise.

studying the picture

Have the children note that the index and middle fingers are used to note the pulse rate. The thumb should not be used.

responses to 20/compare

1. A difference of a second should be noticed between the beat felt in the neck and that felt in the ankle.

again. Do you know how fast your heart beats? You can find out in the following activity.

19/Count

Let your hand bend forward a little at the wrist. Press the first two fingers of your other hand into the little hollow spot under the wrist just in back of the thumb, as shown in the picture. Sit quietly so that you can feel something pushing up against your fingers. This repeated pushing and throbbing is something called a pulse. You can feel your pulse beating. When your teacher says, "Start," begin counting to yourself the number of times you feel a push against your fingers. When the teacher says, "Stop," stop counting and write down the number of beats you counted in your pulse. Repeat this several times. How many times does your heart beat in one minute when you are sitting

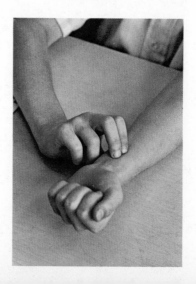

quietly? How many times does your heart beat after you do some exercise? ■

Every time your heart muscles contract, blood is pumped out into the blood tubes. This contraction of the heart muscles is your heartbeat. At certain points in your body you can feel the repeated push of blood through your body. Does it take some time for the blood to move to different parts of the body? Let us see if we can find out?

20/Compare

Locate the beating of the pulse in your neck (under the hinge of the jawbone alongside the windpipe). Now locate the pulse in the blood vessel on the inside of the ankle (just behind the knob of the ankle bone). Place your middle finger on the pulse in the neck and the middle finger of your other hand on the pulse in the ankle. Sit quietly for a minute and note what happens. What difference do you find in these two points where you feel the pulse? ■

Your heart pumps blood to all parts of the body, the head, the arms, the intestines, and the lungs. Your heart also pumps blood to itself by means of small blood tubes that are located in the heart muscles themselves.

As your heart pumps, many changes take place in the blood. To find out more about these changes let us suppose that we can follow one drop of blood as it makes a trip through the body.

The blood has to travel along two main routes. It goes to the lungs to pick up oxygen and release waste gases that are breathed out. It also carries this oxygen

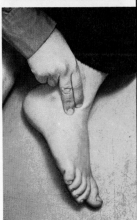

119

Have the class make a model heart from a shoebox. It will not look much like a heart, but it can help them to understand how the heart works.

The heart is divided into two halves, the left half and the right half. Each half has two chambers. The upper chambers are the auricles and the lower chambers are the ventricles. The upper chambers are smaller than the lower chambers. The auricles are partly containers where blood collects while the ventricles work to keep it moving to all parts of the body. Make dividers to separate the left and right halves of your model heart.

Blood can enter each ventricle of the heart only through special one-way openings called valves. The valves let the blood move in the proper direction and prevent it from backing up.

(continued)

To help students visualize the movement of a drop of blood in the system, obtain a long transparent plastic tube large enough for a marble to roll through it freely. Show the children that a marble can roll freely from one end of the tube to the other. Once the youngsters have grasped this idea, hold the tube up and tell them to pretend that the tube is the blood system and the marble is a drop of blood. Help them to see that as the blood moves through the system, it passes through smaller and smaller arteries until it is finally in the tiny capillaries threaded through the cells. Once the drop of blood has brought food ma-

terials and oxygen to the cells and picked up waste materials, it starts its return journey to the heart. From the capillaries the blood passes into larger and larger veins, which are equipped with valves to prevent the backflow of blood, until it is in the mainstream. The blood then re-enters the heart through the right auricle.

Remind the class that blood re-entering the heart from the veins contains less oxygen than before. The blood passes into the right ventricle, then into the lungs where its oxygen supply is increased. It then

optional activity
(continued)

There is a valve between the right auricle and the right ventricle, and another between the left auricle and the left ventricle. There are no valves or other openings between the right and left halves of a normal heart. Add the valves to your model heart.

Blood from the trunk, limbs, and head returns to the heart through two great veins. These veins enter the right auricle. Add these veins to the model heart.

Blood from the auricles flows into the ventricles. When the heart muscle tightens, the blood is forced out of the ventricles and pumped into the major blood vessels.

Blood from the right ventricle is pumped through a blood vessel that leads to the lungs. This blood vessel is called the pulmonary artery. Add the pulmonary artery to your model heart.

(continued)

together with digested food from the small intestines to other parts of the body.

Let's trace a drop of blood as it moves through your body. Look at the drawing to help you trace the drop. As a drop of blood leaves the heart, it goes out

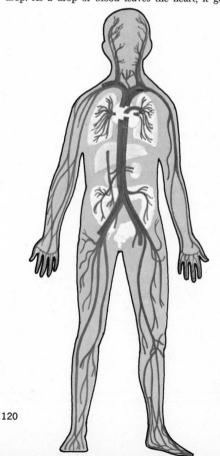

returns to the heart and back into general circulation again.

The composition of the blood is the next topic treated in the textbook. Ask the class what the color of blood is. Explain that the color is due to a red substance contained in the blood's red cells. The red cells and the white cells are suspended in a non-living liquid called plasma. About 12 pints of blood circulate through the body of an adult. Throughout the lifetime of a living animal, new blood is made and worn out blood is discarded.

(continued on page 150)

into a large blood tube that carries blood away from the heart. All tubes carrying blood *away from* the heart are called arteries (AR-tur-ees). The large artery leading out of the heart branches into a tube that leads to the head and another that leads to the lower parts of the body. These smaller arteries branch even more, becoming smaller and smaller in size. After the artery has branched many times, the tiny blood tubes are called capillaries (KAP-i-ler-eez). At this point, the drop of blood passes through a tissue in the body. Here it gives up to the body cells the digested food materials which it has picked up from the small intestine. The blood also gives up the oxygen which it has picked up from the lungs. At the same time, the blood takes up any wastes which are in the tissue and need to be carried away.

On the way back to the heart, the drop of blood goes into larger and larger blood tubes. All blood tubes returning blood *to* the heart are called veins (VAYNZ). The drop of blood moves into one of the big veins that carries blood into the heart. Once here, the journey of each drop of blood begins all over again. The drop of blood leaves the heart by way of an artery that leads to the lungs. Here it picks up oxygen and releases the waste gases you breathe out. The blood finally comes back to the heart by way of veins for another trip around the body.

What happens to one drop of blood will happen to all of the blood. Your body has a very organized system of hollow tubes to get blood from place to place. You can imagine how important it is to have a healthy heart pumping blood through your body every second of your life. Blood is important and necessary for your life because it helps keep all of your body's cells alive. What is blood made of?

121

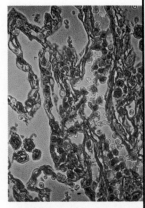

Microscopic view of blood cells in capillaries

optional activity
(continued)

The pulmonary artery branches into two smaller tubes, one of which enters each lung. These two branches divide and subdivide until they become the microscopic capillaries surrounding the air sacs of the lungs.

When the blood reaches the capillaries in the lungs, it absorbs the oxygen from the air that one inhales and gives up carbon dioxide to be exhaled. The pulmonary veins then carry the blood back to the left auricle. Add the pulmonary veins to the model.

The oxygen-bearing blood is pumped from the left auricle into the left ventricle. From here, it is pumped out of the heart through a large artery called the aorta. Add the aorta to the model heart. The aorta branches into many smaller arteries, carrying blood throughout the body.

Have the class trace the flow of the blood through the heart.

Draw red blood cells on the board to show that these cells look like tiny discs, concave on both sides. They carry oxygen from the lungs to the tissues.

The second type of blood cells are the white corpuscles. There are several types of white cells in the blood, and their main function is to destroy disease bacteria and other foreign matter in the body. Red cells are more numerous than white cells.

Red cells and most of the white cells are manufactured in the marrow found in the long bones of the body. The class may be interested in seeing the marrow in a soup bone which has been cut open along its shaft. As cells are worn out, they are removed from the blood, and the liver filters out the hemoglobin (red material) and discards the rest as waste.

optional activity

You will need a sharp needle, glass slides, cover glass, alcohol, Wright's stain (available from a local hospital laboratory or scientific supply house), microscope or microprojector.

Wash the end of your own middle finger with alcohol and sterilize the tip of the needle in the flame of a match for a few seconds. Stroke the finger forward to force the blood to the end and prick the skin to get a drop of blood. You might want to invite the school nurse in for this activity. (Caution: Do not use the same needle for drawing blood from different people. Put a drop of blood on a glass slide and spread it into a thin smear with the edge of another slide. Allow the blood to dry for a few minutes, and then put several drops of Wright's stain on the smear. When the smear turns pink in color (after about 3–5 minutes),

(continued)

Healthy blood cells seen through a microscope

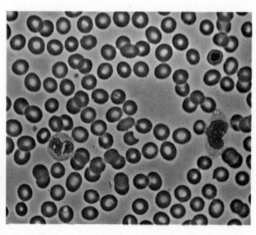

Microscopic view of red blood cells

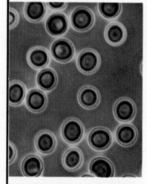

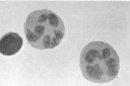

Microscopic view of white blood cells

Look at the picture on this page which shows a sample of blood as you would see it under a microscope. The little cells you see give blood its color. Although each cell is not very red, blood is red in color. Do you know why it is red?

Blood can be thought of as being made up of two parts. The liquid part, or plasma (PLAZ-muh) carries digested food and waste materials. The solid part is made up of cells. Some cells pick up oxygen in the lungs and carry it to the different parts of the body. These are called red cells. Other blood cells, the white cells, attack germs that get into the body and fight infections.

Your growing body makes the materials that form your blood from the food and water in a balanced diet. Try to remember the first step to proper health. Eat the right kinds of foods.

Draw a river on the board with various objects floating along in it. Point out that the blood, like a river, is largely water with various materials carried along in it. Plasma makes up about half the blood, and plasma is mostly made of water. The children should understand again why it is important for them to drink plenty of water each day.

In the first part of Testing Your Ideas the first two statements are false and the second two are true.

TESTING YOUR IDEAS

With which of the following statements do you agree?

The system of the heart, blood tubes, and blood does not depend upon the digestive system.

The digestive system does not depend upon the system of the heart and blood tubes.

No matter where you are cut you will bleed. Therefore, the system of capillaries must be spread throughout the body.

If the system of capillaries is spread throughout the body, then arteries and veins are spread throughout the body too.

optional activity
(*continued*)

rinse the slide in a beaker of water. Put a cover glass on the wet slide and examine it under high magnification. The red cells should show up clearly, and the white cells may be seen as somewhat larger.

optional activity

You will need a live goldfish, absorbent cotton, a Petri dish, a glass microscope slide, and a microscope or microprojector.

Wrap the goldfish in wet absorbent cotton, especially around the gills, and leave the tail uncovered. Place the goldfish in the Petri dish and cover the tail with the glass slide. Hold the tail down with the slide and focus the microprojector on the tail. The movement of the blood in the blood vessels should be visible. (Caution: Do not keep the fish out of water for more than 5 minutes.)

OVERVIEW

The respiratory system and the excretory system are considered in this section. The structure and function of the two systems are described. The main emphasis, however, is on the way the respiratory system functions to supply oxygen the body needs. The need for oxygen as a substance to combine with food in the cells is discussed, and the resulting production of waste products is pointed out. The activities and discussions relate the intake of food and oxygen to the production of energy and the elimination of waste products in the body. Thus, the material dealing with the elimination of wastes rounds out the children's grasp of the major body processes.

how to begin

This lesson should begin with a review of activity 3/Describe to show that when sugar burns, heat is produced. The concept of burning will be further developed in Unit 3, "Heat As Energy." Ask the chil-

process skills

Describing the structure and function of the respiratory system

Describing the structure and function of the urinary-excretory system

Explaining the process by which food is used within the cells of the body, and how waste products are produced and eliminated

materials

mirrors*, drinking glasses*, sugar, dried yeast, empty pop bottles*, rubber or plastic tubes*, modeling clay, limewater, glass chimney (from kerosene lamp)*, rubber sheet (bottom of large rubber balloon can be used)*, rubber balloons*, watch with second hand, drinking straws*, hand magnifiers (or reading glasses)*

---

* one per team

WHAT HAPPENS
WHEN FOOD AND OXYGEN COMBINE?

Have you ever run across the playground and up the stairs? In goes one breath, and out goes another. What do you think is going in and out of your body so fast? If you say it is air, you are right! The most important substance for us in air is oxygen (AHKS-i-jin). We need this substance to stay alive. The air you breathe is made up of several gases, one of which is oxygen.

As you breathe, the air follows a special pathway into the body. Look at the drawing on page 125. With your finger, follow the arrows from the nose to the lungs. The system by which you breathe in oxygen and breathe out other gases is called the respiratory (RES-puh-ruh-taw-ree) system. Can you name some of the organs making up the respiratory system?

Open your mouth and look in a mirror. Can you see a red, moist lining in your mouth? The organs of the respiratory system also have a very thin, moist lining. This kind of tissue has many tiny blood vessels in it. It is always wet, and dry air passing through the nose is warmed and moistened by this lining.

Inside the nostrils of your nose are tiny hairs which catch small particles of dirt and prevent the dust from passing into your lungs.

You can see why it is important that the air passages of your nose be kept open and clean. Air has to be able to go through them easily, and your nose has an important purpose. It warms, cleans, and moistens the air as it goes into your body.

124

dren if they saw the sugar burn in 3/Describe. Ask them what they felt when they touched the outside of the can. Ask them if heat was made when the sugar burned. Then ask them to speculate upon air being present in order for the sugar to burn. To make a preliminary investigation of this problem, repeat activity 3/Describe twice. The second time, however, cover the burning sugar with a Pyrex beaker to see if the flame will burn without air. Have the children compare the time it takes the sugar to burn with and without the Pyrex beaker.

procedure

Tell the children to place their hands on each side of their chests and to inhale and exhale deeply. Ask them what they observed. Encourage different ideas, but look for an answer indicating that as the chest increases in size, air rushes in (inhalation) and when the chest decreases in size, air rushes out (exhalation). Refer to a chart or model of the body, if available, or to the drawing in the textbook, and let the youngsters identify the nose, windpipe, and lungs.

(continued on page 154)

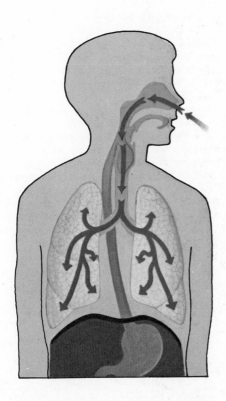

When you have a cold, the moist lining in your nose swells up. The air passages fill with fluids, and you cannot breathe through your nose. Think of your mouth as an extra safety passage for air to be used only when your nose cannot do its job.

125

Have the children follow the path of the air as shown by the arrows in the drawing on page 125. Read the introductory material and then discuss the topic which follows.

Ask the students to look at the lining of their mouths in a mirror. Explain that the same type of moist, warm tissue found there is also found lining the rest of the air tubes leading to the lungs. The blood circulating in the lining warms the air, and the mucous glands in the lining secrete the thick material which coats the mucous membranes.

Draw a lung on the chalkboard similar to the one in the drawing in the text. Explain that the lungs are like two balloons which fill with air, except that the lungs are made up of very tiny, little saclike structures which occur in bunches at the ends of the air tubes. A bunch of grapes held up before the class makes a good model of what a cluster of air sacs looks like under a microscope.

Draw a tree and branches on the board and explain that the windpipe also divides into smaller and smaller air tubes inside each lung. One main branch of the

studying the picture

The picture at the right is a highly magnified cross-section of the tissue of the windpipe. Have the children note the tiny tufts of hairlike threads located at the top of the tissue. The children should understand that the hairlike threads do not move of themselves, but "comb" the air of dust particles as air passes to and fro in the windpipe. *Ask the children how dust particles are removed from the walls of the windpipe.*

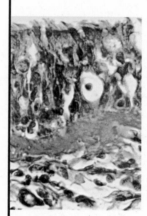

Windpipe tissue with hairlike threads. Magnified 250 times

As you can see in the drawing on page 125, an organ called the windpipe connects the back of the nose and mouth with the lungs. The windpipe is lined with the same kind of tissue as the nose. The lining in the windpipe also has very tiny, hairlike threads which move back and forth and remove dust and germs from the air we breathe in.

Has soap powder or pepper ever made you sneeze? Your body has another way to keep dust and other fine particles out of the respiratory system. If something gets into the air passages which might be dangerous, you cough or sneeze until it is removed.

Look at the drawing of the respiratory system again. Notice how the windpipe branches into two tubes. One goes to the left lung and the other goes to the right lung. The lungs, which are made up of very spongy tissue, are at the ends of these air tubes. The lungs take up most of the space inside the chest. Inside

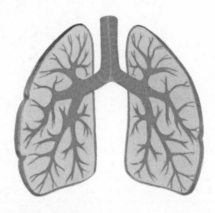

windpipe goes into the right lung and the other branch goes into the left lung. The windpipe and the air tubes are lined with microscopic threadlike cilia which sweep foreign particles upward in the air tubes and into the mouth. These cilia are always moving. Hold up both hands and wiggle your fingers to show the action of cilia. Ask the children if they can explain what happens to the cilia when a person smokes too much. (The ciliary motion slows down. The particles that should be removed by means of their motion accumulate, causing irritation and coughing.) Other

irritating substances which get into the air passages also cause coughing and sneezing as a reflex action to rid the body of these irritants.

Ask the students to tell you what happens to their breathing rate after they play hard. Explain that the harder you exercise, the more air your body needs. Ask them if they know what the essential material is in the air that they breathe (oxygen). Explain that about 1/5 of the air is oxygen, and that the body needs oxygen to combine with food in the cells in order to release energy for all body activities.

(continued on page 156)

the lungs, the air tubes divide into smaller and smaller tubes. At the ends of each of these tiny tubes are very tiny, balloon-like parts called air sacs.

These little "balloons" or air sacs are so tiny that you can see them only with a microscope. The drawing on this page shows you what they might look like. They look like little bunches of grapes. These tiny, hollow sacs make up the spongy tissue of the lungs. Each air sac is surrounded with tiny blood capillaries.

As you breathe in, air goes into the little sacs. Oxygen from the air passes through the thin walls of the air sacs into the blood. At the same time, waste products that are in the blood pass into the air sacs so that the waste can be removed from the body when you breathe out.

As you know, the oxygen taken up by the blood is carried to the tissues of the body. Do you remember what part of the blood carries oxygen? Do you remember what was produced when sugar burned? You will become familiar with burning and its products in the next unit. But when sugar burned, what did you see

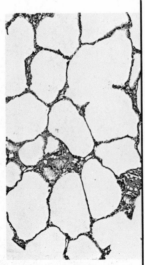

Air sacs of lung magnified 250 times

studying the picture

The microphotograph shows a cross-section of the air sacs where the transfer of oxygen for waste products occurs. *Ask the children to imagine cutting the tiny air sacs in half.* If the cut air sacs were placed under a microscope, tell the students they would see something like what is shown in the microphotograph.

Activity 21/Explain lets the students discover that as sugar and oxygen are combined by the yeast cells, carbon dioxide gas is given off as a waste product. It takes about 10 minutes for the carbon dioxide to begin bubbling out of the delivery tube into the glass of limewater. When this happens, the limewater turns a milky-white color. This reaction is a specific test for carbon dioxide. The gas comes from the oxidation and fermentation of the sugar by the yeast cells as the cells grow and divide.

Tell the children to breathe deeply several times and to note what happens to their chest and ribs as they do so (they rise and fall). To help the class see this action more clearly, have the youngsters place one hand on their abdomens and the other on their ribs. Then let them breathe deeply again and ask what they observed.

Explain that the lungs fill up most of the space inside the chest cavity. A large muscle, the diaphragm, which contracts and relaxes rhythmically, separates the chest cavity from the abdominal cavity. As you inhale, the muscle tightens, creating more space in the chest. The air pressure in the lungs drops, and the air from the outside flows in through the nose and windpipe. As you exhale, the diaphragm relaxes into its normal domelike position. This relaxation decreases the space in the chest cavity and forces air out of the lungs.

(continued on page 158)

responses to 21/explain

1. Bubbles should be seen coming from the tube after a few minutes.
2. The limewater should become milky.
3. The presence of carbon dioxide is apparent when limewater turns milky.
4. Yeast cells acting upon the sugar produce carbon dioxide.

and feel? The oxygen combines with the carbohydrates in the cells in somewhat the same way that sugar combines with oxygen. As the food and oxygen are used by the cells, waste products are formed and energy is given off. Do you know the names of the main waste products formed when carbohydrates and oxygen are used in the body? Let us see if we can find out in the following activity.

21/Explain

Dissolve a level tablespoon of sugar in a glass of warm water. Sprinkle a little powdered yeast into the water and stir. Fill a clean pop bottle half-full with this liquid. Put a plastic or rubber tube into the bottle so that the end of the tube is above the liquid. Seal the opening of the bottle around the tube with modeling clay, as shown in the picture. Put the other end of the tube in a glass of limewater. After a few minutes,

what do you see coming out of the end of the tube in the glass? ②What happens to the color of the limewater? ③Do you know what gas this is a test for? ④Where does the gas come from? ■

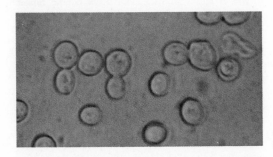

Yeast cells magnified 600 times

The yeast is made up of tiny cells which are in a resting state. When the yeast is added to warm water and sugar, the cells begin to grow and divide. To do this they must have energy. Do you know what these cells use for energy? If you say the sugar, you are only partly right! The cells also take in oxygen from the air and combine it with the sugar to get energy to grow and divide. When this happens, a waste gas is produced. You see it bubbling out of the tube into the glass of limewater. The name of this gas is carbon dioxide. It is also formed by the cells in your body, and you breathe it out in the air leaving your lungs.

Take a deep breath and hold it for about 30 seconds. Slowly let it out. What happens to your chest when you breathe in? What happens when you breathe out? Can you explain how air is able to enter your lungs when you breathe in? Let us do the next activity to see if we can find out.

for your information

The picture at the left shows yeast cells as they appear under a microscope. Yeast is a one-celled fungus. During reproduction, the wall of a yeast cell bulges outward and forms a knob, or bud. This bud eventually separates from the parent cell and is an independent one-celled plant.

studying the picture

Show the children a mixture of baker's yeast, warm water, and sugar.

Ask them if the yeast mixture looks like the yeast in the photograph. What is the difference between the two? If you looked at yeast through a magnifying glass do you think it would look like the picture? Try it.

The children will probably suggest that they try a microscope.

Activity 22/Demonstrate illustrates the action of the diaphragm in the body. Point out that the balloon on top of the lamp chimney represents the lungs and the rubber sheeting on the bottom represents the diaphragm. To help the children set up the demonstration, cut one balloon to fit the bottom of the chimney. Secure this piece with a rubber band or string as shown in the drawing. Insert a second balloon into the top of the chimney and stretch the open end over the lip. A state of equilibrium now exists between the air pressure within and outside the lamp chimney.

When the rubber sheet at the bottom is pulled down, the amount of space inside the chimney is increased. The pressure, therefore, drops. The air outside flows into the balloon and inflates it, as the class can see. When the rubber sheet, representing the diaphragm, flattens out across the bottom of the chimney, the air is forced out of the balloon, in much the same way that air is forced out of the lungs.

Activity 23/Record lets the children observe and count the number of inhale-exhale movements of the chest in one minute of normal breathing. Use a watch with a second hand and tell the class when to start counting. At the end of one minute, say, "Stop," and have the youngsters record their observations in a table. Repeat the procedure five times so that the children observe five different students in the class.

responses to 22/demonstrate

1. When the rubber sheet is stretched across the bottom the air pressure inside the glass chimney is equal to the air pressure outside the chimney. Increasing the volume of the apparatus decreases the air pressure inside. Therefore, air flows into the balloon to equalize the pressures.

22/Demonstrate

Fit the glass chimney of an old-fashioned lamp with a rubber balloon and a piece of rubber sheeting, as shown in the drawing. Pull down on the rubber sheeting and note what happens to the balloon. How does this activity show how the air goes in and out of your lungs? ■

Air is moved in and out of the lungs as the chest expands and contracts. Directly under the ribs is a large muscle, called the diaphragm (DIE-uh-fram), which controls breathing. When the diaphragm is relaxed as you breathe out, it fits up under the ribs and fills the space at the bottom of the chest cavity. When you breathe in, the diaphragm tightens and flattens along the bottom of the chest cavity, making more room for the lungs to fill with air. In the activity you just did, what part of the model acts like the diaphragm?

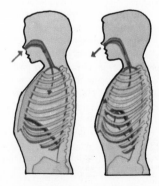

In fourth graders, the breathing rate should average out to about 20 times per minute.

An addition to this activity would be to have the children exercise for a few minutes by jumping up and down on one foot. Then have them sit quietly and repeat the counting activity. They will find that exercise significantly increases the breathing rate. It is important for the children to realize that our rate changes because of the amount of CO_2 in our blood and *not* because of the need for O_2.

The textbook next discusses the processes of excretion in the body. These are closely related to the processes of circulation and respiration. In fact, the respiratory system also acts as an excretory system in ridding the body of carbon dioxide and water. The excretion of undigested food products is not included because this function was already discussed in connection with the digestive process. However, it might be well to review briefly how the body eliminates waste materials from the large intestine.

If the children understand that the systems of the body are interrelated and that some systems perform more than one function, they also should see that the body is not made like a wall of separate, individual units.

(continued on page 160)

How fast does the in and out breathing take place in your body? Let us do the next activity and see how many times a minute you breathe.

23/Record

Everyone in the class should sit quietly for this activity. Look at a classmate and count the number of times his chest rises and falls. When the teacher says "Start," begin to count the number of times the person breathes. When the teacher says "Stop," stop counting and write down the number of times the person breathed. Compare your count with the counts your classmates made. Your teacher will help you figure out the average number of breaths per student. ▪

The blood carries digested foods, water and oxygen to the cells where they are used. As the cells use the materials for repair and growth or to release energy, they produce materials which they cannot use. These are called waste products and must be removed from the body if it is to stay healthy. The blood picks up these waste materials and carries them to special organs which remove them from the blood. The system that gets rid of body wastes is made up of the lungs, the skin, the kidneys, and the bladder. As you can see, an organ may do more than one thing in the body. Do you now see why the living human body is not like a wall of bricks laid together? What two things are done by your lungs?

The lungs are important in getting rid of waste products, as well as in supplying oxygen to the body. Do you know what two waste products are given off by the lungs? Do the next activity to see if you can find out.

131

optional activity

Have the children find out all they can about air pollution. They might investigate the following questions:

How does air pollution affect healthy breathing? How great a threat to good health is air pollution? What is being done about it? What can you do about it?

The waste products which are present in the air we exhale are illustrated in activity 24/Test on page 132. The moisture in the breath will condense into a film on any cool surface. The youngsters can feel this film with their fingers and understand that it is water. The test for carbon dioxide is repeated here by breathing hard through a straw into a glass of limewater. When the limewater turns milky-white, the presence of carbon dioxide is indicated.

The general structure of the urinary excretory system (kidneys, bladder, ureters, and urethra) is shown in the drawing. The children should understand that blood passes through the kidneys where liquid wastes are filtered out. The wastes pass through the ureters from the kidneys into the bladder. There the wastes are stored until they are excreted through the urethra, the tube leading to the outside of the body.

If you wish, a kidney obtained from a butcher shop can be cut lengthwise and used to show the class that the inside of a kidney is hollow. The blood is filtered out in tiny tubules in the outer part of the kidney. The students should understand that the kidneys work continually in filtering the wastes out of the blood,

responses to 24/test

1. Water vapor condenses on the mirror's surface.
2. The water vapor is present in one's breath.
3. The limewater turns milky.
4. Carbon dioxide is produced.

24/Test

Breathe onto the cool surface of a mirror or a glass. 1 What forms on the surface? 2 Where does this material come from? Use a clean drinking straw to blow your breath gently through a glass of limewater. 3 What happens to the color of the limewater? 4 What gas must be given off? Now you can name the two waste products that are given off by the lungs. ■

The two waste products found in the air we breathe out are made by the cells when the cells use carbohydrates to supply energy for the body. Other parts of the body get rid of wastes produced when cells are repaired or destroyed. These parts are the two kidneys, the bladder and the tubes that lead from the kidneys to the bladder to the outside of your body.

132

even though the bladder may be emptied of urine only a few times a day. The urine is a liquid waste produced in protein metabolism.

After the children have read the textbook discussion on the skin, discuss with them the function of the skin as an excretory organ. They will be familiar with sweat, since they have all noticed their own perspiration at one time or another. Ask the youngsters if they know where the sweat comes from (it is produced by the sweat glands in the skin).

Activity 25/Observe lets the students look closely at the surface of the skin. Have them compare what they see with the enlarged cross-section of the skin on page 134. They should be able to make out the creases in the skin, the openings of the sweat glands, and the openings of the hair follicles. The sweat glands on the hands open to the surface of the skin, but the oil glands are inside the hair follicles, and the oil passes up along the hairs to the surface. When these oil ducts become stopped up and infected, blackheads may result. Stress the fact that the skin should be washed regularly and kept clean if it is to function properly.

(continued on page 162)

Look at the drawing on this page. Find the kidneys which are located at the back of the body cavity, a few inches above the waist. Below the kidneys, at the very bottom of the body cavity, is the hollow, muscular bag called the bladder.

Waste materials are collected from the cells of the body by the blood. The blood goes through the kidneys where the liquid waste materials are removed. These then go into the bladder where they are stored. When the bladder fills up, you become aware that liquid waste must be removed from the body.

Although we think of the skin as a covering tissue of the body, it also helps the body get rid of waste materials. Do you remember what happens to the skin of your face and hands when you work in the hot sun? This liquid is formed by the sweat glands in the skin. It is a waste product made up mostly of water with some salts in it. Let us take a closer look at the skin.

25/Observe

Use a magnifier to look at the skin on the back of your hand. Using a mirror, look at the skin on your face. These are the pores through which sweat leaves

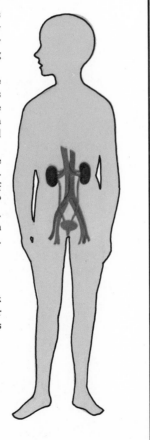

133

The way in which the skin cools the body by the evaporation of sweat can be illustrated by having the youngsters dip their hands in water and then hold them in the stream of air from a fan. The hand which is wet will feel a lot cooler than the hand which is dry, because the evaporation of water uses heat from the body.

In the first part of Testing Your Ideas, the first two statements are true and the last is false. In the second part, the last list best describes the path a particle of oxygen might follow. Students who answer these questions should be asked to give reasons for their answers.

responses to 25/observe

1. Oil is produced by the skin to protect it from drying out.

optional activity

You will need a half-gallon jar with a two-hole stopper to fit it, glass tubes, rubber or plastic tubes, a measuring cup and rubbing alcohol.

Fill the glass jar about three-quarters full of water. Insert two glass tubes through the rubber stopper so that one tube reaches down to the bottom of the jar and the other only goes through the stopper. Attach rubber tubes to the other ends of the two glass tubes. Place one rubber tube in a large jar and put a clean glass mouthpiece in the other rubber tube. The outflow tube should be at least ¼ inch in diameter or the water won't flow fast enough to indicate before the youngsters

(continued)

the body. Rub your finger alongside your nose. Do you feel an oily substance? This oil is produced by oil glands in the skin. Can you guess why we need this oil on our skin? ■

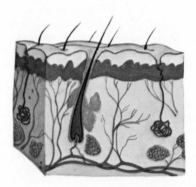

Look at a magnified drawing of the skin on this page. As you can see, the skin is more than just a layer on the outside of the body. The skin gets rid of water and salts by way of sweat. It also helps the body control its temperature. As sweat evaporates from the skin, it cools the body. Can you explain why you sweat a lot when you are exercising?

Because the skin is an important part of your waste removing system, care of the skin is important for good health. If your skin is not properly cared for, the pores may become clogged. Such clogging will prevent the pores from getting rid of wastes. What do you think could happen if the oil glands become filled up with dirt? It is a good habit to bathe yourself with warm water and soap every day.

134

162

With which of the following statements do you agree?

The production of energy in the body makes wastes.

The kidneys are not the only means by which the body rids itself of wastes.

The respiratory system, the digestive system, and the system of the heart and tubes have nothing in common at all.

Which is the correct order a particle of oxygen might follow in the respiratory system?

nose	nose	nose
windpipe	air sacs	windpipe
air sacs	windpipe	air tubes
blood	air tubes	air sacs
air tubes	blood	blood

optional activity
(continued)

have to take another breath. (Caution: Wash the mouthpiece in alcohol before different students put it into their mouths.) Put the mouthpiece in your mouth and exhale into the jar, forcing as much air out from your lungs as you can. With a measuring cup measure the amount of water that flows out of the jar. Determine the average amount of air exhaled by the children in the class.

OVERVIEW

The discussion of the skeletal, muscular, and nervous systems is presented in order to provide the students with an understanding of how food ingested into the body is used to provide energy for the body's movements and activities. To discover this relationship, the children examine the skeletal framework of the body, experiment with muscular actions, and learn how all these activities are under the control of the nervous system.

process skills

Describing the bones as a system which protects and supports the body

Explaining how the muscular system produces all movements in the body

Differentiating between the voluntary and involuntary activities of the body as controlled by the nervous system

Inferring that the energy for the body activities is derived from the conversion of food into energy in the cells

materials

handkerchief°, models or charts of the skeletal and muscular systems, if available

---
° one per team

how to begin

Use a chart or a model of the skeleton, or x-ray pictures (obtained from a doctor's office or a hospital) to show the bones of the body. Show these materials to the class and ask the children what the purpose of the skeleton seems to be in giving form to the body. Let the youngsters think about and discuss this question for a few minutes, but look for an answer which indicates that the skeleton is a framework to which the various structures and organs of the body are attached.

Draw a picture of a house on the board and ask the class what supports the house. Draw in the floor

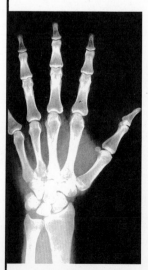

HOW DOES YOUR BODY MOVE?

The food you eat is digested in your body and is carried to all of your cells by the blood. Oxygen in the tissues combines with the food, and energy is released in the cells. What do you think happens to this energy in the body? If you say, "To do all the things we do," you are right. But you may not know the body is able to perform all these actions.

One of the main things you do is to move around. You walk, you run, you write, you comb your hair, and you do many other things every day. How are you able to do all these things?

26/Observe

With your right hand, hold the tip of a finger on your left hand. Squeeze slightly along the sides of the finger, moving your hand up to the wrist, forearm, elbow, upper arm, and shoulder. Do you feel the bones in your hand and arm? Can you feel the different types of bones? ■

Bones form the framework of your body. This system supports the body and gives it the shape you see and feel.

When you were born, your skeleton was not as hard and strong as it is now. Much of it was made of a rubbery tissue called cartilage (KAR-ti-lij). As you grow, most of the cartilage is changed to bone tissue.

136

beams and roof rafters and explain that they support the house. Ask the youngsters how the skeleton compares with this structure (it also supports the body). Ask the class what is on the outside of the house frame (bricks, siding, roof, etc.) and what is found on the inside of the house (plumbing, pipes, wiring, etc.). Have the children compare the structure of the body with that of a house. They should understand that the outside of the skeleton is covered with muscles and skin, and the inside contains vital organs, such as heart, lungs, digestive organs, nervous system, etc. But emphasize again that a house is not a true unit (see page 98 of the Teacher's Edition).

procedure

After the students have read and discussed the introductory material on the skeletal system, have them develop an awareness of their own skeletal structure by completing activity 26/Observe. The children should be able to feel the bones making up their fingers, hands, and arms. The bones of the fingers, hand, forearm, and upper arm are classed as long bones. The bones of the wrist and shoulders are classed as flat bones. These are the two main types of bones making up the skeleton.

(continued on page 166)

responses to 26/observe

1. The answers to the questions of this activity are observational. However, the children should be able to recognize the various bones of the fingers, as opposed to those of the hand, wrist, and forearm.

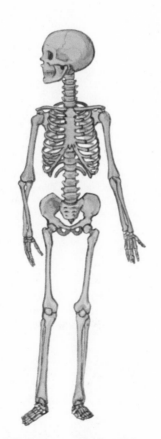

By the time you are fully grown, your body will have 206 bones making up your skeleton. Look at the drawing of the skeleton on this page. Can you find and name some of the main parts of the skeleton?

137

Activity 27/Locate will let the class identify the skull making up the top and sides of the head. The chest structure is made up of the ribs along each side of the chest, the flat breastbone in front, the collarbones on top, and the flat shoulder blades in back. Have the children refer to a chart or the drawing on page 137 of the skeleton to help them identify these bones.

The infant skeleton is largely cartilage. But as the child grows, minerals (calcium phosphate and calcium carbonate) are deposited among the living cells, and the bones become harder and stronger. The students should understand that the skeleton is not fully formed until about 25 years of age. Therefore, a diet rich in minerals (milk, eggs, fruits, vegetables) is essential for proper body growth and development.

Having established the idea that the bones serve as a body frame, point out that the bones are organs, and taken together, make up the skeletal system. The bones serve as places of attachment for muscles and protect the vital organs and tissues which are enclosed by parts of the skeleton (the brain in the

responses to 27/locate

1. The skull.
2. The ribs.
3. The children should have no difficulty in locating the skull, ribs, breastbone, and collarbones, or shoulder blades.

27/Locate

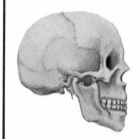

Slide your hand from your forehead across the top of your head and feel the sides of your head. What part of the skeleton do you feel? Move your fingers up and down along the sides of your chest. What bones do you feel there? Feel the large, flat bone in front of your chest. Find the collarbones on each side and on top of the chest. Can you feel two large, flat bones in the upper part of your back? ■

You have been studying where many of the organs of the body are found. Do you remember where the heart and lungs are in the body? What parts of your body are found near the collarbones, breastbone,

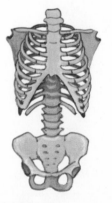
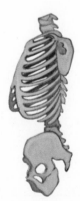

138

166

skull, the heart and lungs in the rib cage, the spinal cord inside the spinal column, etc.). Bone is composed of living cells, the walls of which contain the minerals which make them hard and strong.

Besides providing the supportive and protective functions of the skeleton, some bones are moved by the action of muscles. The bones serve as levers in voluntary motions, such as walking, jumping, bending, etc. To permit freedom of movement for these motions, the bones come together in joints in the skeleton. The bones are held together at the joints by means of strong bands of tissue called ligaments. Muscles are fastened to the bones by a similar formation of tissue, called tendons.

The ends of the bones in the joints are covered with smooth pads of cartilage. A thick membrane filled with fluid surrounds the joint so that the bones can move freely without rubbing. If you can get from your butcher a soup bone which has not been cut apart at the joint, the structure of the cartilage pads and ligaments can be easily shown to the class.

(continued on page 168)

ribs, and shoulder blades? Are these parts inside or outside of the chest? Can you see any reason why the bones of the skull are all around the brain? If you have figured out that these bones help keep your heart, lungs, and brain from being hurt, you have the answers to these questions. An important use of the skeleton is to protect other organs in your body.

Move your arms back and forth. Put your hand on the back of your neck and move your head. Bend over and touch the floor. You are able to do all these things in part because of your skeleton.

In order to be able to move, the bones fit together at places in the skeleton which we call joints (JOYNTS). You have different kinds of joints in your body. See if you can find out which kind of movement each joint can do.

studying the picture

Would the children in the picture be able to climb, swing, run, or kick if they couldn't bend certain parts of their bodies? At what places can the body bend? The neck, shoulder, elbow, wrist, fingers, hip, knee, ankle, toes.

Describe the way parts of the body bend. Up, down, forward, backwards, in circular motion.

139

In activity 28/Describe the children discover that movement takes place in these joints. As the forearm turns from a palms-up to a palms-down position, the youngsters can feel the sliding movement of the two bones (the radius and the ulna). This action is typical for a partially movable joint known as a sliding joint. The elbow and the shoulder are freely movable joints. The elbow illustrates a hinge joint, and the shoulder represents a ball-and-socket joint.

Ask the class to name other examples of sliding joints (bones in wrist and ankle, bones in neck), hinge joints (fingers, toes, lower jaw), ball-and-socket joints (hip, thumb, head on top of neck). Have the children refer to the drawings in the text to see how the bones fit together in these types of joints, and then refer to a chart or the drawing of the skeleton in the text to locate the different joints in the body.

Draw a picture of a domestic animal on the board (a cow, sheep, or other food animal). Ask the students if they have ever seen the muscles of these animals. Let them think about and discuss this point for a few minutes. Then explain that the part of the animal which makes up the steaks and roasts we eat is chiefly muscle meat.

studying the picture

Ask the children to state which picture shows the sliding joint (left), *the hinge joint* (center), *and the socket joint* (right).

responses to 28/describe

1. The kind of motion felt in the elbow is a hinge action.
2. The kind of action felt in the shoulder is a ball-and-socket movement.

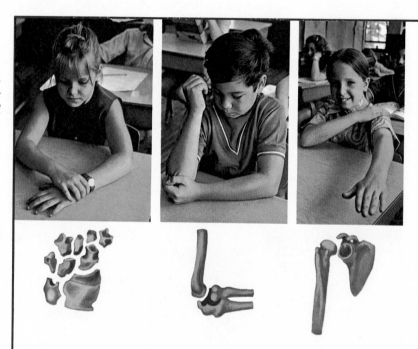

28/Describe

Place your arm on the desk so that the palm is up. Hold your wrist with the other hand and turn your arm over so that the palm is down. Describe what kind of motion you feel in the two bones of the arm.

Hold your arm straight out and put your other hand on the bottom of the elbow. Bend the arm back and forth. What kind of motion do you feel in this kind of joint?

Put your hand on the opposite shoulder of your body. Swing your arm around. What kind of motion do you feel in the shoulder joint? ■

Tell the children to close their hands to make a fist. Have them feel the muscles of the inside of the forearm as the fingers move back and forth. Then explain that the muscles they feel give the hand its ability to move. Ask the students to tell you what system in the body is made up by the muscles (the muscular system).

Discuss with the class the names of several sports requiring the training and use of muscles. Let them list on the board the sports and the muscles used in each (archery uses the hands and arms; hiking uses the back and legs; swimming uses nearly all the muscles of the body, etc.).

(continued on page 170)

Of course, the bones in your body do not move by themselves. You have muscles. The muscles of your muscular (MUS-kyoo-lur) system make the bones move. You can control many of your muscles. You can move when you want to and stop when you want to. Look at the drawings on this page to see where most of these muscles are found.

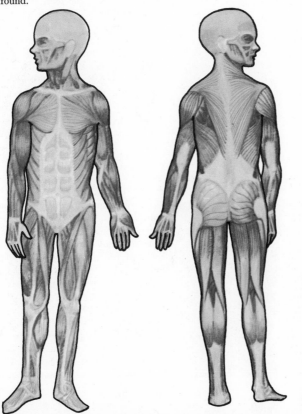

studying the picture

Ask the children where the muscles are attached. They are attached to the skeleton.

169

The muscular system has two main kinds of muscles, voluntary, as in the arms and legs, and involuntary, as in the respiratory and digestive muscles. The children should understand that muscles must have energy for these activities, and that this energy comes from the oxidation of carbohydrates (the chief energy food) in the cells. The class should remember from previous study that as food is converted into energy, carbon dioxide and water are formed as waste products and are carried away by the blood.

Activity 29/Observe illustrates that voluntary muscles usually act in pairs. They oppose each other, producing movement in opposite directions. The two muscles of the upper arm (the biceps and the triceps) provide good examples of this pairing. As one muscle contracts, the opposing muscle relaxes. Let the children compare the action of these muscles with the drawing on page 143 which shows this structure. Other examples of muscles which work in pairs are those that move the fingers, the muscles that open and close the lower jaw, the muscles that move the head, and the muscles that bend the leg at the knee.

Push a book off your desk and then move rapidly to catch it. Ask the class why it was possible for you to move in such a way as to catch the book before it hit the floor. Let the children discuss this point and

studying the picture

The microphotograph shows a section of voluntary muscle tissue. *Ask the children if they note something like threads in the muscle tissue.* The threadlike structures are called fibrils, but the student need not know this name. Tell the children that the threads can shorten and then relax to return to their original size. *Ask the class how these threads might help the muscle to move.*

responses to 29/observe

1. When the muscle of the upper arm contracts, the forearm is pulled toward the shoulder.
2. When the muscle over the back part of the upper arm contracts, the forearm is extended out from the body.
3. Other muscles of the body which work in the same way as the muscles of the upper arm are those of the thigh.

There are other muscles in the body that you do not have to think about to make them move. Do you have to think about moving the diaphragm in order to breathe? Can you name other muscles that move without your thinking about them?

Muscles must have energy to move. Now do you understand why you must have energy foods in your diet? The carbohydrates you eat are digested into forms that can be carried by the blood and taken in by the cells. There oxygen changes the digested food into other materials, and small amounts of energy are given off. Every time you take a step, bend your finger, or take a breath, muscle cells are using some of this energy. Do you remember what else is formed in the body when food materials are used? Energy is needed by all of the muscle cells of the body. Let us see how some of your muscles work.

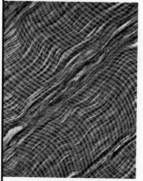

Cells of muscle tissue magnified 800 times

29/Observe

Feel the muscles of your upper arm. When the muscle on the front of the upper arm contracts, it becomes shorter and fatter. 1 What happens to the forearm when this muscle contracts? Feel the muscle over the back part of your upper arm. 2 What happens to the forearm when this muscle contracts? 3 Can you find other muscles in your body which work in pairs like these two muscles? ■

The drawing on page 143 shows you how these two muscles act to move the forearm. They are made up of long strands of muscle tissue. Each strand is made up of thousands of muscle cells. When a muscle contracts, each cell in the muscle contracts. This action

suggest answers. Look for an answer indicating that muscles must work together, or be coordinated with each other and with the sense organs in order to carry on man's activities. Explain that for the muscles to be coordinated, they must be under some central control. The controlling center in the body is the nervous system.

Introduce the nervous system by drawing an outline of a man on the board. Draw in the brain, spinal cord, and main nerves in the arms and legs of this figure. Tell the children that the nervous system is like a telegraph network along which are sent messages to control the actions of the muscles. Except for reflex actions, the central physical source of the messages is the brain. But state that this is only a comparison since a telegraph system is not organic, is not alive, does not grow, and has no mind.

Ask the students if they have ever seen a calf's brain in a butcher shop, and let someone describe it (soft, gelatinous mass with many ridges and furrows). It would be helpful to have a calf's brain in the classroom. Ask the youngsters if they remember what part of the skeleton protects the brain (the skull) and the spinal cord (the spinal column).

(continued on page 172)

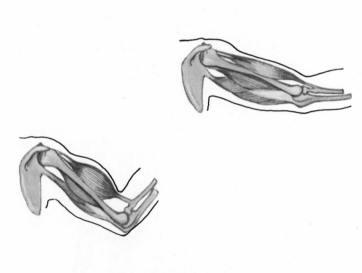

moves the bone or bones to which the muscle is attached. In order for the muscle cells to contract, they must have energy. Where does this energy come from?

Energy can be stored in the tissues which make up your muscles. Using your muscles a lot uses up stored energy very quickly. Can you explain why many sport activities have rest periods for the players?

As you look back at the activity you just did, do you know why the muscles which move the forearm contract at the same time? Do you know how the muscles in your digestive tube are able to move the food along? In order for your body to perform all the different actions it does, there must be some way of controlling the actions of the muscles. The system that controls all the activities of the body is the nervous (NUR-vuhs) system.

143

optional activities

Boil some chicken bones to remove all the meat. Let the bones dry in the sun for a few days. Let the children try to assemble a part of the chicken skeleton using pictures and models to help them see how the bones fit together. Other skeletons of small birds or animals may be assembled in the same way.

Obtain a chicken foot from a freshly killed chicken. Trim the skin from the cut end to expose the white, stringlike tendons. Separate them carefully. Use a tweezers and pull on each tendon. Let the children see that each tendon pulls up one toe and causes it to move. Lead the youngsters to understand that in our bodies muscles are attached to bones by means of similar tendons.

Activity 30/Observe can be used to help the children understand the difference between a voluntary and involuntary action of the organism. The activity shows the pupillary reflex in the eye. As light strikes the eye, the pupil, the small opening in the eyeball through which light enters the eye, becomes smaller. This action reduces the amount of light entering the eye, thus protecting the retina from damage. As the eye is kept in the dark, its pupil opens up. This change is an involuntary action controlled by the nervous system, and the person is not aware of what is happening. The children need to observe this reflex carefully, because the change in size of the pupil takes place very quickly. Other reflex actions which the students have experienced are sneezing and coughing to clear the air passages, the knee jerk reflex, and the blinking of an eye to avoid an object.

studying the picture

Have the children look at the drawing of the nervous system. Then, simply have them touch a chair or desk, and ask them if they feel the object touched. Have them wiggle their toes and ask if they feel the movement. Have them look at the drawing again and note that nerves are throughout the body. *Ask them if they think all the nerves in the body are shown.* All major nerves are indicated. *Ask them if there are nerves which are too small to be drawn in one picture and if there might be some nerves which are too small to be seen.*

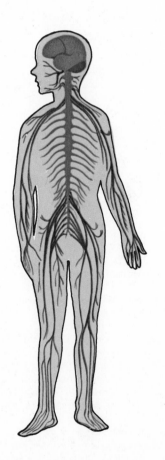

144

The nervous system is made up of organs called the brain, the spinal cord, the nerves, and the sense organs. Some nerves go from the place where a thing is touched or felt to the spinal cord and brain. Other nerves carry "messages" from the brain and spinal cord to the muscles and cause them to move. By means of these nerves you perform such activities as walking, writing, swimming, scratching, and using knives, forks, and spoons for eating.

Some parts of the nervous system tell your muscles to act without your knowing about it. Let us look at one of these actions.

30/Observe

Have one of your classmates sit so that he faces the windows in the room. Have him hold a clean handkerchief over one of his eyes for a minute. Now tell him to quickly take away the handkerchief. As he does this, look very carefully at the dark round area in the

In Testing Your Ideas, all of the statements apply to the movement of the arm. Be sure the children can explain how each statement relates to the arm's movement.

responses to 30/observe

1. The pupil of the eye becomes smaller.
2. The student is not aware that this is happening.
3. Change in size of the pupil is an automatic reflex which protects the retina by reducing the amount of light entering the eye.

middle of his eye. ①What kind of change do you see? ②Does your classmate know that this is happening? ③What do you think causes this change in his eye? Before telling him what you think has happened, exchange places and have your classmate do the activity. Share your observations and your ideas with the rest of the class. ■

An action which happens so quickly that you do not know about it until after it has taken place is called a reflex (REE-fleks) action. Can you name other reflex actions in the body. Why do you think we have reflex actions?

TESTING YOUR IDEAS

Slowly move your arm in all the directions you can. Which of the following statements do you think can be related to what you have just done?

Food gives the body the energy it needs.
Waste materials made when food is used by the cells are eventually removed by the body.
The system of the heart and blood tubes carries food to cells and removes wastes.
The skeletal system gives support to the system of muscles.
The system of muscles enables the skeleton to move.
The nervous system causes muscles to move.

OVERVIEW

The intent of this lesson is to introduce the child to the fact that his rate of growth and his state of health are unique to him alone and can be affected by proper diet, exercise, posture, and personal habits. The meaning of healthy growth, therefore, is two-fold, referring to healthy living as well as to growth.

how to begin

Ask the children how many of them can wear the same size shoe today that they wore two years ago. Ask them if they can wear the hats, gloves, and other clothes which they wore in the second grade. Then ask them why they cannot. You should attempt to have them answer specifically that they are growing. An answer such as their old shoes or gloves are too small should only be accepted tentatively and used to lead them to the discovery that they are now a different size because they have grown.

(continued on page 176)

WHAT IS HEALTHY GROWING?

Food is used in the body to give you energy to run, jump, sing, read, and grow. As you think back to how small you were a few years ago, you know that you have grown. You grow because food materials are used to make new cells in your body.

Do you keep track of how much you grow from month to month? If not, why not start now?

31/Measure

Tack a tapemeasure to the wall. Stand up straight with your back against the tapemeasure. Ask a classmate to place a ruler on your head, as shown in the pictures, and measure your height in inches. Be sure the ruler is held level.

147

process skills

Observing, measuring, and recording the height of classmates
Inferring that different individuals grow at different rates
Deducing that the rate of growth can be affected positively or negatively

materials

tacks, tape measure°, ruler°, colored paper one-half inch wide, Scotch tape

---

° one per team

Once the idea of growth is established, interest them in the concept by asking questions which suggest how differently this idea can be approached. Will they ever stop growing? When? Could they grow faster? Could they hurt their growth? Why are some people of the same age taller or shorter than others? These questions should whet the children's curiosity and be answered as they appear in the lesson.

procedure

Ask one of the pupils to read the title of the lesson aloud. Then have the children speculate on the meaning of the phrase "healthy growing." The purpose of such speculation is to have the class discover what the subject of the lesson is and to establish the idea that to grow one must be healthy. It is important to draw from the class the notion that the rate of healthy growing is uniquely particular to the individual. This idea can be discovered by doing 31/Measure.

responses to 31/measure

1. Emphasize the *average* heights, comparing the heights of all the boys as a group with the heights of all the girls as a group. Some students may be overly sensitive about being "too tall" or "too short," so be tactful when discussing individuals.

Cut a strip of colored paper 1/2 inch wide, and as tall as you are. All the girls in the class can tape their paper strips to one wall of the classroom. All the boys can tape their strips to another wall.  How does the height of the boys and the height of the girls in the class compare? Are there more tall boys or more tall girls in the class? ■

By studying the pictures you have made, you can easily see that your classmates grow at different rates. Perhaps you are shorter than your friends this year, but someday you may be taller than they.

How old are you? How tall are you? How much do you weigh? Look at the chart on page 149. It tells you the average weights of some boys and girls according to their ages and heights. Do you weigh more or less than the average for your age and weight? How much do you think you have grown this past year?

You are still growing. Your body is making new cells and your bones are still being formed. The way you stand, sit, and walk will affect the way your bones form. Look at the drawings on this page. Explain how the children in the picture are helping or hurting good growth of their bodies. How can you improve your own growth?

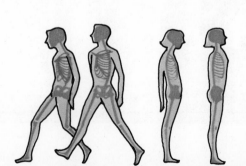

If feasible, all members of the class should be involved in 31/Measure. If the class is too large, select enough boys and girls to suggest the entire spectrum of heights in the age group of the class. At this time you should also, if possible, have the children weighed so that they can use the chart on page 149 to their advantage. Activity 31 should suggest to the class that growth is an individual matter unique to every person.

In the chart on page 149, average weight can be found where appropriate age and height columns intersect. Weight depends on many things besides diet. A large-boned child will generally weigh more than a small-boned child of the same age and height. Rate of growth also affects weight. A child's weight may be below average if the child has just grown two inches. An above-average weight may mean that the child is getting ready for a growth spurt. The chart may be used again to suggest how rate of growth is unique to the individual.

(continued on page 178)

Average Weights

BOYS

HEIGHT	9 YEARS	10 YEARS	11 YEARS
48″	53 lbs.	53 lbs.	
49″	55	55	55 lbs.
50″	58	58	58
51″	61	61	61
52″	64	64	64
53″	67	67	67
54″	70	70	70
55″	72	72	72
56″	76	76	76
57″	79	80	81
58″	83	84	84
59″		87	88
60″		91	92

GIRLS

HEIGHT	9 YEARS	10 YEARS	11 YEARS
48″	52 lbs.	53 lbs.	53 lbs.
49″	55	56	56
50″	58	59	61
51″	61	61	63
52″	64	64	65
53″	67	68	68
54″	70	70	71
55″	74	74	74
56″	76	78	78
57″	80	82	82
58″		84	86
59″		87	90
60″		91	95

149

Proper health habits may at this point be introduced, and you might first poll the class as to what habits they feel insure health. Proper diet, exercise, adequate sleep are some responses toward which the children should be directed. Your interest alone in a certain health habit such as exercise should imply the important role this factor plays in good health. A Project for You is a good launching pad for such a discussion.

The responses that might be listed in A Project for You depend in part on the individual concerned. Among the habits that are known to insure healthy growth are sleep, diet, exercise, vitamins, and, of course, a healthy emotional attitude. You may suggest to them that many of these habits should be continued in adulthood. Smoking and drugs are a possible topic for discussion of habits that should not be adopted.

Because you are yourself, you will be growing in your own special way. Because you are you, there is much you can do to make sure you stay healthy and grow properly. Do you sit, stand, and walk properly? Do you eat a balanced diet so that your body has the proper foods? Do you take care of your body? These are some of the things you can do to help yourself grow up to be healthy.

Your body is composed of cells which form tissues. The tissues go together as organs, and the organs form systems. The systems form a single living unit, an organism which is you. Throughout this unit you have been reminded that you are one single organism which is not like bricks laid together to make a wall. Your systems interact with each other in special ways, and some perform more than one function. You are not only a unit as an individual, you are unlike anyone else. You are the same single person from birth to death. The foods you eat now, the exercise you take, your posture, your habits of chewing, breathing, and training yourself in all the actions you can control will have an influence on you at present, and the influence of your present habits can extend throughout your future life.

A PROJECT FOR YOU

Proper health habits should be learned at an early age to insure a strong body and mind in adulthood. How do you care for yourself now? Make a list of the habits you have that make you strong. Also, make a list of any habits which you feel you should change. Finally, list habits you would like as an adult to keep your body healthy.

SUMMING UP THE UNIT

review

A. 1,3,4
B. 1,3,4
C. 2,5
D. 2,5

SUMMING UP THE UNIT

REVIEW

Below are listed particular statements about food and your growing body and general statements about them too. Which of the general statements about food and your growing body helps to explain each of the particular statements? A general statement may explain more than one particular statement.

Particular Statement

1. Proteins are the main foods used to build and repair body tissue.
2. Without the muscular system, foods could not be digested.
3. A balanced diet is made up of four basic food groups, minerals, vitamins, and water.
4. Carbohydrates and fats are the main energy foods.
5. Without the system of capillaries, blood could not circulate.

General Statement

A. Your body must have the right kinds of food in order to grow properly.
B. Certain kinds of materials used by the body are found in foods.
C. The human body is made of systems working together as a unit.
D. A system is made of many parts working together as a unit.

151

self-test

In the self-test, Vera was unwise not to test the food for protein as well as for carbohydrates. Some foods, such as milk, contain all three kinds of these substances.

Paula and Vera were testing a food to see if it contained starch, fat, or protein. Paula had grated the food into small pieces. Vera put some iodine into a bowl of water. The grated food was then mixed with the water. The color of the mixture turned blue-black.

"There!" said Vera. "The food contains starch!"

"Yes," said Paula, "that's true. But it might also contain fat or protein."

"Nonsense," Vera replied. "Iodine is a test for starch. There are no other things in the food."

"Isn't it possible?" Paula asked. "Why not do some tests?"

"We need no other tests," Vera commanded.

Was Vera wise not to test the food further? Try to explain your answer.

HOME PROJECTS

Construct models of the kinds of joints found in the body, using wood, screw hooks, and eyes. Show how the muscles move the bones in a hinge joint and in a ball-and-socket joint.

Obtain four hamsters and prepare a cage for each. Select healthy animals of the same size and age. To the first hamster feed a balanced diet made up of small

152

amounts of vegetables, fruits, cereals, meat, and fat, such as butter. Feed the same diet to the second hamster, but do not include cereal foods. To the third hamster, feed the same diet but do not include meat, and to the fourth hamster, give everything on the diet except fruit and vegetables. Clean the cages daily and see that the animals have enough water. Run the experiment for three weeks, feeding the animals every four hours during the day, if possible. Keep a record of the weight and condition of each animal, and make a chart showing some of the changes you have observed.

Examine a detailed illustration of the human body, showing organs, muscles, and bones. Find each of the major organs of the body, such as the lungs and heart, and then find some of the main systems. Be able to explain how each system helps the body. Look at drawings of the skeleton and the body's system of muscles, and determine in your mind how the muscles and bones work together. Be able to talk about the pictures that you have looked at and what each one represents.

Look up a good drawing of the circulatory system. Using tracing paper, draw it, using one color for the arteries and another for the veins. Display a drawing of the digestive system, which you have made in a similar manner, to your classmates. By means of arrows, show the movement of food through the digestive system. Be able to show both your charts and explain what is in them.

153

unit three
Heat as Energy

unit three

Heat as Energy

SCIENCE INFORMATION FOR THE TEACHER

Heat energy is an integral part of daily life and work. In its many forms, it is a constant accompaniment to our experience. In the human body, heat from the oxidation of food maintains an average temperature of 98.6°F. The temperature of the surrounding atmosphere is sensed by the body as comfortable or uncomfortable. When radiant energy, such as that given off by the sun, is absorbed by the skin, the sensation of heat is experienced. Plants, the ultimate source of food for animal life, use the sun's radiant energy in producing food. Heat energy cooks our food to make it tastier and easier to digest. Fuels are burned to release heat energy. Much of this heat energy can be converted to mechanical energy in machines.

Heat causes physical changes; that is, changes in appearance. As a rule, solids, liquids, and gases expand when heated. This general statement is illustrated by the increase in length of a wire when it is heated and by the increase in volume of a fluid when it is heated. It is usually true that adding heat causes a material to expand and removing heat from the material causes it to contract. An exception to this behavior is exhibited by water, which expands as it is cooled from 39°F (4°C) to its freezing point, 32°F (0°C). Because of this, the density of ice is less than the density of water. Consequently, ice floats on water.

The addition of a sufficient amount of heat can cause changes of state. Solids melt; liquids evaporate. If sufficient heat is withdrawn from a gas or vapor, it will condense to the liquid state; liquids, in turn, solidify upon loss of heat.

Heat causes chemical changes; that is, changes in the identity of substances. The original substances are destroyed and new ones are formed.

Oxidation, in its simplest interpretation, is the union of oxygen with another substance. It may occur slowly or rapidly. Slow oxidation is the gradual union of oxygen with another substance. Rusting of iron, decay of organic matter, and combustion of food in the body are examples of slow oxidation. In every oxidation, heat energy is released. In the examples just cited, it is released so gradually that there is no light, and the heat is not noticeable.

Burning is rapid oxidation. Energy is released in the form of noticeable heat and light. To start a fire, three things are needed: a material that will burn; a supply of heat at sufficiently high temperature and applied long enough to raise the material to its kindling temperature; and a supply of oxygen to support the burning.

In emphasizing the value of instruments, the teacher should not dismiss sense knowledge, especially the knowledge we get through our sense of touch, as unimportant. Were it not for our sense of touch, we would never really know what heat is, and hence not know what it is that we are measuring. By means of the sense of touch, we become aware of the physical reality of things, their weight, heat, impenetrability, and inertia. The instruments that we use in science are always refinements of sense knowledge, never an abolition of sense knowledge. If we could not trust our senses at all, we could not trust them to read our instruments.

To measure temperature, a thermometer is used. The principle of expansion is utilized in the construction of a thermometer. The body of the common liquid thermometer is formed by a glass tube with a narrow bore through its center and a bulb at its lower end. The bulb is filled with a substance such as mercury or colored alcohol. When the mercury-filled bulb comes into contact with warmer materials, the mercury expands and rises up the bore of the tube. When the bulb comes into contact with cooler materials, the mercury contracts and falls. (The expansion of the glass is minor.)

The markings on a thermometer indicate a scale. There are two scales in common use, the Celsius or centigrade, and the Fahrenheit. To calibrate a thermometer, it is necessary to establish two fixed temperature points, mark them, and divide the space between them into equal parts. The temperatures at which water freezes and boils at sea level are the fixed points on both the Celsius and Fahrenheit scales. If the thermometer is to have a Celsius scale, the points are labeled 0 and 100. The space between them is subdivided into 100 equal parts. Each space represents one degree. If the scale is to be a Fahrenheit scale, the fixed points are labeled 32 and 212. Fahrenheit, who invented this scale, used a mixture of salt and ice water to establish a fixed point lower than the freezing point of water. He then marked the scale above this point into equal parts. Thus water freezes in this scale at 32° and boils at 212°. The space between the fixed points contains 180 equal parts, each space representing one degree. This means that mercury expands or contracts through one of these spaces for each degree change in temperature it undergoes.

Three basic types of thermometers are studied in this unit: liquid, gas, and metal thermometers. The type used is governed by the range of temperatures to be measured. Alcohol boils at 172°F and freezes at

−175°F. An alcohol thermometer is good for measuring low temperatures, but it could not be used to measure the temperature of boiling water; alcohol will boil before water boils. Mercury boils at 675°F and freezes at −40°F. It is useful for measuring high temperatures. However, ovens of various kinds require a thermometer which will measure temperatures higher than 675°F. Liquid thermometers are not practical for such purposes.

A gas thermometer is a very sensitive and accurate instrument. Usually hydrogen is used as the gas, but air will serve for demonstration. The air is trapped in a bulb at the top of the thermometer tube. When the bulb comes in contact with a warmer substance, the air in the bulb gains heat and expands. The expansion of the air forces the liquid in the tube downward. Since heating the air causes the liquid to move down the tube, the higher numbers of the scale are at the bottom of the tube. The gas thermometer has two limitations. It is not practical for very high temperatures and the readings must be corrected for changes in atmospheric pressure.

A useful thermometer for measuring high temperatures is the bimetallic thermometer. It consists of two strips of different metals welded together side by side, and bent to a coil-like shape. The two metal strips expand by different amounts when they are heated. The metal having the greater rate of expansion is on the outside of the coil. Since the two strips cannot move independently, the result of heating is a tightening of the coil. A pointer is attached to the free end of the coil by means of a chain. The movement of the coil governs the movement of the pointer across a scale.

A thermometer is able to function because when two substances of different temperatures are brought in contact, heat flows from the hotter to the cooler. This transfer continues until both substances are at the same temperature. Put a thermometer at room temperature into a pot of boiling water and the thermometer will take in heat until the mercury stands at 212°F. Remove the thermometer from the water and the thermometer will lose heat to the surrounding air until the mercury stands at room temperature again.

Heat transfer is accomplished in different ways through different kinds of materials. Heat travels through solids by conduction. All metals, whether in the solid or liquid state, are good conductors of heat. Some solids, such as wood, are not good conductors. Fluids (liquids and gases) are poor conductors of heat. Poor conductors are good insulators.

Heat is transferred through the air in a room to all parts of the room. If a pot full of water is heated at its base, all the water in the pot will eventually boil, showing that the heat is transferred to all parts of the water. Fluids do not readily conduct heat. The process by which heat is transferred from one part of a fluid to another is called convection. This process should be contrasted with the first method of heat transfer, that of conduction. Convection currents are set up in a fluid because of differences in density between the warm and cold parts of the fluid. For example, when the mercury in the thermometer gains heat, it expands. The amount of mercury has not changed, but it is occupying more space. When we talk about density, we are talking about the amount of matter in a unit of volume. Thus, a cupful of hot water is less dense than a cupful of cold water. If a fluid is being heated in one area and not in all areas, the fluid near the source of heat becomes hotter; it expands and becomes less dense. The cooler, more dense fluid pushes it away and replaces it. In this way, rising and falling currents are established. Heat is transferred through fluids by the actual physical movement of heated portions of the fluid to other regions which are initially cooler.

Besides being transferred by conduction and convection, heat travels in all directions from a hot body by radiation. Radiation does not involve the movement of particles but of waves like those of light. Radiant energy becomes heat when it is absorbed by a material.

The association of heat with motion is relatively new. Some of the ancient ideas about heat were held by thinkers who did not have the instruments to test the validity of their ideas by experimentation. Heraclitus taught that heat was tiny particles that flowed from some objects with such speed that they penetrated liquid and solid materials. In early modern times, scientists advanced the idea that heat was a kind of invisible fluid. They called this fluid "caloric." This theory was held until the last century when heat came to be associated with the motion of molecules. When we speak of the flow of heat, our language still contains a relic of this view that considered heat a fluid.

The first great breakthroughs in the area of heat study were the invention of the thermometer and the establishment of objective temperature scales. Without such tools, Count Rumford's studies would have been impossible. Rumford's work made it clear beyond a doubt that heat is associated with motion, but still another half century passed before the kinetic molecular theory was developed and accepted.

At the present grade level, we do not attempt to go beyond the statement that heat is *associated* with motion because this is all that we can learn through introductory science. The idea of heat as the motion of molecules can only be indoctrination when the students must take the idea of a "molecule" on faith. This unit concentrates primarily on observable phenomena.

Because heat is capable of doing work, we can define it as a form of energy. Heat energy can be transformed into energy of other kinds. Some radiant energy of the sun is absorbed by green plants, and in photosynthesis it is transformed into chemical energy. A heated wire glows. This transformation of heat to light is utilized in the incandescent bulb. Other forms of energy can be transformed into heat energy. Chemical energy becomes heat in the burning of fuels. Electrical energy is changed to heat in toasters, irons, and heaters. Mechanical energy is transformed to heat through muscular activity and friction.

Generalization I

The gain or loss of heat can cause physical changes.

Contributing Principles and Sub-principles

A. Most materials expand when they gain heat and contract when they lose heat.
B. Many materials change state when they gain or lose heat.
    1. When enough heat is gained by a solid, it melts to a liquid; when enough heat is gained by a liquid, it evaporates to a gas.
    2. When enough heat is lost by a gas, it condenses to a liquid; when enough heat is lost by a liquid, it freezes to a solid.

Generalization II

Heat can cause chemical changes.

Contributing Principles and Sub-principles

A. Heating can separate a complex substance into its components.
B. Heating can combine simple substances to form a new, complex substance.
    1. Rusting is the combination of iron with oxygen; it exemplifies slow oxidation.
    2. Burning is rapid oxidation.

Generalization III

Heat travels from a hotter to a cooler place.

Contributing Principles and Sub-principles

A. Heat travels in solids by conduction.
    1. Some materials conduct heat better than others.
    2. Poor conductors make good insulators.
B. Heat travels in fluids by convection.
    1. Fluids (e.g., air) expand when heated; thus cold air is denser than heated air.
    2. Cold air displaces heated air, forcing it to rise.
    3. Differences in density cause convection currents in fluids.
C. No medium is required for heat travel by radiation.
    1. Radiated heat travels in all directions from any hot object.
    2. Some surfaces absorb radiated heat; some reflect it.

Generalization IV

Temperature is the measure of the degree of hotness or coldness of a substance.

Contributing Principles and Sub-principles

A. The sense of touch does not enable us to determine temperature accurately.
B. The thermometer is an instrument that is used to measure temperature accurately.
      1. Thermometers are marked with a scale based on the freezing and boiling temperatures of water.
      2. In most thermometers, temperature changes are indicated by the expansion and contraction of a gas, liquid, or solid.

Generalization V

Heat is a form of energy.

Contributing Principles

A. Heat is associated with motion.
B. Heat is capable of doing work.
C. Heat energy can be transformed into other forms of energy; other forms of energy can be transformed into heat energy.

before you begin

NEW WORDS FOR THE STUDENT

This list contains science words that will be introduced in the course of the unit. Mastery of the vocabulary is not essential. Use this list to help your students understand what they read. Do not require memorization of its contents.

Celsius a thermometer scale on which the freezing point of water is marked 0° and the boiling point of water is marked 100°

centigrade another name for the Celsius thermometer scale, a reference to the fact that this scale has 100 intervals between its fixed points *chemical change* a change in which the original substance is destroyed and one or more new substances are formed

conduction the method by which heat travels in solids, by transmission from one portion of the substance to the next

contraction decrease in volume of a substance, caused by loss of heat

convection the transfer of heat in fluids by upward and downward currents, due to local differences in density

density the amount of matter in a given volume of a substance

energy the ability to do work

expansion increase in volume of a substance, caused by gaining heat

Fahrenheit a thermometer scale on which the freezing point of water is marked 32° and the boiling point of water is marked 212°

fluid a substance that has no definite shape but flows to conform to the shape of its container; gases and liquids are fluids

gas the state of matter in which a substance has no definite shape and no definite volume; it expands to fill its container

infrared radiation invisible radiant energy that produces heat

insulator a material that conducts heat poorly, or not at all

liquid the state of matter in which a substance has a definite volume but no definite shape; it takes the shape of its container

oxidation a chemical change in which a substance combines with oxygen

physical change a change of appearance of a substance, in which the substance remains the same; e.g., expansion, contraction, change of state

radiation the method by which heat travels through space in all directions from a hot object

solid the state of matter in which a substance has both a definite volume and a definite shape

temperature the measurement of the degree of hotness or coldness of a substance

work movement of an object through a distance by a force

SCIENTISTS

Anders Celsius, 1701–1744, Swedish astronomer

Gabriel Daniel Fahrenheit, 1686–1736, German physicist

William Herschel, 1738–1822, German-born English astronomer

Benjamin Thompson, Count Rumford, 1753–1814, American-born British physicist and statesman

BOOKS FOR THE STUDENT

Adler, Irving and Ruth, *Heat*. New York. John Day, 1964.

Feravolo, Rocco V., *Junior Science Book of Heat*. Champaign, Ill. Garrard, 1964.

Feravolo, Rocco V., *Easy Physics Projects: Air, Water, Heat*. Englewood Cliffs, N.J. Prentice-Hall, 1966.

Harrison, George R., *First Book of Energy*. New York. Franklin Watts, 1965.

Lieberg, Owen S., *Wonders of Heat and Light*. New York. Dodd, Mead, 1966.

Munch, Theodore W., *What Is Heat?* Westchester, Ill. Benefic Press, 1960.

Posin, Dan Q., *What Is Energy?* Westchester, Ill. Benefic Press, 1962.

BOOKS FOR THE TEACHER

Ashford, Theodore A., *The Physical Sciences: From Atoms to Stars*. New York. Holt, Rinehart and Winston, Inc., 1967.

Blanc, Sam S., and others, *Modern Science: Earth, Space, and Environment*. New York. Holt, Rinehart and Winston, Inc., 1970.

Blough, Glenn O., and Julius Schwartz, *Elementary School Science and How to Teach It*, 4th edition. New York. Holt, Rinehart and Winston, Inc., 1969.

Gega, Peter C., *Science in Elementary Education*. New York. John Wiley, 1970.

Hone, Elizabeth, and others, *A Sourcebook for Elementary Science*. New York. Harcourt, Brace & World, 1962.

Ramsey, William, and others, *Foundations of Physical Science*. New York. Holt, Rinehart and Winston, Inc., 1967.

Wilson, Mitchell, and others, *Energy*. New York. LIFE Science Library, Time-Life Inc., 1963.

FILMS

Energy Does Work   11 minutes   B&W   COR
   Describes ways in which energy is used to do work; indicates that work is done only when something is moved. A number of sources of energy are mentioned, including food which provides energy for human muscles and gasoline which serves as an energy source for automobiles.

The Fire Triangle   13 minutes   color   FAC
   Explains that fire can occur only when fuel, heat, and oxygen are present, and shows that if any of these is withdrawn the fire will go out. Shows how firemen control fires by removing fuel so that nothing is left to burn, apply water to help reduce heat, or smother the fire with chemicals to keep oxygen away.

The Story of Heat   14 minutes   color   IFB
   Uses animation and live–action photography to describe heat, the action of molecules when heated, and kinds of fuel. Shows how to make fire by focusing sunlight through a magnifying glass and by use of a "fire horn" which produces heat through friction. Describes heat transfer by conduction, convection, and radiation.

Thermometers and How They Work   10 minutes   color   EBF
   Pictures gas, liquid, and solid thermometers and shows how they are used. Illustrates importance of temperature in everyday life. Explains the difference between Fahrenheit and Celsius scales. Relates temperature to the operation of airplanes, refrigerators, and other common devices.

Thermometers—How We Use Them   11 minutes   color   BFI
   Describes the structure and use of liquid thermometers and shows measurement of temperature in degrees on the Fahrenheit scale.

Things Expand When Heated   9 minutes   color   MGH

Illustrates that heat is essential to life and explains through animation the molecular theory that is involved. Shows some everyday
examples of expansion and contraction that pupils can see in operation about them. Revised edition.

BFI	Bailey Films, Inc.
COR	Coronet Films
EBF	Encyclopaedia Britannica Films
FAC	Film Associates of California
IFB	International Film Bureau
MGH	McGraw-Hill Textfilms

BULLETIN BOARDS

Fire: "A Good Servant but a Bad Master"

Draw or cut out pictures of fires, both controlled (e.g., gas burners on
stove, campfire) and uncontrolled (e.g. forest fire, burning house). Group
the pictures under "A Good Servant" and "A Bad Master."

Changes

Collect pictures that show changes of various kinds: ice cream melting, water boiling, a frosty windowpane, a match burning, a rusty tool,
and so on. Scatter them on the bulletin board. When the first two lessons
of this unit have been completed, challenge the students to tell you which
changes are physical and which are chemical. Or use such a bulletin
board game for review at the end of the unit.

Heat at Home

The students can collaborate on a mural showing how heat is used
in the home. Preliminary steps will include a class discussion to decide
what will be shown in the picture, choice of an art medium, and delega-
tion of roles.

Candles

Candles exemplify heat, light, radiation, convection, melting, and
chemical change. They are symbols in our private and family lives also.
Discuss how candles are used at home in family matters and in religious
celebrations. Students can plan a bulletin board to illustrate their discussion.

THE HISTORY OF THE IDEA

The sun is the major source of heat energy for the earth. Without the sun's energy, there could be no life on earth. Our planet would be exposed to the absolute cold of deep space.

One of man's very greatest steps toward civilization was gaining control of fire. This accomplishment enabled man to change his environment to suit him. All other living things must seek surroundings that are favorable to their ways of life. In unfavorable surroundings, they simply do not survive. Man alone can adjust an unfavorable environment and make it support him.

In addition to making it possible for man to live in cool climates, control of heat also makes man's life easier. We use heat to help run the complex machines that build and maintain our cities, transport us from one place to another, and allow us to communicate over long distances.

studying the picture

While the two pictures appearing on this page are illustrative of the text on page 157, they can be used to direct a child's attention to the general question of the unit: what is heat? Introduce the class to the concept of heat by asking them what heat can do. *Ask them if they can feel the sun's rays warming their bodies during summer. Can the sun, you may ask, cause a frozen pond to begin to melt on warm days? Do they think that a burning tree struck by lightning looks the same after the fires have died out? Ask them if they think heat can cause change.* Such questions will introduce the class to the first lessons of the unit.

The sun shines down and warms the earth. Heat from the sun makes the earth suitable for living things, for plants and animals. At the beginning of man's history, his only source of heat was the sun. Men had to live in parts of the earth where the weather was always warm.

As time went on, people discovered other ways of keeping warm. They learned to make clothing from animal skins and plant fibers. They "tamed" the fires that started when lightning struck trees. They took some fire home with them to give heat during the cool night hours. They discovered that heat changes food, making it easier to chew. They learned to bake a clay pot in the fire to make it hard and waterproof.

Once men knew how to control heat, they did not have to depend on the sun for all their warmth. They could live in places where the weather was sometimes cold. They were free to travel and to settle in the cold lands. They were able to spread all over the earth.

How are you using heat right now? What kind of clothes are keeping you warm? What kind of food did you eat to keep your body warm? How was heat used to prepare the food? How is your classroom kept warm? Was heat used to make the furniture in the classroom? Do you suppose heat was used to make this book? Is heat still important in our modern-day world?

the unit at a glance

Heat as energy is, at the outset, studied through experiences concerning the physical and chemical changes heat can cause. How heat travels through solids, liquids, and gases is next introduced and the means by which a quantity of heat (temperature) is measured is developed through inquiry and activities. All of the foregoing experiences provide a basis upon which heat can be defined as a movement of particles or molecules. This definition is developed through experiences and is extended, by analogy, to show that when the particles (molecules and atoms) of which matter is made have heat, they are in motion.

OVERVIEW

This lesson deals with physical changes caused by gain or loss of heat. Activities 1 and 2 review changes of state. Activities 3 to 5 demonstrate expansion and contraction in a solid, a liquid, and a gas. The student is led to define contraction and expansion through his observations. Testing Your Ideas asks the student to show his understanding of these terms by using one of them to describe what happens in a model situation.

how to begin

Recall what was learned in grade 3 in the unit "Mystery Solids, Liquids, and Gases." Ask the students to name some substances in each group. Ask, "Do you know of anything that is sometimes a liquid and sometimes a solid?" Ask, "Do you know of any one substance that can be either a solid, a liquid, or a gas?" Write the students' responses on the board for later evaluation.

process skills

Observing changes of state caused by heat

Observing expansion and contraction of solids, liquids, and gases when heated and cooled

Defining expansion, contraction, and physical change on the basis of observation

materials

ice cubes°, pan°, hot plate°, water, kettle°, 3 feet of bare copper wire°, 2 ringstands (optional), fishing sinker or bunch of metal nuts°, small soda pop bottle°, large soda pop bottle°, modeling clay, clear plastic straw°, oven mitts°, asbestos pad°, balloons°, bowl°

° per team

CAN HEAT CAUSE CHANGES?

Last year, you learned something about how chemists work. You learned about materials representing the three states of matter: solids, liquids, and gases. Most materials in our everyday world can be grouped as solids, liquids, and gases. Name some of each. Can a material be sometimes a solid and sometimes a liquid? What can make it change?

1/Observe

Put an ice cube in a pan and heat the pan on a hot plate. What is the state of matter of the ice cube? What happens to the ice cube when you heat it? Does

158

Some familiar solids the students might mention are: metal, wood, ice, paper, cloth, sugar, butter, and paraffin. Some liquids are: water, milk, soda, gasoline, liquid detergent, cooking oil, vinegar, melted butter, and melted paraffin. Some gases are: air, oxygen, nitrogen, carbon dioxide, and water vapor.

procedure

Activities 1 and 2 can be done by the teacher, with the class observing and discussing the changes. In 1/Observe, we begin with water in the solid state: an ice cube. When heat is applied, it changes to liquid water. With the addition of still more heat, the liquid evaporates to water vapor.

In 2/Compare, we see a change of state caused by loss of heat. When the water vapor strikes the ice-filled pan, it loses heat to the pan and condenses to liquid water. Ask the class, "When you have an iced drink, do you ever find that the outside of the glass gets wet? Do you suppose that there is water vapor in the air? What would happen if that water vapor touched an icy cold glass? Would it lose heat? Would it change its state?"

(continued on page 198)

---

it change to a different state of matter? What do you call this state? Keep heating the pan. How many changes of state take place, in all?

Ice is water in the solid state. When ice is heated, it melts and becomes water. When water is heated, it boils and becomes a gas called water vapor. Water is one substance that is very familiar to us in all three states of matter. Have you ever changed liquid water to a solid? Can you change water vapor to a liquid?

2/Compare

Heat some water in a kettle until it boils. Put some ice into a small pan to cool the pan. Hold the side of the cool pan near the spout of the kettle. What do you see on the side of the pan? What state was the water in as it came out of the kettle? What state was the water in after it touched the cold pan?

When a material gains enough heat, it may change from one state of matter to another. When a material loses enough heat, it may change from one state of matter to another. Which of the changes you observed were caused by gaining heat? Which were caused by losing heat?

Can heat change materials in another way? What would happen, for example, if you heated a solid but did not heat it enough to change its state?

159

responses to 1/observe

1. The ice cube is a solid.
2. The ice cube melts when heated.
3. Yes.
4. It is called the liquid state.
5. Two changes take place—from a solid to a liquid and then from a liquid to a gas.

responses to 2/compare

1. Moisture appears on the side of the pan.
2. When water came out of the kettle, it was in the form of a gas, water vapor.
3. When water vapor touched the cold pan, it changed to a liquid.

Use the questions that follow activity 2 to review change of state and introduce the next topic. The next activity sequence deals with expansion and contraction. Have the students set up the equipment for 3/Observe. Any method of suspending the weighted wire can be subsituted for the method described. Heat the wire with a candle, cigarette lighter, or propane torch, moving the flame back and forth along the wire. *Do not let the students work with an open flame.*

When the wire is heated, it will expand and become longer. The weight will hang lower. A chalk mark at this point will help the class to see the change. Label the mark "when heat was gained." As the wire returns to room temperature, it will shorten and the weight will hang higher. The upper chalk mark can be labeled "when heat was lost."

Activity 4/Compare demonstrates expansion and contraction in a liquid. When heated, the colored water will rise in the straw. As the water loses heat, it will go down again in the straw.

(continued on page 200)

for your information

It is incorrect to say that steam is water in the gaseous state. The gaseous state of water is water vapor. Steam is droplets of liquid water, formed when water vapor condenses. When you look at a kettle boiling, you notice that the steam starts a little distance away from the kettle's spout. The boiling water becomes water vapor, which comes out of the spout. As it strikes the cooler air, the water vapor condenses to steam.

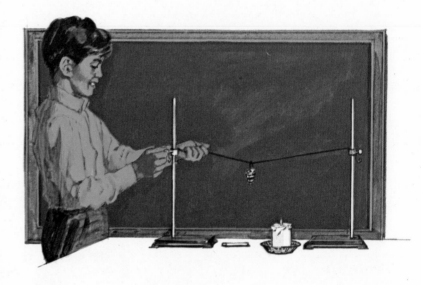

3/Observe

Take 3 feet of bare copper wire. Twist one end of the wire around the clamp of a ring stand. Hang a weight (a fishing sinker or a bunch of metal nuts) on the wire. Fasten the other end of the wire to another ring stand. Set this equipment on a table next to the chalkboard. Make a chalk mark where the weight hangs.

Your teacher will heat the wire. Where does the weight hang now? Make another mark on the chalkboard. What has happened to the length of the wire? Let the wire cool. What happens to its length now? ■

What will happen if you heat a liquid, but do not heat it enough to change its state?

160

4/Compare

Fill a small soda pop bottle with colored water. Use modeling clay to fasten a clear plastic straw into the top of the bottle, as the picture shows. Set the bottle in a small pan of water. Heat the pan and bottle on a hot plate. ① What do you see in the plastic straw?

With oven mitts on your hands, take the bottle out of the pan and put it on an asbestos pad. Let the bottle cool. ② What happens now in the plastic straw? ■

The wire is a solid. The colored water is a liquid. What was the same about the way heating changed them? Do you think that a gas will show the same kind of change when it is heated?

161

responses to 3/observe

1. Measurements should indicate that the weight hangs lower.
2. The length of the wire has increased.
3. The length of the wire will decrease.

responses to 4/compare

1. The colored water in the straw will rise.
2. The colored water in the straw will sink.

Similarly, in 5/Observe, the heated air in the bottle expands into the balloon, filling it. (Adding a few drops of water, which will change to water vapor, causes the balloon to expand more rapidly than it would if it contained only air.) Be sure to use a balloon that has been well stretched. When heat is lost to the cold water, the air contracts and the balloon goes limp again.

On the basis of these observations, the students should be able to define "expand" as meaning "get bigger (or longer)." "Contract" likewise would be defined as "get smaller (or shorter)."

The reading plateau tells of some of the ways we apply our knowledge of expansion and contraction to practical matters. Look for spaces where the rails are joined the next time you are near train tracks. The photo of the buckled pavement shows what happened to the Long Island Expressway in New York during the July 4th weekend of 1966, when the temperature hovered near 100° for three days. If there is a bridge in or near your city, a class research team might be appointed to find out what feature of the bridge's design allows for expansion and contraction.

(continued on page 202)

responses to 5/observe

1. The balloon will expand.
2. The balloon will contract.

for your information

The amount that a given liquid or solid will expand depends on how great is the increase in temperature and on how much liquid or solid is present before the heating. The larger the amount of the substance and the greater the increase in temperature, the more the substance will expand.

5/Observe

Put 2 or 3 drops of water into a large empty soda pop bottle. Fit a small balloon over the neck of the bottle as the picture shows. Heat the bottle in a pan of water on a hot plate. What happens to the balloon? Pick up the bottle with oven mitts and hold it in a bowl of cold water. What happens to the balloon now? ■

The length of the wire changed when it was heated. The water level in the plastic straw changed when the water in the bottle was heated. The size of the balloon changed when the air in the bottle was heated. What did you observe? How did all these things change?

In the language of science, we say that heating causes these materials to expand (eck-SPAND). From your observations, what do you think "expand" means?

162

When the wire lost heat, its length changed. When the water in the bottle lost heat, the water level in the straw changed. When the air in the bottle lost heat, the size of the balloon changed. What did you observe? How did all these things change?

In the language of science, we say that loss of heat causes these materials to contract (kun-TRAKT). From your observations, what do you think "contract" means?

When train tracks are put down, the rails are not placed tight against each other. A little space is left between one rail and the next. Then when the hot summer weather comes, there is room for the rails to expand. The pavement on highways has grooves in it for the same reason. If the grooves are not wide enough, or if the weather gets too hot, the paving may bump up, or "buckle." A metal bridge must be built so that one end is free to move. Then the metal of the bridge can expand in summer and contract in winter without damaging the bridge.

163

Have the children explain why the Long Island Expressway pavement buckled under extremely high temperatures. You may attempt to assess their understanding of the terms *expand* and *contract* in their study of the picture.

The latter part of the reading plateau reviews the lesson's observations and uses them to define physical change. All the changes demonstrated in this lesson are physical changes.

Evaluate the students' responses to the question posed at the beginning of the lesson. Did anyone name water? Mercury is familiar to us in two of its forms: mercury vapor is used for street and highway lighting (bluish color); liquid mercury is used in fever thermometers. Children whose mothers do some home preserving may name paraffin as being familiar in both its solid and liquid states. Most children will know butter and margarine both as solids and as liquids. To boys, solder may be familiar in both these states.

In Testing Your Ideas, the basketball will get softer when it is taken outdoors. It is filled with warm air in a warm room. It is then taken outdoors on a cold day. The air in the basketball loses heat to the cold air around it, and contracts. The material in the cover of the ball contracts, too, but not nearly so much as the air.

for your information

While things generally expand when heated and contract when cool, there are exceptions to the rule. *To emphasize the exceptions to the general rule, ask the students what happens to water when it freezes* (cools to its freezing temperature). Have the students perform this activity at home: Fill a small jar to the brim with water. Screw the cap on tightly. Place the jar in an empty tin can. Put the can with its jar of water into the freezing compartment of the refrigerator overnight. Have the students report their findings. (The jar should crack.) Ask the class to state what happens to *water* when it is cooled and freezes.

You have seen materials change from one state of matter to another as they gained and lost heat. You have seen materials expand and contract as they gained and lost heat. The materials changed in appearance, but they were still the same materials. Ice is water in the solid state, but it is still water. The copper wire gets longer and shorter as it is heated and cooled, but it is still copper wire.

When a material changes in appearance but is still the same material, the change is called a physical (FIZZ-i-k'l) change. From what you observed, can you say that heat causes physical changes?

TESTING YOUR IDEAS

If a basketball is pumped up in a warm room and then taken outdoors on a cold day, will it get harder or softer? When you answer this question, use one of these words in your explanation: expand, contract.

OVERVIEW

This lesson deals with burning in relation to chemical change. The first two activities exemplify different types of chemical change: one in which heat breaks a material down into its components (6/Compare) and one in which heat is liberated as two substances combine chemically (7/Explain). The activity sequence 8 to 11 investigates burning as a chemical change and the new substances formed by it.

how to begin

Recall that all the changes made in the previous lesson were reversible. Water can be changed to water vapor by adding heat; water vapor can be changed to liquid water by taking heat away. The air expands in the bottle when it is heated; when it loses heat, it contracts. Ask: "Can you think of some changes, caused by heat, that cannot be undone by taking heat away?"

WHAT OTHER CHANGES CAN HEAT CAUSE?

In activity 2, you heated water until it turned to water vapor. Then, with a cold pan, you turned the water vapor back to liquid water. Heat makes many kinds of changes. Can the changed material always be changed back again to its original form?

6/Compare

Put a spoonful of sugar in a metal jar lid. Heat the lid on a hot plate until the sugar melts and then chars. 1What color is the substance that is left? 2Does it look like sugar? Does it taste like sugar? 3When it cools, does it turn back to sugar? ■

The substance left in the pan is carbon. It is one of the substances that make up sugar. When you heated the sugar, it broke down into different substances. When a material is broken down and one or more new substances are formed, the change is called a chemical (KEM-i-k'l) change.

165

process skills

Defining chemical change in terms of observations and experiences

Identifying the products of burning by tests

Identifying the conditions needed for burning

materials

sugar, 2 metal jar lids*, steel wool*, detergent, water, 2 candles, modeling clay, aluminum foil dish, oven mitts, limewater, pint jar with lid to fit, quart jar

---

* per team

responses to 6/compare

1. The substance is black.
2. It does not look or taste like sugar.
3. It does not turn back to sugar.

203

procedure

The sugar in 6/Compare is decomposed by heating; it is broken down into its components. Sugar is composed of hydrogen, oxygen, and carbon. What is left in the lid is carbon, the substance that makes up coal and charcoal, and is contained in the "lead" in your pencil. The reaction began with sugar. Heat was supplied, and the result was carbon. When it cooled, it was still carbon. The sugar has been changed permanently into another substance because the other components were given off as water vapor.

The steel wool in 7/Explain should be plain steel wool, purchased in a hardware store. Do not use scouring pads, even the soapless ones; nearly all scouring pads are treated to prevent rusting. The steel wool from the hardware store will have a light coating of oil as a rust preventive; this is removed when you wash the steel wool in detergent and water. After being left overnight, the steel wool will show spots of rust. If it is left a week or more, the whole pad will have turned to rust. Instead of being hard, metallic and resilient, it will be crumbly and reddish-brown.

responses to 7/explain

1. The steel wool has partly turned rusty.
2. The rust spots are crumbly and flaky.
3. The student's fingers should be rusty red.
4. A new substance has formed.
5. A chemical change has taken place.

responses to 8/observe

1. The candle is producing heat.

7/Explain

Wash some steel wool in detergent and water. Rinse it thoroughly. Place the damp steel wool on a jar lid and leave it overnight. Look at it the next day. Touch it. Does it look the same? Does it feel the same? What do you see on your fingers? Has a new substance been formed? What kind of change has taken place? ■

Steel is a form of iron. The iron combines with oxygen (AHK-si-j'n) in the air to form a new substance called rust. Another name for rust is iron oxide (AHK-side). Rusting is a slow combination of iron with oxygen. It produces a little heat, but so little that you cannot feel it. Fast combination with oxygen produces enough heat to feel—in fact, enough to burn!

Set a candle upright with modeling clay in an aluminum foil dish. Your teacher will light the candle and place an empty pint jar over it.

8/Observe

Touch the side of the jar very carefully and quickly. Is the candle producing heat? ■

When something burns, it joins quickly with oxygen. Did you notice the heat from this fast burning in

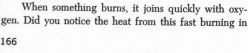

The rusting of iron is slow oxidation. Burning is rapid oxidation. Activity 8/Observe shows that this reaction produces noticeable heat. The new substances produced are water, identified in activity 9, and carbon dioxide, identified in activity 10. The students should be familiar with the limewater test for carbon dioxide from their study of "Mystery Solids, Liquids, and Gases" in grade 3, but they will benefit from a brief review.

(continued on page 206)

oxygen? If burning is a chemical change, one or more new substances must come from it. You can find out what they are.

9/Identify

1. Is the candle still burning inside the jar? Look at the inside surface of the jar. Do you see small drops of moisture? Can you guess what this moisture is?

Your teacher will pick up the jar with oven mitts and place it on a pad or pot holder. Cover the jar with a saucer and set it aside for a few minutes. When the jar has cooled, touch the moisture with your finger. Taste it. Now do you know what it is? ■

167

1. The candle will burn for as long as there is oxygen in the jar.
2. The moisture is water.

note

Chemical and physical changes will be discussed at much greater length and in much greater detail in grade 5. At this level, the discussion in the student text is quite adequate.

Note that the jar is turned upside down in activity 10. Carbon dioxide is heavier than air. If you just lifted the jar off the plate, you would lose all the carbon dioxide.

Use the questions that follow activity 10 to review the definition of chemical change and to identify burning as a chemical change. You did not time the burning of the candle in activity 10, so the question "How long did it take to stop burning?" can be answered only in general terms.

In 11/Compare, you will time the two candles burning under jars of different sizes. Use two candles of the same size and type, so that the only difference will be the size of the jar (and thus the amount of oxygen supplied to the candle). When all the available oxygen is used up, the oxidation reaction will stop. The candle will go out. The reading plateau that follows activity 11 discusses the other conditions for burning.

(continued on page 208)

responses to 10/identify

1. The limewater turns milky.
2. Carbon dioxide is in the jar.

responses to 11/compare

1. The candle in the quart jar burned longer.
2. There are different amounts of oxygen in the jar.
3. The quart jar contained more oxygen.

10/Identify

Your teacher will replace the jar over the burning candle. Leave it until the candle goes out. Using oven mitts, turn the dish and jar upside down. Take the dish away and quickly cover the jar with a lid. Lift the lid just far enough to let you pour some limewater into the jar. Then screw the lid on firmly and swirl the limewater around in the jar. 1 What happens to the limewater? 2 What gas do you think is in the jar? ▪

These two activities tell you what new substances are formed when a candle burns. Is burning a chemical change? How do you know?

In activity 10, how long did it take for the candle to stop burning? Why did the candle stop burning?

Set up two candles in aluminum dishes. Your teacher will light them both, and then cover one with a pint jar and the other with a quart jar.

11/Compare

Record the time it takes for each to stop burning. What do your records tell you? ①Which candle burned longer? ②What was different when the two candles started burning? ③What did one jar contain more of? ■

If burning is combining with oxygen, what will happen when most of the oxygen is used up? Can a material combine with oxygen when there is too little oxygen left?

For burning, three things are needed. First you must have a material that is able to burn. Was the candle wax able to burn? Why did it stop burning? The second thing you need is a supply of oxygen. Did the candles have a supply of oxygen? What happens when the supply is used up?

The third thing you need is heat. How did you start the candle burning? You can light a candle with a match, but can you set a log burning with just one match? Different materials start to burn at different temperatures. So you need not just *some* heat, but *enough* heat to start a particular material burning.

When you build a fire, you start with crumpled paper. Then you add some chips and small sticks of

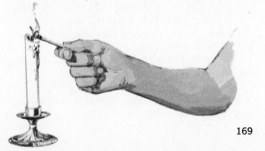

To show another type of chemical change, heat a piece of bare copper wire in the flame. *Caution: hold the wire with insulated gloves.* When the oxygen in the air unites with the hot copper, a coating of black copper oxide is formed. Scrape some of this material onto a plate and ask the students to examine it. Distinguish this black copper oxide from black carbon. They both have similar *physical* appearances, but they differ *chemically.*

In Testing Your Ideas, only the rusting of Rose's bicycle was not caused by gaining or losing heat. (Note that some heat is produced by rusting, but heat does not cause the reaction.) The expansion of the balloon and the melting of the snowman are physical changes. The burning of wood is a chemical change.

optional questions

Ask the students if small wood chips are made of a different material than a large log. They may be different kinds of wood, but they are both wood. Ask, *"Why, then, does it require more heat to ignite small wood chips than to ignite a large log?"* It might be that one kind of wood requires more heat than another to reach its kindling temperature, but it might also be that the amount of material being ignited makes the difference. Lead the students to see that these two possibilities exist, if they don't suggest them themselves. *Ask the students how they might test to find out which is actually the reason.* They could try to ignite a large log made of a certain kind of wood and then try to ignite small chips of the same kind of wood, using the same amount of heat in each case. This would indicate whether or not the amount of material makes a difference.

wood. On top of that, you put large sticks and small logs. A match sets fire to the paper. The burning paper produces enough heat to start the chips and small sticks burning. The burning sticks and chips give off enough heat to start the big sticks and small logs burning. When the small logs are burning, the fire is hot enough for a big log.

TESTING YOUR IDEAS

Jack blew some air into a balloon. He put the balloon on a sunny windowsill. The balloon got bigger.

Rose left her bicycle out in the rain. It got rusty.

Peter and Emily built a snowman in their backyard. After a week, it had melted away.

When Tom's Boy Scout troop went camping, they burned some wood to cook their dinner.

Which of these changes were caused by gaining or losing heat? Which were physical changes? Which were chemical changes?

170

OVERVIEW

Conduction, the method by which heat travels through solids, is the subject of this lesson. Activities 12 and 13 establish the fact that heat does travel through solids. Activities 14 and 15 investigate the way in which heat travels through solids. Relative speeds of heat traveling through different solids are explored in activities 16 and 17, and in the process insulators are defined. Testing Your Ideas evaluates the students' understanding of conductors and insulators.

how to begin

Recall activity 1/Observe. Discuss with the class what happened. You put an ice cube in a pan. You heated the pan. Heat melted the ice cube; heat caused the water to boil away as water vapor. Where did the heat come from? (Hot plate) How did the heat get through the pan to the ice?

HOW DOES HEAT TRAVEL THROUGH SOLIDS?

When you boil water in a pan, how does the heat get through the pan to the water? How does heat get to you from the heating unit on the other side of the classroom? How does heat get from the sun to the earth? How does heat travel? You can find out about the way heat travels by doing a few activities.

12/Observe

At lunchtime today, put a metal spoon into a bowl of hot soup. Leave it there for a few minutes. From time to time, touch the handle of the spoon. What do you notice? Does heat travel through the spoon? ■

171

process skills

Observing conduction of heat in solids

Comparing the rates at which heat is conducted through various solids

Defining conductor and insulator on the basis of observations

materials

hot water, cold water, 2 metal cups*, 2 solid metal curtain rods of different metals*, wooden rod*, glass rod*, coffee can*, hot plate, plastic cup*

For the teacher: candle, flame source

---

* per team

responses to 12/observe

1. The handle of the spoon becomes warm.
2. Heat travels through the spoon.

procedure

The questions posed at the beginning of this lesson will be answered in the course of the next three lessons. Do not expect answers immediately.

Activity 12 is an observation that the students can make at leisure. If you want, you can put a spoon in a cup of hot water and have the children make the observation in the classroom. Having observed that heat travels through solids, the students can use

13/Observe to determine the direction in which heat travels.

Heat travels from a place of greater heat to a place of less heat. The hot tumbler has more heat than my hand. Heat is transferred to my hand from the tumbler. My hand has more heat than the cold tumbler. Heat is transferred from my hand to the cold tumbler.

The rod for 14/Test can be prepared by the class and the teacher together. Students can mark the spacing on the rod. The teacher can drip the candle wax

responses to 13/observe

1. The cup feels hot.
2. The cup is hotter than your hand.
3. Heat travels from a place of greater heat (the cup) to a place of lesser heat (your hand).
4. The cup feels cold.
5. Your hand is hotter than the cup.
6. Heat travels from your hand to the cup.

The metal spoon carries the heat of the soup to your hand. Which was hotter, the soup or the spoon? Which was hotter, the spoon or your hand? Which way does the heat travel: from hot to cold or from cold to hot?

13/Observe

Pour some very hot water into a metal cup. Touch the cup with your hand. 1 What do you feel? 2 Which is hotter, the cup or your hand? 3 In which direction is heat traveling?

Pour some very cold water into a metal cup. Touch the cup with your hand. 4 What do you feel? 5 Which is hotter, the cup or your hand? 6 In which direction is heat traveling? ■

Do you think it is true to say that heat travels from a place where there is more heat to a place where there is less heat? The spoon and the cup were both made of metal. Both of them were made of solid materials. How does heat travel through solid materials?

210

on the marks and the students can place the tacks. The teacher can then hold one end of the rod in the candle flame. Use a potholder or oven mitt to hold the rod. The tacks will fall off in order of increasing distance from the flame. Heat is transferred from the portion of the rod in the flame, to the next portion, and so on to the end. Activity 15 presents a model of this method of heat travel, which is then identified as conduction.

(continued on page 212)

14/Test

Take a solid metal curtain rod. Attach tacks to it with a few drops of candle wax. Space the tacks about 2 inches apart. Watch as your teacher holds one end of the rod in a flame. Which tack drops off first? In what order do the rest of the tacks fall off? Which one falls off last? What does this test tell you about the way heat travels through the rod? ▪

15/Model

Take six of these textbooks. Set them up on a table top about 4 inches apart. Look at the picture. Tap the first book just hard enough to knock it over. What happens to the rest of the books? How is this model like what happened in activity 14? Does heat seem to be passed on from one portion of the rod to the next? ▪

173

responses to 14/test

1. The tack closest to the flame drops off first.
2. The tacks fall off in order of increasing distance from the flame.
3. The tack farthest from the flame drops off last.
4. Heat travels from a place of greater heat (the flame) to a place of lesser heat (the other end of the rod).

responses to 15/model

1. The books fall over one after another in a direction away from the first book tapped.
2. In activity 14, there was also movement in a direction, i.e., away from the heat source.
3. Heat seems to be passed from one portion of the rod to the next.

In 16/Compare, the students will discover that heat travels through different solids at different rates. The metal rods will prove to be good conductors; the glass rod and the wooden rod are poor conductors, and thus good insulators. Use the material that follows activity 16 to define insulator and to discuss the use of insulators in our daily lives.

Insulation is placed in the spaces between walls of most homes. Ceilings and floors are also insulated. Most insulation is made of a fireproof, fibrous material that reduces the flow of heat from the warm interior of the house to the colder outside; and likewise, from the warm outside, during the summer, to the cooler inside.

Metal cooking pots often have wooden handles because wood is a poor conductor of heat.

The material of a pot holder (cloth and cotton padding) is a poor conductor of heat.

Activity 17/Compare reviews the concepts learned in the lesson: conduction, direction of heat

for your information

Heat is transferred from place to place by conduction, convection, and radiation, each of which is studied in this lesson and the following two lessons. In this lesson, we are concerned with how heat travels through solids by conduction. Conduction is direct transfer of heat from molecule to molecule within the material. Solids are better conductors of heat than are liquids, and liquids are better conductors than are gases. The explanation for this lies in the fact that molecules of a solid are much closer together than are molecules of a liquid and the molecules of a liquid are much closer together than molecules of a gas.

This method is the way heat travels in solid materials. It is called conduction (kun-DUCK-shun). Do all solid materials conduct heat at the same speed?

16/Compare

Cut off a 7-inch piece of the curtain rod you used in activity 14. Get three other rods of the same size, but of different materials. Another metal, wood, and glass are good examples.

Make four holes in the lid of a coffee can. The holes should be just big enough to hold the rods. Pour 1 inch of water into the can and put the lid on the can. Push one rod through each hole so that the end of the rod is in the water. Use wax to attach a tack to the upper end of each rod.

Put the can on a hot plate. Heat the water in the can. 1 Which tack drops off first? 2 Which one drops off last? 3 Which material is the best conductor of heat? 4 Which is the poorest conductor of heat? ■

travel, and insulation. The metal cup is a good conductor. Heat is transferred rapidly from your hand to the metal, and so your hand feels very cold. The plastic cup is a poor conductor (good insulator). Heat is transferred much less rapidly from your hand to the plastic cup, and so your hand feels much less cold. The plastic is more comfortable to hold. For similar reasons, you would choose the wooden stick for toasting marshmallows. The metal rod would transfer heat rapidly to your hand and might burn it.

(continued on page 214)

Different solids conduct heat at different speeds. Metals are generally good conductors of heat. Heat travels through them fast. Wood is a poor conductor. Heat travels through it much more slowly. Materials that are poor conductors of heat are called insulators (IN-suh-late'rz).

Are the walls of your home insulated? How do you suppose insulated walls help to keep your home warmer in winter and cooler in summer? Why do metal cooking pots often have wooden handles? What is the use of pot holders?

17/Compare

Fill the metal cup with very cold water again. Fill a plastic cup of the same size with very cold water. Touch the metal cup with your left hand. Touch the plastic cup with your right hand. Which hand feels colder? Which cup is conducting heat away from your

175

responses to 16/compare

1. The tack on the metal rod drops off first.
2. The tack on the wooden rod will drop off last.
3. Metal is the best conductor of heat.
4. Wood is the poorest conductor of heat.

responses to 17/compare

1. The hand on the metal cup feels colder.
2. The metal cup conducts heat away from your hand faster.

(continued)

In Testing Your Ideas, heat will be conducted through rod A in the manner you demonstrated in activity 15/Model. Heat will be conducted through rod B until it reaches the wooden section. Wood is an insulator. Little or no heat will be conducted through the wood to the remaining portion of the rod. The tack will fall off rod A but not off rod B.

responses to 17/compare

(continued)

3. The metal cup is the better conductor.
4. The plastic cup is the better insulator.
5. Metal would make a better pot.
6. Plastic would make a better handle.

hand faster? 3 Which is the better conductor? 4 Which is the better insulator? 5 Which material would make a better pot? 6 Which would make a better handle for a pot? ■

Suppose you made a campfire to toast marshmallows. You looked around for something you could use to hold the marshmallows in the fire. You found a long thin metal rod and a long thin wooden stick. Which would you use for toasting the marshmallows? Explain your choice.

TESTING YOUR IDEAS

The picture below shows two metal rods. Rod A is one single piece of metal. Rod B has had a section cut out of it and replaced with wood. Both rods have tacks attached to them with candle wax at the right-hand end. Both rods are being heated at the left-hand end. Which tack will fall off first, the one on rod A or the one on rod B? When you explain your prediction, use the words conduct and insulate.

a

b

OVERVIEW

Convection, the method by which heat travels through fluids, is the subject of this lesson. Activity sequence 18-19 tests a liquid and a gas for conductivity and leads the student to conclude that heat does not travel through fluids by conduction. Activity 20 demonstrates currents in a gas. The currents are identified as convection currents, the means by which heat is transferred in fluids. Activity 21 and the reading plateau help the student understand that differences in density explain why convection currents form. Convection currents in a liquid are demonstrated in activity 22. Activity 23 asks the student to put his learnings to work predicting what convection currents he expects to find in a concrete situation: the classroom. Testing Your Ideas asks the student to explain the results of activities 18 and 19 in terms of convection.

how to begin

Ask, "How does heat travel through solids? (Conduction, from one portion of the object to the next) How do you think heat travels through liquids; for example, water? Can you boil some ice water without melting the ice?"

HOW DOES HEAT TRAVEL THROUGH LIQUIDS AND GASES?

You have tested some solid materials to find out how they conduct heat. Now test a common liquid, water.

18/Test

Drop a small piece of ice into a test tube and wedge it in place with some steel wool. Fill the test tube with water. The steel wool will hold the ice in place but will let the water pass through.

Watch while your teacher heats the test tube over a flame. Notice that the test tube is being heated at the top, as the picture shows. When the water at the top

process skills

Testing a liquid and a gas for conduction of heat

Observing convection currents as the method of heat transfer in fluids

Identifying differences in density as the cause of convection currents in fluids

materials

ice, test tube, test tube holder, steel wool, water, strong wire, milk bottle, cardboard, rope, brick*, large sponge*, scale*, Pyrex glass coffee pot*, hot plate, sawdust (or shavings from a pencil sharpener), tissue paper, long stick (broomstick, mop handle)*

For the teacher: flame source, candle

---
* one per team

215

Activity 18/Test is a surprising demonstration of the lack of conduction in a liquid. The class is likely to be amazed at the results. Do not try to investigate the "why" of this activity now; by the end of the lesson it should be clear to the students.

responses to 18/test

1. Water is a poor conductor of heat.

optional questions

Obtain some small samples of fur for the students to examine in connection with the following. *Ask the students to describe all the differences they can notice between fur and other clothing materials.* Someone should note that the individual hairs have air spaces between them. *Ask the students why they think fur coats are warmer than cloth coats in winter.* The air between the individual hairs acts as an insulator and helps to retain body heat.

procedure

Having shown that water is not a good conductor of heat, you can now test whether air conducts heat, using 19/Compare. The student will feel intense heat from the flame only when his hand is held above the flame. At a distance of 10 inches to either side of the flame, he will detect little heat. (This heat is due to radiation.)

of the test tube is boiling, look at the bottom of the tube. 1 If the ice has not melted away, what can you say about water as a conductor of heat? ■

If you had time to make enough tests, you would find that almost all liquids, except liquid metals like mercury, are poor heat conductors. How about gases? Air is the most common gas. Is air a good heat conductor?

19/Compare

Your teacher will light a candle. Hold your hand about 10 inches above the candle flame. 1 Can you feel the heat? Now hold your hand 10 inches from the side of the flame. 2 Do you feel the heat? 3 Is heat traveling sideways from the candle flame? ■

Air is all around the flame. If air conducts heat, you should find no difference at the same distance above and to the sides of the flame. Is air a good or poor conductor of heat? There is a layer of air between the storm window and the regular window of a house. How does this air space help to insulate the house?

You have tested the heat properties of a common liquid and a common gas. What have you discovered about them as conductors of heat? Liquids and gases can be grouped under the name of fluids (FLOO-idz). You see every day that heat can travel through water and through air. If it does not travel by conduction, how does heat travel through fluids?

Liquids and gases are identified as fluids. Ask the class to name some fluids in addition to the water and air discussed in the text. The students can prepare the materials for 20/Observe. *The handling of the lighted candle should be reserved to the teacher.* The first time the candle is lowered into the bottle, it goes out after a little while. When the candle is lowered into the bottle the second time, and the cardboard T is placed in the neck of the bottle, the candle burns on. Smoke from the rope is observed to drift down on one side of the T and up on the other. Simply make these observations; do not seek an explanation until after density has been discussed later in this lesson. The paragraph following activity 20 identifies the currents on opposite sides of the T as convection currents.

(continued on page 218)

20/Observe

Wrap a few turns of wire around a candle. Leave about 15 inches of wire for a handle. Bend the handle straight up next to the candle and bend the end of it into a hook. Your teacher will light the candle and lower it into a milk bottle by its wire handle. 1 What happens to the candle flame in a little while?

Take the candle out of the bottle. Blow into the bottle two or three times to change the air in the bottle. Cut a T-shaped piece out of cardboard. The stem of the T should just fit into the neck of the milk bottle. Your teacher will light the candle and lower it into the bottle again. Quickly put the cardboard T into the neck of the bottle. 2 What happens to the candle flame this time?

Is there a difference? Why? Your teacher will light one end of a piece of rope and then blow out the flame.

179

responses to 19/compare

1. Yes, the heat can be felt.
2. No, the heat cannot be felt.
3. Heat is not traveling sideways from the flame.

responses to 20/observe

1. The candle flame goes out.
2. The candle continues to burn.

(continued)

Convection currents are caused by differences in density in adjacent portions of the fluid. To understand convection, we must investigate density. Activity 21/Compare establishes the definition of density:

Density is weight per unit volume or, in the students' vocabulary:

When you have two things that are exactly the same size, but they differ in weight, then they have different densities.

Read and discuss the reading plateau that follows activity 21. To evaluate the students' grasp of the concept, do 22/Observe. Ask the students to explain what is happening. The water is being heated only at one point. The sawdust will trace the currents of cooler water down toward the point where the water is being heated, and the currents of heated water up away from this point.

(continued on page 220)

responses to 20/observe

(continued)

3. The smoke goes out of the bottle on one side of the T, and air goes into the bottle on the other side of the T.

responses to 21/compare

1. The brick weighs more than the sponge.

responses to 22/observe

1. There is a down current on the side of the pan which is not being heated.
2. The water is being heated on one side of the pan only.
3. There is an up current on the side of the pan which is being heated.
4. Different parts of the water are moving.

While the rope is still smoking, hold it next to one side of the T. **3** Where does the smoke go? Now hold the smoking rope on the other side of the T. Where does the smoke go? ■

Hot air is carrying the smoke upward on one side of the T. What is happening on the other side? The smoke shows that cool air is sinking into the bottle on the other side of the T. The upward and downward drafts of air are called convection (kun-VECK-shun) currents. Heat travels through fluids by the method called convection.

To understand the reason for convection currents in fluids, you must understand the meaning of the word "dense." What do you think of when you read about a "dense forest"? The word "dense" can be applied to all matter. Let's find out why.

21/Compare

Weigh a brick and record the weight. Measure the brick carefully and cut a large sponge to the exact same size as the brick. Weigh the sponge and record its weight. **1** Which weighs more, the brick or the sponge? Which weighs less? ■

The brick and the sponge occupy exactly the same amount of space. Which one weighs more? When you have two things that are exactly the same size, but differ in weight, then they have different densities (DEN-si-teez). The one with the greater weight for the same size has the greater density. The one with the lower weight for the same size has the lower density.

Now apply this idea to fluids. You know that water and air expand when they are heated and therefore become less dense. If you poured a cupful of very hot water and let it cool, you would have a little less than a cupful of cool water. If you measured out a cupful of very hot water and a cupful of cold water, the cupful of very hot water would weigh a little less.

The cupful of cold water, being a little bit heavier than the cupful of hot water would really have a little more water in it. Cold water is denser than hot water. Likewise, cold air is denser than hot air. The greater weight of the denser material makes it fall to the bottom of the container. It pushes up the less dense material. Can you use these facts to explain what you saw happening in activity 20?

Convection takes place in fluids because different parts of the fluid have different densities. The different densities result from one part of the fluid being heated more than another. What happens when you heat a pot of water unevenly?

22/Observe

Fill a Pyrex glass coffee pot with water. Set the pot on a hot plate so that only one side of the pot is on the heating unit. Look at the picture. When the water has come to a full boil, add a teaspoonful of sawdust to the water in the pot. The sawdust will help you to see the movement of the water. (1)Where is there a down current? (2)Where is the water being heated? (3)Where is there an up current? (4)Is heat traveling through the water or are different parts of the water actually moving? ■

181

In the metric system, the density of fresh water is 1 gram/cubic centimeter at a temperature of 4°C. By comparison, the density of lead is 11.3 grams/cubic centimeter; that of air is 0.0013 grams/cubic centimeter; and that of cork is 124 grams/cubic centimeter. The density of any substance can be found by simply dividing its weight by its volume.

Apply the concept of convection currents to the classroom air, as directed in 23/Predict. You can expect to find rising air currents over heat sources, falling air currents near sources of cold air; at the top of the window, heated air will generally be found streaming out of the room; at the bottom of the window, cool fresh air will be spilling into the room.

Discuss with the class the results that were observed in activity 20. Why did the candle go out when it was first lowered into the bottle? The candle flame warmed the air in the bottle. The air expanded. The expanding warm air "plugged" the neck of the bottle and prevented fresh air from coming in to keep the candle burning. As a model of this condition, you might refer to someone trying to come in to the doorway of the school at dismissal time when the students are rushing out.

When the T is inserted in the neck of the bottle, it is as if the departing students were allowed to use only one half of the doorway. The other half remains free for traffic in the opposite direction. Cold air can push down on one side of the T and force the less dense warm air to pass out on the other side.

responses to 23/predict

1. At the top of an open window, the streamers will probably flutter toward the out-of-doors.

2. Near the bottom of an open window, the streamers will probably flutter toward the inside of the room.

3. Near a heating unit, streamers will flutter upwards. Near an air conditioner, the streamers will flutter downwards. (Caution: the streamers should not be placed too closely to the air conditioner because they will extend straight out from the force of the blowing air.)

Cut some narrow streamers of very thin tissue paper. Tape them to the end of a long stick. Use this stick to test for air currents in different parts of the classroom. But first, tell what you expect to find in each place you will test.

23/Predict

1. What do you expect to find near the top of an open window? 2. What do you expect to find near the bottom of an open window? 3. What do you expect to find near the heating unit or air conditioner? Test these places and as many others as you can think of. Were your guesses correct? ■

If you have a window that opens at top and bottom, how would you arrange the openings to get the best circulation of air?

In Testing Your Ideas, the students are asked to explain two other observations in terms of convection. In 18/Test, the test tube was heated at the *top;* the ice was confined to the *bottom* of the tube. The cooler water would tend to sink to the bottom and the warmer water to rise to the top. So no convection was taking place. The hot water stayed at the top of the tube and got hotter; the water in the middle of the tube insulated the ice cube against the heat.

In 19/Compare, rising currents of heated air were felt when you held your hand above the candle flame. The heated air travels up, not sideways, so you did not feel the heat at the sides of the flame.

In activity 18, water was boiled in a test tube containing an ice cube. Explain what happened, in terms of convection currents.

In activity 19, you held your hand 10 inches above a candle flame, and then 10 inches to the side of the candle flame. Explain what you observed, in terms of convection.

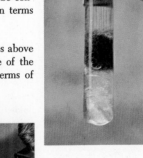

183

OVERVIEW

A third method of heat transfer, radiation, is investigated in this lesson. The first activity establishes that there is a method of heat transfer that is neither conduction nor convection. The investigations grouped under 25/Compare help the students determine that radiant heat is reflected from light and shiny surfaces, and absorbed by dark and dull surfaces. On the basis of the lesson's experiences, the students are asked to predict the result of activity 26. The reading plateau describes a Thermos bottle, an everyday application of our knowledge of heat transfer by conduction, convection, and radiation. Testing Your Ideas evaluates the student's grasp of the principles of reflection and absorption of radiated heat.

how to begin

Read and discuss the first paragraph to define the problem. For heat transfer by conduction or convection, a medium is needed; heat must travel *through something* when it travels by these methods. The distance between the sun and the earth is not filled with a solid material, so heat from the sun does not reach the earth by conduction. The distance is not filled

process skills

Comparing absorption of radiated heat by light colored objects and dark colored objects

Defining reflection and absorption

Predicting the results of a test

materials

unshaded electric lamp, 2 thermometers*, white cloth*, black cloth*, 2 pint jars*, water, white paper*, black paper*, cardboard, empty tin cans all the same size (e.g., soup cans), paints of various colors, large juice can, 2 tacks

For the teacher: can opener, candle

*per team

HOW DOES HEAT TRAVEL THROUGH SPACE?

The sun is far off in space. There is no solid material between the earth and the sun. There is no liquid or gas filling the space between the earth and the sun. How does heat travel from the sun to the earth? Heat travels in solids by conduction. Heat travels through fluids by convection. But how does heat travel through airless space?

24/Observe

Move your hand around an unlighted electric bulb. Do you feel any heat from it in any position? Turn the light on and move your hand around the bulb again. In which position do you feel the heat from the bulb?

184

with a liquid or a gas; the air ends a few hundred miles above the earth's surface. So heat from the sun does not reach the earth by convection. Yet we know that the sun's heat does reach the earth. How does it travel?

procedure

Have each student in turn feel for heat in all directions around an unlighted electric bulb, as directed in 24/Observe. No heat will be felt from the unlighted bulb. Have each one try it again with the light turned on. Heat will be felt in all directions around the bulb.

There is air between the bulb and your hand. Heat travels through air by convection. The heated air rises, so your hand will receive heat from the bulb by convection only when your hand is above the bulb. Yet you will feel the heat when your hand is below the bulb and beside it. In this case, the heat is traveling through a gas, but it does not depend on the gas to carry it. When heat reaches the earth from the sun, it travels by radiation through airless space.

(continued on page 224)

3 What is between the bulb and your hand? **4** Where must your hand be to receive heat from the bulb by convection? **5** Did you feel heat from the bulb when your hand was in any other position? ■

Heat travels in all directions from any hot object. This kind of heat travel is called radiation (ray-dee-AY-shun). When heat travels by radiation, it moves outward from the hot object without needing a solid or a fluid to carry it.

Hold your hand in the sunlight. Do you feel warmth? Does heat come from the sun? What happens to the heat that radiates from hot objects? What happens to heat from the sun? What happens when it strikes an object on the earth?

25/Compare

a. Place two thermometers in the sunlight. Put a white cloth over one thermometer and a black cloth over the other. **1** Every 5 minutes for half an hour, read and record the temperature on each thermometer.

responses to 24/observe

1. No.
2. Heat is felt in all positions.
3. Air is between the bulb and your hand.
4. Your hand must be above the bulb to receive heat by convection.
5. Yes, heat can be felt in other positions.

responses to 25/compare

1. The thermometer under the black cloth shows the greater temperature change.

(continued)

The three activities in 25/Compare show what happens when light strikes a surface. Direct half the work teams in the class to make comparison A. Make sure that both thermometers show the same temperature to begin with. Record this temperature. The A teams will find that the thermometer under the black cloth shows a greater temperature change.

At the same time, the remaining teams can be doing comparison B. Fill the jars from a single container so that the water in both jars will be at the same temperature. Tape the paper in place or fasten it with a rubber band. Make sure that both thermometers show the same temperature at the start of the activity. Record this temperature. The thermome-

ter in the black-wrapped jar will show the greater temperature change.

A tentative conclusion the class might draw from comparisons A and B could be: black things take in heat better than white things. This assumption can be tested by doing comparison C. In addition to the suggestions in the activity, paint some cans in light colors and some in dark colors. Try painting one can in red enamel and another in red flat paint. (You can paint the can for 26/Predict at the same time.)

Fill the cans, cover them, and insert the thermometers. Each team can be responsible for one can. After 5 minutes, each team will record the starting temperature for its can on a large sheet of paper. Set

responses to 25/compare
(*continued*)

2. The thermometer in the black-wrapped jar shows the greater temperature change.
3. The black can painted with "flat" paint should show the greatest difference.
4. A light, shiny can should show the least difference.

responses to 26/predict

1. The tack on the black side of the can will fall off first.

b. Fill two pint jars with cool water. Wrap white paper around one jar. Wrap black paper around the other jar. Put a thermometer in each jar. Place both jars in the sunlight. ②Read and record the temperature in each jar every 15 minutes for one hour.

c. Collect a lot of cans, all exactly the same size. Make cardboard covers for them. Each cover should have a hole just big enough to let a thermometer fit snugly through. Paint one can black, using "flat" paint. Paint one can white. Leave one can shiny. Paint the other cans as many different colors as you have paint for. Fill the cans with water. Put a cardboard cover on each can. Put a thermometer in each can. Wait 5 minutes and then record the temperature for each can. Put the cans in the sunlight. Wait 15 minutes and then record the temperature for each can again. ③Which can showed the greatest difference between the first and second temperature? ④Which showed the least? ■

186

the can on this piece of paper in the sunlight. After 15 minutes, record the second temperature on the paper. What is the difference? How many degrees did the temperature rise?

On the chalkboard, record each team's results along with the color of the can and whether the surface was dull or shiny. This table, used with the paragraph that follows activity 25, should help the students conclude that light and shiny surfaces reflect heat; dark and dull surfaces absorb heat. To reinforce this concept, do 26/Predict.

The teacher should remove the ends of the can with an electric can opener, so that there are no sharp edges. Paint the right side of the can with flat black paint. Drip wax from a lighted candle onto one side of the can, at about the height the candle flame will reach when the can is placed over the candle. Let the students place the tack in the wax. Repeat for the other side of the can. The class's predictions will help you gauge whether they have understood reflection and absorption.

Examine the diagram of the Thermos bottle; read and discuss the reading plateau. Heat can travel through the outer case of the Thermos bottle only by conduction. The "vacuum" space between the outer and inner cases will not conduct heat; with so little air in the space, convection is at a minimum. Heat can travel through this space only by radiation.

(continued on page 226)

When radiated heat strikes an object, what happens depends on the kind of surface the object has. Heat bounces off some surfaces; we say it is reflected (ree-FLECK-ted). Heat sinks into some surfaces; we say it is absorbed (ab-SORBD). In the activities you just did, what kind of surface seemed to reflect heat? What kind of surface seemed to absorb heat? From what you have seen, do you think you can guess what will happen in the next activity?

26/Predict

With a can opener, remove the top and bottom from a large juice can. Paint one half of the can black, inside and out. Leave the other half of the can shiny. With candle wax, fasten a tack to the black side of the can. Fasten another tack to the shiny side of the can. Your teacher will place the can over a lighted candle. Which tack would you think will fall off first? Watch and see whether your guess was correct. ■

Was your prediction right? Which side of the can absorbed more heat? Which side reflected more heat?

Have you ever taken a Thermos bottle on a picnic? How does a Thermos bottle keep the milk cold until you are ready to drink it? Look at the picture which shows the layers of a Thermos bottle.

The outside layer is made of metal or plastic. The center section is made of glass. Both the glass and the inside of the metal or plastic case have a shiny coating, like a mirror. Most of the air has been pumped out of the space between the outer case and the center section.

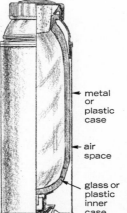

metal
or
plastic
case

air
space

glass or
plastic
inner
case

187

optional activity

A hand held 10 inches above a lighted bulb detects heat. Heat travels to the hand by convection and radiation. To demonstrate how heat travels by radiation alone to a hand, hold a pane of glass between the lighted bulb and your hand. The hand feels the heat through the glass, but the glass is not hot to the touch. Radiant energy does not heat transparent materials. It passes through them. When radiant energy is absorbed by a material, it is converted into heat. The hand absorbs the radiant energy, and heat is produced.

The shiny surface of the inner case reflects radiated heat, so that the material of the case does not transmit the heat. Thus the contents of the inner case are protected against heat. If the inner case is filled with a hot liquid, on the other hand, the contents are protected against losing heat by radiation, convection, or conduction.

In answer to Testing Your Ideas, a white jacket will protect you more at the beach because the heat will bounce off (be reflected from) the white jacket. The black jacket would absorb heat and be very warm. Heat from the sun travels through space as radiation. The astronauts' white suits protect them from excessive radiant energy.

responses to 27/compare

1. To the left hand, the lukewarm water feels warmer than it really is.
2. To the right hand, the lukewarm water feels cooler than it really is.
3. It feels as though there is a difference. Actually, both hands are in water of the same temperature.

Metal and plastic are both solids. How does heat travel through solids? Would a space that is almost empty of air conduct heat? Would heat travel by convection through such a space? What type of heat travel does not need a solid or a fluid? What does a shiny surface do to radiated heat?

Now can you explain: How does a Thermos bottle keep drinks cold? How does it stop all three methods of heat travel? If you filled a Thermos bottle with hot soup, would it keep the soup hot? Why?

TESTING YOUR IDEAS

At the beach on a hot day, which will give you more protection from the sun's heat: a white jacket or a black jacket?

Why do astronauts wear white suits? How does heat travel to a spacecraft from the sun?

OVERVIEW

This lesson and the next deal with temperature measurement. The present lesson deals with liquid thermometers. It explores the way in which we mark, or calibrate, a thermometer. The two most familiar thermometer scales and their uses are discussed in the reading plateau and some equivalent temperatures are mentioned. Testing Your Ideas considers suitability of the thermometer liquid to the purpose of the thermometer.

how to begin

Activity 27/Compare offers a good start for the lesson. The difference in sensations is surprising. As many students as possible should do the activity. The hot and cold water should be renewed after every 3 or 4 students. If it is impossible for the whole class to have this experience now, encourage the students to try it at home. Any three containers will do; they should be set in the sink or bathtub to prevent damage in case of spillage.

process skills

Comparing sensations of heat and cold
Marking (calibrating) a liquid thermometer
Comparing the Fahrenheit and Celsius thermometer scales

materials

3 large bowls, hot water, cold water, lukewarm water, soda pop bottle*, food coloring, one-hole stopper*, clear plastic straw*, pan*, hot plate, china marker or felt-tipped pen*, ice

---

* one per team

HOW DO WE MEASURE
TEMPERATURE?

What is hot? Can you tell? Can you *always* tell? Try this and see.

27/Compare

Take three large bowls. Fill the first with cold water and add a few ice cubes to make the water very cold. Fill the second bowl with lukewarm water. Fill the third with hot water, not too hot for your hand to touch.

Put your left hand in the bowl of cold water. Put your right hand in the bowl of hot water. Leave them there for two minutes. Then put both hands at once into the bowl of lukewarm water. ① How does the lukewarm water feel to your left hand? ② How does it feel to your right hand? ③ Is there a difference? ■

Is your temperature sense exact? Does your temperature sense tell you "exactly 72 degrees"? Or does it say "hotter than this, less hot than that"? Why are hot and cold not exact terms? To know exactly how hot or cold something is, you use a thermometer. How can a thermometer show the exact temperature?

Most of the thermometers you use contain a liquid.

189

procedure

Hot and cold are relative terms. Each person senses them differently. The cocoa that is too hot for me to drink is just right for you. In order to make measurements, we need some objective standards of "hot" and "cold."

Before the beginning of the 18th century, there were no objective standards for heat measurement. About 1593, Galileo had made an air thermometer similar to the one the class will construct in the next lesson. This instrument was not reliable since it was affected not by temperature alone but also by weather conditions and altitude. Other thermometer designs followed, but their scales were arbitrary. Early liquid thermometers were of the type described in 28/Mark.

Assemble the liquid thermometer as directed. "What happens to liquids when they are heated? What do you expect to happen if you heat the liquid in the bottle of the thermometer? What happens to liquids when they lose heat? What do you expect will happen if the liquid in the bottle is cooled? How could you use this instrument to measure temperature?"

Fahrenheit is said to have invented the mercury thermometer consisting of a sealed glass tube with mercury inside. The high and low points from which

responses to 28/mark

1. The water moves downward.

28/Mark

Fill an empty soda pop bottle with colored water. Hold a plastic straw in the neck of a bottle with modeling clay. Press down on the clay so that the colored water rises in the tube about 3 inches above the stopper.

Place the bottle in a pan of water and heat it on a hot plate. Allow the water in the pan to boil. When the colored water has stopped rising in the straw, mark the water level with a felt-tipped pen.

Take the bottle out of the pan, using oven mitts. Do not shake the bottle. Let it cool to room temperature. Then put it into a deep bowl. Fill the bowl with ice. Pack the ice around the bottle. Watch the water in the straw. Which way does it move? When it has stopped moving, mark the water level.

190

he calibrated his thermometer are described in the reading plateau. Fahrenheit's greatest contribution was the establishment of standards for temperature measurement that would be the same everywhere in the world. With his reliable thermometer and the partial scale established from his fixed points, he found that ice always melted into water at the same temperature and that water (at constant altitude) always boiled at the same temperature. At last there was an objective standard for temperature measurement. Instead of merely "hot," we now have "as hot as boiling water." Instead of merely "cold," we now have "as cold as melting ice."

Fahrenheit's scale is used in the United States and some other English-speaking countries for everyday temperature measurements. The fact that its degrees are smaller than those of the Celsius scale makes it a good scale for weather records. Most scientific work, however, uses the Celsius scale.

Celsius proposed a scale of 100 intervals, but originally he proposed that the freezing point be 100° and the boiling point 0°. His scale was soon reversed. The 100 intervals between boiling and freezing points make his scale fit nearly into a decimal system. For this reason it is used by many nations in everyday life, and is used widely by scientists all over the world.

(continued on page 230)

The two marks give you a high point and a low point for a temperature scale. This method is like the way a thermometer is marked.

When you mark a thermometer, you first find the level to which the liquid expands when it is heated to the temperature of boiling water. Then you find the level to which the liquid contracts when it is cooled to the temperature of melting ice. These two levels are called the fixed points of the thermometer. You can make a scale from these points when you have learned more about thermometers.

The thermometer scale we use in everyday life in the United States is the Fahrenheit (FAR-en-hite) thermometer scale. It was invented in the beginning of the 18th century by Gabriel Fahrenheit, a German physicist. For the low point of his scale, he took the temperature of a mixture of ice and salt, and marked it zero degrees. The sign for degrees is °. Temperatures on the Fahrenheit scale are followed by the letter F. We can write zero degrees Fahrenheit as 0°F.

For a high point, Fahrenheit used what he thought was the normal temperature of the human body, and marked it 96°F. He made a scale from his fixed points. Using his scale, he found the temperature of boiling water to be 212°F, and the temperature of melting ice to be 32°F.

At about the same time, Anders Celsius (SELL-see-us), a Swedish astronomer, invented another thermometer scale. Temperatures on this scale are followed by the letter C. He marked the freezing and boiling points of water 0°C and 100°C. Scientists all over the world use the Celsius scale.

The Celsius scale is also called the centigrade (SENT-uh-grade) scale. "Centigrade" means "one

for your information

Water does not make a useful thermometer liquid. When atmospheric temperature falls below 32°F, the water freezes. Because of its peculiar behavior of expanding as it freezes, it would break the thermometer tube.

Alcohol (colored red) and mercury are effective thermometer liquids. Alcohol's low freezing point makes it more useful in cold climates. An alcohol thermometer is not used to measure the temperature of boiling water because it boils at a temperature below that of boiling water.

Celsius

191

The Celsius scale is also known as the centigrade scale.

In the picture of the two thermometer scales, each line on each scale represents two degrees. By holding a ruler across from one scale to the other, the students should find that 68°F is equivalent to 20°C. A temperature of −17°C (17 degrees below zero Celsius) is about equal to 0°F.

To make a scale for your liquid thermometer, tape a strip of paper behind the straw. For a Fahrenheit scale, mark the low point 32° and the high point 212°. There are 180 degrees between the high and low points, so if you mark off the space into ten intervals, each will represent 18 degrees. Of course, you can divide the space in any other way that the students suggest and create a new scale.

For a Celsius scale, mark the low point 0° and the high point 100°. If you mark off the space between these points into ten intervals, each will represent 10 degrees.

The students' liquid thermometers use water, colored to make the water level more visible. Ask, "Could you use this thermometer to measure outdoor temperatures if you live where winters are cold?

note

Guide the student through the comparison of Fahrenheit and centigrade scales pictured on this page. Drill by asking the students to locate corresponding points on the scales. A sheet of paper or a ruler will help to guide their eyes.

hundred steps." Do you think this is a good name for a scale that has one hundred degrees between its fixed points? How many degrees are there between the fixed points of the Fahrenheit scale?

Look at the diagram of the two scales. How many degrees does each line on each scale represent? What Celsius temperature is equal to 68°F? These are comfortable indoor temperatures. What Celsius temperature is equal to 0°F?

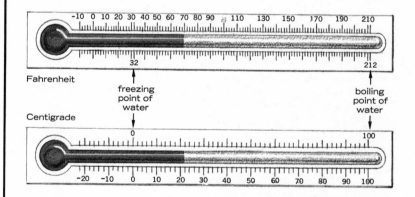

You should be able now to make either a Fahrenheit or Celsius thermometer scale by using the fixed points that you marked on the straw in activity 28. What liquid did you use in your thermometer? Why did you color it? Most liquid thermometers use alcohol or mercury. Why is water not a useful liquid for thermometers?

192

230

What would happen when the temperature went below 32°F?"

Testing Your Ideas compares the usefulness of mercury and alcohol as thermometer liquids. Note that alcohol has a low freezing point, but it has a low boiling point, too. Mercury has a higher freezing point, but a much higher boiling point. To measure low temperatures (e.g., temperatures at the North Pole), you would use an alcohol thermometer. You could not use the same thermometer to measure the temperature of boiling water because the alcohol would boil before the water did.

TESTING YOUR IDEAS

The table shows the freezing and boiling temperatures of two common thermometer liquids. Which liquid would be more useful if you wanted to measure temperatures at the North Pole? Could you use an alcohol thermometer to measure the temperature of boiling water?

	FREEZING POINT	BOILING POINT
Mercury	−40°F	675°F
Alcohol	−175°F	172°F

OVERVIEW

This lesson investigates the workings and uses of a fever thermometer, a gas thermometer, and a metal thermometer. A gas thermometer is constructed and, in 29/Measure, it is calibrated. A model of a bimetallic thermometer is made and it is tested in 30/Test. Testing Your Ideas is concerned with reading thermometers and with comparing the various types of thermometers.

process skills

Calibrating a home-made gas thermometer

Testing a model bimetallic thermometer to demonstrate how it works

materials

soda pop bottle*, clear plastic straw*, one-hole stopper*, modeling clay, tape, paper, jar*, food coloring, large cardboard carton*, paper-backed metal foil wrapping paper, small cardboard box*, tape, scissors, lightweight cardboard, stapler

For the teacher: oven thermometer, candle

---

* one per team

how to begin

Investigate an outdoor-indoor thermometer. What kind of thermometer is it? (Liquid thermometer) Which scale does it use? (F or C) How many degrees does each line stand for? (Usually 2) Would it be easy to measure parts of one degree on this thermometer? Can you think of a way to make it easier?

procedure

The fever thermometer shown on the first page of this lesson has a very narrow opening through the

ARE THERE DIFFERENT THERMOMETERS?

The thermometer you made in activity 28 is a liquid thermometer. The thermometer shown in the margin is a liquid thermometer, too. It is marked with the Fahrenheit scale. What part of the full scale is shown? Look at the scale of the thermometer in the picture. Each degree is divided into five parts. Each line stands for two tenths of a degree. To read a temperature on this thermometer, you say the last whole number before the end of the liquid column. Then you count the number of tenths until you reach the end of the liquid column.

What temperature is shown on the thermometer in the picture? This is the average body temperature for man. What did Fahrenheit think was the normal temperature of the human body?

Some people may have a normal temperature a little above or a little below 98.6°F. Usually a tempera-

center of its tube. A very small rise in temperature, causing a slight expansion of the mercury in the bulb, therefore causes an appreciable change in the length of the mercury column. For the students, it is sufficient to note that this thermometer shows only a small part of the scale, and that each line represents 2/10 degree.

Note that the mercury column in the fever thermometer remains at the highest point to which it has risen until you shake it down. This fact enables you to get an accurate reading. If the mercury column began to fall as soon as you took the thermometer out of your mouth, you would not be able to tell what your exact temperature was.

Each work team should construct a gas thermometer according to the directions in the student text. Because the air will expand considerably with only a small rise in temperature, you may want to substitute a length of flexible, clear plastic tubing, such as is used with aquarium air pumps, for the plastic straw. A 3-foot length of tubing will give you a much longer air column than the straw can provide.

Tell the class, "The first instrument for measuring temperature was like the one you have just made. Galileo, an Italian scientist, designed it almost 400 years ago." Ask, "How accurate do you think this instrument is? Do you think it will make exact measurements of temperature?"

(continued on page 234)

ture above 98.6°F means that you have a fever. Why is this thermometer sometimes called a fever thermometer? Why does a fever thermometer show only 92°F to 110°F?

In most liquid thermometers, the liquid can move freely up and down. If the mercury started to go down as soon as you took the thermometer out of your mouth, could you ever know exactly what your temperature was? Notice that the tube holding the liquid is pinched together near the bottom. The mercury cannot fall back past this pinched place. You have to shake the thermometer hard to force the mercury down.

Another kind of thermometer is a gas thermometer. You can make one with a soda pop bottle. Fix a clear plastic straw in the neck of a bottle with modeling clay. Be sure that the straw and clay are airtight. Wire or tap the bottle to the side of a large carton, as shown in the picture. Tape a strip of paper to the carton next to the plastic straw. You will mark your scale on this paper.

Put the free end of the straw into a jar of colored cold water. Heat the bottle gently with an unshaded lamp or with your hands to drive out some of the air. Let the bottle cool. When the bottle cools, the colored water should be about halfway up the straw.

29/Measure

To make a scale for your gas thermometer, let it stand for half an hour in a warm place. Put an ordinary indoor-outdoor thermometer beside it. Mark the level of the water on the paper. Next to the mark, write the temperature that the indoor-outdoor thermometer shows. Put the two thermometers in a cool

note

Guide the calibration of the gas thermometer with questions such as the following: *Why is some of the air driven out of the pop bottle?* This occurs in order for the pressure inside the pop bottle to be reduced. *Why is the thermometer placed in both a warm and a cool place?* You do this to obtain two fixed points on the thermometer. *How many degrees lie between the two fixed points?* Answers will vary. *How does a gas thermometer work?* (If warmed hands do not cause an appreciable expansion of gas, try heating a piece of woolen cloth on a radiator and wrapping it around the pop bottle.) As gas in the pop bottle is heated, the gas will expand. You may point out to the students that the principle on which the gas thermometer operates is demonstrated in activity 5/Observe.

To answer the preceding question, do 29/Measure. Notice, in calibrating the thermometer, that the higher temperatures appear lower on the scale. Ask, "In this thermometer, what is expanding? (Air) Where is the air in the thermometer?" (At the top of the tube, in the bottle) As the bottle is warmed, the air in it expands, pushing down the colored water in the tube. The purpose of the water is to confine the air in the tube and bottle. The reason for coloring the water is to make the level of the air column more visible by contrast.

When you rub your hands together, the result will probably be a higher temperature than that of the high point on your scale. If so, you will not be able to read this temperature on the scale. You can extrapolate to the higher temperature, though, in the following manner. If the temperature difference between your high and low points is 15°, for example, and the distance between these points on the scale is 5 inches, you can assume that a temperature rise of 3° will move the air column downward 1 inch. If the temperature of your rubbed hands pushed the air column to a point 3 inches below your previous high point, you could assume that the temperature of your rubbed hands was "high point + 9°."

In a fever thermometer, expansion of a column of mercury indicates temperature. In an indoor-outdoor thermometer, the liquid is colored alcohol. In a

responses to 29/measure

1. Answers will vary.
2. Answers again will vary.
3. The answers to the remaining questions are strictly observational.

responses to 30/test

1. The curled strip will straighten out.
2. The pointer will move to the right.
3. The pointer will move to its original position or slightly to the left of it.
4. When heated, the foil strip is expanding. When cooled, the foil strip is contracting.

place for half an hour. Mark the water level again and write the temperature next to this mark. 1 How many fixed points do you have on your scale? 2 How many degrees difference is there between these fixed points? Divide the space between the marks on the paper into the proper number of degrees.

Rub your hands together until they become very warm. Gently place them around the bottle. 3 When the water stops moving in the straw, where does it reach on the scale? Are your hands hotter or cooler than the highest temperature on the scale? Can you read the temperature of your hands on the scale? ■

What material expands in a fever thermometer to show the temperature? What material expands in an indoor-outdoor thermometer to show the temperature? What material expands in this gas thermometer? Where are the higher numbers on the scale of the gas thermometer? Is the gas thermometer different in this way from a liquid thermometer?

You have shown that gases expand when they are heated. The gas thermometer uses this expansion to show temperature. The expanding gas in the bottle pushes on the liquid in the straw. The higher the temperature, the more the gas expands. Where are the higher numbers on the scale of the gas thermometer?

What temperatures does an oven thermometer show? Would air be a good expansion material in an oven thermometer? Would alcohol? Would mercury?

Most oven thermometers work by the expansion and contraction of a bar made of two kinds of metal. When the bar is heated, one metal expands more than the other. When the bar cools, one metal contracts more than the other. Make a model of a metal thermometer to see how it works.

liquid thermometer, the higher temperatures are at the top of the scale. In the gas thermometer, the higher temperatures are located at the bottom of the scale.

Gas thermometers suffer from the disadvantage of needing a very long tube to show any useful range of temperatures. An oven thermometer has to have a range of several hundred degrees. Obviously, a gas thermometer would not be a useful oven thermometer. Recall the boiling points of water and alcohol. Ask, "Would these liquids be useful to measure an oven temperature of 350°F?" Mercury has a very high boiling point, but the glass of the thermometer would melt long before that temperature was reached.

Thus, a mercury thermometer would not be a useful oven thermometer.

A common type of oven thermometer works by the uneven expansion of a bimetallic strip. A model of a metal thermometer, made according to the directions in the student text, will help the class to see how such a device works. Paper-backed foil from a chewing gum wrapper can be substituted for the wrapping paper.

In 30/Test, you will find that your model does not give very useful readings. However, the activity will show the "curling" and "uncurling" effect of uneven expansion and contraction of the two materials that are bonded together.

(continued on page 236)

Take some wrapping paper that is metal foil on one side and paper on the other. Cut a strip that is three inches long and 3/4 inch wide. Tape the strip to the top of a cardboard box. Cut a pointer from lightweight cardboard and staple it to the end of the foil-paper strip. Look at the drawing to see how the instrument should look when it is finished.

30/Test

Place the instrument on a warm radiator. 1 What happens to the strip? 2 In which direction does the pointer move? Mark that side of the box WARMER. Put the instrument in a refrigerator. 3 In which direction does the pointer move? Mark that side of the box COOLER. 4 What is happening to the foil-paper strip? ■

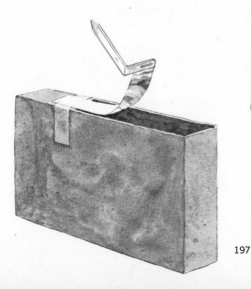

optional activity

To suggest to the students that cold temperatures cause a gas to contract, place a bag of crushed ice around the pop bottle of the gas thermometer. Make sure that the thermometer is air tight. Colored water should rise up the tube and enter the pop bottle, because the contraction of the gas (air) inside the pop bottle has decreased its air pressure. *Ask the children what they can determine about the temperature of the ice bag.*

197

The first three questions in Testing Your Ideas can be answered by observation; the last two require the student to make comparisons and contrasts. The gas, metal, and liquid thermometer differ in the expansion material used and in their construction. All three are alike because, in each, *something expands*.

optional activity

The following should be done as a teacher demonstration. Obtain an inexpensive metal oven thermometer (usually available at a hardware or novelty store). Remove the back of the case to show the workings inside. A coiled metal strip, made of two different metals, is connected to a pointer. Heat the coil with a candle flame while the students watch at the front of the oven thermometer. The heated coil winds tighter as the outer metal expands more than the inner one. The pointer moves toward the higher temperature on the scale. An ice cube applied to the coil will cause contraction. The outer metal contracts more than the inner, relaxing the coil so that it moves the pointer toward the lower temperature on the scale.

When the foil-paper strip is heated, the foil expands more than the paper. What happens to the strip? When the foil-paper strip is cooled, the foil contracts more than the paper. What happens to the strip?

TESTING YOUR IDEAS

Which gives you more readings on the Fahrenheit scale, a fever thermometer or an indoor-outdoor thermometer?

Where are the higher temperatures shown on the scale of a gas thermometer?

Where are the higher temperatures shown on the scale of the model metal thermometer that you made?

How are the gas and metal thermometers different from the liquid thermometer? How are they all alike?

OVERVIEW

This lesson looks at some early ideas of the nature of heat. It relates the studies of Count Rumford (Benjamin Thompson), which gave the first indication of a relationship between heat and motion. In two activities the student investigates this relationship for himself. Testing Your Ideas asks the student to predict, on the basis of his experiences, the outcome of a heat-motion situation.

how to begin

What have you learned about heat? Can it cause changes? What kinds of changes? How does heat travel? How do we measure temperature?

You can tell a lot of things about heat now, but do you know what it is? What is heat? Let's see how scientists have tried to answer this question.

process skills

Comparing the weights of equal quantities of water, frozen and not frozen

Measuring a change in temperature caused by friction

materials

measuring cup*, water, 2 plastic freezer containers*, scale, indoor-outdoor thermometer*, 2 bowls*, ice cubes

———————
* per team

WHAT IS HEAT?

Heat can be passed on from one part of an object to another part of the same object. It can travel from one object to another object. It flows from one place to another place. What is heat?

Aristotle (AR-uh-staht'l) was a Greek who lived in the 4th century B.C. He taught that everything in the world was made up of four basic materials: earth, air, fire, and water. Some objects had more fire and some had less. The more fire an object contained, the hotter it was.

Over the centuries, ideas changed. By the time that Gabriel Fahrenheit and Anders Celsius were making their thermometer scales, heat was thought to be a fluid. The fluid was called caloric (ka-LOR-ick) and it was thought to be present in every material. Some materials had more of it and some had less. Caloric flowed from warm objects to cooler ones. You could squeeze caloric out of materials. You could add caloric to materials by holding them over flames. Ice combined with caloric to form water.

Some thinkers did not agree with the caloric explanation of heat. One of them was Benjamin Thompson, Count Rumford, an American who was the minister of war of Bavaria in the late 18th century. He suspected that heat was not a form of material. Materials, he reasoned, had weight. If heat were particles or a fluid, it would have weight. A warm material would weigh more than a cold one.

Rumford

199

procedure

Read and discuss the historical material. Follow up with 31/Compare. If heat were particles or a fluid, it would have weight. A warm material would weigh more than a cold one. A cupful of water at room temperature should contain more "caloric" than a cupful of water that has frozen solid. The freezing should squeeze "caloric" out of the water.

Be careful to wipe off any frost on the outside of the container that is at room temperature. The weight of each will be about ½ pound plus the weight of the container (hence the importance of using identical containers). The container of water that has lost heat has not lost weight.

Read about Rumford's observation of the drilling of the cannon. Many people had seen what Rumford saw, but none had the same ideas from the sight. A scientist is not someone who knows all the answers; a scientist is someone who knows the right questions to ask.

(continued on page 240)

responses to 31/compare

1. The weight should be the same.
2. The container that was in the freezer lost heat.
3. It did not lose weight.
4. Heat does not seem to have weight.

31/Compare

Measure one cup of water exactly. Pour it into a plastic freezer container. Cover the container tightly so that no water can get in or out. Put the container into a freezer until the water has frozen solid.

Measure another cup of water exactly. Pour it into a plastic freezer container that is exactly like the first one you used. Again, cover the container tightly. Leave the container on a table or shelf until the water has come to room temperature. It should take about one hour.

Weigh the container of water at room temperature. Record this weight. Take the other container out of the freezer. If any frost has formed on the outside of the container, wipe it off. What do you expect to find when you weigh this container? Weigh it, and record the weight. Compare the two weights that you recorded. Which container lost heat? Did it lose weight also? Does heat seem to have weight? ■

200

Rumford tried many experiments. He filled jars with alcohol and water, and placed them in rooms with temperatures hot enough to boil the liquids or cold enough to freeze them. He weighed the jars and compared their weights, but he could find no signs that heat had weight.

As part of his job as minister of war, Rumford had to inspect the places where cannons were made. He watched the workmen as they took a solid brass rod and drilled a hole down the length of the rod. During the drilling, the brass got very hot.

Count Rumford asked himself where this heat came from. He measured the temperature of chips of metal that were drilled out of the rod. They were hotter than boiling water! But the metal was not changed in any way. The only change that happened during the making of the cannon was the movement of the drill against the metal. Did the movement cause the heat? Is there a connection between heat and motion?

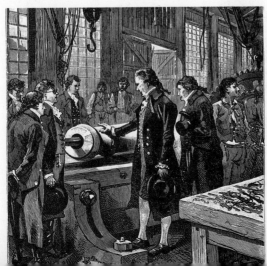

for your information

Contrary to early opinions about heat, Count Rumford maintained that heat had no weight. To demonstrate his theory, he bored a cannon in a large tank of water. The drill was turned by a team of horses. Thompson took the temperature of the water from time to time during the drilling. After two and one-half hours, the water actually boiled. Where had the heat come from? Nothing had entered the water. The only thing that was different before the experiment to its ending was that there had been movement. Count Rumford concluded that heat was not a material substance as men had thought earlier. Heat seemed to be related to motion.

Do 32/Test. Your hands will feel warm when rubbed together. The pencil eraser will feel warm when touched to your cheek. However, recall what you discovered in 27/Compare. Is your sense of touch always a reliable indicator of hotness and coldness?

The thermometer in 33/Measure will give a more dependable indication of the heat of your hands. If the second reading is higher (as it will be, by a couple of degrees), you know that rubbing your hands together has really increased the heat of your hands. The class will then be able to conclude that there is a connection between motion and heat.

Testing Your Ideas calls for a prediction. On the basis of their experiences, the students should be able to predict that the cube in the water that is stirred will melt first.

responses to 32/test

1. Your hands feel hotter.
2. The eraser is warm.

responses to 33/measure

1. Yes, your hands are hotter; the thermometer indicates a higher temperature.

32/Test

Rub your hands together.①What do you feel? Rub a pencil eraser on a sheet of paper while you count slowly to twenty. Then touch the eraser to your cheek. ②What do you feel? ■

Are you really heating things by rubbing them together, or do they just feel hot? Measure, and find out.

33/Measure

Hold an indoor-outdoor thermometer between your hands until the liquid column stops rising. Record the temperature it shows. Rub your hands together hard while you count slowly to two hundred. Again hold the thermometer between your hands until the liquid stops rising.①Are your hands actually hotter after rubbing them together, or do they only feel that way? ■

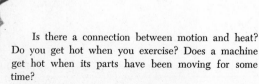

Is there a connection between motion and heat? Do you get hot when you exercise? Does a machine get hot when its parts have been moving for some time?

What do you think will happen in the following case? You have a pitcher full of water. You measure out exactly one cup of water into each of two bowls. The bowls are exactly the same. You put one ice cube into each bowl. You leave one bowl alone until the ice cube melts. You stir the water in the other bowl until the ice cube melts.

Do the ice cubes in both bowls melt in the same amount of time?

Does one melt before the other? If so, which one melts first?

Try it and find out if your prediction was right.

note

The fact that the ice in the stirred bowl melts first will probably be explained by the students in terms of the heating of the water due to the friction of the stirring. More likely, this ice melts first because of the speeded-up convection of fresh warm water against the surface of the ice. However, do not expect the students to know this. The main point is that there is a definite connection between heat and motion.

OVERVIEW

In this lesson, heat is identified as a form of energy. The definition of work (developed in grade 3) is reviewed as involving motion of an object through a distance. Movement in thermometers is recalled and a demonstration (34/Observe) is given of heat causing motion through a distance. The reading plateau and 35/Measure show that heat energy is related to light energy and to the other kinds of energy that make up the electromagnetic spectrum.

process skills

Observing that heat can move an object through a distance

Concluding that, since heat can do work, heat is a form of energy

materials

water, Pyrex glass flask, cork to fit flask, hot plate, indoor-outdoor thermometer°, white cardboard, tape, prism°, ring stand°, black construction paper

° one per team

responses to 34/observe

1. The cork pops out of the flask.
2. Heat caused the cork to move a certain distance.

how to begin

Review the concept of work from grade 3. Work is done when an object is moved through a distance. If the object is not moved, no work is done, regardless of the amount of force exerted on it.

procedure

Recall the results of activities 27, 28, and 29. In each of the thermometers, something moved a certain distance. What was causing each thing to move?

IS HEAT A FORM OF ENERGY?

When you studied machines and work, you learned that the word "work" has a special meaning in the language of science. Work is done when something is moved a certain distance. You can push on a brick wall until you are tired out, but you won't be doing any work—unless you *move* the wall! On the other hand, if you push a book across your desk, you are doing work.

You need energy to do work. Can heat do work? Can heat move things? Is heat energy?

When you warmed the air in the gas thermometer, what happened? Did something move a certain distance? When you put a fever thermometer in your mouth, what happens? Does something move a certain distance?

Discuss the students' observations and the question "Can heat do work?"

Activity 34/Observe should be done by the teacher while the students watch and comment. Heating causes the water to boil. When the water has boiled for two or three minutes, the pressure of the steam blows the cork out of the flask. Thus, heat has caused an object to move through a distance; heat has done work.

In doing 34/Observe, be careful about the fit of the cork. If it is too loose, the steam will leak out; there will be no build-up of pressure to blow the cork out. On the other hand, if the cork is too tightly wedged into the flask, too much pressure will build up. Either the cork will blow out violently, causing damage, or the pressure may shatter the flask. *The teacher should do 34/Observe a couple of times for practice before doing it in class.* With experience, you will be able to predict when the cork will blow out.

Discuss the questions that follow activity 34. What other kinds of energy do the students suggest? Again emphasize that work involves moving an object through a distance. The questions about energy transformations can be answered from experience.

(continued on page 244)

34/Observe

Pour one inch of water into a Pyrex glass flask. Put a cork into the neck of the flask and push it down lightly. Do not press hard on the cork. Watch while your teacher heats the flask on a hot plate. When the water has been boiling for a little while, what happens? 2 Does something move a certain distance? ■

Can heat do work? Do you think it is fair to say that heat is energy? What other kinds of energy do you know of? Do they all move things a large or small distance?

You saw that heat is connected with the energy of motion. Do you suppose there is a connection between heat and some other kinds of energy? Does heat cause chemical changes? Do you think there might be a connection between heat and chemical energy? What happens when you plug in an electric iron? Can electrical energy produce heat?

optional questions

Ask the students which of the following are examples of work being done. For those examples which do indicate that work is done, have the students name the source of energy:

A car driving down the street This does illustrate that work is being done because the car moves. The source of energy is the fuel in the car.

An electric mix-master plugged in the wall. This does not illustrate work being done because nothing is moving.

An electric mix-master which is mixing cake batter. This is work, because the blades of the mixer are moving. The source of energy is the electric current.

An electric shaver in use. Work is being done as the blades of the shaver move. Again, the source of energy is electricity.

Next, the reading plateau tells how Herschel identified heat as related to the visible radiation we call light. His classic experiment is repeated by the students in 35/Measure. For this activity, it will probably be best to set up one apparatus. All the students can make readings of the thermometer and can keep individual records. If you feel that your students are ready for it, you can introduce the word "spectrum" to describe the bands of colored light that are produced when white light passes through a prism.

Sum up by reading the last three paragraphs aloud. All kinds of energy are interrelated. You can take pictures by infrared light as well as by visible light. Light energy can be transformed into the energy of motion, as when an "electric eye" opens doors for you. Ask the class to describe some more energy changes. Emphasize heat production in relation to energy changes. Even in a refrigerator or freezer, you can feel heat if you put your hand near the motor.

Use Testing Your Ideas to review the concepts of work, energy, and heat as a form of energy.

responses to 35/measure

1. The temperature is higher than when the bulb was in the red light.

Herschel

Is there a connection between heat and light energy? In 1800, this question was asked by Sir William Herschel (HERR-shell), an English scientist. He was studying light so that he could learn more about the sun and the stars. He knew that when he held a prism in a beam of light, the white light was broken up into all the colors of the rainbow.

Herschel measured the temperature of each color of light coming out of a prism. He found that the red light had the highest temperature. Then he moved the thermometer below the red, where there was no light to be seen. Surprise! This was by far the hottest place!

You can do Sir William Herschel's experiment. Choose a window where the sun shines in. Cover it with black construction paper, except for a slit 1/2 inch wide and 2 inches long. Draw the shades on the other windows to darken the room as much as possible. Turn a prism in the beam of light until the light makes a rainbow on the wall. Then fasten the prism to a stand. Put a piece of white cardboard close to the prism so that the rainbow shows on the cardboard.

35/Measure

Take an indoor-outdoor thermometer that is at room temperature. Tape the thermometer to the cardboard so that the red light is shining on the thermometer bulb. Wait 5 minutes. You may have to move the cardboard to keep the red light exactly on the thermometer bulb. After 5 minutes, record the temperature that the thermometer shows.

Move the thermometer and tape it to the cardboard so that the bulb is just below the red band of light. Wait 5 minutes. Check the temperature. Is it higher or lower than when the bulb was in red light? ■

There seems to be some radiation that we cannot see, but that is real, all the same. We call it infrared (in-fruh-RED), which means "below red." Infrared rays are given off by all hot objects. Have you ever used a heater that gave off lots of heat, but very little light? Was it giving off infrared rays? Kitchens on airplanes cook dinners very quickly in infrared ovens.

We live in a world full of energy and of energy changes. When you turn on a lamp, electrical energy is changed to light energy and some heat energy. The chemical energy stored in the food you eat is changed to the energy of your muscles. When you use muscular energy, you give off some heat energy, too. When you strike a gong, the energy of motion is changed to sound energy. Hit the gong many times in a row, and it will become warm at the spot where you strike it. Whenever any kind of energy is used, some of it is changed to heat energy.

TESTING YOUR IDEAS

What do scientists mean by "work"?
Can heat do work?
Is heat energy?

studying the picture

Have the students look at the picture and determine which objects or people in the picture are doing work. All of the people who appear to be moving are doing work. The fire is not doing work because nothing is being moved by the heat given off. *Ask the students if it is really possible to know that their answers, with regard to the movement of people in the picture, are accurate.* Because the picture only shows one instant of time, it can only be inferred that the people are, in fact, moving. *Ask the students if the heat from the fire would be doing work if a metal pinwheel were held above the rising heat.* It would, because the pinwheel would begin to turn as the heated air pushed against its blades.

OVERVIEW

This lesson asks the student to examine his ideas of matter and its relationship to heat. It introduces him to an ancient question, "Is matter continuous, or is it made up of particles?" The Greek philosophers argued at length but they did not observe nature. In 36/Observe, the student discovers that there are "empty spaces" in water. In activity 37 and the reading plateau that follows it, he recognizes that there is motion in liquids, gases, and solids. He is led to reason that matter seems to be made up of tiny moving particles. By repeating activity 37 and intro-ducing a difference of heat, he can observe that heat seems to increase the motion of the moving particles of matter.

how to begin

Have the class suggest names of some solids, liquids, and gases. Make a list of familiar materials in each state. How does heat change each of these? Which are conductors of heat? Which are insulators? Discuss with the students whether matter is continuous or made up of "pieces." Suggest, "We may be able to discover the answer."

process skills

Observing the diffusion of matter in its various states

Making the hypothesis that matter is made up of particles that are moving, and that this motion seems to be associated with heat

materials

2 drinking glasses*, 2 cups*, sugar, teaspoon*, water, black ink, instant coffee

* per team

HOW IS HEAT ENERGY CONNECTED WITH MOTION?

How many states of matter do you know? In grade 3 you examined rocks. Some rocks were made of small bits stuck together. Some rocks seemed to be one solid piece, but you could break the rock into smaller and smaller pieces. Are these very small pieces still rock? Are there other materials made of pieces?

36/Observe

Fill a glass to the top with water. Look at it carefully. Do you see any spaces in the water? Do you see any pieces of water? Carefully pour a level teaspoonful of sugar into the water. What happens? How many teaspoonsful of sugar can you drop into the glass of water before it overflows? ■

procedure

Read and discuss the first paragraph. Follow up with 36/Observe. When the teams have filled their glasses with water, ask "What will happen if I drop something into the glass now?" The students will probably predict that the water will overflow. Pour the sugar into the water. Let each team pour one spoonful of sugar into its glass. Ask, "Do you suppose that more sugar can be poured into the water?"

Ask the students to predict how many spoonfuls of sugar can be poured into the full glass before the water overflows. Since two objects cannot occupy the same space at the same time, the amount of sugar poured into the water indicates empty spaces in the water. If water was a continuous material, the first spoonful of sugar would have made the water overflow.

Activity 37/Measure will present the idea of *moving* particles. Ask the students to predict what will happen. The black color of the ink will spread throughout the water in the glass. To emphasize the color, hold a sheet of paper behind the glass. In time, larger particles of ink will settle to the bottom of the glass, due to the pull of gravity.

(continued on page 248)

Do you think there are spaces in water? Could water be made up of tiny pieces, too small to see? Let's test the idea.

37/Measure

Put a drop of black ink into a glass of water. How long does it take for the ink to spread throughout the water? ■

You did not stir the water. Yet the black ink seemed to move through the water. Do you think gases mix together in the same way as liquids do? Can you smell gas in the living room if there is gas leaking in the kitchen? How do you know when someone has used perfume? Do gases seem to mix?

Will solids spread through each other? Here is an experiment that has been done in science laboratories, with special equipment.

responses to 36/observe

1. The water will not overflow.
2. About 4 or 5 teaspoonsful of sugar can be added.

responses to 37/measure

1. You can observe the ink slowly spread throughout the water.

Activity 36/Observe showed that there are empty spaces in water. Activity 37/Measure showed evidence that water is made up of particles that are tiny (since they cannot be observed even with a magnifying glass), and moving (since one material spreads through another).

Read and discuss the material that follows activity 37. Recall smelling things at a distance. Do gases seem to mix together? Read about the gold-lead experiment. Do solids seem to mix together?

Assist the class to reason through what they have seen. Sometimes, what is not observed can be as important as what is observed. Thus, if matter were continuous, the black ink would have settled on top of the water. A scientist must be aware of what happens and of what does not happen.

The fact that there was a spreading of one material throughout another disproves the "continuous" concept of matter. If it is not continuous, matter must be made up of parts. The observations made by the class

note

This lesson introduces the students to the kinetic-molecular theory, but it is never named, as such, nor is the term "molecule" introduced at this grade level. In grade 5, the students will explore the idea of matter being made of "particles" with spaces between them and they will be introduced to the terms "molecule" and "atom" at that time. This lesson is merely to get them thinking about the idea. The conclusion that "It seems as if" matter is made of tiny moving pieces is all that is desired at this level.

A block of gold and a block of lead were held together for a long time by a machine called a vise. After a long time, the surfaces that touched were examined. Gold was found in the surface of the lead block. Lead was found in the surface of the gold block. Some gold had moved into the lead and some lead had moved into the gold.

Is this example like the black ink moving through the water? Is it like the gas moving through the air? Something moved in each form of matter. Some matter spread through other matter without a push or pull from outside the matter.

Matter acts as if it is made up of tiny moving pieces, so different materials mix with each other. These pieces must be very small, for you cannot see them. Even when you look at water through a microscope, you cannot see pieces of water. Of course, you may see pieces *in* the water.

Think of how much sugar you poured into the glass full of water before it overflowed. The sugar took up space, so there must be space between these tiny moving pieces. Many times, scientists will say, "It seems as if." You can say, from what you have observed, "*It seems as if* matter is made up of tiny moving pieces with spaces between them."

38/Explain

Fill a drinking glass with marbles. ①Is the glass full? ②Are there spaces between the marbles? Sift a handful of sand into the glass. ③Where does the sand go? ④Does this model help you to explain how materials mix with each other? ■

210

seem to suggest that these parts must be very small and moving. It is important to use the word "seems," for the observations made in these activities are not conclusive.

Activity 38/Explain should help the students visualize how matter is composed. The marbles are like particles of one substance, with spaces between them. The sand grains are like particles of another substance that mixes with the first by slipping into the spaces. Compare this model with your observation in activity 37. The question about the size of the particles may be raised. Particles of matter are of different sizes, but do not develop this question unless someone asks.

Do 39/Compare. The black ink spreads through the warm water faster than through the cold water. Heat seems to increase the motion of the particles.

Before doing 40/Predict, ask the students to predict what will happen. Record the time that it takes for the coffee to appear to spread throughout the cups of water. The difference will be great enough to notice. The coffee dissolves and spreads faster in hot water than in cold.

(continued on page 250)

You have learned that there is a connection between heat and motion. If this is true, then there should be a connection between heat and matter, which acts as if it is made up of tiny moving particles.

39/Compare

Repeat activity 37. Put a drop of black ink into a glass of cold water. At the same time, put a drop of black ink into a glass of hot water. How long does it take for the ink to move through the cold water? How long does it take for the ink to move through the hot water? Which period of time is shorter? Can you guess why? ■

Can you conclude that matter is made of tiny pieces? Your activities show that tiny particles of matter are moving. Heat seems to increase their motion. You observed that the black ink moved through hot water faster than through cold water.

40/Predict

Take two cups. Put a teaspoonful of instant coffee in each cup. Fill one cup with cold water and the other with hot water. In which cup will the instant coffee mix faster? ■

Is cocoa easier to make with hot milk or cold milk? When do you think odors would spread faster, on a hot day or a cold day?

Count Rumford thought that heat was connected with motion, but he could not explain how. Can you?

211

responses to 38/explain

1. Yes.
2. Yes, there appear to be small spaces between the marbles.
3. The sand goes into the spaces between the marbles.
4. It suggests that pieces of sugar can fit between pieces of water.

responses to 39/compare

1. The ink moves through warm water faster than through cold water.
2. Heat increases the motion of the particles.

responses to 40/predict

1. The coffee mixes faster with hot water.

Testing Your Ideas requires the student to apply what he has learned about particles of matter to an activity performed earlier in the unit. When the class did activity 14, they observed that heat traveled through the rod from one portion to the next, starting with the end nearest to the heat source. If we accept the idea of particles whose motion is increased by heating, then the particles would be moving fastest at the end nearest the heat source, and slowest at the end farthest from the heat source. Recall 15/Model, which helped to explain activity 14. Some of the students may suggest that the particles at the heated end, moving faster, bump into nearby particles, making *them* move faster.

SUMMING UP THE UNIT

review

Water can be a solid, a liquid, or a gas. What makes the difference?
heat
What kind of change do you call this?
physical change; change of state
What do you mean when you say that heating makes materials expand?
answers should be based on the student's experiences and should indicate some increase in size

TESTING YOUR IDEAS

Look back at activity 14/Test on page 173. What did you find out when you did the activity? Suppose the rod is made up of tiny moving pieces? Where would the pieces be moving fastest? Where would they be moving slowest? Can you use the idea of tiny moving pieces to explain what happened in activity 14?

212

What kind of change is burning?
chemical change; oxidation
Is a new substance formed when a candle burns?
yes (carbon dioxide, water)
What three things are needed for burning?
a material that is burnable, enough heat to bring the material to its kindling point, a supply of air (oxygen)
Do you think you could stop a fire by taking away one of these things?
discussion (yes)

How does heat travel through solids?
by conduction; from one portion to the next

Does heat travel through all solid materials at the same speed?
no
What is an insulator?
a material that does not conduct heat, or conducts it poorly
How are insulators used?
discussion

Name some fluids.
e.g., air, water
How does heat travel through fluids?

(continued on page 252)

SUMMING UP THE UNIT

REVIEW

Water can be a solid, a liquid, or a gas. What makes the difference? What kind of change do you call this? What do you mean when you say that heating makes materials expand?

What kind of change is burning? Is a new substance formed when something burns? What three things are needed for burning? Do you think you could stop a fire by taking away one of these three things?

How does heat travel through solids? Does heat travel through all solid materials at the same speed? What is an insulator? How are insulators used?

Name some fluids. How does heat travel through fluids? Do fluids conduct heat? Look at the fluids at the side of the page. Which is denser, A or B?

How does heat travel through space? What kinds of surfaces absorb heat? What kinds of surfaces reflect heat?

How does a thermometer work? Does a thermometer depend on the fact that heat can travel? Does a thermometer depend on the fact that heat makes things expand? How do you make a scale for a thermometer?

213

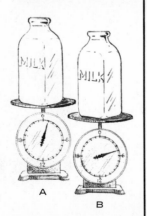

A

B

by convection; by currents of cooler and warmer fluid

Do fluids conduct heat?
no; they are insulators
Which is denser, A or B?
B

How does heat travel through space?
by radiation; without traveling through a solid or a fluid
What kinds of surfaces absorb heat?
dark, dull
What kinds of surfaces reflect heat?
light, bright, shiny

How does a thermometer work?
by something expanding
Does a thermometer depend on the fact that heat can travel?
yes; otherwise it would not take in heat from the thing whose temperature it is measuring

Does a thermometer depend on the fact that heat makes things expand?
yes; otherwise it would not be able to show the temperature
How do you make a scale for a thermometer?
find the fixed points, divide the space between them into a suitable number of spaces

Draw a picture of a Thermos bottle. Show how it prevents heat from traveling in the three ways you learned about.

Is there a connection between heat and motion? Show how motion can produce heat. Tell how heat can produce motion.

What does a scientist mean when he talks about "work"? Can heat do work? Is there a connection between heat and some other kinds of energy? Is there a connection between heat and light?

HOME PROJECTS

How long can you keep an ice cube? What materials do you know of that do not conduct heat? How can you prevent heat from traveling by convection? by radiation? Design and make an ice-cube keeper. Have a contest with your friends to see whose design will keep an ice cube longest.

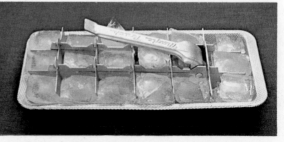

214

Draw a picture of a Thermos bottle. Show how it prevents heat from traveling in the three ways you learned about.

responses should show that the near-empty space between the inner and outer layers prevents conduction and convection, and the silvered surface of the inner layer stops radiation

Is there a connection between heat and motion?
yes
Show how motion can produce heat.
e.g., rubbing hands together
Tell how heat can produce motion.
e.g., recall 34/Observe

What does a scientist mean when he talks about "work"?
moving an object a certain distance
Can heat do work?
yes
Is there a connection between heat and some other kinds of energy?
yes (discuss examples)
Is there a connection between heat and light?
yes (discuss examples)

SELF TEST

a. Wood's ability to conduct heat | is greater than / is the same as / is less than | Iron's ability to conduct heat

b. The number of degrees between the fixed points of Fahrenheit's scale | is greater than / is the same as / is less than | The number of degrees between the fixed points on Celsius' scale

c. The amount of heat we get from the sun by convection | is greater than / is the same as / is less than | The amount of heat we get from the sun by radiation

d. The length of time the candle burns in the pint jar | is greater than / is the same as / is less than | The length of time the candle burns in the quart jar

215

self test

a. is less than
b. is greater than
c. is less than
d. is less than

unit four

The Changing Earth

unit four

The Changing Earth

In this unit the children discover how the earth's surface has changed through the ages. They observe that the same kinds of changes that are going on today have been taking place from the earth's beginning and will probably continue to take place as long as the earth exists. They discover that the forces that have built up the earth's surface, such as deposition, vulcanism, and uplift, have been balanced by the forces of erosion that have worn it away, such as weathering, wind, and water.

Through the planned experiences of the unit, the children realize that there is a relationship between the geological processes and our present concepts of continuity and change. For example, they observe that the surface features of the earth continue from one geologic era to another, and that the major continents and seas have existed for millions of years. Yet, the children also become aware of the fact that the earth today is quite different from the earth yesterday. Since yesterday, rivers have eroded their banks and beds, and carried a few more tons of sediment into the oceans. Winds have blown tons of soil from one area to another, and in the process etched the surface of rocks. Ocean waves have chipped away more rock from cliffs, ground it into sand, and deposited it on beaches or carried it out to be deposited on ocean bottoms.

Through the activities of the unit, children make firsthand observations of the interactions that take place between the earth's surface and the forces of nature that change it—the agents of erosion, vulcanism, weathering, and diastrophism. As the youngsters study the interactions and relate them to the history of the earth, they become aware of the pattern that does exist. They learn that the great pressures in the earth which result in uplift, mountain building, and vulcanism follow a pattern and that the earth's surface is slowly built up only to be gradually eroded, deposited in the seas, and uplifted again.

The surface of the earth has gone through a series of vast changes to reach its present form. We see the changes that are taking place on its surface today, and we assume that forces must have acted in much the same way in the past to create the present surface features.

The large scale changes in the history of the earth cannot be seen in a lifetime or even in many lifetimes. They are the sum total of many smaller changes going on throughout all of geological time. The forces that give the general character to the earth's surface are those that work from within—internal pressures and the movements of magma. The forces that account for the finer features of the earth's surface are those that work from without—wind, moving water, ice, and the expansion of freezing water. Few changes are sudden and dramatic, but most are gradual and inconspicuous.

Unequal heating of the earth's surface as well as the rotation of the earth sets the air in motion, which we call wind. The distance an object will be moved by the wind depends on the object's size, shape, density, and the speed at which the wind is blowing. Dust particles will be blown by the wind more easily than sand grains, and sand grains more easily than pebbles. The stronger the wind, the farther the earth materials will be carried. Dust and sand storms demonstrate the wind's power to erode and transport earth materials. Efforts to prevent wind erosion include the planting of cover crops with very fine spreading roots to hold the soil.

Wind-borne earth particles can cause further erosion. Sharp-edged grains of soil or sand, carried by a strong wind, may carve and polish obstacles such as rocks. Wind erosion of rocks is a very slow process and is effective only in areas of steady wind, abundant loose sand, and soft rock.

Eventually, windblown earth materials must fall to the ground. When the wind loses speed, it deposits its burden of dust or soil. The materials may have been carried thousands of miles or only inches. The deposits are often temporary; the soil is picked up and carried further by the next stiff breeze that comes along. Sometimes though, the deposit remains long enough to become closely packed and to remain as a permanent part of the landscape. Thus, wind is capable of changing the earth's surface by erosion, abrasion, and deposition.

Wind also helps in the evaporation of water from soil and from bodies of water. Atmospheric water condenses and falls as rain. About seventy-five percent of the earth's surface is covered with water. Even the "dry" land that protrudes above the ocean's surface contains much water. Streams and rivers, ponds, lakes, and inland seas are obvious to us. Less obvious is the water that runs beneath the surface of the land, the underground streams and lakes that we tap when we dig wells. The force exerted by running water is dramatically demonstrated to us each time a river overflows its banks or a dam bursts and sends tons of water cascading over the countryside below it. Erosion by running water is not dramatic but, because it is constant, its effects are greater in the long run.

The amount of earth materials that a given amount of water can carry is dependent on the kind of material that is being carried and on the speed at which the water is moving. The water's speed often is related to the slope of the land surface over which the water flows. Thus, a mountain stream will run faster and will erode soil faster than a stream on a plain. Run-off from a hillside or sloping lawn can strip the land of its topsoil in a few seasons. Terracing of hillside farms and contour plowing in rolling country keeps rain water from running straight down the incline of the land and forces it to take a more gradual route. By reducing some of the speed of running water, farmers reduce its capacity to damage their land.

When running water loses speed, it deposits some of the earth materials it carries. The ancient Egyptians depended on the annual Nile floods to renew the fertility of their farms with rice soil carried from the river's headwaters. The fertility of the Mississippi Valley, too, is due to the river. Deposition also can be a problem when rivers deposit soil where man does not want it. Harbors at the mouths of rivers must be dredged periodically, or they will fill up with silt and become impassable to large ocean vessels.

The porosity of soil and rock help water to change the earth's surface in further ways. Wet soil is heavier than dry soil and, thus, is less vulnerable to erosion by wind. However, water is a solvent, and the continual seepage of water through soil can remove valuable minerals from the soil in a process called leaching. The dissolving of minerals in water also helps to explain the formation of underground caverns, although dissolved gases and acids may combine chemically with components of the rock and eat it away.

Water-soaked rocks may undergo further change if the temperature drops below the freezing point. With some exceptions, matter expands regularly when heated and contracts regularly when it is cooled. Water is one of the exceptions. Upon cooling, water contracts until it reaches 4°C, or approximately 32°F, at which point it is at its maximum density. From 4°C to 0°C, its freezing temperature, water expands as it freezes. Thus, when water freezes in a porous rock, the pressure exerted by its expansion can chip and split the rock. Alternation of temperature extremes can break even dry rocks, as in a desert where hot days are followed by cool nights. The alternate expansion and contraction can loosen grains from the surface of rock, eventually breaking the rock down into sandy soil.

Ice is another of the sculptors of the earth's surface. Great ice sheets cover Greenland and the Antarctic continent. Others once covered large portions of the continents in the northern hemisphere. The ice sheets were, in a sense, overgrown glaciers. When weather conditions were favorable, the glaciers grew and spread until they covered vast areas. Periodically, warmer temperatures caused those at lower altitudes to melt. At present we cannot say whether the Ice Age is over, or whether the earth is in an interglacial period.

Glaciers, like wind and water, carve the earth's surface by eroding, transporting, and depositing earth materials. Soil and rock become embedded in the sides and bottom of the glacier as it passes over them, and these in turn help to grind away at other surfaces over which the glacier travels. When the glacier melts, it deposits the materials it has carried with it, and melted water may carry glacial debris still farther.

Ice under pressure will melt. This fact helps to explain how glaciers pick up rocks and earth materials, and how glaciers move over irregular surfaces and around corners. Continual melting under pressure, flowing over and around obstacles, and refreezing when pressure is reduced, may help the glacier to pursue its winding path down a mountainside. It should be noted that other processes, including some not yet understood, are involved in a glacial movement.

Mountains are carved by wind, water, and ice but they are formed by pressures from within the earth. The outermost layer of the earth is a thin rocky crust. Beneath the crust is a mantle which is thought to be hot, plastic, and under great pressure. Pressure exerted against the crust or within the crust may form mountains by faulting, folding, or uplifting parts of the crust. Magma flowing under pressure may form the roots of dome mountains; magma escaping through the crust may form volcanic mountains.

A deep crack in the earth's crust, the edges of which are pressed tightly together, is called a fault. When a mountain is formed by faulting, the rock on one side of the fault is thrust upward while the rock on the other side may remain comparatively level. More often, movement along a fault is lateral. The rock on one side of the fault may be shifted, or both sides may move in opposite directions. The vibration that is set up when the moving rock masses grind each other is an earthquake. Earthquake waves, while most noticeable near their source, travel throughout the earth and may be detected by seismographs. What little we know about the interior of the earth has been learned from the way earthquake vibrations travel through it. Vibrations continue, diminishing in strength, for some time after the initial shock. Scientists state that the violent vibrations of the Alaskan earthquake of 1964 set the earth "ringing like a bell" for months.

Earthquakes also may be caused by volcanic eruptions, but such disturbances are usually feeble by comparison with those caused by shifts in the earth's crust. In the course of a volcanic eruption, molten rock and gases from the earth's interior escape through the surface, sometimes with great force. Once it was thought that, below the crust, all was molten rock. Modern evidence from the study of earthquake vibrations indicates that the earth's interior is largely solid. It is proposed that there are small pockets of molten rock in the crust or in the upper portion of the mantle, the layer underneath the crust. These pockets would be the sources of the molten rock that escapes from volcanoes.

Molten rock under the earth's surface is called magma; when it escapes to the surface it is called lava. Generally, in a volcanic eruption, lava flows through cracks in the sides of a volcano. Gases such as water vapor, carbon dioxide, hydrogen sulfide, and many others stream from the crater of the volcano. Rapidly escaping gases carry with them fine particles of lava called ash and cinder, and large particles called volcanic bombs. The greater the proportion of solid material given off by the volcano, the steeper its cone will be. Most volcanoes are made up of alternate layers of lava and cinder.

Generalization I

The surface of the earth is constantly changing.

Contributing Principles

A. Some changes in the earth's surface take place rapidly.
B. Some changes in the earth's surface take place very slowly.

Generalization II

Changes in the earth's surface may be physical or chemical.

Contributing Principles

A. Wind is air moving over the earth's surface.
B. Wind changes the earth's surface by carrying away dry soil and sand and depositing them elsewhere.
C. Wind-driven sand changes the earth's surface by carving and eroding land surfaces.
D. Water flows from high places to lower places over the earth's surface.
E. Flowing water changes the earth's surface by wearing away land surfaces and depositing sediment.
F. Ocean waves change the earth's surface by wearing away shorelines.
G. Some water is absorbed into the earth's surface and stored in porous soils and porous rocks.
H. Some materials within the earth's surface are dissolved by water and carried away or deposited when the water evaporates.
I. The freezing and melting of water causes rock erosion.
J. Glaciers bearing rocks and soil erode the earth's surface.

Generalization III

Unbalanced forces under the earth's surface cause mountain formations and earthquakes.

Contributing Principles

A. Pressures in the earth raise blocks of crust and fold the surface into mountains.
B. Pressures in the earth cause blocks of crust to shift along deep faults, causing earthquakes.
C. Pressures in the earth force lava, rocks, and gases to the surface, forming volcanic mountains and great lava fields.

before you begin

NEW WORDS FOR THE STUDENT

This list contains science words that will be introduced in the course of the unit. Mastery of the vocabulary is not essential. Use this list to help your students understand what they read. Do not require memorization of its contents.

block mountains mountains formed by the uplifting of a large area of the earth's crust

crust the earth's outer layer, which is made up of soil, rocks, and minerals

delta a low plain at the mouth of a river or sea, built up by the settling out and accumulation of sediment

dome mountains mountains formed by upward pressures beneath a weak spot in the earth's crust

dunes hills of windblown sand, deposited when the speed of a desert wind is checked by plants or other objects

erosion the wearing away of the surface of the earth by water, wind, and ice *fault* a deep break in the earth's crust caused by stresses and pressures

folded mountains mountains formed by the uplifting and wrinkling of the earth's crust because of internal pressures

fossils the remains of ancient plants and animals which have been preserved in rock layers

geology the study of the history, structure, and composition of the earth

lava the material poured out by a volcano and hardened into a porous rock

moraines mounds usually consisting of large, rounded rocks deposited by the melting of glaciers

mountain glacier a mass of ice and snow covering a relatively small area in the high mountains

seismograph an instrument which records the shock waves produced by an earthquake

sedimentary rock rock formed by the settling and cementing together of materials deposited as sediment

vulcanism the changes in the earth's surface produced by the action of volcanoes

weathering the breaking up of rocks on the earth's surface by means of physical and chemical changes produced by the atmosphere

BOOKS FOR THE STUDENT

Ames, Gerald, and Rose Wyler, *The Earth's History*. Mankato, Minn. Creative Educational Society, 1962.

Bergaust, Erik, and William O. Foss, *Oceanographers in Action*. New York. G. P. Putnam's Sons, 1968.

Carona, Philip B., *Our Planet Earth*. Chicago. Follett, 1967.

Clayton, Keith, *The Crust of the Earth: The Story of Geology*. Garden City, N.Y. Natural History Press, 1967.

Lauber, Patricia, *All About Planet Earth*. New York. Random House, 1962.

Poole, Lynn, and Gary Poole, *Volcanoes in Action*. New York. Whittlesey House, 1962.

Stone, A. Harris, and Dale Ingmanson, *Rocks and Rills: A Look At Geology*. Englewood Cliffs, N.J. Prentice-Hall, 1967.

Sutton, Felix, *How and Why Wonder Book of Our Earth*. New York. Grossett & Dunlap, 1960.

Winchester, James H., *Hurricanes, Storms and Tornadoes*. New York. G. P. Putnam's Sons, 1968.

BOOKS FOR THE TEACHER

Blanc, Sam S., Abraham S. Fischler, and Olcott Gardner, *Modern Science: Earth, Space, and Environment*. "The Changes in the Earth," pp. 225–250. New York. Holt, Rinehart and Winston, 1970.

Blough, G. O., and J. Schwartz, *Elementary School Science and How to Teach It*. "The Earth and Its Surface," pp. 81–107. New York. Holt, Rinehart and Winston, 1964.

FILMS

Birth and Death of Mountains   12 minutes   B&W/color   FAC
Shows that though mountains appear to be permanent and unchanging features of the earth's surface, they are constantly being changed. Effects of wind, water, ice, and underground forces are seen in changes that take place in mountain formation and erosion.

Caverns and Geysers   14 minutes   B&W/color   FAC
Illustrates how underground water is constantly changing our earth and the role such water plays in forming both caverns and geysers. Illustrates the mechanism of cavern and geyser formation.

The Earth: Changes in its Surface   11 minutes   B&W/color   COR
Shows the dramatic changes that sometimes take place in the eruption of a volcano. Shows other forces that are changing the earth's surface also. Explains both internal and external forces at work.

The Earth's Changing Surface   11 minutes   B&W/color   MGH
Describes the variety of elements that are continuously wearing away and building up the earth's surface. Shows the spread of glaciers.

The Earth in Change: The Earth's Crust
                              16 minutes   B&W/color   EBF
Tells the story of the changing features of the earth. Shows that the earth's crust is undergoing constant change due to erosion, folding, sedimentation, volcanic action, and earthquakes. Tells a little about geological history.

Earthquakes and Volcanoes   14 minutes   B&W/color   FAC
Presents the causes of both earthquakes and volcanoes and explains the relationship between them. Illustrates faults, volcanic eruptions, and other features or forces related to earthquakes and volcanic activity.

Face of the Earth   12 minutes   color   EBF
Shows how glaciers, frost, landslides, and running water wear down the earth's surface. Also shows how volcanoes and sedimentation build up the earth's surface. Shows views in several national parks.

Our Earth   12 minutes   B&W/color   CEN
Shows that our earth is composed of several layers inside and a blanket of atmosphere outside. Tells about various kinds of rocks in the earth. Compares the amounts of air, land, and water on the earth.

Strata, the Earth's Changing Crust   11 minutes   B&W/color   FAC
Describes the changes that have taken place in the earth. Illustrates how rock layers were originally formed as flat layers, but have been changed by folding and faulting. The processes that produce many of the land features are shown.

Understanding Our Earth: How its Surface Changes
                              11 minutes   B&W/color   COR
Shows the forces which build up and wear away the surface of the earth over long periods of time. Depicts volcanic eruptions and lava flow, wind and water at work, and the geologic evidence offered.

CEN	Cenco Educational Films
COR	Coronet Films
EBF	Encyclopaedia Britannica Films
FAC	Film Associates of California
MGH	McGraw-Hill

BULLETIN BOARDS

What Forces Change the Earth's Surface?

Display pictures or drawings of various eroding agents, such as a muddy stream, windblown sand, a mountain glacier, and waves breaking on a cliff. Let the children describe how each of these agents is wearing away the surface of the earth. List questions that children raise and cannot answer. When you have completed the unit, plan to have a follow-up discussion in which the children can review their questions and answer them.

Why Do We Find Different Kinds of Land?

Display pictures or drawings of different examples of the earth's surface—for example, pictures of rocky deserts, lush farmlands, thick forests, and eroded fields. Let the children discuss the pictures and try to explain what must have happened to change the valuable land into useless land. Make a note of their observations. After they have studied the sections on erosion, let them review their speculations in the light of what they have learned.

Why Are the Earth Formations This Way?

Arrange pictures showing various kinds of eroded formations—for example, wind-eroded rocks, eroded sea cliffs, and gullies. Ask the children if they know how the original formations were changed by the forces of nature. Let them predict what the end results of this action will probably be. In the course of the unit, plan to have other follow-up discussions.

Where Can We See Land That Has Been Worn Away?

On a large, outline map of the United States paste pictures of scenes in national parks, or other areas where examples of erosion are outstanding. For example, Bryce Canyon is a good example of wind erosion; the Grand Canyon of the Yellowstone River and of the Colorado River, of water erosion; and the Rocky Mountains, of glacier erosion. After the children have completed the unit, let them label each picture according to the type of erosion shown.

HISTORY OF THE IDEA

The history of geology can be understood as a growing reliance upon field observation rather than upon speculation. But from the ancients through the seventeenth century, various speculative thinkers did remarkably accurate reasoning upon certain aspects of geology. While Aristotle believed that the earth had grown like a living thing to its present size, the Greek philosopher Herodotus recognized that the sedimentary deposits of the Nile made Egypt a "gift of the river." The discovery of sea shells far inland by Eratosthenes (third century B.C.) led him to speculate that land had once been covered by the sea. Leonardo da Vinci (1452–1519) showed brilliant reasoning on a wide range of geologic phenomena.

The eighteenth and nineteenth centuries, however, showed outstanding advances in discovery and coordination of thought. In the eighteenth century amidst raging controversy, the idea of James Hutton (1726–97) that the earth had developed over a long period of time by forces which would continue to

studying the picture

Ask the students what they might find in a handful of soil. Some possibilities are pebbles, twigs, leaves, ants, seed grains. *Ask how the contents of a handful of soil shows that the earth is changing.* Probably none of the things in a handful of soil were originally formed where you now find them. Also, they are probably in a different form than at some prior time (the twigs, for example, were once part of a tree). Tell the students that the old-time prospector in the picture relied mostly on luck to discover deposits of valuable minerals, such as gold and silver. *Ask how a present-day prospector works, by comparison.* He relies on instruments and methods of geological science and usually has thorough training in mining geology.

bring about change was eventually accepted. Independent studies in the nineteenth century in England and France led to the discovery that identical layers of earth distantly apart contained the same fossil forms. Geology became a field based more solidly on fact rather than speculation.

Aided by advances in biology, chemistry, and physics, twentieth century geology continues to work out its main objective: to discover the full history of the earth and its inhabitants.

Men have not always been able to explain many of the natural events that take place on the earth. The word volcano comes from the name of the Roman god of fire Vulcan. Primitive people living on Pacific islands where volcanoes erupted thought that one of their gods was angry when a volcano began to erupt. The Pacific islanders had strange ceremonies in which they thought they would calm the angry god by sacrificing a beautiful young person to the volcano. The fact that the eruption sometimes did stop was only accidental. We know today that there is nothing we can do to stop an erupting volcano. The best we can do is observe carefully the various instruments that may signal a possible eruption and let people know so that they can prevent great loss of life and property. Today we know that volcanoes are caused by the release of molten materials from beneath the surface of the earth's crust. We do not have to rely on the explanation that a god is angry to explain this spectacular natural event.

On your way to school you may have passed streets and sidewalks, trees and lawns. Do you think any of these things have changed? Will they?

You might see that dirt has been blown into the street or that soil from a lawn has washed across a driveway. You may find places where the sidewalk is cracked. What could have caused it to crack?

Is the surface of the earth today exactly the same as it was yesterday? We have many reasons for believing that the earth was much different thousands of years ago. Scientists who study the uncovered remains of ancient cities are called archaeologists (ahr-kee-ahl-uh-jihsts). These cities have been buried for thousands of years by layers of soil. Such places give us a record not only of what these cities were like, but also what the surface of the earth was like.

the unit at a glance

This unit's overall theme is expressed in its title, "The Changing Earth." The students are made aware of the fact that, though most of the changes in the earth take place on such a small scale and over such a long time as to be virtually unnoticeable in the course of a human lifetime, they are nonetheless occurring. The principal causes of earth changes, wind, water and ice, are given major emphasis because they are the most significant forces operating. In addition, the more spectacular causes, earthquakes and volcanic eruptions, are also discussed.

OVERVIEW

By a series of observations of activities the children will begin to understand that certain changes involve only the moving of objects from one place to another, while other changes affect the objects themselves. This understanding will help them to learn how the earth is constantly changing. To become aware of these changes that take place on the earth's surface, have the class observe those that can be seen from season to season. Others can be seen only over a long period. In these activities the children will see how the action of wind, water, and ice can change the earth. The students will investigate the effects of contraction and expansion on rocks. In another activity the children observe the effects of running water on soil. The action of wind on dry and wet soil are compared by the class. You will contrast changes that occur over thousands of years, such as beach erosion, to those that happen suddenly and dramatically, such as earthquakes and volcanoes.

process skills

Observing evidence that the earth's surface is changing

Observing the chemical and physical effects that running water, wind, and ice have upon soil and rocks

Inferring the approximate length of time of certain geological changes

materials

marble rock*, vinegar, pan*, hot plate, long-handled wooden spoon*, small glass jar with cover*, plastic or cloth bag*, aluminum foil pans (two sizes)*, soft rock such as sandstone or limestone*, shallow box*, ruler*, soil, paper towel*, litmus paper, popsicle stick*, crayons or paints, metal can of cold water*, newspapers

---

* per team

WHAT CHANGES CAN WE SEE ON THE EARTH?

The photograph shows many different features of our earth's surface. Some of these are ones you notice everyday. Hills, for example, are parts of the earth's surface you might often see. Rivers and mountains are familiar features. What other features can you name in the photograph? Have you seen some of them close to your home or during a vacation trip?

how to begin

Depending on the season of the year when the unit is studied, ask the children if they have ever noticed any changes in the earth around them. The changes in plant life that come with the four seasons will be obvious ones that will be mentioned, but it should be emphasized that these are plant life changes and not actual changes in the surface of the earth itself. Some children will mention changes that involve weather conditions. This discussion can lead to how a change in weather can cause a difference in the earth's surface. Discuss the weather conditions of that particular day and ask if the weather has caused any changes in the earth. The children might mention very temporary changes that will last only as long as a few hours. Depending on the surrounding geographical conditions, different changes in the surface of the earth will be noticed.

procedure

The first activity, boiling a small piece of marble in vinegar, must be done under your supervision since it involves the use of heat. Make sure the children examine the marble rock carefully before heating.

(continued on page 270)

You may have noticed changes in lawns, streets or sidewalks. Other changes cannot be noticed from day to day, because they happen so slowly. A small hill may have once been a mountain. A stream could have been a great river. While some valleys are being filled by lakes, some flat lands may be carved into valleys. Such changes would take thousands, even millions, of years. Many features of the earth's surface change, but they do so ever so slowly.

1/Infer

Here is one change you can see in a short time. After boiling a small piece of marble rock in vinegar for about 10-15 minutes, remove the marble from the vinegar with a long-handled wooden spoon. Cool the piece of marble rock on a strip of paper towel. Examine it carefully after it has cooled. 1 How was the marble changed? 2 Was something new formed? 3 What do you think caused the change? Remember you used an indicator called litmus paper to test liquids last year.

221

responses to 1/infer

1. The surface of the marble becomes rough and pock-marked.
2. Bubbles of the gas carbon dioxide (CO_2) can be seen escaping.
3. Marble reacted chemically with the boiling vinegar, causing the marble to undergo a chemical change.

(continued)

Let them feel the rock's surface so they can compare any differences in texture after boiling it. It isn't necessary to first bring to the children's attention that this is a chemical change. That can be done at the end of the group of activities when the children compare the two types of change.

Filling a container with water and freezing it will probably be done at home since a freezer will not be available in the classroom. Emphasize that the container must be wrapped in a cloth or plastic bag, but do not give the class any reason. After the activity is completed, you can ask the children why this precaution was needed.

Showing the physical effects of erosion by running water is a continuing activity that lasts for a week. Have the children keep a daily record of observations so they can compare the progress of the erosion. Help them organize their results in chart form.

(continued on page 272)

responses to 1/infer

(continued)

4. Make them dissolve.

responses to 2/compare

1. The glass jar has cracked.
2. When the water froze it expanded and broke the glass.
3. Hopefully, the students will relate this observation to the effects caused by water freezing in rock, expanding and causing the rock to crack.

note

It should be pointed out to the students that most substances, other than water, will contract when they reach their freezing temperature. Water is somewhat unique in that it expands upon freezing. This will be further discussed later in the unit (see page 312).

Vinegar is an acid and it reacts with marble. There are acids formed in the earth's surface. ④ What might they do to pieces of rock? ■

The next activity will help you observe the effect of cold temperature on water.

2/Compare

Fill a small jar to the top with cold water. Put the cap on tightly and wrap the jar in a plastic bag. Close the end of the bag with rubber bands. Put the jar in a freezer. Let it stand overnight.

The next day remove the jar from the freezer and unwrap it carefully. If you do not have a plastic bag for this activity, put the jar in a large can without a lid. ① How has the jar of water changed? ② What do you think caused the change? ③ Think of ways that cold causes other substances to change. ■

222

3/Compare

Cut a V-shaped notch in one end of an aluminum foil pan. Fill the pan with moistened soil. Place it in another larger pan; then raise the uncut end by resting it on a wooden block. Take a popsicle stick and starting at one end, rule lines 1/2″ apart on the stick. Color the spaces in this order: red, orange, yellow, green, blue and purple. Fasten the stick next to the V-shaped notch, with the red portion at the top as shown in the drawing. Each day for one week, pour one-half cup of water on the soil from the raised end. What have you found out after observing your results for one week? Weigh any soil that has been washed into the larger pan. How many cups of water did you use? If more water was used, would your results have changed? Try tilting the pan more and continuing the activity for a longer time. Compare your results with the first ones. ■

responses to 3/compare

1. Some soil has been washed into the larger pan.
2. Three and a half cups of water have been used.
3. More soil would have been washed into the larger pan.
4. The longer the activity is continued, the more soil there will be in the larger pan. Tilting increases the amount of soil that is washed out of the smaller pan.

note

Have the students observe how the following factors affect the rate of soil deposition: (a) duration of water flow, (b) amount of water, and (c) the tilt or slope of the smaller pan. You might have some students keep a time chart to determine how long it takes to cover the color spaces on the stick when the previous factors are varied.

You should supervise the heating of the sandstone or limestone in water. Have the children compare this activity with the one in which marble is boiled in vinegar to understand the difference between a physical and chemical change.

Comparing how much soil can be blown away when it is dry and wet is another study of physical change. You can have the children weigh the soil in each case for a more accurate observation, but weighing is not absolutely necessary. They will be able to see the difference so that weighing is optional.

The main points to be understood in these activities is the cause of erosion and the difference between physical and chemical changes. In a physical change, as in erosion, a substance remains the same in kind, but changes in shape or position. In a chemical change, as in the rusting of iron, matter changes from one form to another.

(continued on page 274)

responses to 4/observe

1. The rock cracks or breaks.
2. The sudden and extreme temperature change caused the rock to crack.
3. Extremely cold temperatures can cause cracks in sidewalks.

note

Here is an illustration of what is the usual result when objects are heated and cooled. In activity 4, the rock expands when heated. When suddenly cooled, it contracts and the shrinkage causes the rock to crack. This actually happens to rock in nature. In addition, once a tiny crack is formed, water seeps into the crack and freezes, causing the rock to crack further.

The kinds of changes you see correspond to bigger changes on the earth's surface. Few big changes on the surface of the earth take place rapidly. Most of them are the result of small ones taking place daily.

4/Observe

Heat a small piece of some rock, such as sandstone, limestone, or sidewalk cement, on a hot plate for about five minutes. Drop the heated rock into a metal can of cold water. How did the rock change? What might have caused any change? Can you now suggest one reason why a crack may appear in the sidewalk? ■

The next two activities will help you observe another way that the surface of the earth may be changed in appearance.

224

272

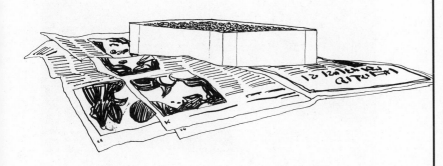

5/Observe

After filling a shallow box with loose, dry soil, place it on a sheet of newspaper. Use a ruler to smooth the surface of the soil. Blow across the surface. ①How has the surface of the soil changed? ■

6/Compare

Now place the box on another sheet of paper. Sprinkle part of the soil with water. Again blow across ①the surface of the soil. ②What do you observe? How do people in various areas prevent the wind from doing too much damage? ③How much soil is there on the first newspaper? ④Is there any on the second newspaper? ⑤How much? ⑥Compare the movement of wet soil and dry soil. ⑦Explain the reason for any difference between them. ⑧What might happen to dry soil in a windstorm? ■

225

responses to 5/observe

1. Some of the soil is blown off the surface.

responses to 6/compare

1. Less soil is blown off the surface than in activity 5/Observe.
2. By irrigating the soil and by planting grass or rows of trees.
3. Answers will vary.
4. Answers will vary.
5. Answers will vary.
6. Dry soil is moved by blowing (wind) to a greater extent than is wet soil.
7. Wet soil helps the particles stick together and prevents the wind from separating them.
8. Dry topsoil gets blown away in a windstorm. Sand dunes are one example of wind-blown soil that has been transported and redeposited.

The answers to Testing Your Ideas are that the first statement is a change by water, the second statement is a change by temperature, the third statement is a change by wind, and the fourth statement is a change by acid.

studying the picture

Have the students study the picture on page 227. It illustrates one of the beneficial effects of wind—it helps to dry the clothes hanging on the line. *Ask the students if they see the wind in the picture.* Lead them to understand that we never see the wind itself—we only see the results of the wind's action. *Ask the students to find a clue in the picture which indicates the direction of the wind.* The direction the clothes are blowing indicates that the wind is blowing from the left.

The earth can be changed by water, wind, acid, and temperature. Which of the statements listed below best illustrates one of these ways:

changed by water   *changed by temperature*
changed by wind   *changed by acid*

At the bottom of the Grand Canyon is the Colorado River.

Sometimes during a period of frost, freezing water may push against the underside of tar roads to make bumps.

Sand dunes change shape.

Sometimes the earth is eaten away to make caverns.

OVERVIEW

By careful observation, children see air in motion on the earth's surface and that it exerts a force. The dust storms of the 1930's are offered as an example of a change by wind. This example is reinforced by measure and compare activities dealing with the erosion of sandy beaches. Students perform activities to investigate how erosion can be retarded. Commercial sandblasting and wind carrying sand particles suggest how rock can be worn away by wind.

how to begin

Student observations of wind in action can begin the discussion of the ways wind can change the surface of the earth. The children can report firsthand examples of how wind blows leaves about, bends bushes over, and blows soil and sand around. The discussion should bring about the knowledge that wind is air in motion. Students might mention that wind can help us as well as cause damage. We can measure its speed and take steps to limit some of its harmful effects.

process skills

Investigating how wind can cause physical changes on the earth's surface

Describing methods of preventing topsoil and seashore areas from eroding

materials

paper, thread, rice, 2 fans (different sizes), puffed rice, dry soil, sand, salt, sugar, talcum powder, yardstick or strip of wood*, grassy soil, chalkboard eraser, sandpaper, piece of hard wood*, piece of soft wood*, light bulb, piece of sandstone*

---

* one per team

HOW DOES WIND CAUSE CHANGES ON THE EARTH?

Have you ever seen a man walking on a windy day? A man's hat can suddenly blow off on a windy day. He may have to run down the street to catch it.

Watch the flag on your school building on a windy day. Is it blowing out straight from the flagpole? On a windy day, leaves may suddenly swirl up into the air. Dust will fly about. Did you really see what knocked the man's hat off or what made the flag move or the leaves swirl?

procedure

The class may be divided into small groups for 7/Observe. The children will observe the turning of a paper propeller over a source of heat. Have the class explain why the propeller turns. From the discussion the youngsters should conclude that the propeller moves because warm arm rises and pushes it. Encourage the children to relate their observations to the nature of wind. Lead them to see that heat from the sun raises temperatures on the surface of the earth. The air above the heated earth is heated in turn and rises. Thus, a pattern of circulatory movement is set up. This is as far as you should expect the students to be able to reason from the activity and from their own experiencial backgrounds. In reality, planetary wind patterns are greatly influenced by the earth's rotation, which causes an east-west deflection of the air surrounding the earth. This effect is called the Coriolis effect. Do not introduce this subject unless the students happen to bring it up.

(continued on page 278)

optional activity

Students can study wind currents at home or school by making a wind stick (see diagram below). Tie two pieces of light-weight string of equal lengths to a stick sunk firmly in the ground at an angle. Tie a metal ring or other weight to one string; let the other hang loose. The students can get a rough idea of the force of the wind by measuring the angle formed between the two pieces of string as the wind blows.

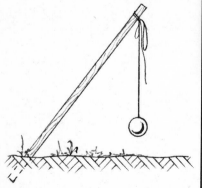

By observing carefully, you can see objects that are moved or changed by wind. Everyone has heard the wind, but who has really seen it? Clothes flapping on a clothesline can show the presence of wind. You can see the effects of wind, but you cannot see the wind itself.

Wind is powerful. It can push over trees or a sailboat on a stormy ocean. It can be gentle and blow softly. Wind can move fast during a storm or slowly in a breeze. The next activity shows you the effects of air in motion.

228

7/Observe

Mark a square piece of paper as shown. Fold up on the solid lines and down on the dotted ones. Now attach a thread to the center of the paper. Hold the paper by the thread over a light bulb. What happens? 2 Do you know the reason for it? ■

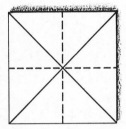

Air has weight. It can push. Air moves. Air moving over the surface of the earth is called wind. Do you think that the heat from the sun can change the movement of air?

Wind is always blowing somewhere on the surface of the earth. It can be a wild hurricane blowing more than 120 miles an hour or a mild breeze that just blows leaves across a lawn. Wind speeds can reach over 200 miles an hour. Most of the time wind is moving less than 15 miles per hour.

responses to 7/observe

1. The paper twirls around.
2. The air above the light bulb is heated and rises, producing a convection current.

studying the picture

For the photographs on these pages, have the children look for evidence that indicates the presence of wind. *From which direction does the wind come in each picture? In which picture is the wind stronger? How can you tell?* In both pictures the wind is blowing from left to right, as indicated by the sails and the direction of the tree branches. The force of the wind in the picture of the tropical storm is greater—strong enough to cause destruction.

Activities 8/Measure and 9/Compare should be performed out of doors and would be better done in groups of about four or five children. While the best results are obtained with the materials listed, the activities may be done with sizes 00, 0, and 1 corks. Care should be taken to avoid mishaps with the blades of the fan. Each group should be encouraged to select a recorder and prepare a chart indicating the distance each material was carried. Ask the children to think of additional materials they might test and how they could prevent the fan from moving the materials they are testing. Then the children can discuss how this applies to actual situations where materials on the earth's surface are displaced by the action of wind.

Ask the children if they notice a particular pattern in the results they get. What they should find is that the heavier materials are blown less than lighter ones and that a larger fan increases the movement of materials tested. To find out what their observations would be like if the materials had been wet, the students could simply repeat activity 9/Compare with wet materials. They should be able to infer that the wet materials would be heavier and therefore would be blown less than the dry materials.

Now you can help the children relate their results to what occurs when wind blows earth materials about.

(continued on page 280)

responses to 8/measure

1. All of the rice grains do not move the same distance, but most of the grains are in the same general area.

2. The puffed rice moves a greater distance than the plain rice.

3. When a larger fan is used, both the rice and the puffed rice move farther.

The force of wind causes changes in the surface of the earth. Some of them can be seen each day. Other changes take longer. A pile of dry leaves can be blown away in a few minutes. Wind blowing sand against a rock can take years to change the shape of that rock.

8/Measure

Use paper that is at least 20 inches by 30 inches. Mark off the paper into one-inch squares. Now tape the paper on a table in front of a fan. Put a table-spoonful of rice on the edge of the paper, just in front of the fan. Turn on the fan and when it reaches a steady speed, count to 15. Turn off the fan. Measure how far the rice moved across the paper. Record the

230

greatest distance the rice moved. Did all grains of rice move the same distance?

Now using a tablespoonful of puffed rice, repeat the activity. Record your observations. Next, you might use a larger fan. Is there any difference when the larger fan is used? Observe what happens and record your results. ■

9/Compare

Use a mixture of puffed rice and plain rice. Repeat the activity. Compare the distances the two kinds of rice moved.

Record your results when testing a tablespoonful of each of the following materials in the same way: dry soil, sand, salt, sugar, talcum powder. ■

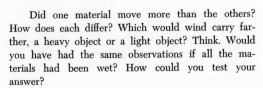

Did one material move more than the others? How does each differ? Which would wind carry farther, a heavy object or a light object? Think. Would you have had the same observations if all the materials had been wet? How could you test your answer?

231

1. The puffed rice moves a greater distance than the plain rice.
2. Lighter materials move farther than heavier materials.

Measuring changes in sand level at a particular spot in 10/Measure and 11/Compare will show how wind moves materials from one place to another. Depending on wind direction, the sand level may rise or fall. The force of the wind at that spot will also determine how much sand is blown there or blown away. If a sandy area is not available, ask some of the children to recall any experiences at a seashore area on a windy day. They can also use what they have observed in a previous activity with a fan to predict what would happen.

(continued on page 282)

studying the picture

This is a striking photo of a dust storm in action. Have the students study it and then ask them the following questions: *Do you think this land was once green pasture? Why? What does the presence of the cattle tell you?* The students should be able to infer that this was pasture land, because there are cattle in the picture and because there are bits of dry, brown grass in the scene.

Ask the students to think back to some of the experiments they have done in this unit and then ask the following questions, which are related to the picture and the experiments. *Which would be better for the soil at this time, a light rain or a heavy downpour? Why?* A light rain would be the best because it would allow the water enough time to sink into the ground.

(continued)

In the 1930's the middle western United States had several years of very dry weather called a drought (DROWT). The drought destroyed farm crops. The soil dried out. Strong, dry winds blew the soil great distances. In 1934 a single windstorm blew an estimated 300 million tons of soil eastward to the Atlantic Ocean. Thousands of farms were ruined because their topsoil was carried away by the wind.

Suppose grass and other plants had been growing in the soil. Would less soil have been lost if there had been more rain? Think of some activities you could do to find out.

232

Wearing away of the earth by wind may cause the level of the land to become lower. During a long time period, the land level in southern Wyoming has dropped 150 feet. Wind carried dust and loose soil away. Compare your height with 150 feet. Measure 150 feet in the hall outside your classroom. Do you think that a lot of soil was moved in the 150 foot drop?

10/Measure

Measure changes in the depth of the sand if you live near a sandlot or beach. Mark one-inch lines on a strip of wood to use as a yardstick or use a ready-made one. Push one end of your measuring stick firmly into the sand. Record the reading.

Observe the level of the sand each day for three weeks or longer. Record your observations. ■

233

A sudden downpour might create a flash flood. Because the soil is loose and dry, the topsoil would be easily washed away by strong, sudden and intense rainfall.

An essay question for some of your faster students is: *If you were the owner of this land, how would you go about trying to get it back to its original condition? Devise a step-by-step plan for the job.* The students should be able to come up with a good plan based on what they have learned in this lesson, plus what they can learn from library research.

responses to 10/measure

1. Changes in the depth of the sand will vary according to wind and precipitation.

12/Compare prepares the children to see that erosion can be retarded by certain practices. Before doing the activity have the children explore ways they would take to lessen the erosive effects of wind. You might help the children conclude that if cover crops had been growing, their roots would have helped to hold down valuable topsoil during a wind-storm.

13/Investigate suggests another method to retard erosion and is done with a barrier (eraser) to air movement. The important point is to relate the activity to the way actual barriers are set up in areas subject to wind erosion. Mention wind fences and planting of sand grass at seashore areas to reduce erosion. Discuss what precautions must be taken when gale or hurricane warnings are given by the weather bureau.

(continued on page 284)

responses to 11/compare

1. The changes might be more extreme—the stick might be buried, or it might fall over if enough sand is blown away.
2. If the area is sheltered, it is likely that there will be fewer changes in the level of the sand.

responses to 12/compare

1. Less soil is washed away.
2. Yes.

responses to 13/investigate

1. The rice directly in front of the eraser does not move as far as the other rice.

11/Compare

Compare the results you get after one week with those after three weeks. Suppose the record was kept for one year. What changes might you discover? Think of some of the causes for such changes. Why will the place where the stick is pushed into the sand make any difference in your findings? Predict if the sand level will be raised or lowered. ■

The wearing away of land by wind is called erosion (e-ROE-shun). Many deserts have been formed mostly by wind erosion. The first step in desert formation is the loss of grass and other plant life. When the topsoil dries up and its particles separate, the wind can carry it away. Once topsoil is gone, the wind continues to carry away the remaining dust, sand, and soil until sometimes only bare rock remains. This kind of change may take place in a few years.

Topsoil contains all the nutrients which the plant must obtain in order to grow. Topsoil is very important to the farmer. Without it he cannot grow food crops.

12/Compare

Repeat the activity with the V-shaped notch pan. This time use soil which has grass growing in it. How do your results compare? Can grass slow the erosion of soil by wind as well as water? ■

Sand or soil carried away by wind is deposited as the wind loses speed. The topsoil that wind picks up in one place may be deposited in another, thousands of miles away. Check the records you kept doing the activity with the two electric fans. Was there a difference in how far materials were moved with each fan?

Windblown topsoils often form rich farmlands, such as those in the Mississippi Valley. What else can cause the wind to deposit soil and other material that it carries?

13/Investigate

Set up the electric fan, the marked paper, and the grains of rice again. Place a chalkboard eraser at half the greatest distance the rice moved. Turn on the fan and count to 15. Turn off the fan. What did you observe? ■

To illustrate how sand dunes are formed, fill a flat box with dry, clean soil or fine sand. Cut "trees" and "bushes" out of cardboard (or use actual twigs and bits of plants). Stick these upright into the soil and use an electric fan to blow a stream of air over the box. *Ask the students to explain what happens.* The soil is blown away by the air stream, but is deflected by the obstructions so that tiny dunes form on the side away from the fan. *Ask the students to explain what would have happened if the twigs and plants had not been there.* The soil would have blown away and no dunes would form.

Sand dunes are hills of windblown sand. A dune is started by an obstruction which reduces the speed of the wind. A small deposit of sand accumulates on the sheltered side of the obstacle. As the amount of sand grows, it acts as a larger and larger windbreak, thus increasing the amount deposited.

A sand dune has a gentle slope on its windward side because the force of the wind tends to flatten the side of the dune against which it blows. The sheltered side has a steeper slope since the wind pushes the sand over the crest, where it tumbles down.

The wind sweeping around the sides of a growing dune often builds two long pointed extensions. These give the dune a crescent shape when viewed from above. Such a dune is called a barchan. In the photograph below, the wind was blowing from the left. If the wind direction changed, the formation of the dunes would be reversed.

The students should compare the difference between changing the shape of a dune made of loose

for your information

In the United States, sand dunes are found along the shores of the Atlantic and Pacific Oceans, along the east coast of Lake Michigan, and in some of the larger stream valleys of the West.

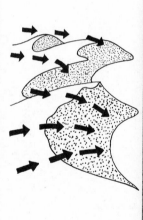

An object in the path of the wind will lessen its speed. This is the way huge piles of sand, called dunes, are formed. Sand grass can be used to keep the sand from blowing near the seacoast. Rocks and wooden slat fences lessen the speed of the wind. Such objects make the wind deposit some of the sand it may be carrying. A large dune builds up with a gentle slope on the side toward the wind. Examine a sand dune if possible. Figure out which side was toward the wind. Looking at the picture, decide the direction the wind was blowing when the dunes were formed. What happens to the shape of the sand dunes if the wind direction changes?

236

sand and changing the shape and character of hard rock by bombarding it with sand. In the one case, we are talking about simply moving materials from one place to another, while in the other case, we are talking about completely wearing down solid, hard rock. The students should be able to infer that it might take millions of years to wear away hard rock. The amount of time it would take would depend on wind velocity, the amount of contact the rock surface has with wind-blown sand, and composition of the original rock.

(continued on page 286)

studying the picture

Ask the students to imagine what the land in this photograph might have looked like before the erosion took place. *What peaks might have been joined? How can you tell?* Bands or layers of rock (sedimentation lines) stand out distinctly in the picture. These bands indicate that many of the adjacent peaks were once part of an unbroken formation.

Wind-blown sand travels close to the earth. A rock is worn away as the sand blows against it. The wearing away of rocks and soil by wind and water is called weathering. The rocks in the photograph were changed in shape by the sand blown against them. Estimate how long it might have taken to shape these rocks. Could you predict what factors would determine how long the wearing away of the rock surface would take?

237

Testing the action of sandpaper on various materials is compared in 14/Compare to the abrasive action of windblown sand. Using surfaces that vary in hardness will show the difference in the effects of erosion on materials. The amount of time a substance is exposed to erosion is a most important factor, and this should be stressed when the results of the activity are discussed. Rocks vary in their degree of hardness. Softer rocks are, of course, worn away more quickly than harder rocks.

(continued on page 288)

responses to 14/compare

1. The amount of sawdust accumulates quickly from the piece of soft wood.
2. The sandpaper scratches the surface of the marble, but does not produce a noticeable amount of particles. Some particles of sandstone are rubbed off.
3. Marble is smooth; sandstone is rough. Marble is harder than sandstone.
4. More particles of sandstone are worn off; the surface of the marble is scratched more.
5. Answers will vary. The point of this prediction and the activity is to show the great amount of time necessary for erosion.

14/Compare

Take a piece of hard wood and rub it with rough sandpaper for one minute. Do this over a sheet of paper. Now use a piece of soft wood. Compare the amount of sawdust from each.

Use medium-weight sandpaper to rub a small piece of marble rock. Rub it 100 times and note your results. Use another piece of the same grade of sandpaper to rub a chunk of sandstone 100 times. Compare the two results. Explain the difference between the two kinds of rock. Repeat using 500 strokes. Compare the results. Suppose you had sanded each rock 1000 times. Predict how long it would take to wear away the rocks to dust. ∎

When stone buildings become dark and dirty-looking, they are cleaned with air-blown sand. A high-speed stream of air and sand is blown at the surface of the building from a spray gun. This sandblasting quickly wears away the outer dirty layer of stone. The clean stone underneath is exposed.

Men who operate sand-blasting machinery must wear heavy protective clothing. Why is this safety measure necessary? Commercial sandblasting is a very rapid process. Compare it to sandblasting in nature. Are all rocks the same hardness? Which factors will determine how quickly the rocks are worn away?

239

Ask the students if any of them have ever seen a sandblasting job in operation. If they have, let them discuss the things they noticed. *Ask if a person could stand right next to a building which was being sandblasted and comfortably watch the proceedings.* This would be impossible without protective glasses to prevent the sand from getting in your eyes. In addition, everything for several blocks around becomes coated with the particles of dirty stone as they are blasted away from the building. *Ask why this process is so rapid when done commercially and so slow in nature.* The force of the machine-blown sand is much greater than that exerted by wind-blown sand, for one thing, and in addition, the blowing is continuous from the machine, while in nature, the wind changes its speed frequently.

In Testing Your Ideas the first two statements are false, and the last two are true.

note

Be sure to point out to the students that the wind is actually an indirect erosional agent. The wind itself does no eroding. Rather, it is the constant battering of tiny sand particles against the surface of a rock which wears off the rock's surface.

TESTING YOUR IDEAS

With which of the following statements do you agree?

Wind changes the earth, but only by wearing it away.

Nothing can be done to stop or to slow the wearing away of the earth by wind.

Wind can be helpful as well as harmful.

Some of the earth's surfaces are more quickly worn away than others.

OVERVIEW

The first two activities introduce the fact that the earth can be changed by water by showing that this substance has weight and can exert a force. Building on these activities, the lesson elaborates upon water's erosive effects, its ability to carry soil, and to build up land, as in the case of deltas. The ocean's effect upon land is suggested by a comparison of smooth stones found at the shore and those found inland. Activities indicate that soil absorbs water and that plants and decaying animal matter prevent runoff and combat erosion. As a final point, water's action as a solvent upon the earth in the formation of caverns is suggested. The length of the lesson makes unlikely a thorough coverage of the material in less than a week. The list of materials, consequently, has been divided to allow the teacher to obtain what she needs on a staggered basis.

how to begin

Use photographs to show land formations and deformations caused by the action of running water. Ask the students what the photographs show. Relate responses to the idea that water exerts a force.

(continued on page 290)

HOW DOES WATER CHANGE THE SURFACE OF THE EARTH?

Many changes in the earth's surface are caused by wind. But wind alone does not cause all change. About three-fourths of our earth is covered by water. Look around you. In what ways do you think water could change the surface of the earth?

The oceans of the world contain most of the earth's water. Water flows on and below the earth's surface to form springs, lakes, ponds, rivers and streams.

The heat of the sun evaporates water into the air surrounding the earth. Clouds form. Water returns to the surface of the earth as snow, rain, sleet, or hail.

process skills

Describing how running water can wear away land

Observing that objects of different weight settle out of water at different rates

Explaining how land areas are built up through the action of running water and the sediment that it carries

Describing how shore lines are changed through the process of erosion

Observing how water can form caverns

289

Ask for a description of the kinds of materials carried along a curb during and just after a heavy rainstorm. A filmstrip or movie can emphasize the great force with which ocean waves pound against the shore. The film could graphically point out how the continual wearing away effect of water occurs over a given period of time.

procedure

To understand how water can change the earth, the children are shown in 15/Compare and 16/Observe that water has weight and that when this weight is combined with motion, materials can be picked up by water and carried from one place to another. Ask the children to apply what they observed in 16/Observe to the filmstrips and photographs they have seen.

(continued on page 292)

materials

scales, glass*, water, shallow pan of thin aluminum*, soil, sprinkling bottle*, pint jar*, tablespoon*, hammer*, soft red brick*, plastic container*, 2 plastic bags*

cupful of soil with bits of rock, sand, pebbles*, quart jar with lid*, 3 sugar cubes*, small jar with lid*, pebbles, plastic bag*, hammer*, magnifying glass*, clean sand

paper towel*, colored water, sprinkling bottle*, water, sponge*, wax paper, hard rock (marble or granite)*, soft rock (sandstone)*, jar of water*, scales

quart jar*, dry soil, pebbles or rock chips, sand, coarse dry soil, fine topsoil, water, smooth round jar*, deep pan*, sand, glass baking dish*, scoop, salt, iron nail or tack*, wet sponge*

---

* per team

Water leaving the surface of the earth and then returning to it is called the water cycle. All the earth's water is part of a water cycle.

When was the last rainy day? How long did it continue to rain? Is any of that rainwater still around? Watch the rain falling on the ground the next time it rains. Observe where it goes. Can you follow the water cycle?

15/Compare

First weigh an empty glass. Weigh it again after filling it with water. Explain the difference. ■

Gravity pulls water down as it does on all materials on the surface of the earth. Therefore, water has weight. Rain is pulled down to the earth by gravity. Some rain soaks into the earth. What happens to the rest of the rainwater? What happens to the water that soaks into the earth?

242

16/Observe

Fill a shallow pan with soil. Keep sprinkling the dirt with water until it cannot absorb any more. Put the pan in a larger one and tilt it slightly. Continue sprinkling. Observe what happens when more water falls than the soil can absorb. How does gravity affect water on the surface? Punch a hole in the bottom of the pan. Watch the water leak out of the hole. ■

There is a difference between water which runs off the surface of the soil and water which runs through the soil. Which do you think is of benefit to the plants?

243

1. The glass of water weighs more than the empty glass. Water has weight.

responses to 16/observe

1. The water drips off into the larger pan, taking some soil with it.
2. Gravity pulls surface water down into the soil until the soil becomes saturated.

17/Observe reinforces the idea of water's ability to move rocks and soil and enables the children to imagine how water can erode stream beds, the sides of streams, and mountain sides. Studying gully erosion and the formation of gullies directly requires very concentrated observation. Your more interested students may like to do something like this: Ask them to find a vacant lot or a spot where there is no vegetative cover; that is, any bare area. Have them make notes about the condition of the area, including an indication of where there are cracks or crevices in the soil. Their notes should be as complete as possible. Then, ask them to look at the same spot after *every* rain and to note whether or not the original cracks or crevices have changed since the initial observations. They can even measure the width of the gully as each rain makes it wider. This study should take several weeks, depending on how much rainfall your part of the country gets, but it is most satisfactory in giving the students a first-hand picture of how gullies are formed in nature.

(continued on page 294)

studying the picture

Heavy rains may set off landslides in which whole sections of a slope slide abruptly downhill. *Ask the students what indication there is that erosion will continue to take place in the section where the natural plant cover has been removed.* Gullies in the soil provide a natural pathway for water that washes down the hillside. This water will continue to erode the bare soil.

responses to 17/observe

1. Some particles of soil remain suspended in the water longer than others. Some particles sink to the bottom immediately.
2. The heavier, larger particles sink first.

Water running off a field or hill makes changes in the earth's surface. Where there is plenty of rain it wears away mountains and washes out valleys. Water is the main carver of the earth. It ruins good fertile soil by dissolving minerals and washing them away. Running water in nature is always on the move, wearing down and carrying away the earth's surface.

244

Running water moving from place to place, carries soil, sand, and other materials along with it. The surfaces over which water flows are carved by sharp-edged particles of rock and soil.

17/Observe

Put two tablespoonsful of soil in a pint jar of water. Shake the jar. ① What did you notice? ② Can you explain what you saw? ∎

Water running off a mountainside forms swiftly flowing streams. Rocks and pebbles, caught up by the moving water smash against the stream beds and cut them away.

245

optional activity

To show the effects of the slope of the land on water erosion, fill three shallow aluminum pans with the same kind of soil. With a stick make a furrow the same depth down the length of each pan. Prop one end of the first pan to a height of 1 inch, the second pan to a height of 2 inches, and the third pan to a height of 3 inches. Measure one quart of water and sprinkle this amount on the upper end of each pan in turn. (Be sure to put the pans on several layers of newspaper and have a pan to catch the overflow water at the lower end of each pan.) The students should compare the depths of the "gully" formed in each pan. *Ask them how the erosion is related to the slope of the pan.* Their observations should indicate that the greater the slope, the greater the erosion.

Activities 18/Investigate and 19/Compare elaborate upon water's erosive effects. 19/Compare may become tiresome if 1000 shakes are given to the container each day for a week. The desired result is to show that water crashing rocks together can break them down. If this result can be indicated before the end of the week, the activity may be considered a success, discussed and terminated.

The reading plateau which follows activity 19 discusses three striking examples of earth evolution due to the slow process of erosion: the Grand Canyon, Niagara Falls, and the Mississippi complex. Find out if any of your students have visited either the Grand Canyon or Niagara Falls. It seems incredible when standing on the edge of the canyon and looking down at that seemingly tiny river winding its way through the maze of canyons, that such an unassuming-looking body of water could have created the great gouge in the earth's surface that we see today. And yet, there is no doubt that the river is responsible. The canyon formed by the Colorado, despite what seems like great age to us, is actually a youngster in terms of the evolution of a landform. The canyon is formed

responses to 18/investigate

1. The pieces of brick have decreased in size.
2. The water has turned a reddish color.
3. Particles of brick, broken off the larger pieces, have colored the water.

responses to 19/compare

1. The rocks are chipped and broken.
2. Soil at the sides of the streams is worn away.

18/Investigate

Break a soft red brick with a hammer. Put several sharp pieces of the brick into a plastic container. Fill the container about half full with water. Screw on the top and place the container in a plastic bag in case it should break.

Have 10 friends shake the container 100 times each. Examine the brick pieces. What do you observe? What is the color of the water? Why? ■

19/Compare

Repeat the activity. Shake the container 1000 times each day for one week. Examine the contents of the container. What happens to rocks as they are carried along by fast moving streams? What do these rocks do to the sides of the streams? ■

and continues to deepen, only until the river reaches its base level (the lowest level it is possible for the stream to cut). Once this level is reached, the speed of the water decreases and thus, downward erosion proceeds more slowly. However, the sides of the canyon continue to erode. As the canyon walls begin to wear down, the valley itself becomes wider, and the walls become increasingly gentle in slope. In this way, the shape of the canyon changes from a sharp V-shape to a more gentle U-shape.

(continued on page 296)

Have you ever seen a valley with a stream or a small river winding through it? Such a valley may once have been level land as high as the surrounding hills. Earth materials that once filled the valley may have been carried away by the water, during many thousands of years.

The Grand Canyon of the Colorado River is one of the most amazing examples of river erosion. For 30 million years or more, the river has been cutting its way through a great plain of rock. It has carved a tremendous canyon that is 6000 feet deep in some places.

optional questions

Ask the students to imagine that for some reason, the Colorado suddenly was unable to continue eroding downward into the Canyon. *What would happen? Would all erosion stop?* They should be able to infer that, as long as the river is moving, it is carrying rocks and other materials which have the ability to wear away rock. If, for some reason, the river were unable to cut downward, it would begin to cut sideways into the walls of the Canyon. Once they recognize that this would happen, have them predict the final appearance of the area. As the river cuts into the walls of the Canyon, the cliffs would become top-heavy and fall into the canyon, thus widening the valley. Eventually, the area would flatten out.

Niagara Falls came into existence simply because the Niagara River had to pass over a steep cliff on its travels from Lake Erie to Lake Ontario. But like canyons, waterfalls are only temporary features in the lifetime of a river. As the river waters plunge over the cliff, they begin to wear away at the base of the falls. In this way, the cliff becomes "top heavy" and the rock at the edge of the cliff begins to crumble and fall to the base of the cliff. Each time this happens, of course, the waterfall moves backwards from its original position. In other words, it recedes. It has been estimated that it has taken the Niagara River 10,000 years to move upstream seven miles. While this may seem like a long time, in terms of human lifetimes, it represents less than 5% of the river's lifetime.

(continued on page 298)

studying the picture

Have the children try to locate a photograph of Niagara Falls which is similar to this one, but which is at least twenty-five years older. Let them compare the two photographs, looking for changes and remaining landmarks. As a research project, some students might like to contact the local newspaper and ask for reprints of back issues which contain articles on changes in the Falls. Periodically, great chunks of rock break from the edge of the cliffs and fall to the base and these occasions are always reported by the press.

Another spot where erosion is always taking place is Niagara Falls. The Niagara River flows over a cliff of hard limestone and soft shale. The rock is being worn away at the rate of five feet per year by the moving water. Which rock would wear away faster? The shape of the falls has changed greatly because of this constant erosion. If you were to compare the shape of the falls today with a photograph taken 20 years ago, the changes could be easily seen.

Running water carries soil, bits of rocks and earth materials with it. As the swift moving streams broaden

248

out, they flow more slowly. The stream deposits some of the earth materials. These materials, called sediments, gradually build up the river bottom.

Two or more rivers may join to form a river system. The largest one in our country is the Mississippi River system. Picking up earth materials in some places and dropping them in others, the Mississippi flows for more than 2300 miles. When it finally reaches the quiet waters of the Gulf of Mexico, the Mississippi deposits the last of its earth materials, over a million tons a day.

Most of the Mississippi's sediment is carried farther by the Gulf waters, but much is deposited to form a low plain where the river meets the sea. A plain built up at the mouth of a stream or river is called a delta. Pushing its way farther out into the Gulf of Mexico, the Mississippi delta continues to grow every day.

for your information

Not all rivers have deltas. A river that is relatively free of silt will not form a delta. Some rivers do not build deltas because tidal currents at the mouth of the river carry away the earth materials.

When doing 20/Compare, divide the class into small groups. Some students might want to predict what will happen even before they do the activity. Be sure each group records its observations accurately and have each draw sketches of the jar containing the settled materials. To let the children apply what they have seen, ask them why harbors where the mouth of a river flows into the ocean have to be dredged over a period of time. Point out that deltas at the mouth of rivers are formed by the sediment picked up by rivers as they flow towards the ocean. Have the children explain what happened to the various kinds of materials that were put into suspension and why they got the results they did. The class should use its observations to reach the conclusion that some materials settle faster than others because of their weight.

(continued on page 300)

responses to 20/compare

1. The rock and pebbles drop to the bottom first.
2. The sand remains suspended the longest.
3. The heavier materials sink to the bottom first. The lighter materials remain suspended longer.

Deltas are built up as running water carries soil, bits of rock, and other earth materials with it. These substances are deposited on the bottom where the river broadens out and slows down. See for yourself what happens when a narrow, swift-flowing stream broadens out and flows more slowly.

20/Compare

Take a cupful of soil containing bits of rock, sand, and pebbles. Put the soil into a quart jar. Fill the jar almost to the top with water. Cover the jar tightly; shake it hard. Set the jar down and watch carefully as the earth materials settle.

250

1 Identify the material that drops to the bottom first. **2** Which substance remains suspended in the water longest? **3** Compare the differences between the materials. When running water loses speed which of the materials will be dropped first? Predict which materials will be carried farthest by the running water. ▪

Have you seen washouts, gullies, or other changes made by rushing water? Wherever the ocean meets the land there is constant change. Sometimes the change is great and sudden such as when a single storm washes away part of an island. Usually the change is only a few shells or small amounts of sand washed back into the ocean or thrown up on the beach.

The kind of change produced when, as in the example in the text, a storm washes away part of an island, is due to the force of the wind itself. This is a spectacular, but less significant kind of erosion than the kind which occurs over long periods of time. Long-term erosion is due to three things: the battering of rocks by water; the battering of rocks by solid particles carried by the waves; and the dissolving of the surface layers of rock by water.

Activities 21/Discover and 22/Predict, while similar to others, prepare the children to appreciate activity 23/Compare. In activity 21/Discover, have the children be sure to shake the jar vigorously for several minutes. It is important that the class see what effect the shaking has on the sugar. Some groups of children will get a more dramatic effect if they shake the jar for a longer time and put more effort into it. The children can use their observational skills in 22/Predict to explain differences in the stones. Most pebbles taken from the shore area will be rounded and smooth. Some children might also bring in small pieces of wood they have found along the beach. Ask the children if this smoothing process takes place over a long or short time period. Having seen how rocks may be broken down by water, the students can be made dramatically aware of the similarity between broken pieces of pebbles and particles of sand. Summarize this idea of the lesson by having a volunteer explain how he might show a classmate how sand has been made.

(continued on page 302)

optional activity

If you are fortunate enough to be located near a beach, have students in the class collect objects, other than rocks and pebbles, that show signs of erosion by waves. Pieces of glass, whole shells or pieces of shells, driftwood, bits of iron and other metals will all show signs of erosion if they have been on the beach long enough. They will be smooth and rounded. This activity may have even more meaning to the students than their observations of rocks because, for all they know, the apparently eroded rock they observed may have always looked that way. The objects they collect for this activity, however, are objects with which they are previously familiar.

21/Discover

Place three sugar cubes in a small jar. Put the lid on tightly and shake the jar for a few minutes. Open it and examine the sugar cubes. 1 Look at the corners of the cubes. 2 What do you find at the bottom of the jar? ■

22/Predict

1 If you used pieces of sandstone what do you think you would find at the bottom of the jar? 2 Where does sand come from? Most of the stones you find on a beach are smooth and rounded. Compare their shapes with those found in a backyard area. 3 How does the action of waves change the shape? ■

Rocks are tumbled against each other as waves wash up on the beach. Gradually, the rocks on beaches are broken down into sand. The change from rock to sand does not occur overnight. Many thousands of years are needed to change a rocky coastline to an area of soft, rolling sand dunes. Predict which would take longer to change, a coastline of soft rock or one of hard rock, such as that found along the Maine coast.

23/Compare

Take a few pebbles and break them up into some pieces by wrapping them in a plastic bag and hitting them with a hammer. Examine a piece with a magnifying glass. Examine some clean sand with a magnifying glass. How does it compare to the rock pieces? ■

responses to 21/discover

1. The corners of the cubes are worn away.
2. Some grains of sugar are at the bottom of the jar.

responses to 22/predict

1. Grains of sand would be at the bottom of the jar.
2. Sand comes from rocks that have been broken down into smaller particles.
3. The action of the waves wears away the surface of the stones, making them smooth.

responses to 23/compare

1. In each there are particles visible. In the rock pieces, the particles have not broken off.

Having studied the erosive effects of water, the students can now examine the absorptive qualities of soil. This idea is related to the formation of rivers, streams, caverns, and wells. The ground work for 26/Compare is laid by activities 24 and 25. In 24/Observe, the children see that the colored water is slowly absorbed by the paper towel. They can test materials other than the paper towel to see how liquid is absorbed. A piece of blotting paper will work very well, and cloth can also be used. To elaborate upon 24/Observe, one is asked to use a sponge in 25/Explain.

(continued on page 304)

for your information

The waterfalls and V-shaped valley in the photograph on this page are typical features of a young stream or river (a stream's age is determined by the extent to which it has eroded its valley). A complete discussion of the lifetimes of streams appears on pages 324–325 of the teacher's edition. You may want to refer back to this picture when discussing stream ages with your class.

Rain falls on mountainsides, and runs off as a swift-moving stream. Streams join and form broad rivers that flow across plains and broad valleys to the ocean. All the way from falling rain to the sea, water is changing the earth's surface. How would a hard rain affect the soil by just striking it repeatedly?

Does all rain run off the land it falls upon? Plants would not be able to stay alive if this were so. Think what happens to water when someone waters a plant. Why do you often have to hill the earth around a plant? Where does the water go when a lawn or garden is watered?

24/Observe

Dip the end of a piece of paper towel into colored water. Note what happens. How far does the paper towel soak up the colored water? ■

25/Explain

Fill a sprinkling bottle with water. Now put a sponge on a sheet of wax paper and sprinkle it with water. Don't let any water run down the sides of the sponge. Continue sprinkling the sponge as long as water will disappear into it. Look at the sponge. ①Where does the water go? ■

The materials used in the activities retained water. Were all of them the same? Were they alike in any way?

Each of the materials used contained many empty spaces. Such materials are said to be porous (PAWR-us). Porous materials can soak up water and other liquids.

responses to 24/observe

1. The towel soaks up some of the water.
2. The towel soaks up the water beyond the point where the towel is submerged.

responses to 25/explain

1. The water is absorbed by the sponge. (The water goes into the empty spaces in the sponge.)

In activity 26/Compare, the students learn that both rocks weigh more after having been soaked in water. The soft limestone, however, shows a greater increase in weight than the hard marble. Capitalizing on these past activities, get the children to relate in 27/Describe that various types of soil differ in their capacity to absorb and hold water. Soil that has a high sand content will hold less water than soil containing clay. The jar should be set up as shown in the diagram on the right.

(continued on page 306)

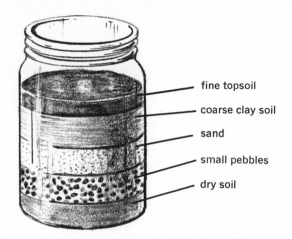

fine topsoil

coarse clay soil

sand

small pebbles

dry soil

responses to 26/compare

1. The rocks which soak overnight weigh more than the dry rocks. The soft rocks gain more weight (absorb more water) than the hard rocks.

responses to 27/describe

1. The water will pass through the fine topsoil layer and becomes trapped in the next layer of coarse clay soil.
2. As you add more water, it will eventually saturate the fine topsoil layer. The coarse clay soil prevents most of the water from passing through to the lower layers.
3. A portion of the rainwater passes through the porous layer of topsoil and collects above non-porous layers such as clay soil.

Is soil porous? Does it absorb water? Is more water absorbed by some soils than others? Name some other materials of the earth that soak up water.

26/Compare

Weigh pieces of a very hard rock, like marble or granite, and a very soft one like sandstone. Place both rocks in a jar of water. After soaking them overnight, wipe them dry. Weigh the pieces of rock again. Compare the differences between the dry rocks and the rocks which soaked overnight. What did you find out? Do all rocks soak up the same amount of water? ■

Layers of soil differ in the way they are able to hold water. The next activity will help you to see how water travels through different underground areas.

27/Describe

Fill a jar with layers of dry soil, small pebbles or rock chips, sand, coarse clay soil, and fine topsoil. Begin with the dry soil, as the picture shows, then build your layers to within two inches of the top of the jar. These layers are similar to the ones making up the crust of the earth. Now pour enough water onto the top layer to cover it well. Examine the jar after a few hours. 1 Explain what has happened to the water. Add more water, but be careful not to let any water stay above the top layer of soil. 2 What happens now? 3 What happens to rainwater when it falls on the earth's surface? ■

257

After the students have finished activity 27, in which they should find that different kinds of soils have different abilities to absorb water (that is, different porosities), ask them the following: *Do you think that the porosity of the soil in a given location can affect the amount of surface erosion that takes place? Would an area which has very porous soil have as many streams as an area that has less porous soil?* The students should be able to infer that if the soil is very porous, much of the rainfall will sink into the soil, rather than running over the surface as streams. In turn, the less surface runoff there is, the less surface erosion will take place.

This fact is developed in 28/Observe where the absorptive and porous qualities of sand enable a "well" to be made. Care should be taken removing the smooth round jar from the sand so that a well-formed pocket is made. 29/Explain allows the students to visualize and explain what occurs on a far larger scale in the formation of rivers.

(continued on page 308)

responses to 28/observe

1. Water seeps into the hole.
2. The water that was poured on the sand moved through the sand and into the hole.
3. The water moves between the particles of sand.
4. Rainwater seeps into the ground and then moves through the soil. This underground water fills wells in much the same way the water in this activity seeped into the hole.
5. When there is no rain for a very long time, underground water diminishes or disappears in some places.

Water from the surface of the earth slowly collects underground. Do the next activity to observe the action of underground water.

28/Observe

Put a smooth round jar in the center of a deep pan. Fill the pan with sand. Pack down the sand and smooth out the surface. Pour water slowly on the sand until all of it is wet.

Wait a few minutes, then lift the jar carefully with a slow twisting motion. Watch the hole formed by the jar. 1 Note what happens after a short time. 2 Where does the water come from? 3 Explain how it moves through the sand. 4 How does this underground water fill wells? 5 Explain why wells often go dry when there is no rain for a very long time. ■

The continual action of water on the earth's surface causes it to change. Do the next activity to help you understand how this occurs.

29/Explain

Fill a glass baking dish half-way with soil. Scoop some of it out of the center. Pack this soil against the sides to form a "valley" and two "hills". Now pour water gently on the soil. Keep packing the soil so it doesn't slide into the valley. Look through the sides of the dish and watch the water rise in the soil. Note what happens in the valley. This can help you explain how underground water helps to form streams and rivers. What happens to rivers and streams during a long dry period? ■

1. The valley begins to fill with water that seeps sideways through the soil.

2. During a long dry period, rivers and streams become smaller and may even dry up, because there is no underground water to "feed" them.

The three following activities are very simple to carry out. Their main point is that water is a solvent and will also form rust as it reacts with iron. Since water is such a good solvent, it can cause certain minerals in rocks to form solutions. This dissolving out of the minerals eventually causes the rocks to erode over a long period of time. The combination of water with minerals causes a chemical change. One example is the formation of rust as water combines with iron contained in rocks. The rust formation gradually weakens the rock itself and erosion takes place, causing the rock to crumble.

Since field trips to caves will be very limited except for those schools in certain geographic areas, you can have the children do library research on caves which have been discovered. Call on your school librarian to suggest books about the exploring of caves. Children can write to various state chambers of commerce about caves located in those states in order to get further information about this subject.

(continued on page 310)

optional activity

To illustrate how mineral deposits are formed in limestone caves, make a saturated solution of epsom salts in a jar of water. Pour the clear liquid into two smaller jars and place them a few inches apart on a sheet of cardboard. Wet a piece of heavy string and put an end in each of the two jars. After a few hours, the children should see liquid beginning to drip down from the center of the string. In a few days a mineral deposit will build up on the cardboard sheet.

Some of the minerals in rocks are dissolved by underground water. Gases as well as these dissolved minerals slowly wear away the underground rocks. Underground water often hollows out large caves in the earth. If you have ever visited a cave, describe it for the class.

260

30/Observe

Put a tablespoonful of salt into a glass of warm water. Stir the water until all the salt is gone. Now the salt has been dissolved by the water. ■

A material able to dissolve others is called a solvent. Water is a solvent for many materials. Name others beside salt that dissolve in it.

31/Describe

Fill a glass with water. Let it stand for 30 minutes. Describe what you see on the insides of the glass. Where does this come from? Do you think air dissolves in water? ■

The next activity will help you to see another way that water causes rocks to change. Such changes take place over a long period of time.

32/Observe

Some rocks contain iron. Do water and oxygen from the air affect iron? Place an iron nail or tack on a wet sponge. Leave it there for one week. Add water to the sponge when it dries out. Observe what happens to the nail or tack. Try scraping its surface. ■

Rocks that contain iron will rust. Rust weakens the rock. The carbon dioxide in the air also dissolves in water. It forms an acid that dissolves certain rocks in the earth. The marble rocks that you boiled in vinegar were changed by an acid. Could such acids also change rocks in nature?

responses to 31/describe

1. There are bubbles in the water (on the inside surface of the glass).
2. The bubbles come from the air that was already dissolved in the water.
3. Air will dissolve in water.

note

Point out to the class that all carbonated drinks contain a gas (carbon dioxide) dissolved in the soda. A bottle of soda left open will taste "flat" after the gas escapes.

responses to 32/observe

1. The nail or tack rusts.
2. Some of this rust can be scraped off.

The first activity in Testing Your Ideas can be matched with the second statement in Column B. The second activity can be matched with the first statement in Column B. The third activity can be matched with the last statement, and the last activity can be matched with the third statement.

optional activity

To illustrate further the variations in porosity of different types of soil, some students may do the following activity as a home project and report their findings to the class. Tell them to collect empty soup cans and remove both the tops and bottoms (warn them to be careful of sharp edges). Tell them to embed the cans in as many different areas of soil as they can find. They should be sure to embed each can to the same depth (about an inch into the soil). Then they should fill each can to the brim with water and note how long it takes for the water in each can to be absorbed by the soil it is in (this may take several hours for some soils). When they report to the class, the students should bring a little sample of each kind of soil they tested so the rest of the class can relate porosity to the type of soil.

Below are two columns. The first lists activities like the ones given to you to do. The second lists what water can do to the earth. Which of the statements of Column A is the best example of the statements in Column B?

A	B
Tilt a pan of loose soil five inches. Pour water down the soil. What happens?	Land is built up at the mouth of a river.
Fill a jar halfway with soil, and fill the remainder with water. Shake for thirty seconds. What happens to the soil when it stops moving?	When water runs off a hill, the earth's surface can be eroded.
Using a hand lens, compare pieces of broken pebbles with some rock.	Different kinds of rock and soil can hold different amounts of water.
Weigh a hard rock and a soft one. Soak both in water overnight, and compare their weights.	Waves which crash rocks into other rocks can eventually make sand of them.

310

262

OVERVIEW

Children discover some of the effects on the earth's surface produced by temperature changes, particularly of water. The primary focus here is on the results of the temperature changes which produce melting and freezing of water.

The children learn that as water freezes, it expands; thus, any water trapped in cracks between rocks or within the pores of rocks themselves can cause the rocks to crack and crumble.

The children also discover how pressure affects temperature. Pressure on ice, for example, can cause it to melt, as is the case at the bottom of glaciers.

The children investigate how, in this process, the ice can pick up sand and other debris, which then acts as an abrasive as it moves over the surface of the earth, scraping and gouging the land. It is shown that areas over which a glacier has passed have distinct characteristics due to the fact that the glacier deposits its rocky load as it melts.

how to begin

Ask the students if they have ever seen what happens to a bottle of milk after it is left outside for a long time in freezing weather. (The bottle cracks or the lid is pushed up.)

(continued on page 312)

HOW DOES TEMPERATURE CAUSE CHANGE?

The temperature differences over the earth's surface cause noticeable changes. After a long, cold winter you can see some of these changes. Try to remember some you may have seen and think of what might have caused them to occur.

33/Explain

Fill two half-pint cartons with water. Measure them to be sure they are the same size. Put one of the cartons in the freezer, until the water is frozen solid. Take the carton of ice from the freezer and compare it with the carton of water. 1 Are the two cartons still the same size? ■

263

process skills

Describing how the freezing and melting of water causes rock erosion

Describing how pressure causes ice to melt

Inferring how glacial movements change the earth's surface

materials

2 half-pint milk cartons°, water, sandstone, plastic bag, ice cubes, heavy book°, brick°, 2 squares of cardboard, dish of sand°, painted board°

° per team

responses to 33/explain

1. The carton that was frozen is larger. The freezing water expanded.

311

Then ask the students if they can suggest two possible reasons for the cracking of the milk bottle under these circumstances. In this case, the water in the milk has expanded upon freezing; and, in addition, the bottle has contracted. Thus, either the bottle cracks or the lid is pushed up by the frozen liquid.

procedure

33/Explain requires the use of a freezer, and for this reason it might better be done at home with a report and discussion held in class. The activity shows that as water freezes, it expands, unlike most substances. The ice which forms from a given amount of water takes up about one-ninth more space than the liquid water took up. After the students have reported the results of the activity, ask how this peculiar property of water might be responsible for breaking up rocks. The children should be able to conclude that water trapped in the spaces in rock, upon freezing, will expand and push outward. It should be stressed that the actual breaking of rock by this process takes a great deal of time and, of course, can only occur in locations where the temperature ranges above and

responses to 34/compare

1. Some cracks are visible in the sandstone.

Most materials contract as they cool. Water is an exception to this rule. As water cools, it first contracts. Then, as it nears the freezing point, it expands. This expansion is so great that the ice takes up about 1/9th more space than the water did. If you want to test this you can place some water in a glass, mark the height, and then put it in the freezer at home. See if the ice, when it is formed, is higher than the mark you made on the glass.

Rocks with spaces in them can take in water. In cold weather, the water freezes and expands, causing the rocks to break and crumble into smaller pieces. Gradually, the rocks are broken down into soil for plants.

34/Compare

Take several pieces of porous sandstone. Soak them in a jar of water overnight. Place the stones in a plastic bag in the freezer of your refrigerator the next day. Examine the bag of stones one day later. How has the sandstone changed? ■

below the freezing point of water. In activity 34/ Compare, the students observe the actual effect of this process on rocks. Sandstone was selected because it is a very porous rock and absorbs water easily. Most sedimentary rocks are porous and many can be used in place of sandstone (shale, limestone, conglomerate). The students should soak the rocks for about 24 hours, in order for enough water to be absorbed. After being frozen for 24 hours, the rocks should show some erosive effects, such as tiny cracks and some crumbling. Ask the students if it would take a long time for this rock to be completely broken down by this process.

(continued on page 314)

The upper slopes of most high mountain ranges, such as the Rocky Mountains, the Sierra Nevadas, and the Alaska Range, are white with snow all year. Snow sometimes lies hundreds of feet deep in protected hollows on these mountains. The top surface of the snow is soft, but toward the bottom it is packed to icy hardness by the weight of the snow above. These masses of snow are called snow fields.

265

optional questions

Ask the students why they think tall mountains are capped with snow even though their valleys may not receive snow. The students will not study the reasons for decrease in temperature with elevation until Grade 5. However, they should be able to infer that the temperature must be lower at the higher altitudes in order for the tops of the mountains to retain snow. *Ask if they think this fact would have anything to do with the amount of vegetation on the mountains.* Again, they should be able to infer that there would be little vegetation on the high slopes because of the extreme temperatures.

35/Think and 36/Compare demonstrate the effect of pressure on the temperature of ice and give evidence for one theory of why glaciers may move. A control is used and the children should discuss why it is necessary. The ice cubes in both activities will melt, partly because of the heat in the room, but the results will show that those ice cubes with more weight on top will melt more and faster. Relate these observations to the movement of glaciers. Since glaciers are made up of great amounts of snow and ice, the pressure above the bottom layers causes them to melt. Ask the children to imagine a glacier on a slope. What effect would the melting and freezing of the bottom of the glacier have on the glacier as a whole? According to one theory, the glacier begins to slide downslope as the bottom melts. Thus, it is the alternate melting and refreezing which may produce movement of the glacier.

(continued on page 316)

optional activity

Students sometimes have the erroneous idea that glaciers are, and always have been, confined to the North and South Poles. Some students can be assigned research projects to find out and report on the extent of continental glaciers in the past which occurred on the North American continent. They can report their findings by indicating the various glaciers on an outline map of North America with colored pencils.

If the snow doesn't melt in summer, the snow fields grow larger each winter. The snow-and-ice mass will begin to move downhill when its weight becomes great enough. A glacier (GLAY-sher) has started.

Glaciers, which carve the earth's surface, are slow-moving rivers of ice. Just how the glaciers move is not fully understood. Gravity helps the glaciers move downhill. But how do these solid, icy masses manage to turn corners and even to creep uphill at times? Again, we don't have the answer to this question.

266

35/Think

Take a tray of ice cubes, two square pieces of cardboard, and a brick. Place two groups of four ice cubes each on a table top. Put a cardboard square on top of each group of ice cubes. Now place the brick on top of one group of ice cubes. Time which ice cubes melt faster. Do you think pressure has anything to do with melting? ■

36/Compare

Take four ice cubes and place them in pairs, so that a book can be balanced on top. Let the book stay for a few minutes. Examine the ice cubes. What has happened? Compare this time with the brick. ■

Ice at the bottom of a glacier will melt because of the weight of the upper layers. According to one theory, the continuous process of melting, refreezing, and melting again somehow helps glaciers in their movements. However, this process appears to be more complicated than just melting and refreezing.

267

1. The ice cubes with the brick on them melt faster.
2. Pressure increases the rate of melting.

responses to 36/compare

1. The ice cubes appear to start melting at the bottom, as small puddles of water can be seen forming.
2. The ice cubes with the brick on them melted faster than those with the book on them.

315

37/Compare demonstrates how debris can be picked up and frozen into ice as it melts and freezes, and in addition, how this debris acts as an abrasive agent on surfaces over which it passes. Have the students relate this activity to glaciers. They should be able to see how a moving glacier can leave great scratches in the rock over which it passes (assuming the rock carried by the glacier is harder than that over which it passes).

(continued on page 318)

optional activity

Another way to show the effect of pressure on the melting point of ice is to simply hold an ice cube or a piece of broken ice in each hand and press them together over a piece of paper. The students will observe that water drips down to the paper, indicating that the ice has melted. If the two pieces of ice are pushed forcibly together and then the pressure is released, the ice pieces will remain stuck together. What occurs is that the ice melts when the pressure is applied, but as soon as the pressure is released, the ice refreezes, causing the two pieces to stick together.

Glacial movement, though not completely understood, can be measured. Some glaciers move a few inches a year, others almost 100 feet each day. Most glacial movement is very slow, but glaciers are still very powerful in shaping the surface of the earth.

As the bottom and sides of a glacier melt and refreeze, the glacier picks up soil, sand, small rocks, and even huge boulders. Such earth materials become frozen in the edges of the moving glacier. When rock rubs against rock and soil, surfaces wear down.

37/Compare

Press an ice cube into a dish of sand. When it starts to melt, put the dish and the ice cube into the freezer for one hour. Take the ice cube out and see if it has picked up some of the sand. (If not, let the ice cube melt and refreeze it.) Now rub the sandy ice cube on a painted board. Note any change. ■

Glaciers, carrying earth materials, grind away at rocks and soil under them and along their sides. River valleys through which they travel are deepened and widened. Rock on mountainsides is scoured and scratched. Land once covered by a glacier would show the marks of this rubbing. What could you find in a stream flowing from a melting glacier?

While glaciers are always growing from their sources in the snow fields, they are always melting at their lower ends. A glacier will melt away entirely, if it melts faster than it can grow. When glaciers melt, much of their earth materials are deposited.

responses to 37/compare

1. The ice cube containing particles of sand scratches the paint. Also, some grains of sand are rubbed off the ice cube.

optional questions

Ask the students to imagine what would happen to the sand if the ice cube were left alone to melt. As the ice cube melted, the sand would remain where it is. If the melt-water moves, some of the sand may move with it. When the water from the cube evaporates, the sand will remain.

studying the picture

Tell the students that the small hill they see in the photo is actually a mound of debris (rocks, pebbles, dirt) left when a glacier melted.

Much of the material carried by glaciers, like that carried by the wind and by bodies of moving water, is deposited on the land. The reason for the deposition of this material, however, differs from the reasons for the deposition of wind or water-transported materials. The latter occurs when the velocity of the wind or water drops. When this happens, the wind or water can no longer carry its load, and thus, materials are deposited. Glacier-carried rock and dirt, however, is deposited almost entirely when and where the glacier melts.

This is one way geologists have of determining the extent of past glacial movements. Because the mounds of rock and dirt (moraines) form in nearly the same relative positions as they occupied in the glacier, the movement of the glacier can be quite accurately mapped by noting the positions of the moraines.

All the statements in Testing Your Ideas are true.

A melting glacier may often leave a great pile of earth materials it has gathered at the foot of a valley. Such materials then act as a dam, keeping back the water from the melting glacier. A lake is formed as water fills the valley.

Streams flowing from melting glaciers also deposit earth materials. Ice can carry heavy materials such as boulders, but its melting water carries only the finer, lighter earth materials such as sand and soil. In areas where these finer materials are deposited, large hills are formed.

270

Several times during the past million years North America and Europe were covered with huge sheets of ice, more than a mile thick. Many glaciers on the earth today are the remains of those great ice sheets.

Great ice sheets still bury the land masses of Greenland and Antarctica. Such glaciers are so large that if they were to melt, the sea level would rise more than 200 feet. Many of our cities would be flooded.

38/Think

①Could you say that we are still in the Ice Age or that it passed thousands of years ago?②Might we be at the beginning of a new Ice Age?③Think what changes a new Ice Age might make in the earth's surface. ■

TESTING YOUR IDEAS

Do you agree with the following statements?

Glaciers grind away at mountains and carry boulders and soil.

Glaciers make streams, lakes, and hills.

It is mostly the temperature at which water freezes and melts which causes glacial changes.

responses to 38/think

1. Although the earth still has glaciers, the term Ice Age refers to a time, thousands of years ago, when a large part of the earth was covered with glaciers.

2. Scientists explain that conditions necessary for a new ice age, which would allow glaciers to grow, would require a drop in temperature and an increase in the amount of snowfall, both at the same time.

3. A new ice age would drastically alter the earth's surface. New lakes, rivers, and mountains would be formed, the level of the oceans would drop (because large amounts of the earth's water would be frozen into the glaciers), and new land areas would appear.

OVERVIEW

In the activity, children will observe how sedimentary rock layers fold when pressure is applied. They can relate what they observe to how pressures long ago in the history of the earth's formation caused the rocks of the earth's surface to bend and fold, eventually forming mountains. By the use of a balloon and clay, they can surmise how unequal pressure causes a shifting of materials, as in the case of the formation of mountains.

process skills

Describing the process of mountain formation

Explaining how mountains occur through faulting

materials

large pan*, plaster of paris, shells, fish bones, crab claws, bits of coral, different colored blotting or construction paper, modeling clay, long balloon*

---

*one per team

how to begin

Use photographs of various types of mountains to initiate this section of the material. Different varieties of mountains classed according to their formation can be seen as well as various stages of each type of mountain building. If you can show a series of one type of mountain forming from its earliest stages, have the students put these stages in the proper order.

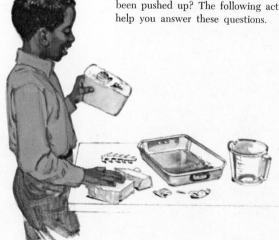

HOW COULD MOUNTAINS BE MADE?

We know that water, wind, and glaciers can wear away mountains. We also know that this erosion has been taking place for a very long time. Why shouldn't the earth be a flat plain? How is it possible that there are mountains? Must we not say that the surface of the earth is rising as well as being worn away? Can we show that the surface of the earth in fact has been pushed up? The following activity will begin to help you answer these questions.

39/Observe

Fill a large pan half full of plaster of paris. Fill the remainder of the pan with water and stir care-

272

procedure

It should be possible to have each child in the class carry out the activities individually. Before doing the activities, you can review some of the forces the children have observed that change mountains and wear them away. A discussion of sedimentary rock formation should be related to the simple activity the class will carry out.

(continued on page 322)

fully until it is as smooth as cake batter. Drop in shells, fish bones, crab claws, and bits of coral. Put the pan aside until the plaster dries. When it is completely dry, break it apart and observe the "fossils." ■

Fossils of ancient sea animals have been found in rocks of very high mountains. Therefore, does not this fact tell us that land once under the sea might have been pushed up in some way to make mountains? What might be one kind of push needed to make mountains?

273

studying the picture

The photograph shows a fossil fish discovered in Wyoming. By examining the remains of such marine animals (and plants), scientists have been able to trace the boundaries of prehistoric seas.

optional questions

Scientists have discovered fossils of tropical plants in rocks close to the Arctic Circle. Fossil corals have been found in rocks in almost all regions of the earth. What does such evidence indicate about the regions where the fossils were found? Such fossils provide clues to weather and climate conditions at the time the organisms existed. They are also evidence of great environmental changes in the past.

In 40/Compare the children should form a good idea of how great forces have bent and folded the earth's surface. As the children pushed the layers of paper, the layers rose in the center to form a small raised area. This is a simple example of one type of mountain formation. Discuss the statement that the remains of sea animals have been found in the sedi-mentary rocks of very high mountains. Have the children relate this fact to the way they formed a "mountain" with the colored paper.

In 41/Compare, care should be taken to assure that the modeling clay is sufficiently stiff so that it will "fault."

(continued on page 324)

responses to 40/compare

1. The sheets of paper begin to bulge and rise in the center.
2. The sheets of blotting paper and the layers in the photograph are similar in that they both show upward folds of layers.
3. The formation of mountains is an extremely slow process (The Rocky Mountains are over 60 million years old and are still considered youthful mountains).

40/Compare

Lay several pieces of brightly-colored blotting paper in a pile. These layers will represent rock layers. Placing your hands firmly on the ends of the pile, slowly bring your hands together. Watch carefully as you push. What happens? Does the blotting paper begin to bulge or rise? Compare the blotting paper with the layers in the photograph. Do you think that mountains are uplifted quickly or slowly? ■

Geologists (jee-AHL-uh-jists) are scientists who study the changing earth. They believe that the land at the base of some mountains was once further apart.

274

Some points of land once 81 miles apart in the Appalachian mountains in Pennsylvania are now only 66 miles apart. What happened to the distance between your hands as you pushed the ends of the blotting paper together? Did the distance "shrink"? Do you think a shrinking earth can make mountains? Some geologists think it may be so.

The kind of mountain suggested by your activity is called a folded mountain. It is a bend in the earth's crust. Some rocks may bend. But can you imagine that some rocks may break to form mountains? Do the following activity to find out how this might happen.

41/Compare

Get some modeling clay which will dry out. Mold the clay into a piece one-half inch thick, six inches long, four inches wide. With your teacher's help, cut the clay along its width into two equal pieces. Make sure the cut is on a slant and does not go through the clay entirely. Turn the clay over to hide the cut and let the clay dry for an hour. Then, press down with one hand

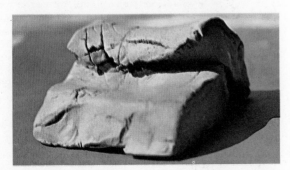

To help children understand how a geologist thinks and works, place a layer of soft modeling clay in a cookie sheet. Make imprints in the clay to resemble animal footprints, and be sure that some of them overlap. Ask the children to study the model and have them decide the sequence in which these events occurred. They should learn that the way the imprints overlap is a clue to the time order of the events. The bottom layer represents an event which occurred at an earlier age than the top layers.

In 42/Compare, the modeling clay should be wet and pliable to enable it to rise when the balloon is inflated.

At this point, you may wish to introduce the concept of the life history of mountains. Mountains go through periods of youth, maturity, and finally, old age.

Youth. This period is characterized by jagged peaks which have not yet been eroded. They are steep and high and usually rise well above the snow line. Many are capped with snow the year round. Valleys are very narrow and streams are fast moving, often torrents of water. Examples are: the Alps, the Himalayas, the Rockies, and the Sierras.

Maturity. Here, growth has more or less ceased, and the rugged slopes have been worn down by the forces of wind, water, and ice. There is some rounding of peaks and less snow than on young mountains. Valleys are wider and streams are slower-moving, with deeper pools that make good hiding spots for fish. Examples are: the White and Green Mountains of New England, the Appalachians of the mid-Atlantic area, and the Adirondacks of New York.

responses to 41 / compare

1. A break or weakness in the earth's crust.

2. As pressure is applied to the break or "zone of weakness," the crust will finally give way along the crack.

3. The block of clay on the upper side of the crack will be forced to move up above the lower block (see diagram below).

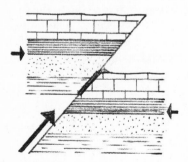

along the cut and push the other half of the clay towards the cut. **1** What does the cut represent? **2** Does the clay begin to crack at the cut? **3** After you have pushed, is one side of the clay higher? ■

Pressures can push up large volumes of rock as blocks along weaknesses or cracks in the earth's crust. These cracks, called faults, go deep in the earth's crust. Mountains pushed up along a fault are called block mountains. A sidewalk broken by tree roots growing underneath it is a tiny example of the way block mountains may have formed. But once the mountain is raised above the earth's surface, what do you think begins to happen? Might weather begin to erode the mountain and change its appearance after many years? The Sierra Nevada mountains shown in the picture are block mountains. Do you think they have been worn away by water, wind, and ice?

Old Age. At this stage, there are really no mountains as the students generally think of mountains. Instead, these are gently rolling hills. Valleys are very wide and streams in them are also wide and sluggish or slow-moving. Examples are: the hills of southern New England, and the Piedmont area in Georgia. Use photographs of the various age mountains as you discuss their features so that the students will have a visual picture as well as the descriptions.

(continued on page 326)

While the earth's surface may fold or fault, is it possible that it can also be pushed up from underneath the crust? As you will see in the next lesson, a part of the inside of the earth is magma, a thick, "syrup-like" rock that has melted. Find out if a fluid can push up a mountain by doing the next activity.

42/Compare

Place several layers of modeling clay softened with warm water over a balloon. Blow into the balloon. While air is not liquid like melted rock, it is still a fluid and can cause a push. What happens to the layers of soft clay as you blow the balloon up? ■

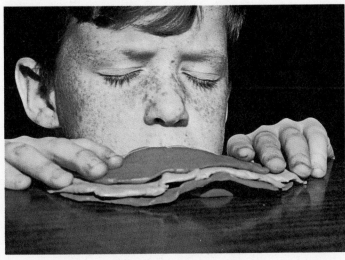

277

responses to 42/compare

1. The layers of clay are forced to rise.

optional activity

If you discuss ages of mountains with your students, you can do the following activity: Have the students collect as many photographs of mountains as they can. Their collection should include the names of the mountains, and also their location in the state, country, or continent. Then they should attempt to classify the mountains according to whether they are young, mature, or old. You may refer back to page 302 (student page 254) for an example of a young mountain.

The first statement in Testing Your Ideas refers to a block mountain. The second statement refers to a dome mountain, and the last statement refers to a fold mountain.

for your information

The photograph on this page shows a dome mountain—a mountain formed when a sedimentary bed is uplifted into a broad circular dome. Erosion of the dome results in the circular ridges that can be seen in the picture. The Black Hills of South Dakota are typical dome mountains.

Liquid rock seeping between rock layers in the earth may raise the layers up. Mountains formed when liquid rock causes a lifting push are dome mountains. When the melted rock cools slowly under the earth's surface, the rock formed is very hard and durable. When weather wears away the surface layers of rock, the hard and durable rock is exposed.

You know that the earth's crust must be pushed in some way to form a mountain. But what causes the push? Is the earth shrinking? Or is the rock beneath the crust moving in some way to cause the crust to fold, fault, or rise? The questions suggest possible explanations, but geologists are not yet sure.

Which of the following kinds of mountains may have been produced by the causes found below?

block mountain
fold mountain
dome mountain

Large volumes of rock separated by faults may be pushed up by pressures in the earth's crust.

The pressure of magma under the crust may push up large areas of earth.

A mountain may rise because the earth's crust bends.

for your information

Although the specifics of mountain-building evade geologists, there are certain features which almost all mountain ranges share in common. Most mountain ranges are found along the coasts of large land masses, and they are large features, in the sense that they may be thousands of miles long. In addition, sedimentary units are thicker in mountain ranges than in other land formations, and the type of sediment most prevalent in these sedimentary units is marine in nature. This has led some geologists to conclude that the formation of mountains proceeds in the following way: A long, troughlike depression forms in the sea, near a coast. Sediments are deposited in this trough (or geosyncline) and the bottom of the trough begins to sink. Then a large-scale earth movement takes place, lifting the deposits above land.

OVERVIEW

While previous lessons have dealt with changes taking place over a long period of time, the students are now exposed to changes which occur suddenly and with little warning. The concept of excessive force breaking materials begins this section and is related to earthquakes. Moreover, that these changes cause vibrations and can be measured is shown. An activity sequence on volcanoes follows which relates pressure to eruption. The student is then introduced to how lava can flow.

how to begin

Photographs of earthquake destruction can graphically show the class the dramatic results of the shifting of the earth's crust. Few students will have experienced an earthquake, but often recent news of an earthquake can be found in newspapers. These articles can be used when available to initiate discussion of this section.

process skills

Explaining the causes of earthquakes

Using a model to observe what happens when a volcano erupts

Describing how volcanoes rapidly change the surface of the earth

materials

stick*, paper circle 5″ in diameter*, tape, jar*, grass seed or wood shavings, cardboard, rubber tubing, clothespin*, 2 books*, large rock*, cloth*, hammer*, cup of water, flashlight, support to hold flashlight, cake pan filled with mud*

---

*per team

responses to 43/observe

1. Apply more force.

HOW DOES THE EARTH CHANGE SUDDENLY?

Most changes in the earth's surface come about slowly. There are other changes that can take place suddenly and violently. Late one Friday afternoon in 1964, the people of Alaska were going about their normal activities. Some were shopping, some were still at work, and others were getting ready for dinner.

Suddenly the earth began to shake. The ground cracked, and sections of it dropped several feet. Buildings crumbled and fell. Cars bounced around like rubber balls. The disturbance caused great waves in the Pacific Ocean that smashed shoreline cities along the Alaskan coast. Some effects from these waves were felt even in California, 2000 miles away.

These were not the kinds of changes usually made by water, wind, or ice. What caused this great change in the surface of the earth?

procedure

Ask the children to explain in their own words the cause of most earthquakes. (Scientists believe earthquakes are the result of vibrations in the earth produced by a slipping of great blocks of crust along a fault.) Activity 43/Observe will help the children understand how the rocks of the earth's crust break and shift under great pressures. Ask the children what they felt as their sticks broke. If the stick didn't break immediately, they should have applied more force.

Help the children understand the force with which the stick broke. Rock formations of the earth are under great force at various times, and depending on the amount of force, some rock sections will move suddenly, causing an earthquake.

Earthquakes occur all over the world. They are most frequent and intensive, however, along two great belts, one of which circles the Pacific Ocean and the other of which includes southern Europe, North Africa, and parts of southwest Asia.

(continued on page 330)

43/Observe

Hold a stick by the ends. Bend it until it breaks. What must you do if it doesn't break immediately? The stick can withstand a certain amount of force. It breaks when you exert more force than the stick can withstand. ■

The earth's rocks are subject to many forces. They break and shift when these forces become more than they can withstand. When rocks break and shift, this movement causes vibrations. These vibrations of the earth are called an earthquake.

Earthquakes most often occur along faults in the earth's crust. Rocks, deep in the crust, on either side of the fault, are being pushed in opposite directions. They begin to slide sideways against each other.

One great fault in the earth's crust located in North America is along the Alaskan coast. Another is in California. Probably the most serious earthquakes in our country would always be along these fault lines. Do other countries have these also?

281

for your information

The idea that most earth changes have occurred through the slow processes of erosion and deposition has not always been accepted. Up until the 18th century, most people believed that the earth itself was only about 6000 years old. This would hardly be enough time, for example, for a landform as spectacular as the Grand Canyon to be formed by the Colorado, cutting away at its present slow rate. Because people believed the earth to be so young, they had to devise a theory of earth change which could account for large changes over short periods of time. Thus, a *catastrophic* view of geologic change was popular. That is, it was believed that great catastrophes (floods, earthquakes, etc.) were responsible. As the age of the earth was pushed further and further back, this view became less and less popular, until today, when it is discounted completely by geologists, in favor of the "slow change" theory.

Before doing 44/Discover, ask the children to describe in their own words what a fault is. Be sure to correct any false impression it is an open crack. It is a break in a rock surface which permits the rock to change position. The activity will help the children understand how earthquakes occur along a fault. Have enough pieces of rock on hand so that each child can participate. Instruct the children to fit the jagged pieces of the broken rocks tightly together.

Ask the class to relate the jagged line formed by the fitting of the two edges to a fault. When the youngsters rub the edges of the rocks against each other, they will feel vibrations. When an earthquake occurs, its seriousness can be measured by a seismograph which records the quake's vibrations traveling through the earth. The fundamental principle of how a seismograph works is made clear by 45/Observe.

(continued on page 332)

responses to 44/discover

1. The rough, irregular surfaces, when rubbed together, will cause a grinding noise that can be felt as a vibration.

note

The idea of vibrations traveling through something as solid as rock and dirt can be further illustrated by having a student stand barefoot at one end of the room while you drop something heavy on the floor at the other end. The student should be able to feel the vibrations produced through his feet.

Large landslides and volcanoes can also cause earthquakes. These disturbances are generally not as strong as those caused by the breaking and shifting of rocks. Even so, volcanoes and landslides can cause much damage.

44/Discover

Wrap a large rock in a cloth. Take it outside and break it with a hammer. Take two pieces of the rock that fit together and rub their edges together. (1) Describe what you feel. ■

Vibration waves travel out in all directions from the place where an earthquake occurs. These waves can be recorded on a sensitive instrument called a seismograph (SYZ-ma-graf). Scientists can learn where the

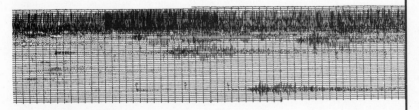

earthquake is taking place and how serious it is by studying seismograph recordings.

45/Observe.

Put a dish or cup of water in the middle of a table. Fasten a flashlight to a support to hold it steady and aim it so that the light shines down at an angle on the water, as shown in the picture. Darken the room so that the light reflected from the water forms a spot on the wall. Now, rap the table gently and note the movement of the spot of light on the wall. Walk across

studying the picture

Explain to the students that each vertical line on the seismograph sample indicates a time interval. By counting the number of vertical lines during which the tremor occurred, the observer can determine how long the tremor lasted.

331

Actual seismographs, used by geologists, look like that shown in the diagram on the right. Because it is suspended as it is, the weight does not move when the earth vibrates. The drum revolves, and in addition, is embedded in bedrock. Thus, when the earth vibrates, the drum also vibrates. The pen, attached to the stationary weight, remains stationary, but since the drum it touches is moving back and forth with the earth, the movements are recorded on the paper which is wrapped around the drum.

(continued on page 334)

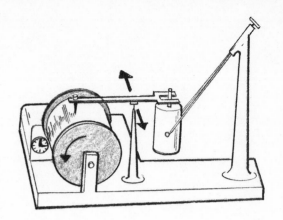

responses to 45/observe

1. Vibrations are set up.
2. Vibrations set up by a truck going down the street may not be strong enough to be picked up by such an instrument.

the floor near the table and note what happens. Jump up and down in the corner of the room away from the table. 1 Describe what happens each time something moves in the room. 2 Will your instrument pick up the vibrations of a truck going down the street? ■

Vibrations travel through the air, the floor, and the table every time something moves in the room. You might say that when you walk you are making a tiny earthquake. When these vibrations reach the water in the dish, they set up tiny waves on the water, and the reflected light begins to move. If the vibrations are weak the movement is small; if the vibrations are strong the movement is great. This is the way a real seismograph works, but, of course, it uses a recorder very much more complicated than a cup of water to detect the vibrations in the earth.

The numbers 1 to 12 are used to indicate the intensity of earthquakes. A reading between 8 and 9 on one such scale was made for the Alaskan earthquake of March, 1964. A reading of 1 would be a vibration almost unnoticed. Readings at the high end of the scale would be earthquakes causing great destruction and loss of life.

There are about 150,000 earthquakes a year. Most of them are so slight that we don't notice them. Earthquakes are happening all the time. They change the earth's surface in great and small ways.

In Hawaii, many people farm the fertile soil near the crater Kilauea (kee-low-AY-a). When the earth begins to tremble under their feet, the people know it may soon be time to move to another part of the island. Soon, hot lava may flow down the mountainside. It burns and buries everything in its path. The crater Kilauea is the mouth of the volcano.

284

This photograph, taken at night, shows Kilauea volcano in eruption. The temperature of the lava from this volcano is about 1830°F. The 1959 eruption of Kilauea gave scientists a great opportunity to study the volcanic process.

Volcanoes are mountains formed by hot materials escaping from the earth's crust. Lava, steam, rocks, and hot gases may be thrown out by an erupting volcano. Kilauea has gently sloping sides since it gives off mostly liquid lava. Volcanoes giving off more solid material, such as ash and chunks of rock, have steeper sides.

285

Before the children start to construct their model volcanoes in 46/Compare, ask them to explain what volcanoes are and how they are formed. (Volcanoes are mountains formed of hot materials such as lava escaping from the earth's crust.) From what the children have learned, they should know that pressures within the earth force the materials to the surface. Ask the children if volcanoes give any warning before they erupt. (Usually there is rumbling and earth tremors.) Eventually scientists hope to develop a warning system that will give advance notice of the eruption of volcanoes.

(continued on page 336)

optional activity

A great deal of interesting research can be done on the general subject of volcanism. Books on earth science, general science, or physical science have good discussions on the topic. Some topics for either written or oral reports are as follows: *Location of important volcanoes today; Volcanic activity in the past; Economic importance of volcanoes; and Predicting volcanoes.* In the course of their research, students may find other related topics they wish to explore. Encourage them to do so.

46/Compare

Take a paper circle which measures 5 inches across. Cut a slit from the edge of the circle to the center. Overlap the edges of the slit one inch to form a cone. Hold the overlapped edges in position with tape. Now put the cone upside down in the mouth of a jar. Use grass seed, sawdust, or wood shavings from a pencil sharpener to fill the cone. Lay a flat piece of cardboard over the cone's open end and tape the cone firmly to the cardboard. Make a hole in the cardboard, just big enough for a piece of rubber tubing. Pinch the tubing closed with a spring-type clothespin. Turn the cardboard over so the cone is on top and place it on two books, with space between them for the tubing, as shown in the drawing. Cut off the tip of the cone. Coat the outside of the cone with paper cement. Blow into the rubber tube until it is full of air. Remove the clothespin and keep blowing. This model is like a volcano that has already been formed and is erupting again. You can see how an eruption increases the size of a volcanic mountain. ■

Volcanoes are classified as active, dormant, or extinct. One that is erupting or has recently erupted is said to be active. If its activity ceases for a considerable time it is called dormant. If there is evidence to suggest that it will not erupt again it is called extinct. Nobody can really be sure, however, that a volcano is extinct and not just dormant. Paricutín, shown erupting in the photograph at the left, is now dormant.

It was February 20, 1943. A Mexican farmer heard a rumbling noise in the earth, and smoke began to rise out of the ground. He ran into the village to tell his neighbors. The birth of a volcano had begun. The next day his cornfield was gone. In its place stood a cone 100 feet high, pouring out clouds of smoke and ash. Small earthquakes shook the ground for weeks. Rocks and ash were blasted high into the air. The cone continued to grow. Lava poured out of cracks that appeared in the earth.

When the erupting stopped in 1952, the volcano was 1350 feet high. It was called Paricutín (pa-REE-koo-teen), after the nearby village that it buried. Today the volcano is quiet, but it may waken again.

Sometimes volcanoes destroy their cones instead of making them higher. Paricutín blasted away parts of its cone in some of its explosions.

This activity as well as 47/Observe will help the children understand that pressures within the earth build up, causing a volcanic eruption. It is probably better to divide the class into groups for the construction of model volcanoes. Encourage the children to discuss the activity. Some of them might want to repeat building a model volcano at home and to report the results.

Groups can do 48/Describe. It will help the class see how lava is forced by internal pressures through cracks in the earth's surface. Encourage the children to discuss the result of great lava flows in building up land. Examples are the building up of the Columbia and Snake River Plateaus.

Discuss with the children what happens to volcanic material as it hardens on the earth's surface and is

studying the picture

This old engraving shows Krakatoa before the eruption of 1883. This kind of volcano blasts hot gases, lava, and rocks into the air with great violence. The tall steep cone is indicative of this explosive kind of eruption.

responses to 47/observe

1. The seeds or shavings are dispersed, but not with the force that was seen in 46/compare.

Krakatoa (kra-ka-TOW-a) was an East Indian island that had begun as a volcano on the ocean floor. It grew slowly until its cone towered high above the sea. In 1883, it blasted itself to pieces in a series of eruptions. The crumbled remains of the island collapsed into a great hole in the ocean bottom. A small new cone is building now where Krakatoa once stood. Someday there may be a repeat performance.

47/Observe

Set up the cardboard and rubber tubing again. You won't need the paper cone this time. Pinch the

weathered. The soil that is formed by the weathering of volcanic materials is rich in minerals and forms fertile farmland. Although volcanoes can be destructive, they also help make the earth suitable for living things. In addition to building up the land and soil, they supply water vapor to fill oceans and supply carbon dioxide needed by plants.

(continued on page 338)

rubber tubing closed. Make a mound of seeds or shavings over the opening of the tube. Remove the clothespin. Note what happens as you blow through the tube. ■

Volcanic action is not always spectacular. Lava sometimes flows out onto the earth's surface from long cracks. Such lava flows more gently than lava that has had to force its way through a small opening.

Many of the earth's regions have been covered by lava flowing from long cracks. A hilly part of Iceland was changed to a high level mound by such a lava flow. The Columbia and Snake River Plateau in the western United States was formed by lava flows.

48/Describe

Fill a cake pan with runny mud. Cut a piece of heavy cardboard to fit the pan. Now make two slits in the cardboard, 6 inches long and 1/4 inch wide. Press the cardboard down into the loose mud. Describe what happens. ■

Volcanic action builds and destroys mountains. Undersea volcanoes build up volcanic islands and sometimes destroy them, as in the case of Krakatoa. Hilly regions can be changed to high, flat plateaus by flowing lava.

Magma and lava cool to form rocks. Such heat-formed rocks are called igneous (IG-nee-us). Granite and basalt are examples of igneous rocks. Volcanic ash hardens to form a rock called tuff. Soil that forms from tiny pieces of volcanic material is very fertile. It makes excellent farmland.

289

responses to 48/describe

1. The mud seeps through the slits in the cardboard.

note

If possible, obtain samples of the igneous rock mentioned in the student text so that the students can have the chance to study them firsthand. If this is not possible, good photographs of these rocks can be found in most geology books.

The first statement in Testing Your Ideas is about erosion, earthquakes, and volcanoes. The second is about erosion only. The third is about volcanoes and earthquakes, and the last is about erosion only.

for your information

Lava is molten rock which has reached the surface; magma is liquid rock that does not come to the surface. In reality, no one has ever seen magma; rather it is assumed or inferred that liquid rock exists under the earth from two facts: First, lava reaches the surface; thus, there must be a molten source (magma) somewhere beneath the surface. Second, because of motion of the earth's crust and erosion, rock becomes exposed at the surface which, on the basis of its composition and structure, can only be attributed to the cooling of molten lava under the surface. Rock formed from magma, that is, molten rock which has hardened beneath the surface, has a similar composition to lava; however, it has a different structure and different properties than rock formed from lava because it cooled much more slowly than lava which reaches the surface.

(continued)

Volcanoes also give off water vapor and carbon dioxide. In the early days of the earth's formation water vapor given off by volcanoes condensed and helped to fill the oceans. Plants could not live without carbon dioxide in the atmosphere. So you see that although volcanoes can cause great destruction, they have helped make the earth suitable for living things.

Which of the statements given below are about earthquakes, volcanoes, and erosion? Which are only about earthquakes and volcanoes? Which are only about erosion?

The earth can change.
The earth can change slowly.
The earth can change quickly and with little warning.
Changes in the earth can sometimes be controlled.

for your information
(continued)

Because it cooled so slowly, the minerals of which this rock is composed had time to arrange themselves into definite crystalline patterns. Granite is formed in this way.

Lava flowing from a volcano, on the other hand, cools quickly as it makes contact with the air. There is not time for the formation of crystals and the rock thus formed has a glassy, non-crystalline character. Obsidian is a rock formed in this way.

Sometimes the force of a volcanic explosion blasts lava into the air, and when this happens, the gases in it expand, making the lava foamy. When this foamy, frothy lava drops to the ground and cools, the result is a rock such as pumice, which is full of spaces left when the gases escaped. Such rock is so light that it will float in water.

OVERVIEW

The influence that man has had on changes in the earth's surface is discussed in this section. In three activities the children can see how man, by the use of machines to clear land or his abuse of natural resources, has changed the world around him. His clearing of land for homes is not an abuse of land if the natural vegetation can be partially retained by the builder. This is not always done, and often many trees are needlessly lost in the process.

how to begin

Ask the children to think of as many ways as possible in which man has caused the earth's surface to change. An initial listing will include clearing of land to build cities, towns, factories, and roads. The class should be encouraged to see how many of the changes were essential to the progress of civilization, but at the same time were abusive to natural resources.

process skills

Observing what man has done to change the earth's surface around him

materials

responses to 49/observe

1. Much of the topsoil is removed. Probably some vegetation is destroyed.
2. If the run-off is muddy, soil erosion is taking place.

HOW DOES MAN CHANGE THE EARTH'S SURFACE?

When the first colonist arrived in what is now called the United States, he found great forests extending from the Atlantic Ocean to the Mississippi River. Today, as we fly over this same land, we see large cities, many towns and villages and some forest land. Man, too, changes the surface of the earth and he has not always been careful in how he did it.

There was so much forest land that man was careless in how he cut down the trees and he did not plant new ones. Topsoil was washed away. It poured into the streams so that sewer systems overflowed and also poured into the streams. Great destruction to land, property, and life resulted.

Today man has learned to save the forests by more careful cutting of trees and replanting of forest land.

49/Observe

Find a place where new houses are being built. What changes in the earth's surface do you observe? Examine any water run-off from the land. What do you notice? ■

Farmlands and forest areas must be used carefully. Soil and forest conservation must be practiced not only to preserve the land from erosion, but also to preserve living places for animal life.

procedure

The abundance of information that is available to the children on problems that we face because of the abuse of natural resources can be utilized here. Air and water pollution are major problems for many of our cities. Newspaper and magazine articles can be the basis here for class discussion. Each child should be able to point out around him some possible abuse of natural resources. At the same time there are many forward-looking conservation programs in operation that serve to protect natural resources for future use. The improper use of insecticides has been curbed to protect the wild life in various regions. There are many of our water resources that become almost impossible to use because of pollution by industrial wastes. Discussion in class can bring out from the children examples they have seen personally. First-hand observation of many of these changes can be described to show what changes man has caused, some of them beneficial, others detrimental.

Activities 49 and 50 can provide the basis for these discussions. Before the students set out to perform them, be sure to develop, through discussion, a check-list which the students can use as a guide for their observations.

(continued on page 342)

Man has changed the earth's surface by changing the surroundings of living things. He has learned to use many chemicals to keep plants from being destroyed by insects and disease. Do you remember what happened to the salt that was dropped into the glass of water? What do you think happens to many of the chemicals on the plants as the rain falls on the plants and washes the chemicals off?

Many of these chemicals, called insecticides, are poisonous to fish, birds, or animals that drink from the streams.

Sewage is allowed to drain off into lakes and seas. As our cities have grown, our streams have become dangerous to drink from and swim in, and they have changed in appearance.

50/Observe

If you live near a stream or lake, do you find evidence of man's use or abuse? ■

note

The subject of man's contribution to our changing environment is pursued in great detail in Grade 6, Unit 1, "The Community of Animals and Plants." The focus in that unit, however, is on how man's behavior directly affects living things. In this unit, the emphasis is less direct—we concentrate on how man has changed the physical environment. A good research activity for your students is to have them investigate conservation programs which aim to preserve the land, vegetation, and water—all of which contribute to the physical, as well as biological, maintenance of our environment.

Activity 51 points out, subtly, that man's misuse of the environment has made it necessary for him to take corrective measures in order to safeguard his own welfare.

After the students have discussed this result of man's use of the environment, ask the students whether they think man has any major effect on the actual earth changes they have been discussing throughout this unit. The emphasis in this lesson has been that earth changes take many, many years, and except for violent or unusual events (floods, earth-quakes, and the like), one rarely sees a major change during the course of a lifetime. Ask the students to imagine the following situation: A heavy forest occupies the slopes of a hilly region, which receives a large amount of rainfall. The trees help to prevent the rainwater from rapidly running into the valley. In the valley itself, farmers raise crops of one kind or another. A lumber company buys up the forested land and proceeds to cut down all the trees. Ask the students what results this might have. Quite probably, the streams, now unchecked by the forest, will bring

responses to
51/investigate

1. The water supply comes from rivers, lakes, and the ground (underground water from rain that soaks into the ground). Some rivers are dammed so that a reservoir is created for the storage of water.
2. Do research on (or, if possible, visit) a water filtration plant.

51/Investigate

①Where does the water supply come from? ②Find out how it is made safe for you to drink. If you have a swimming pool in a nearby public park, find out what is done to keep the water safe to use. ■

The age of the earth is figured in billions of years. The landscape you see today is only a moment in the long history of the changing earth.

The ocean waves may plunge massive cliffs into the sea overnight. A volcano may build up a high mountain in a week or month. But most changes in the earth's surface come about gradually, during hundreds of thousands or millions of years.

periodic flood conditions to the valley, forcing the farmers out. The hillside will erode rapidly as the rushing waters pick up rocks and dirt. The life of the hillside is shortened as a result of man's behavior. Ask the students if they can think of other situations in which man's activities might contribute to drastic changes in the earth's surface.

In Testing Your Ideas, a combination of Helen's view and Bud's view showing how man has both beneficially as well as harmfully changed the earth's surface is appropriate.

Ages from now, there may be high mountains where you see only hills today. The great mountain ranges of the earth today may have vanished ten million years from now. Over the ages of time, the surface of the earth is built up in some areas and worn down in others. Tell what you know about the changing surface of the earth that you can see about you.

TESTING YOUR IDEAS

Helen and Bud were discussing how man had changed the earth's surface. Helen said that the changes were all for the best. Bud disagreed. Helen said that man had built cities, towns, and villages. He had also turned forests and plains into useful farmland. In addition, man had built canals and waterways to make travel easier. Dams had been built to give man enough water.

Bud said that man had not learned to change the earth's surface usefully. He had spoiled rivers, streams, and lakes with sewage and dangerous chemicals. He had cut down entire forests without reseeding. As a result, the beauty of the land was spoiled. Rains also washed away the soil once held in place by roots. All of this damage disturbed and in many cases destroyed wildlife.

With which point of view, Helen's or Bud's, do you agree? Do you think that to combine their views in some way would be best?

review

The answers to the review questions are listed below.

A. 4, 6. B. 4, 8, 9, 10. C. 1, 5. D. 1, 2, 5. E. 2, 3, 7.
F. 2, 3, 7. G. 4, 9.

Below are listed particular statements about the changing earth and general statements about it too. Which of the particular statements about the changing earth are contained in the general statements? A general statement may explain more than one particular statement.

Particular Statement	General Statement
1. Ice can break up rocks.	A. Wind can carry away dry topsoil and deposit it elsewhere.
2. Land once below the surface of the sea is now above it.	B. Water can wear away land and deposit it elsewhere.
3. A large fault area in the United States lies on the coast of California.	C. Freezing and melting water can erode rocks.
4. Planting grass can prevent erosion.	D. Glaciers cause the earth's surface to change.
5. A glacier sometimes makes at its foot a hill or lake.	E. Pressures in the earth can cause changes in the surface.

Particular Statement	*General Statement*
6. In 1934, a single windstorm blew about 300 million tons of soil from the midwestern United States to the Atlantic Ocean.	F. Sometimes a volcano or earthquake can change the earth's surface quickly.
7. In Alaska late one Friday afternoon in 1964, the ground cracked, and sections fell several feet.	G. Man can change the earth's surface.
8. The rock of Niagara Falls is being worn away five feet a year.	
9. If trees are cut down and not replaced, harsh rains can wear away forest topsoil.	
10. Land built up at the mouth of a river is called a delta.	

297

self-test

Edward is right about how a small force given a long period of time can change mountains. The effect of the question is to give the student a sense of how immense geologic time is.

John and Edward were talking about how the earth had changed. Both students agreed that the forces which were changing the earth today were the forces which changed it in the past. John, however, thought that the changes could not have been very great. After all, how could streams, winds, and glaciers wear down mountains? Edward said that in northern Wisconsin, Michigan, and Minnesota there were only the "roots" of what were once great mountains. Edward said that streams, winds, and glaciers had worn these mountains down. John laughed, "Impossible." "Streams and things are too weak. How could they cause great change?" "Simple," said Edward. "It's a one word answer—time!"

What do you think Edward meant by his answer?

Keep a scrapbook of all sorts of unusual occurrences such as earthquakes, volcanic eruptions, new volcanoes, tornadoes, hurricanes, and severe ice storms that you can find in the daily newspapers. Keep this for at least four months and possibly even one year.

Find an area near your home that shows erosion and try to discover how it occurred and what preventative measures could have been taken. Can you do anything about it now to stop the erosion?

Find out how seacoast areas prepare for the damage that wind and water do to these regions during the winter. Write to the Department of Interior, Washington, D.C. and see what information you can get about the prevention of erosion from our seacoast areas.

Make a collection of different types of rocks and soil and find about as much information about the rocks and soil as you can from various sourcebooks.

GLOSSARY

absorbed heat (ab-SORBD HEET)   heat that sinks into some surfaces

air sacs (AIR SACKS)   balloon-like sacs where oxygen and waste materials are exchanged

air tubes (AIR TUBZ)   branches of the windpipe that carry air to the air sacs

armadillo (AR-muh-DILL-oe)   small burrowing animal whose head and body have a hard bony covering

artery (ART-uh-ree)   a blood tube that carries blood away from the heart

balanced diet (BAL-unst DIE-uht)   a diet that gives the healthy amounts of each food group

beriberi (BER-ee-BER-ee)   a disease caused by a lack of vitamin B

block mountain (BLOK moun-tin)   a mountain formed by the uplifting of a large area of the earth's crust

body system (SIS-tem)   the parts of an organism that work together to carry on a life activity

bread group (BRED GROOHP)   an important food group that includes breads, cereals, and cakes and should be included in a daily diet

capillary (KAP-i-ler-ee)   a tiny blood tube that gives up digested food materials and oxygen to the cells and picks up waste materials from the cells

carbohydrates (cahr-bo-HIE-drayts)   food that contains sugar and starch and provides a good source of energy

cartilage (KAR-ti-lij)   a rubbery tissue that makes up most of an infant's skeleton

cells (SELLZ)   the smallest units of living matter that make up the body

Celsius scale (SELL-see-us SKALE)   a thermometer scale on which the freezing point of water is marked 0° and the boiling point of water is 100 °

chemical change (KEM-i-k'l CHANJE)   when a material is broken down and one or more new substances are formed

conduction (kun-DUCK-shun)   the way heat travels through solids

contract (kun-TRAKT)   to decrease in size

convection currents (Kun-VECK-shun KUR-entz)   upward and downward movement of a fluid because of changes in heating.

crust (KRUST)   the earth's outer layer which is make up of soil, rocks, and minerals

delta (DELL-tuh)   a low plain at the mouth of a river or sea, built up by the settling out and accumulation of sediment

density (DEN-sa-tee)   the weight of a unit volume

desert (DEZ-ert)   a region with little rainfall and often very little life

diaphragm (DIE-uh-fram)   a large muscle directly under the ribs that controls breathing

diet (DIE-uht)   all the food that you eat every day

digestion (di-JES-chun)   process by which the body changes food into a form that can be used

dispersal (dis-PER-sal)   all the ways in which seeds are carried to different places

350

dome mountain (DOME MOUN-tin)   a mountain formed by upward pressures beneath a weak spot in the earth's crust

dormancy (DAWR-mun-see)   a period of seasonal inactivity in certain plants

drought (DROWT)   several years of very dry weather

dune (DOOHN)   a huge pile of sand formed by the wind

energy (EN-ur-jee)   the ability to do work

erosion (ee-ROE-zhun)   the wearing away of the earth's surface by water, wind, and ice

estivation (ess-tuh-VAY-shun)   a resting state that some animals go into during the summer

expand (eck-SPAND)   to increase in size

Fahrenheit (FAR-en-HITE)   a thermometer scale on which the freezing point of water is marked 32° and the boiling point of water is marked 212°

fats (FATS)   food found in butter, lard, egg yolks, and bacon and provides a good source of energy

fault (FAWLT)   a deep break in the earth's crust caused by stress and pressure

fluids (FLOO-idz)   a name for liquids and gases

folded mountain (FOLD-ed MOUN-tin)   a mountain formed by the uplifting and wrinkling of the earth's crust

food chain (FOOD CHANE)   food relationships between plants and animals

fossil (FOSS-ul)   remains of ancient animals found buried in rocks

gas (GASS)   a substance which has no definite shape or volume; it expands to fill its container

glacier (GLAY-shur)   large mass of ice formed from snow in high, old mountains

glands (GLANDZ) organs which produce special body substances such as digestive juices and saliva

gravity (GRAV-uh-tee) pull of the earth that draws all objects on or near the earth toward its center

grub (GRUB) fat, white worms which are a stage in the development of a beetle

habitat (HAB-i-tat) the place where a plant or animal usually lives

heart (HART) a powerful muscle that pumps blood to all parts of the body

heart valve (HART VALV) fold of tissue in the heart that keeps the blood flowing in one direction

hibernation (hy-ber-NAY-shun) a resting state that some animals go into during the winter shown by sleeping, lowered body temperature and sluggishness

igneous rock (IG-nee-us ROCK) rocks formed from the heat of a volcano

insulators (IN-suh-LATE'rz) materials that are poor conductors of heat

kelp (KELP) large brown sea plants frequently found in the Pacific Ocean

large intestine (in-TESS-tin) an organ of digestion where water is taken back into the blood and waste materials are passed out of the body

life zone (LIFE ZONE) area of plant and animal life. On a mountainside, changes appear as different coloring in plants, as you climb.

liquid (LI-quid) a substance that has a definite volume but no definite shape; it takes the shape of its container

litmus paper (LIT-muss PAY-pur) a chemical indicator used to test for acids and bases.

liver (LIV-uhr) an organ that produces bile which aids in the digestion of fats

magma (MAG-muh) melted rock materials below the surface of the earth; may flow from volcano

meat group (MEET GROOHP) an important food group that includes meat, fish, and poultry and should be included in your daily diet

migrate (MY-grayt) the movement of animals in large numbers from one place to a distant place

milk group (MILK GROOHP) an important food group that includes milk, butter, cheese, cream, and ice cream and should be included in your daily diet

milt (MILT) whitish fluid released from a male fish which fertilizes the eggs of the female fish

minerals (MIN-ur-uhlz) a food substance that builds strong bones, hard teeth, and healthy blood

muscular system (MUS-kyoo-lur SIS-tem) the muscles of the body that make the bones move

nervous system (NUR-vuhs SIS-tem) the system that controls all of the body's activities

organism (OR-gan-izm) any living thing whose parts act together as a unit

organs (OAR-gunz) the different parts that make up the systems of organisms

pancreas (PAN-kree-uhs) a large gland near the stomach which produces a digestive juice

physical change (FIZZ-i-k'l CHANJE) when a material changes in appearance but remains the same material

plankton (PLANK-tun) free-floating algae and microscopic animals found in water

plasma (PLAZ-muh)   the liquid part of the blood that carries digested food and waste materials

porous (PAWR-us)   materials that can soak up water and other liquids

protective coloration (pruh-TEK-tiv KUL-uh-ray-shun)   the blending of an animal with the color of its surroundings

proteins (PRO- teenz)   food that builds up and repairs body tissues

pulse (PULS)   the throb felt in a blood tube caused by the contraction of the heart muscle

radiation (RAY-dee-AY-shun)   when heat travels in all directions from a hot object

reflected heat (ree-FLECK-ted HEET)   heat that bounces off some substances

reflex action (REE-fleks ACK-shun)   an action that happens quickly and without our control

respiratory system (RES-puh-ruh-taw-ree SIS-tem)   the system which regulates the oxygen you breathe in and the other gases you breathe out.

sandstone (SAND-stone)   rock formed by particles that have been under great pressure.

scurvy (SKUR-vee)   disease caused by lack of Vitamin C

sediment (SED-uh-munt)   particles of rock and soil that settle to the bottom of a river

seismograph (SYZ-ma-graf)   a sensitive instrument that records the vibrations of an earthquake

skeletal system (SKEL-uh-t'l SIS-tem)   all the bones of an organism

small intestine (in-TESS-tin)   an organ of digestion where food is broken down and absorbed into the blood

spawning (SPAWN-ing)   the depositing of eggs by a female fish

stomach (STOM-uck)   an organ of digestion where food is mixed with digestive juices and begins to be broken down

terrarium (tuh-RAIR-ee-um)   a self-contained area for growing plants indoors and keeping small land animals.

thermometer (thur-MOM-eh-tur)   an instrument used to take temperature

timberline (TIM-bur-line)   a definite line on a mountain where the growth of trees stops

tissues (TISH-yooz)   the special material that makes up the organs of the body

topsoil (TOP-soyl)   a rich soil that contains all the nutrients which a plant needs in order to grow

vegetable group (VEJ-eh-tuh-bull GROOHP) an important food group that includes vegetables and fruit and should be included in your daily diet

vegetarian (veh-juh-TAIR-ee-unz)   animals that feed only on plants

vein (VAYN)   a blood tube that carries blood toward the heart

vitamins (VY-tuh-minz)   substances found in food that aid and regulate body activity and growth.

water cycle (WAH-tur SIE-kul)   movement of water from the earth's surface into the atmosphere and back again

water vapor (WAH-tur VAY-pur)   a gas formed when water is heated

weathering (WETH-ur-ing)   wearing away of rocks due to the action of wind and water over a long period of time

work (WURK)   movement of an object through a distance by force

INDEX

Key to Publishers

Arco Publishing Company, Inc., 219 Park Avenue South, New York, N.Y. 10003

Atheneum Publishers, 122 East 42nd Street, New York, N.Y. 10017

Avon Books, 959 Eighth Avenue, New York, N.Y. 10019

Basic Books, Inc., 404 Park Avenue South, New York, N.Y. 10016

Belknap, Harvard University Press, 79 Garden Street, Cambridge, Mass. 02163

Blaisdell Publishing Company, Division of Ginn and Co., 135 W. 50th St., New York, N.Y. 10020

Bobbs-Merrill Co., Inc., 4300 W. 62nd St., Indianapolis, Indiana 46268

Bowmar Pub. Corp., 622 Radier Dr., Glendale, California 91201

Childrens Press, 1224 W. Van Buren St., Chicago, Ill. 60607

Chilton Book Company, 401 Walnut Street, Philadelphia, Pa. 19106

Coward-McCann, Inc., 200 Madison Ave., New York, N.Y. 10016

Crowell-Collier Press, 866 Third Avenue, New York, N.Y. 10022

Dodd, Mead and Company, Inc., 79 Madison Avenue, New York, N.Y. 10016

Doubleday and Co., Inc., 501 Franklin Avenue, Garden City, N.Y. 11531

Dover Publications, Inc., 180 Varick St., New York, N.Y. 10014

Dutton. E. P. Dutton and Company, Inc., 201 Park Avenue South, New York, N.Y. 10003

Edmund Scientific Co., 400 Edscorp Bldg., Barrington, New Jersey 08007

Follett Publishing Co., 1010 West Washington Blvd., Chicago, Ill. 60607

Golden Press, 850 Third Avenue, New York, N.Y. 10022

Grosset and Dunlap, Inc., 51 Madison Avenue, New York, N.Y. 10010

Hale. E. M. Hale and Co., 1201 S. Hastings Way, Eau Claire, Wisc. 54701

Harcourt, Brace and World, Inc., 757 Third Avenue, New York, N.Y. 10017

Harper and Row, Publishers, 49 East 33 Street, New York, N.Y. 10016

Harvey House, Inc., Irvington-on-Hudson, N.Y. 10533

Hayden Book Company, Inc., 116 West 14 Street, New York, N.Y. 10011

Holiday House, Inc., 18 East 56 Street, New York, N.Y. 10022

Holt, Rinehart and Winston, Inc., 383 Madison Ave., New York, N.Y. 10017

International Publishers, 381 Park Avenue South, New York, N.Y. 10016

Lippincott. J. B. Lippincott Company, East Washington Square, Philadelphia, Pa. 19105

Lothrop, Lee and Shepard Company, Inc., 425 Park Avenue South, New York, N.Y. 10016

Lynn. Austin Lynn Publishing Co., 2424 West Granville Rd., Worthington, Ohio 43085

McGraw-Hill Book Company, Inc., 330 West 42 Street, New York, N.Y. 10036

McKnight, Division of Taplinger Publishing Co., Inc., 20 E. 10th St., New York, N.Y. 10003

Morrow. William Morrow and Company, Inc., 425 Park Avenue South, New York, N.Y. 10016

Natural History Press, Central Park West at 79th Street, New York, N.Y. 10024

New American Library, Inc., 1301 Avenue of the Americas, New York, N.Y. 10019

Norton. W. W. Norton and Company, Inc., 55 Fifth Avenue, New York, N.Y. 10003

Odyssey Press, 55 Fifth Avenue, New York, N.Y. 10003

Pergamon Press, Inc., Maxwell House, Fairview Park, Elmsford, N.Y. 10523

Prentice-Hall, Inc., Englewood Cliffs, N.J. 07632

Putnam's. G. P. Putnam's Sons, 200 Madison Avenue, New York, N.Y. 10016

Random House, Inc., 201 East 50th Street, New York, N.Y. 10022

Ronald Press Co., 79 Madison Ave., New York, N.Y. 10016

Roy Publishers, Inc., 30 East 74 Street, New York, N.Y. 10021

Simon (Messner). Julian Messner, Division of Simon and Schuster, Inc., 1 West 39 Street, New York, N.Y. 10018

St. Martin's Press, Inc., 175 Fifth Avenue, New York, N.Y. 10010

Sterling Publishing Co., 419 Park Ave. So., New York, N.Y. 10014

Tab Books, Blue Ridge, Summit, Pa. 17214

Thomas Y. Crowell Co., 426 So. 6th St., Minneapolis, Minnesota

Time-Life Books, Time and Life Building, Rockefeller Center, New York, N.Y. 10020

Van Nostrand. D. Van Nostrand Co., Inc., 120 Alexander St., Princeton, N.J. 08540

Van Nostrand-Reinhold Company, 430 Park Avenue, New York, N.Y. 10022

Walker and Co., 720 Fifth Ave., New York, N.Y. 10019

Watts. Franklin Watts, Inc., 575 Lexington Ave., New York, N.Y. 10022

World Publishing Co., 2231 West 110 St., Cleveland, Ohio 44102

Key to Manufacturers, Distributors, and Supply Houses

Allied Radio Corp., 833 N. Jefferson Blvd., Chicago, Ill. 60607. Radio equipment, meters, etc.

America Basic Science Club, 501 E. Crockett, San Antonio, Tex. 78206. Kits and manuals on projects in physics.

Baker Science Packets, 650 Concord Dr., Holland, Mich. 49423. Card file of 153 indexed science experiments.

Cambosco Scientific Co., 37 Antwerp St., Brighton, Mass. 02324. General.

Carolina Biological Supply Co., Elon College, N.C. 27244. Biological apparatus, supplies, living and preserved specimens. Models, charts.

Central Scientific Co., 1700 Irving Park Rd., Chicago, Ill. 60613; 79 Amherst St., Cambridge, Mass. 01922; 6446 Telegraph Rd., Los Angeles, Calif. 90022. Hobby kits for electronics, medicine, geology, optics, weather. General.

Denoyer-Geppert Co., 5235–39 Ravenswood Ave., Chicago, Ill. 60640. Biological models, charts on biology and astronomy.

Eastman Kodak Co., Rochester, N.Y. 14600. Photographic supplies, equipment, and literature.

Edmund Scientific Corp., Barrington, N.J. 08007. "America's greatest optical marketplace."

Fischer Scientific Co., 717 Forbes St., Pittsburgh, Pa. 15219; 635 Greenwich St., New York, N.Y. 10014. Molecular models, general.

General Biological Supply House, 8200 S. Hoyne Ave., Chicago, Ill. 60620. Biological apparatus, supplies, living and preserved specimens, models, charts.

A. C. Gilbert Co., New Haven, Conn. 06500. Gilbert toys, including microscope sets, tool cabinets, model telephone and electric construction sets, chemical labs.

C. S. Hammond Co., Maplewood, N.J. 07040. Space and weather kits, color maps.

Hubbard Scientific Co., P.O. Box 105, Northbrook, Ill. 60062. Instructional media and models for biological, natural, and earth sciences.

Los Angeles Biological Laboratories, 2977 W. 14th St., Los Angeles, Calif. 90006. Biological apparatus, supplies, living and preserved specimens, models, charts.

National Audubon Society, 1130 Fifth Ave., New York, N.Y. 10028. Inexpensive nature charts and bulletins.

Nature Games, 8339 W. Dry Creek Rd., Healdsburg, Calif. 95448. Card games using colorful, authentic pictures of scientific names.

OMSI/Kit, Inc., 10655 S.W. Greenburg Rd., Portland, Oregon 97223. Special science apparatus and laboratory equipment for elementary and junior high school.

A. J. Nystrom and Co., 3333 Elston Ave., Chicago, Ill. 60618. Biological models; charts on health, biological sciences, general science, atmosphere, and weather.

E. H. Sargent and Co., 155 E. Superior St., Chicago, Ill. 60600. General.

Science Associates, P.O. Box 216, Princeton, N.J. 08540. Special instruments and teaching aids for meteorology, astronomy, optics, and earth sciences.

Science Kit, Box 69, Tonawanda, N.Y. 14150. Standard laboratory equipment, teacher's manual, astronomy manual and star chart.

Science Materials Center, Div. of Library of Science, 59 Fourth Ave., New York, N.Y. 10003. Equipment; teaching aids.

Standard Oil of California, Public Relations, 225 Bush St., San Francisco, Calif. 94100. Catalog of free teaching materials and services.

Stansi Scientific Co., 1231 N. Honore St., Chicago, Ill. 60622. Teaching kits in electricity and electronics. Science kits for elementary school. General.

Taylor Instrument Co., Rochester, N.Y. 14600. Weather and temperature instruments.

Things of Science, Science Service, 1719 N St., N.W., Washington, D.C. 20006. Monthly kits on various subjects.

Turtox General Biological Supply House, 8200 S. Hoyne Ave., Chicago, Ill. 60620. Biological supplies, living and preserved specimens. Models. charts.

Ward's Natural Science Establishment, Inc., P.O. Box 24, Beechwood Sta., Rochester, N.Y. 14603. Teaching aids, charts, equipment, geology specimens, and other materials for biological, natural, and earth sciences.

W. M. Welch Manufacturing Co., 1515 N. Sedgwick St., Chicago, Ill. 60610. General.

Key to Film Distributors

Bailey Films, Inc., 6509 De Longpre Ave., Hollywood, California 90028

Babcock and Wilcox Co., 161 East 42nd St., New York, N.Y. 10016

Bureau of Mines, 4800 Forbes Ave., Pittsburgh, Pa. 15213

Coronet Instructional Films, 65 E. South Water St., Chicago, Ill. 60601

DeVry Technical Institute, Film Svc. Dept., 4141 Belmont Ave., Chicago, Ill. 60641

Ealing, The Ealing Corp., 2225 Massachusetts Ave., Cambridge, Mass. 02140

EBEd Corp. - Encyclopedia Brittanica Education Corporation, 425 N. Michigan Ave., Chicago 60611

Film Associates of California, 11014 Santa Monica Blvd., Los Angeles, California 90025

Filmstrip of the Month Club, 355 Lexington Ave., New York, N.Y. 10017

International Communication Films, Division of Doubleday, 870 Monterey Park, California 91754

Jam Handy, 2821 E. Grand Blvd., Detroit 11, Michigan 48211

Long Film Slide Svc., 7505 Fairmont Ave., El Cerrito, California 94530

3M Company, Visual Products Divisions, P.O. Box 3344, St. Paul, Minn. 55101

McGraw-Hill Films, McGraw-Hill Book Co., Text Film Dept., 330 W. 42nd St., N.Y. 10036

MLA. Modern Learning Aids, 3 East 54th St., New York, N.Y. 10022

Moody Institute of Science, Educational Film Division, 11428 Santa Monica Blvd., Los Angeles, California 90025

MTP. Modern Talking Picture Co., 3 East 54th St., New York, N.Y. 10022

Photo Laboratory, Inc., 3825 Georgia Ave., N.W., Washington, D.C. 20011

Shell Oil Co., 149 Northern Blvd., Flushing, N.Y. 11354

USOE. United States Office of Education, Washington, D.C. 20202

PHOTO CREDITS

George Zimbel: 80, 81, 82, 84, 96, 100B, 102, 103, 109, 118, 119, 128, 133, 139, 140, 145, 147, 158, 159, 161, 166T, 167, 168, 170, 172, 173, 175, 177, 178, 180, 181, 183, 184B, 185, 186, 189, 196, 200, 203, 205, 208, 209, 210, 211, 218T, 256, 258, 274, 275, 277, 283B

UNIT ONE: 1, John Clawson; 2 *top*, John Clawson; 2 *bottom*, Douglas Baglin, Freelance Photographers Guild; 3, Stephen Dalton from National Audubon Society; 4, Suzanne Szasz; 5, Roche Photography; 6, Walter Dawn; 8, W. Dawn; 9, Grant Heilman; 10, J. Clawson; 11, Alvin E. Staffan from NAS; 12, Leonard Lee Rue III from NAS; 13, Allan Roberts; 14, Roche Photography; 15 *top*, W. A. Pluemer courtesy of American Museum of Natural History; 15B, Janet Stone from NAS; 16T, M, W. Dawn; 16B, J. Clawson; 17, A. Roberts; Hans Wendler, FPG; 20, Ellis-Sawyer, FPG; 21T, W. Dawn; 21B, Anthony Mercieca from NAS; 22, Verna Johnson; 23, Larry West, Full Moon Studio; 24T, Miami Seaquarium; 24B, Russ Kinne, Photo Researchers; 25, W. Dawn; 26, Fred Ragsdale, FPG; 27, L. L. Rue III; 28T, J. Clawson; 28B, Wilford Millar from NAS; 29, George Hunter, FPG; 30, Fred Baldwin from NAS; 31L, L. L. Rue III; 31R, Hal Kanzler, FPG; 32, Jacques Jangoux; 33, Harry Thompson from NAS; 34, Jacques Jangoux; 35, W. Dawn; 36, Willis Peterson; 37T, Treat Davidson from NAS; 38, S. Dalton from NAS; 39, L. L. Rue III; 40, L. West, FMS; 42, L. L. Rue III; 44, Edward Degginer; 46, Herbert Weihrich; 48, L. West, FMS; 49, L. West, FMS; 50, L. L. Rue III; 51T, Dr. Sigurdur Thorarinsson; 51B, Icelandic Airlines, Inc.; 52, Dr. S. Thorarinsson; 53, H. Weihrich; 54, L. L. Rue III from NAS; 56T, H. Weihrich; 56B, L. West, FMS; 57, Allan Roberts; 59, W. Dawn; 60, Robert Ellison from NAS; 61. R. Kinne from PR; 62, Harold V. Green; 66, Marineland of the Pacific; 72, H. Wendler, FPG; 74, Grant Heilman; 75, Allan Cruickshank from NAS; 76, Courtesy of AMNH; 79, Purno, FPG.

UNIT TWO: 85, National Dairy Council; 86, NDC; 87, W. Dawn; 91, W. Dawn; 93, W. Dawn; 95, Otto Fenn, FPG; 100T, W. Dawn; 101, W. Dawn; 113, Lester Bergman & Associates; 117, Courtesy of Hubbard Scientific Co., Northbrook, Illinois; 121, W. Dawn; 122 T, M, W. Dawn; 122B, L. Bergman & Assoc.; 126, Phillip Harrington; 127, P. Harrington; 129, Hugh Spencer; 136, L. Bergman & Assoc.

UNIT THREE: 154, 155, L. Willinger, FPG; 156T, Dr. Richard Orville; 156B, Peter Gridley, FPG; 157, Sinclair, FPG; 163 T, Association of American Railroads; 163 B, United Press International; 166 B, James Foote; 184 T, F. Schulze, FPG; 188, NASA; 193 T, Rudolf Newman, FPG; 193 B, E. Degginger; 194, Burton Neeley, FPG; 201, The Granger Collection; 204, L. Willinger, FPG; 213, Howard Kritchell, FPG; 214, J. Foote.

UNIT FOUR: 216, 217, Albert J. Hill; 218 B, James Goodwin, PR; 219, E. Degginger; 220, George Schwartz, FPG; 226, John H. Burnett, FPG; 227, E. Degginger; 228, Camera Hawaii, FPG; 229, American Red Cross; 232, Soil Conservation Service; 236, H. Roberts, FPG; 237, Dennis Hallinen, FPG; 239, E. Degginger; 240, F. Ragsdale, FPG; 241, E. Degginger; 244, J. Jangoux; 245, Hans Wendler, FPG; 245, H. Wendler, FPG; 247, H. Wendler, FPG; 248, Jack Zerht, FPG; 249, E. Degginger; 251, Camera Hawaii, FPG; 252, Herman Kessler; 254, Alvin Upitis, FPG; 260, Ellis-Sawyer, FPG; 262, Katherine Jensen; 264, William Ramsey; 265, J. M. Burnett, FPG; 266, E. Degginger; 268, L. West, FMS; 269, K. Jensen; 270, J. H. Burnett, FPG; 271, U.S. Geological Survey; 273, K. Jensen; 276, David Meunch, Alpha Photos; 278, E. Degginger; 279, V. Johnston; 280, D. Hallinan, FPG; 282, ESSA; 283T, ESSA; 285, Camera Hawaii, FPG; 287, Rafael Garcia, Black Star; 288, Culver Pictures; 290, Franz Lazi, FPG; 292, John Atkinson, FPG; 293, Betty Barford from NAS; 294, E. Degginger; 295, Ellis-Sawyer, FPG; 297, H. L. Parent from NAS; 299, *ESSA*.

Photo research by
Picturebook Photo Research

Designed by
Frank Lamacchia and Angela Pozzi

Cover photo by John Clawson